NEO-BABYLONIAN TRIAL RECORDS

Society of Biblical Literature

Writings from the Ancient World

Theodore J. Lewis, General Editor

Associate Editors

Daniel Fleming
Theo van den Hout
Martti Nissinen
William Schniedewind
Mark S. Smith
Emily Teeter
Terry Wilfong

Number 35
Neo-Babylonian Trial Records
Volume Editor: Cornelia Wunsch

NEO-BABYLONIAN TRIAL RECORDS

by Shalom E. Holtz

Society of Biblical Literature
Atlanta

NEO-BABYLONIAN TRIAL RECORDS

Library of Congress Cataloging-in-Publication Data

Holtz, Shalom E., author.
Neo-Babylonian trial records / by Shalom E. Holtz.
p. cm. — (Writings from the ancient world society of biblical literature number 35)
Includes bibliographical references and indexes.
ISBN 978-1-58983-943-4 (paper binding : alk. paper) — ISBN 978-1-58983-945-8 (electronic format) — ISBN 978-1-58983-944-1 (hardcover binding : alk. paper)
1. Law, Assyro-Babylonian—Sources. 2. Civil procedure (Assyro-Babylonian law)—Sources. 3. Trials—Iraq—Babylonia—Sources.
4. Court records—Iraq—Babylonia. I. Title.
KL707.H65 2014
347.35'507—dc23

2014003157

Printed on acid-free, recycled paper conforming to ANSI/NISO Z39.48-1992 (R1997) and ISO 9706:1994 standards for paper permanence.

Contents

Series Editor Foreword vii
Acknowledgments ix
Conventions and Abbreviations xi
Remarks on the Transcriptions and Translations xiv
Chronology of Neo-Babylonian and Achaemenid Kings (605–424 BCE) xvi

Introduction 1
General Historical Context 3
The Trial Records and Neo-Babylonian Archival Texts 4
Imagining the Courtroom Drama 5
The Adjudicatory System 7
On the Organization of This Book 9

Chapter 1: Preliminaries to Trials 13
1. A Confession 13
2. Apprehension for Cultic Crimes 17
3. Reports about Theft in High Places 20
4. An Accusation of Burglary 24
5. An Interrogation about Sheep 27
6. An Interrogation about Missing Gold 31
7. Testimony about a Stolen Ox 34
8. Examination of a Tablet as Evidence 36
9. A Conditional Verdict 38
10. Another Conditional Verdict 41
11. Prelude to a Trial for Manslaughter 43
12. Requirement to Present Witnesses 45
13. An Oath to Argue a Case 48
14. A Counterclaim Regarding Misappropriated Sheep 52
15. A Summons to Babylon 55
16. Testimony and a Summons 57
17. A Summons to the Esagil at Babylon 60
18. A Settled Case 62

Chapter 2: Completed Trials 67
19. A Dispute over the Sale of a Slave 67
20. A Slave's Attempt at Self-Liberation 70
21. A Misappropriated Temple Slave 74
22. A Boatman's Fraud 80
23. Inheritance 84
24. Undivided Inheritance 87
25. A Property Dispute 94
26. A Property Dispute with the Eanna Temple 102
27. A Dispute over a House 107
28. Dispute over a Theft 110
29. An Attempted Fraud 114
30. A Violent Theft 118
31. The Case of a Branded Temple Servant 122
32. Settling a Debt 125
33. A Case from the Ebabbar at Sippar 129
34. A Case regarding Prebends 132
35. A Widow and Her Husband's Creditors 137
36. Settling Dowry Obligations 141

Chapter 3: Four Trial Dossiers 147
The Infamous Gimillu (Documents 37–41) 147
37. Suspected Misappropriation 148
38. Gimillu on Trial 151
39. The King's Court of Law 163
40. Oral and Written Evidence 166
41. A Suspicion of Contract for Murder 169
The Case of Anu-šarra-uṣur's Branded Sheep (Documents 42–43) 172
42. Testimony regarding Five Branded Sheep 172
43. A Decision regarding Branded Sheep 178
The Case of Lā-tubāšinni and Her Children (Documents 44–48) 182
44. Lā-tubāšinni's Marriage Contract 183
45. Nabû-ēda-uṣur's Slave Wages 186
46. Sale of Four Slaves 188
47. Sale of a Slave 191
48. The Status of Lā-tubāšinni's Children 194
An Unauthorized Marriage (Documents 49–50) 198
49. A Guarantee for Testimony 198
50. An Unauthorized Marriage 201

Normalized Texts 205

Bibliography 241
Indexes 249

Series Editor Foreword

Writings from the Ancient World is designed to provide up-to-date, readable English translations of writings recovered from the ancient Near East.

The series is intended to serve the interests of general readers, students, and educators who wish to explore the ancient Near Eastern roots of Western civilization or to compare these earliest written expressions of human thought and activity with writings from other parts of the world. It should also be useful to scholars in the humanities or social sciences who need clear, reliable translations of ancient Near Eastern materials for comparative purposes. Specialists in particular areas of the ancient Near East who need access to texts in the scripts and languages of other areas will also find these translations helpful. Given the wide range of materials translated in the series, different volumes will appeal to different interests. However, these translations make available to all readers of English the world's earliest traditions as well as valuable sources of information on daily life, history, religion, and the like in the preclassical world.

The translators of the various volumes in this series are specialists in the particular languages and have based their work on the original sources and the most recent research. In their translations they attempt to convey as much as possible of the original texts in fluent, current English. In the introductions, notes, glossaries, maps, and chronological tables, they aim to provide the essential information for an appreciation of these ancient documents.

The ancient Near East reached from Egypt to Iran and, for the purposes of our volumes, ranged in time from the invention of writing (by 3000 BCE) to the conquests of Alexander the Great (ca. 330 BCE). The cultures represented within these limits include especially Egyptian, Sumerian, Babylonian, Assyrian, Hittite, Ugaritic, Aramean, Phoenician, and Israelite. It is hoped that Writings from the Ancient World will eventually produce translations from most of the many different genres attested in these cultures: letters (official and private), myths, diplomatic documents, hymns, law collections, monumental inscriptions, tales, and administrative records, to mention but a few.

Significant funding was made available by the Society of Biblical Literature for the preparation of this volume. In addition, those involved in preparing this volume have received financial and clerical assistance from their respective institutions. Were it not for these expressions of confidence in our work, the arduous tasks of preparation, translation, editing, and publication could not have been accomplished or even undertaken. It is the hope of all who have worked with the Writings from the Ancient World series that our translations will open up new horizons and deepen the humanity of all who read these volumes.

Theodore J. Lewis
The Johns Hopkins University

Acknowledgments

This book grows out of research that I conducted for *Neo-Babylonian Court Procedure* (Holtz 2009). That work brought me into contact with Cornelia Wunsch, editor of the present volume. Her insights have improved every aspect of this book, from its general organization to specific readings based on her own collations. I am honored that she agreed to participate in this project, grateful to her for the hours we spent together in virtual meetings, and humbled to share credit with her.

Bruce Wells planted the idea for this volume in my mind and suggested that I propose it to the Writings from the Ancient World series. He, together with Cornelia and Rachel Magdalene, led the "Neo-Babylonian Trial Procedure" project, funded by a Collaborative Research Grant from the U.S. National Endowment for the Humanities. This grant partially supported my research, including a trip to collate tablets at the Yale Babylonian Collection. Any views, findings, conclusions, or recommendations expressed in this book are mine alone and do not necessarily represent those of the National Endowment for the Humanities. I thank Bruce, Cornelia and Rachel for inviting me to serve as a consultant to their project and for the valuable scholarly interactions we have had.

I am also pleased to acknowledge the help, advice and encouragement I have received from various other scholars, including Kathleen Abraham, Paul-Alain Beaulieu, Grant Frame, Michael Jursa, Elizabeth Payne, Małgorzata Sandowicz and Benjamin Sommer. Theodore Lewis, series editor for the Writings from the Ancient World, gave helpful guidance, as did Billie Jean Collins, Acquisitions Editor at the Society of Biblical Literature.

While working on this volume, I benefited from two research leaves from my teaching and administrative duties at Yeshiva University. During the first leave (2009–2010), I served as a visiting fellow in Jewish law and interdisciplinary studies at the Center for Jewish Law and Contemporary Civilization of Yeshiva University's Benjamin N. Cardozo School of Law. Thanks for this fellowship are due to Suzanne Stone, director of the center, her assistant (my friend for some twenty years, and now my colleague), Ari Mermelstein, and to Yeshiva University's provost, Morton Lowengrub, who provided a supplemental grant. For the second leave (Fall, 2013), I thank Barry L. Eichler, Dean of Yeshiva College, and my colleagues who led the Robert M. Beren Department of Jewish Studies as its Executive Committee: David Berger, Shalom Carmy, Debra Kaplan and Aaron Koller.

Last, but certainly not least, I thank my family: my parents, Avraham and Toby Holtz; my wife, Leebie Mallin; and our three children, Zev (Billy), Avigayil and Tal. All of them have contributed in their own ways to this project.

New York, NY
February 2014

Conventions and Abbreviations

Babylonian Months

I	Nisannu-BAR_2 (March–April)
II	Ayaru-GU_4 (April–May)
III	Simānu-SIG_4 (May–June)
IV	Dûzu-ŠU (June–July)
V	Abu-NE (July–August)
VI	Ulūlu-KIN (August–September)
VII	Tašrītu-DU_6 (September–October)
VIII	Araḫšamna-APIN (October–November)
IX	Kislīmu-GAN (November–December)
X	Ṭebētu-AB (December–January)
XI	Šabāṭu- ZIZ_2 (January–February)
XII	Addaru- ŠE (February–March)

Royal Names

Camb	Cambyses
Cyr	Cyrus
Dar	Darius I
Nbk	Nebuchadnezzar
Nbn	Nabonidus
Ngl	Neriglissar

Weights and Measures (for full discussion, see Powell 1987)

1 mina	60 šeqels (approximately 500 grams)
1 šeqel	24 *girû* (approximately 8.3 grams)
1 *kur*	5 *pi* (approximately 180 liters)
1 *pi*	6 BAN_2 (approximately 36 liters)
1 BAN_2	6 $SILA_3$ (approximately 6 liters)

1 $SILA_3$	10 GAR (approximately 1 liter)
1 GAR	14 *ammatu* (approximately 7 meters)

1 GI (*qanû*, "reed") 7 *ammatu* (approximately 3.5 meters)
1 $KUŠ_3$ (*ammatu*, "cubit") 24 *ubānu* ("fingerlengths") (approximately 0.5 meter)

Museum Sigla

AO	Musée du Louvre, Paris, Antiquités orientales
BM	British Museum, London (Old accession numbers in parentheses)
CBS	University Museum, Philadelphia, Catalogue of the Babylonian Section
HSM	Harvard Semitic Museum, Cambridge, Massachusetts
MNB	Musée du Louvre, Paris, Musées Nationaux
NBC	Nies Babylonian Collection, Yale Babylonian Collection, New Haven
RSM	Royal Scottish Museum, Edinburgh
VAT	Vorderasiatisches Museum, Berlin, Vorderasiatische Abteilung–Tontafeln
YBC	Yale Babylonian Collection, New Haven

Other Abbreviations

AASOR	*Annual of the American Schools of Oriental Research*
ADOG	Abhandlungen der deutschen Orientgesellschaft
AfO	*Archiv für Orientforschung*
AfOB	*Archiv für Orientforschung* Beiheft
AHw	*Akkadisches Handwörterbuch*. W. von Soden. 3 vols. Wiesbaden, 1965–1981
AJSL	*American Journal of Semitic Languages and Literature*
AnOr	Analecta Orientalia
AOAT	Alter Orient und Altes Testament
ArOr	*Archiv Orientální*
AS	Assyriological Studies
BASOR	*Bulletin of the American Schools of Oriental Research*
BE	Babylonian Expedition of the University of Pennsylvania, Series A: Cueniform Texts
BIN	Babylonian Inscriptions in the Collection of J.B. Nies
BiOr	*Bibliotheca Orientalis*
BJS	Brown Judaic Studies
CAD	*The Assyrian Dictionary of the Oriental Institute of the University of Chicago*. Chicago: The Oriental Institute of the University of Chicago. 1956–2010

CBQ	*Catholic Biblical Quarterly*
JAOS	*Journal of the American Oriental Society*
JBL	*Journal of Biblical Literature*
JCS	*Journal of Cuneiform Studies*
JEOL	*Jaarbericht van het Vooraziatisch-Egyptisch Gezelschap (Genootschap) Ex oriente lux*
JESHO	*Journal of the Economic and Social History of the Orient*
KB	Keilinschriftliche Bibliothek
MBPF	Münchener Beiträge zur Papyrusforschung und antiken Rechtsgeschichte
NABU	*Nouvelles Assyriologiques Brèves et Utilitaires*
Or (NS)	*Orientalia* (New Series)
RA	*Revue d'assyriologie et d'archéologie orientale*
RlA	*Reallexikon der Assyriologie*
SBLWAW	Society of Biblical Literature Writings from the Ancient World
TCL	Textes cunéiformes du Louvre
TUAT, NF	*Texte aus der Umwelt des Alten Testament, Neue Folge*
WO	*Die Welt des Orients*
WZKM	*Wiener Zeitschrift für die Kunde des Morgenlandes*
YNER	Yale Near Eastern Researches
YOS	Yale Oriental Series, Babylonian Texts
YOSR	Yale Oriental Series, Researches
ZA	*Zeitschrift für Assyriologie*

Remarks on the Transcriptions and Translations

The purpose of the transcriptions is to represent, in Latin characters, the cuneiform writing on the original tablets. By following the transcription, a trained Assyriologist can imagine the cuneiform. Nonspecialists can use the transcriptions to get some sense of what the original language sounds like, and may consult the normalizations at the end of the volume to get a better sense of the language and the grammar that underlie the translations. It should, however, be noted that there is a considerable gap between the actual utterances and their representations on the tablets.

The transcriptions also reflect a certain degree of interpretation of the original writing. On almost every level, from the decoding of the script to the division of the words and phrases, there may be some room for dispute. Most often, context is a very helpful guide to determining the correct reading, with the result that the best reading is usually evident because the final result makes good sense. Moreover, because the texts in the present volume have all been read by others before, one can follow scholarly consensus. Matters of dispute are mentioned in the notes to the transcriptions.

The transcriptions have been made in consultation with previously published hand drawings, transliterations, and other studies. In addition, texts in the Yale Babylonian collection (sigla NBC and YBC) and the University Museum (siglum CBS) were collated by the author in June 2010. Texts in the British Museum (siglum BM) were collated based on digital photographs provided by Cornelia Wunsch or Małgorzata Sandowicz of the University of Warsaw. Additional collations by Cornelia Wunsch are noted in the comments to the texts.

On the tablets, each cuneiform sign, or combination of signs, can be read in one of two ways: as a syllable in an Akkadian word or as a Sumerian logogram that was interpreted as a complete Akkadian word. In the transcriptions, lower case italic letters reflect Akkadian syllables, with each syllable separated by a space (between words) or by a dash (between syllables in the same word). Uppercase roman letters reflect Sumerian logograms. The logographic and syllabic values in the transcriptions follow those published in Labat 1999. The following are other symbols used to indicate other aspects of the texts:

PN	personal name
m	masculine
f	feminine
d	deity
[ ]	restorations to a broken text
⸢ ⸣	likely readings of a partially damaged text
< >	insertion of text omitted by ancient scribes
<< >>	deletion of originally erroneous text
X	illegible sign
...	broken text that cannot be restored
?	possible reading that does not fully accord with writing

Lines are numbered consecutively in Arabic numerals. After a large gap, line numbering begins with 1'. If there are two large gaps, line numbering resumes with 1" after the second gap.

The translations attempt to render the original texts as faithfully and as consistently as possible. Neo-Babylonian court records are marked by convoluted and, at times, repetitive language. These aspects of the original records make for somewhat cumbersome translations. Perhaps the best way to justify this unfortunate aspect of the translations is to note that, in this respect at least, Neo-Babylonian court records resemble legal writing from any other time or place.

Making even basic sense of the Akkadian sometimes requires repositioning parts of speech and breaking up one originally long sentence into two or more. This is done mostly without any indication in the translations. Line numbers at the beginning of each part of the translations guide the reader who wishes to refer back to the original. When English words are added for sense, the added words are placed between parentheses.

In most cases, the various titles, such as *šatammu*, *qīpu,* or *kizû*, are left untranslated. Proper interpretation of terms like these requires more than a simple one- or two-word translation can provide. Fuller pictures can be found in works that examine the institutions in which these functionaries played a role, such as the Ebabbar (Bongenaar 1997) and the Eanna (Kümmel 1979). The entries for the specific titles in *CAD* and *AHw* also provide useful data and interpretations.

Chronology of Neo-Babylonian and Achaemenid Kings (605–424 BCE)

Name in Akkadian	Common English Name	Dates (BCE)
Nabû-kudurrī-uṣur	Nebuchadnezzar (II)	605–562
Amēl-Marduk	Evil-Merodach	561–559
Nergal-šarra-uṣur	Neriglissar	559–555
Nabû-nāʾid	Nabonidus	555–539
Kuraš	Cyrus	538–530
Kambuziya	Cambyses	530–522
Darimuš	Darius I	522–486
Akšiarši	Xerxes	486–465
Artaḫšassu	Artaxerxes I	465–424

INTRODUCTION

The rediscovery of the Code of Hammurabi in the early twentieth century at Susa has ensured that, even among the general public today, ancient Mesopotamia is remembered for its legal legacy. This legacy, however, extends beyond formal law collections like Hammurabi's, to include thousands of much less familiar legal records that attest to the practical use of law in the day-to-day affairs of people who lived millennia ago in the region that stretches from the Persian Gulf to the Levant. Ancient scribes, writing in cuneiform script on clay tablets, recorded transactions, such as loans, contracts, sales, marriages, and adoptions. These mundane documents are attested for almost as long as cuneiform writing was used, that is, for nearly three millennia until just before the beginning of the Common Era.

Neo-Babylonian Mesopotamia is known, for the most part, from a wealth of these kinds of legal and administrative records. Some sixteen thousand Neo-Babylonian legal tablets have been published, out of the approximately one hundred thousand (according to some estimates) that survive in museum collections (Jursa 2005; Wunsch 2010, 41). Originally, these tablets were kept by families or temples, as records of their property, in much the same way that modern files are kept. Assyriologists refer to different sets of documents, that represent the holdings of different families or institutions, as the families' or institutions' "archives."

The fifty trial records that this book presents belong to this vast corpus of Neo-Babylonian archival texts. They are the written remains of litigation pertaining to the property or other interests of the individuals or institutions that kept them. For example, the owner of a parcel of land whose ownership was disputed and then confirmed in court would retain a record of the ruling as proof of ownership. Similarly, temples would conduct investigations and hearings into mishandlings of their property and keep records in order to recoup losses.

Compared to other Neo-Babylonian legal and administrative texts, trial records are among the most exciting to read. Most of the Neo-Babylonian archival texts reflect "business as usual." Trial records, on the other hand, stem from unusual moments, such as disputes over property or cases of institutional malfeasance. Instead of reflecting normal states of affairs, these texts record rather dramatic moments as conflicts are resolved. The drama of the situation is enhanced by the fact that, unlike most Neo-Babylonian archival texts, the trial records usually quote statements by the various parties involved. In other words, even though the cases were closed two and a half millennia ago, one can still "hear" plaintiffs arguing their case or judges questioning a suspect. With just a little imagination, one can conjure up the courtroom dramas as they unfold from the cuneiform records.

By reading trial records like the ones this volume presents, one gets a close-up view of a particular moment in the lives of people who lived in Mesopotamia during the Neo-Babylonian period. The wealth of available documentation often makes it possible not only to read the records of these individuals' days in court, but also to relate the trial records to other documents pertaining to the same litigants. This task is often difficult, since documents that were probably held together in antiquity may be scattered in modern museums around the world. Modern scholarship has, however, successfully overcome this barrier through careful study of personal names and other identifying information. As a result, one can appreciate the courtroom dramas' "background stories," including the events that led up to the lawsuits, the litigants' social or institutional positions, the later history of the subjects in question, as well as the lawsuits' legal bases. The broad view that can emerge from reading the trial records together with other pertinent texts is almost unrivaled by similar records from other periods of ancient Mesopotamian history.

The stories that these lawsuit records tell about particular cases are, of themselves, the stuff of legal and social history. Historians of law can see not only what the law was, but can also observe the machinery of justice at work in an ancient society: its adjudicators, its courtroom procedure and its legal vocabulary. In addition, like all other Neo-Babylonian archival texts, the lawsuit records are also a window into "daily life" in this period. They contain information about topics such as real-estate ownership, land use, personal status, inheritance, business practices, temple management, and agriculture, to name just a few. Most importantly, the trial records tell their stories "from below," meaning from the relatively unfiltered, unofficial perspectives of the men and women who actually participated in the lawsuits. One sees the society, particularly its law, not through an idealized statement on a monumental royal inscription, but as it existed on the ground.

General Historical Context

Most of the texts in this volume were composed during the sixth century BCE. This century saw the flourish and decline of the last native Babylonian rulers in Mesopotamia. During the immediately preceding years, the Babylonians, led by Nabopolassar (r. 626–605 BCE), released themselves from Assyrian hegemony and brought down what remained of the once mighty Assyrian Empire. The oldest texts in this anthology date to the reign of Nabopolassar's son, Nebuchadnezzar (r. 605–562 BCE), whose empire extended beyond the Euphrates River and who made great investments in large-scale building at home. Native Babylonian rule continued through the short reigns of Nebuchadnezzar's two immediate successors, Amēl-Marduk (biblical Evil-Merodach; r. 561–559 BCE) and Neriglissar (r. 559–555 BCE), until the reign of Nabonidus (r. 555–539 BCE), which ended with Cyrus the Great's conquest of Babylonia. The region then became part of the Persian, or Achaemenid, Empire; it would remain so until the arrival of Alexander the Great, who gained control in 330 BCE and incorporated Mesopotamia into his vast empire.

Although Babylonia's political status changed in the later part of the sixth century BCE, local institutions, including legal practice, were not affected at that time. Thus, the cuneiform legal texts from after the Persian conquest, including some of those presented here, closely resemble those from before. The most noticeable difference occurs in the dates written on the texts: the later texts count years by the reigns of the Achaemenid, instead of Babylonian, kings. From the point-of-view of strict political history, then, these later texts are Achaemenid, rather than Neo-Babylonian. However, because of the continuity of the documentation, Assyriologists refer to both pre-Achaemenid and Achaemenid texts as "Neo-Babylonian."

A change in the nature of the available records occurs shortly after the conclusion of the sixth century BCE. Many of the most important family archives come to an abrupt end around the second year of the Achaemenid king Xerxes (484 BCE). Recent revisionary study of the data has determined that this break in the record is not accidental (Waerzeggers 2003–4). Rather, the interruption of the archives provides important evidence for royal intervention in the affairs of the archive-holding families. These families had ties to the old, native Babylonian elite, especially to the management of the ancient temples, and would have had every reason to chafe under the new, Achaemenid regime. Revolts broke out in northern Babylonia and Xerxes quelled them decisively. Xerxes's actions have left their mark on the textual record; the end of the native elite's activities corresponds to the so-called end of archives. Later cuneiform archives are much more limited in number and scope of activity (Jursa 2005, 1; Wunsch 2010, 41).

The Trial Records and Neo-Babylonian Archival Texts: Some Limitations

The relatively small number of texts in this volume is clearly insufficient to provide a meaningfully complete picture of "daily life" in Neo-Babylonian Mesopotamia. It is perhaps less obvious, but just as crucial, that texts like the fifty examples here were hardly typical even when they were originally written. To some degree, this is true of all Neo-Babylonian archival records, regardless of their subject matter. In strictly numerical terms, the overwhelming majority of Neo-Babylonian legal and administrative records come from the archives of just two temples: the Ebabbar at Sippar and the Eanna at Uruk. And the considerable, if much smaller, number of texts from the private archives of ancient families come from just five cities: Babylon, Borsippa, Nippur, Sippar, and Uruk. The available records leave life beyond these centers mostly out of view.

Apart from their restricted provenance, a further limitation stems from the very purpose for which the Neo-Babylonian legal and administrative records were composed. As in other periods of Mesopotamian history, the texts were written with the often explicit goal of protecting the property or interests of those who retained the records. With a written record, there could be no question of who owned a plot of land or who owed debts to whom. But if there was no need to prevent this kind of question, then there was probably no need for a written record. As one author has put it, "where there is no property, or more precisely, no possibility for future disagreement over property (or status or material interests in general), there is no writing" (Jursa 2005, 9). Consequently, the people and institutions attested in the records were those who would have had property and interests to protect and the resources to do so. These are the people whose "daily lives" one can know from the archival records. People without some connection to a temple or from outside the native, landed urban elite (who were also usually connected to the temples) are largely missing from the available documents.

People without such connections did, of course, exist. The personal names in the records show interactions between archive holders and people from outside the more limited circle of the "cuneiform archival class." The archive holders themselves usually have traditional Akkadian personal names, which are recorded with two-part filiation: X son of Y descendant of the Z family. Alongside these traditional names, non-Akkadian names, especially in Aramaic, occur in the records on occasion. But in the vast majority of cases, people with these nonnative names appear as "outsiders" interacting with the archives' main protagonists; by one count, there are only twenty cuneiform documents without any native Babylonian principal involved (Zadok 2003, 553). One must conclude, then, that when these "outsiders" conducted business among themselves, they used other media to record their transactions (Zadok 2003, 553; Jursa 2005, 8). Writing in Aramaic would have been a natural choice; elsewhere in the Persian Empire, Aramaic became the main language of jurisprudence. Thus, in Babylonia, there could well have been a parallel Aramaic legal sphere. Aramaic records, however, would have been written in ink on perishable materials, so, unlike Akkadian records on clay tablets, they would not have survived. Therefore, for the purposes of Assyriologists and other ancient historians, Aramaic records are largely lost.

Trial records, as a distinct subset of the Neo-Babylonian archival corpus, are even less representative than most of the available documentation. A Neo-Babylonian archive usually consists of business documents, most commonly debt obligations, and other contracts. Records pertaining to litigation are much rarer, and may not occur at all. For example, the archive of the Murašû family from the city of Nippur consists of over seven hundred tablets, but contains almost no litigation records (Stolper 1976, 195). Similarly, the Nappāḫu-family archive, the second-largest private family archive from the city of Babylon, contains 266 distinct records. Of these, there are more than 170 "business documents," such as promissory notes, receipts and leases, and some forty documents recording purchases of property, but only about ten documents pertaining to litigation in some way (Baker 2003, 8–10). Because of this trend in the available documentation, studies of Neo-Babylonian court procedure usually find less than four hundred relevant documents, altogether (Magdalene 2007, 55; Holtz 2009, 329–33).

Imagining the Courtroom Drama

As was stated near the outset, the Neo-Babylonian trial records stand out for their immediate, almost dramatic quality. Other documents, such as debt-notes or bills of sale, are often abstract, with only minimal references to the reasons for the transactions. For example, the most common Neo-Babylonian archival text, the debt-note (*u*ʾ*iltu*), typically reads, quite simply, "(object) owed by B to A; on (date), B will give (it) to A" (Jursa 2005, 41–42). Based on this spare formulation, it is impossible to determine why B is indebted to A.

On occasion, even a basic debt-note actually does reveal a trial background. For example, one such note records a debt incurred as the result of a court ruling; the document describes the sum owed as a payment "in lieu of (not) cutting off the hand" of the debtor (Roth 2007, 217–18). In other words, this particular debt-note reflects the substitution of a monetary payment for a physical punishment for theft (Roth 2007). But a nugget of information like this is more the exception than the rule, and, moreover, leaves much to the imagination of anyone who wishes to get a good picture of Neo-Babylonian adjudicatory procedure.

The spare, "boiler plate" language of the debt-note was also of only limited use to the ancient scribes who composed the trial records. The differences between the circumstances of each trial required including details like quotations of direct speech and descriptions of specific procedures. As a result, each record seems like a page torn from the ledger of the ancient professional ancestors of modern-day court stenographers. In fact, many of these documents are often called "protocols," using a modern term that indicates their similarity, at least in terms of content, to the written records of courts today.

Not all trial records narrate the proceedings in court to the same degree of completeness. Some records, especially those of cases tried by the royal judges in Babylon and elsewhere, read almost like minute-to-minute trial accounts. They begin with the plaintiff's initiation of the lawsuit, continue with notices of judicial investigative actions, and conclude with the judges' decision. Assuming that a tablet is reasonably well preserved, one can read individual records like these and, in effect, follow cases from beginning to end. Other texts, rather than telling nearly complete stories, record individual stages of the trial, such as reports to the authorities, summonses to appear in court, or the debt obligations that result from the judges' decision. Texts like these are more like scenes than complete dramas. They require imagination to fill in the surrounding narrative of the lawsuit, including, at times, how the case might have ended (see Wunsch 2012).

Regardless of the type of action the texts record, it is important to remember that the hands of the recording scribes came between the actions as they actually transpired and the written account of these actions preserved on the tablets. While these scribes probably did not consciously invent actions from whole cloth, they did not simply write down speeches and actions as they saw them take place, either. Instead, the scribes followed formal conventions that are immediately noticeable when one compares the records of different cases. Despite the obvious differences in content, different records follow consistent patterns of fixed terminology and order of elements. The highest degree of stylization occurs in the set of records from the courts of the royal judges in Babylon, and other, similar ones (e.g., Documents 19–24). For example, in these texts, the plaintiffs' speeches usually end with a formulaic demand for judgment addressed directly to the judges, followed by a notice that the judges "heard" the arguments. Because these features occur in multiple texts pertaining to different trials, it seems that the very production of the court records required some artificial "staging" of the drama.

One obvious consequence is that events recorded as continuous did not necessarily occur as such in "real time." For example, a document may indicate that, following a complaint, the judges "brought," or summoned, a party before them. In the written record, there is no break between the complaint, the judges' actions and the appearance of the summoned party; all the action seems to occur at one sitting, on one day. In reality, as can be seen from texts that record summonses and other individual actions, some time must have elapsed before the trial could proceed.

In part, this kind of gap between the reality of the lawsuit and its representation in the written record is to be expected. One probably encounters similar problems, to a greater or lesser extent, whenever one relies on court records to reconstruct what took place during a lawsuit. In the case of the Neo-Babylonian records, however, it is important to remember that recording legal proceedings was not the documents' primary purpose. Rather, they were often intended to serve as the prevailing parties' irrefutable proof of the decision in their favor and to prevent reopening the litigation in the future (see Holtz 2009, 302–6). Document 35 makes this purpose very explicit: "So that (the decision) would not be changed, the governor and the judges wrote a tablet. They sealed (it) with their seals and gave (it) to [the prevailing parties]." Thus, these records' reports of the actions that transpired during the trial are ancillary to their original purpose as evidence that the decision was made. Despite their obvious similarities to "protocols," they were never intended to be read as such.

The Adjudicatory System

The courtroom dramas usually take place in one of two main settings: in the presence of temple tribunals or before panels of royal judges. The cases that appear in these two settings are, to some extent, of different kinds. In broadest terms, temple tribunals prosecute matters internal to the temple, while royal judges adjudicate disputes at large. On the surface, this suggests a distinction between "civil" and "criminal" cases, with each handled in its own "stream of justice." It would be artificial, however, to distinguish so rigidly. The separate venues mainly reflect the two main kinds of archival sources, rather than anything inherent in the nature of the litigation. Trial procedures are similar in both venues, and, at times, the same adjudicating authorities are involved.

The essential unity of the Neo-Babylonian adjudicatory process is best explained by considering the role of the king. Judicial authority ultimately stemmed from him, and he was also the highest legal authority. In this capacity, the king upheld a longstanding ancient Near Eastern royal tradition, according to which the king must provide justice for his people. A unique Neo-Babylonian literary text extols a king, probably Nebuchadnezzar II, as follows:

> With regard to true and righteous judgment, he was not negligent; he did not rest night or day. Judgments and decisions designed to be pleasing to the great lord, Marduk, for the benefit of all people and for settling the land of Akkad,

> he inscribed with council and deliberation, and he drew up regulations for the improvement of the city. He built anew the court of law. (Lambert 1965, 8)

The evidence from the actual practice of law confirms the king's legal and legislative activities for which this text sings his praises. Some texts record how temple officials consulted written records of the king's rulings, possibly even the ruler's own written law code (Jursa, Paszkowiak, Waerzeggers 2003–4, 256–59; MacGinnis 2008). Several summonses, including some in this anthology, show the progress of cases from local adjudication by authorities in the Eanna to adjudication by royal judges (Document 16) and even to "the king's court of law" (*bīt dīni ša šarri*) in Babylon (Document 39).

The most consistent indications of the king's connection to the judiciary, however, are the title and office of the royal judges. In the records, they are known as "judges of the king" (*dayyānū ša šarri*) or, more frequently, "the judges of" (*dayyānū ša*) a named king. A good number of texts from their courts survive in the Egibi family archive because one holder of the archive, Nabû-aḫḫē-iddin, was himself a royal judge (van Driel 1985–6, 55). A comprehensive study of the institution of the royal judges as it is reflected in these texts has found that the judges belonged to the same limited circle of families generally attested in the Neo-Babylonian cuneiform records (Wunsch 2000b). This fact further underscores this elite group's connections to power and their "insider" status.

The royal judges were organized in a recognizable hierarchy based on seniority and were overseen by royal officials called the *sartennu* and the *sukallu*. The judges sat in tribunal panels, with usually no more than one representative of any particular family per panel (Wunsch 2000b). A team of court scribes, usually in a pair, served the judges and recorded the proceedings during the trials. Service as a court scribe may have been the first step towards appointment as a royal judge (Holtz 2008).

Despite the connection to the king that their title implies, however, the royal judges apparently enjoyed a degree of independence. Royal judges were not removed from office when the monarch changed. In fact, some royal judges of Nabonidus, the last Neo-Babylonian ruler, continued to serve as royal judges of Cyrus, the first Achaemenid emperor (Wunsch 2000b). More generally, the king's own obligation and commitment to the rule of law probably prevented him from acting arbitrarily against his subjects. One remarkable record shows that even Nebuchadnezzar himself had to follow due process, and in the extreme case of treason, no less:

> Bau-aḫa-iddin son of Nabû-aḫḫē-bulliṭ descendant of Ašared-… committed crimes and planned evil. He did not keep the treaty of the king, his lord, and acted treacherously.

> At that time, Nebuchadnezzar—king of Babylon, judicious prince, shepherd of broad humanity, who, like Šamaš, examines all lands, establisher of truth and justice, who destroys evildoer and enemy—discovered the machinations of Bau-aḫa-iddin; he intercepted his plot.
>
> In the assembly of the people, he testified (regarding) the crime he committed against him. He gazed at him angrily, he commanded that he not live, so they slit his throat. (Weidner 1954–1956, 1–5; Jursa 2001, 2004b)

In light of the severe crime, the ultimate outcome of this case is not very surprising. And given the offense and the offended party, one has to question just how fair the proceedings were, even by ancient standards. As significant, however, is the text's indication that the king publicly convicts the traitor ("in the assembly of the people") before he slits the traitor's throat. Even as he plays the role of judge, he must also "follow the rules," just like any other litigant. The king, at least as far as he wished to be depicted, was also subject to the law.

Apart from the royal judges, and their titular patron, the king (who appears only rarely in the available documents), the Neo-Babylonian records attest to other adjudicating authorities, as well. Higher-level temple bureaucrats, namely the *qīpu*, the *šatammu*, and the royal administrator (*ša rēš šarri bēl piqitti*) of the Eanna frequently oversaw legal proceedings. Alongside these administrative officials, temple records indicate that an "assembly" (UKKIN=*puḫru*) participated in the adjudication. This assembly consisted of "free citizens" (*mār banî*), who, in addition to their role as adjudicators, are often listed as "witnesses" (*mukinnū*) before whom depositions were made.

The participation of these various authorities in the adjudicatory process raises the question of jurisdiction: what determined which authority tried which cases? Temple authorities usually oversee cases related to temple affairs, and the involvement of outside authorities in a temple-related case can usually be explained by the context (Magdalene 2007, 62). When it comes to private affairs, however, determining jurisdiction becomes more difficult. There is evidence for adjudicators who do not bear the title of "judge" (*dayyānu*), such as elders and local governors, but the jurisdictional reason for their participation is not immediately apparent (Wells 2011, 86).

On the Organization of This Book

The first chapter of this book brings together a sample of documents (Documents 1–18) that record legal actions preliminary to the actual trials. These documents pertain to lawsuits from different times and locations and on different subjects. Overall, however, they reflect the variety of actions that might have preceded a trial, such as various evidence-gathering procedures, like the recording of a confession (Document 1) and interrogations (Documents 5–7), and summoning to court in advance of a trial (Documents 15–17). Based on these texts, one can imagine the progress of a hypothetical trial. The order of the documents in this chapter situates them, as best as possible, within the sequence of events leading to the trials themselves.

The second chapter contains formally composed records of trials that end with judicial decisions (Documents 19–36). These decision records come mostly from the courts of the royal judges in Babylon, although other venues are attested, too. They begin with a record of plaintiffs' appearances and statements before the adjudicating authorities, followed by investigative and evidentiary actions, with the decision recorded as the final result. Within the chapter, the documents are arranged according to the subjects of the lawsuits.

The third, and final, chapter presents groups of documents, or "dossiers," that pertain to four different trials. As one might imagine, the variety of documents tell the cases' legal stories more completely than any individual legal text can. Just as importantly, however, the various documents allow one to situate the litigants and their cases within their broader social settings.

Each document in this volume is transliterated and translated into English. Introductory material provides additional information about each document. This introductory material is organized as follows:

1. A number (1–50)

2. An English title assigned to the document that gives a very brief idea of its subject.

3. Text: The specific museum acquisition number assigned to the clay tablet on which the document is written. The combinations of letters and numbers are familiar to trained Assyriologists, who use them to locate the physical artifacts on which the transliterations and translations are ultimately based.

4. Copy: Bibliographic references to published drawings of the tablet. These are useful for anyone who wishes to read (or at least see) the original cuneiform writing, without having to travel to the tablet itself.

5. Translation/Discussion: Bibliographic references to previous complete translations of the document and to other discussions that devote significant attention to the document. With regard to translations, the information under this heading aims to include any full translation of the document. The decision to include references to quotations of shorter passages and other discussions is based on a subjective evaluation of these references' treatment of the issues that the document treats. It is quite likely that there are other scholarly discussions (including references in dictionaries) that mention the document, but which are not listed. For additional references, Assyriologists usually consult the "Register Assyriologie" published in the journal *Archiv für Orientforschung*, and, for earlier publications, Borger 1967–1973.

6. Place of Composition: The location in which the document was written. This is usually based on the information that the document provides.

7. Date: The date on which the document was written, as indicated by the document itself. The date is given first according to the Babylonian calendar, followed by the corresponding date on the modern calendar, in parentheses, calculated according to the tables in Parker and Dubberstein 1956. The Babylonian date is given with the day of the month in Arabic numerals, followed by the month, indicated by a Roman numeral corresponding to that month's place on the calendar. The year is given by an Arabic numeral followed by a three letter abbreviation of the name of the king. The corresponding modern date is indicated by the day of the month, followed by the name of the month and the year BCE. Thus, the date 3.VI.1 Cyr (21 August, 538 BCE) shows that the document was written on the third day of the sixth Babylonian month (Ulūlu) in year 1 of Cyrus, which corresponds to 21 August, 538 BCE. Originally, all the documents contained a specific notice of their date of composition, although this notice may not be preserved today. In cases where the date is damaged, the parts of the date that are not certain are indicated by a question mark.

8. A one-paragraph summary of the main contents of each document follows. This paragraph sketches the main points of each document's "plot," that is, the actions and statements that the document records. The remaining introductory paragraphs survey important contextual topics that emerge from the document's contents, such as the people named in the document or the legal significance of the actions that take place. Keeping the document at the center of the discussion, these introductory paragraphs identify key elements that expose aspects of the proceedings that may not be apparent upon reading the text by itself. Very often, these later paragraphs contextualize by referring to other texts, including other documents in this collection.

Chapter 1
Preliminaries to Trials

1. A Confession

Text: VAT 8461
Copy: Pohl 1933 (AnOr 8), No. 27
Translation/Discussion: Ebeling 1952–53, 68–69; Joannès 2000b, No. 155 (pp. 213–14); Holtz 2009, 273–75.
Place of Composition: Uruk
Date: 10.IV.12 Nbn (4 July, 544 BCE)

Iltameš-baraku has caught Lū-dānu stealing property and has handed the thief to Nergal-nāṣir. Lū-dānu confesses that he and four accomplices made a hole in Nergal-nāṣir's house in order to steal a variety of tools, garments, and commodities, which they gave to the father of one of the thieves. Following the confession, the authorities take one spade, which was marked with a star as temple property, to the Eanna.

Consideration of the parties involved in this case indicates that the very act of theft was probably quite bold. Specifically, Nergal-nāṣir, the man from whose house the temple property was stolen, was serving as the "chief farmer" (*ša muḫḫi sūti*) at the time of the present document's composition (Kümmel 1979, 105; Joannès 2000b, 213). When they broke into his house, the thieves not only took property illegally, but also flouted Nergal-nāṣir's authority as an important temple functionary. In addition, Nergal-nāṣir's role in the management of the Eanna's agricultural enterprises might also explain why the agricultural implements were in his house in the first place.

The present document belongs to pretrial documentation. As such, it illustrates a number of features of the Eanna's procedure of evidence gathering. In general, this process was formally documented; records were maintained that are separate from those of the trials themselves. In the present case, Lū-dānu makes his statement and names his accomplices "without interrogation," which contrasts with reports of confessions made under interrogation (see Documents 5 and 6, below). Furthermore, the placing of the marked spade in the Eanna might be more than simply the restoration of the stolen property. It might, instead, reflect a concern for the preservation of physical evidence, known from other texts (like Documents 2 and 40 below) that record similar procedures.

1. ^{m}*lu-u-da-a-nu* A-*šú šá* ^{m}*ib-ni-*[^{d}INNIN A … *šá*]
2. ^{md}*il-ta-meš-ba-ra-ku*$^{!}$ A-*šú šá* ^{md}⸢NA$_{3}$⸣-⸢NUMUN⸣-[X]
3. *ina sa-áš-tu*$_{4}$ *iṣ-ba-ta-áš-šim-ma a-na* ^{md}U.GUR-PAP

(1–4) Lū-dānu son of Ibni-[Ištar descendant of … whom] Iltameš-baraku son of Nabû-zēra-[X] caught in (an act of) theft and handed him over to Nergal-nāṣir son of Nanaya-ibni.

4. A-*šú šá* ^{md}*na-na-a-*DU$_{3}$ *id-di-nu-uš šá la ma-áš-a-a-al-tu*$_{4}$

(4–5) Without interrogation he said thus:

5. *iq-bi um-ma a-*⸢*na*⸣-[*ku*] ^{m}*mu-ra-šu-ú* A-*šú šá* ^{m}NUMUN-DU$_{3}$
6. ^{md}INNIN-ŠEŠ-MU A-*šú* [*šá*…] ^{m}*ba-si-a u* ^{md}INNIN-*na*-ŠEŠ.ME-MU
7. A.MEŠ *šá* ^{m}*ib-ni-*^{d}INNIN *ina mu-ši ni-ik-su a-na*
8. E$_{2}$ ^{md}U.GUR-*na-ṣir* A-*šú šá* ^{md}*na-na-a-ib-ni*
9. *šá ina* UGU $^{id_{2}}$*tak-ki-ru ki-i ni-ik-ki-su*
10. *ki-i ni-ru-bu* 1 *na-áš-ḫi-ip-tu*$_{4}$ *ap-pa-tu*$_{4}$ AN.BAR
11. [*ka-la*]-*ab-ba-tu*$_{4}$ AN.BAR 3 *mar* AN.BAR.MEŠ *ù* $^{tug_{2}}$*mu-ṣip-e-tu*$_{4}$
12. 1 (GUR) ŠE.BAR 1 GUR ZU$_{2}$.LUM.MA
13. *ki-i ni-iš-šu-ú a-na* ^{m}NUMUN-DU$_{3}$ AD *šá* ^{m}*mu-*[*ra-šu-ú*]
14. $^{lu_{2}}$ŠU.HA *šá it-ti-ni ni-ip-ta*$^{!}$*-qí-id*

(5–14) "I, Murašû son of Zēra-ibni, Ištar-aḫa-iddin son [of PN], Basiya and Innin-aḫḫē-iddin sons of Ibni-Ištar—at night, when we cut a hole in the house of Nergal-nāṣir son of Nanaya-ibni, which is near the Takkiru canal—when we entered and took 1 iron-tipped spade, an iron a[x], 3 iron shovels, a *muṣipetu* garment, 1 *kur* of barley and 1 *kur* of dates, we deposited it with Zēra-ibni, father of Mu[rašû], the fisherman, who was with us."

15. 1 *na-áš-ḫi-ip-tu*$_4$ *šá kak*$^!$*-kab-tu*$_4$ *še-en-*[*de-ti*]	(15–18) 1 spade, mark[ed] with a star, which they took from the house of Nergal-nāṣir, which Iltameš-baraku took from his (i.e., Lū-dānu's) hands—the evidence against him (Lū-dānu)—they placed in the Eanna.
16. *šá ul-tu* E$_2$ ^{md}U.GUR-*na-ṣir iš-šu*	
17. *šá* ^{md}*il-ta-meš-ba-ra-ku ina* ŠU.2-*šú iš-šá*	
18. SU.2 *ṣi-bit-ti-šú ina* E$_2$.AN.NA *iš-ku-nu*	
19. *ina* DU-*zu šá* ^{md}NA$_3$-LUGAL-URI$_3$ ^{lu_2}SAG-LUGAL ^{lu_2}EN *pi-qit-tu*$_4$ E$_2$.AN.NA	(19) In the presence of: Nabû-šarra-uṣur, the royal official in charge of the Eanna;
20. ^{m}*gab-bi*-DINGIR.MEŠ-LUGAL-URI$_3$ ^{lu_2}*qí-i-pi šá* E$_2$.AN.NA	(20) Gabbi-ilī-šarra-uṣur, the *qīpu*-official of Eanna;
21. ^{m}NUMUN-*ia* ^{lu_2}ŠA$_3$.TAM E$_2$.AN.NA A-*šú šá* ^{m}*ib-na-a*	(21–22) Zēriya, the *šatammu* of the Eanna, son of Ibnaya descendant of Egibi.
22. A ^{m}*e-gi-bi* ^{lu_2}*mu-kin-nu* ^{md}30-APIN-*eš*	(22–23) Witnesses: Sîn-ēreš son of Nabû-šumu-līšir descendant of Ibni-ilī;
23. A-*šú šá* ^{md}NA$_3$-MU-SI.SA$_2$ A ^{m}DU$_3$-DINGIR ^{md}DI.KU$_5$-ŠEŠ.ME-⌜MU⌝	(23–24) Madānu-aḫḫē-iddin son of Gimillu descendant of Šigûa;
24. A-*šú šá* ^{m}*gi-mil-lu* A ^{m}*ši-gu-ú-a* ^{m}*ki-na-a*	(24–25) Kīnaya son of Zēriya;
25. A-*šú šá* ^{m}NUMUN-*ia* ^{m}*mu-ra-nu* A-*šú šá* ^{md}NA$_3$-DU$_3$-ŠEŠ	(25–26) Mūrānu son of Nabû-bāni-aḫi descendant of Ekur-zakir;
26. A ^{m}*e-kur-za-kir* ^{m}*ba-la-ṭu* A-*šú šá* ^{md}30-DU$_3$	(26–27) Balāṭu son of Sîn-ibni descendant of Rē'i-alpi.
27. A ^{lu_2}SIPA GU$_4$ ^{lu_2}UMBISAG ^{m}*na-di-nu* A-*šú*	(27–28) Scribe: Nādinu son of Bēl-aḫḫē-iqīša descendant of Egibi.
28. *šá* ^{md}EN-ŠEŠ.MEŠ-BA-*šá* A ^{m}*e-gi-bi*	
29. UNUG^{ki} ITI ŠU U$_4$ 10-*kám* MU 12-*kám*	(29–30) Uruk. 10 Dûzu, year 12 of Nabonidus, king of Babylon.
30. ^{d}NA$_3$-IM.TUK LUGAL TIN.TIR^{ki}	

NOTES

18. As it occurs here, the term *qāṭ ṣibitti* refers to the *corpus delicti,* the stolen property that has been found in the thief's possession (see *CAD* Ṣ, 156).

2. Apprehension for Cultic Crimes

Text: YBC 3981
Copy: Dougherty 1920 (YOS 6), No. 222
Translation/Discussion: Coquerillat 1973–1974, 113–14.
Place of Composition: Uruk
Date: 4.VI.12 Nbn (27 August, 544 BCE)

Anum-šumu-līšir has presented rotten dates and pomegranates as offerings. Because they could not be used, there was a cessation of the cultic offerings, which had to be resolved by using the Eanna's own produce. The šatammu *places Anum-šumu-līšir in shackles and places the rotten fruit under seal in the Eanna.*

The present document provides a rare glimpse into the daily rituals in the Eanna. Based on the description of the obligatory offering that Anum-šumu-līšir, the defendant, was required to bring, he is an "orchard-keeper" (*rāb bani*). In this position, he would have been in charge of the temple's sacred orchard (*kirû ḫallatu*), and would have been responsible for providing the fruits for the gods' consumption (Cocquerillat 1973–1974, 133). Other temple functionaries would have received Anum-šumu-līšir's fruit and, if all had been in order, would have made the actual offering (Cocquerillat 1973–1974, 114). It is probably the temple functionaries in charge of the actual offerings who would have reported the poor quality of Anum-šumu-līšir's dates and pomegranates to the Eanna authorities.

Like Document 1 above, the present document records the very first stages of the legal proceedings. In fact, this document was composed on the very same date upon which the ritual offense was committed. Two preliminary actions are recorded: the apprehension of the defendant and the preservation of the evidence. The defendant here, and in other cases as well, is placed in shackles until the time of his trial. The rotten fruits, like other evidence and *corpora delicti*, are tied and sealed in a bundle (see San Nicolò 1945, 16–17 and Holtz 2009, 272–75). They would probably have been presented before the adjudicating authorities when Anum-šumu-līšir's punishment was decided.

Confirmation of the preliminary nature of the present document comes from another document, composed on the same date (Weisberg 1967, No. 3 [pp. 19–21]). In this other document, Šamaš-zēra-ibni (the witness in line 21 in the present document) and another man assume responsibility for Anum-šumu-līšir (Kümmel 1979, 95 n. 5). Thus, Anum-šumu-līšir was released from the shackles to be presented "on the day that the royal official in charge of the Eanna summons him," presumably for a hearing.

1. U$_4$ 4-*kám šá* ITI KIN MU 12-*kám* ^{d}NA$_3$-IM.TUK LUGAL TIN.TIR^{ki} 2. ^{lú_2}GAL.DU$_3$-*ú-tu* IGI ^{d}GAŠAN *šá* UNUG^{ki} ^{d}*na-na-a* 3. *ù* ^{d}GAŠAN *šá* SAG *šá* ^{md}*a-num*-MU-SI.SA$_2$ A-*šú* 4. *šá* ^{md}NA$_3$-A-MU ZU$_2$.LUM.MA *ù lu-ri-in-du* 5. *a-na nap-ta-nu šá* ^{d}GAŠAN *šá* UNUG^{ki} *ú-še-lam-ma*	(1–5) On 4 Ulūlu, year 12 of Nabonidus, king of Babylon, (in fulfillment of) the obligation of the orchard-keepers before the Lady of Uruk, Nanaya and Bēlet-ša-rēši, incumbent upon Anum-šumu-līšir son of Nabû-apla-iddin, he presented dates and pomegranates for the meal of the Lady of Uruk.
6. *ku-um be-ʾ-e-šú a-na* ^{d}GAŠAN *šá* UNUG^{ki} *la iq-ru-bu*	(6) Because they were rotten, they were not offered before the Lady of Uruk.
7. *baṭ-lu iš-ku-nu-ma* ^{m}NUMUN-*ia* ^{lú_2}ŠA$_3$.TAM E$_2$.AN.NA	(7) A cessation was caused.
8. A-*šú šá* ^{m}*ib-na-a* A ^{m}*e-gi-bi ù* ^{lú_2}UMBISAG.MEŠ *šá* E$_2$.AN.NA 9. ZU$_2$.LUM.MA *ù lu-ri-in-du ul-tu* E$_2$.AN.NA	(7–10) Zēriya, the *šatammu* of the Eanna, son of Ibnaya descendant of Egibi and the scribes of the Eanna offered dates and pomegranates from the Eanna to the Lady of Uruk.
10. *a-na* ^{d}GAŠAN *šá* UNUG^{ki} *ú-qar-ri-bu* ^{md}*a-num*-MU-SI.SA$_2$	(10–11) He cast Anum-šumu-līšir in the shackles which are in the Eanna.
11. *si-me-re-e šá ina* E$_2$.AN.NA *id-di ù* ZU$_2$.LUM.MA 12. *ù lu-ri-in-du šá a-na nap-ta-nu* 13. *ú-še-lam-ma ku-um be-ʾ-e-šú la iq-ru-bu* 14. *ina* E$_2$.AN.NA *ik-nu-uk*	(11–14) In the Eanna, he (Zēriya) placed the dates and pomegranates, which he (Anum-šumu-līšir) presented for the meal and which were not offered because they were rotten, under seal.
15. ^{lú_2}*mu-kin-nu* ^{m}*mu-še-zib*-^{d}EN A-*šú šá* ^{md}UTU-SIG$_{15}$ A ^{m}DU$_3$-*eš*-⌜DINGIR⌝	(15) Witnesses: Mušēzib-Bēl son of Šamaš-mudammiq descendant of Eppeš-ili;
16. ^{md}30-KAM$_2$ A-*šú šá* ^{md}NA$_3$-MU-SI.SA$_2$ A ^{m}DU$_3$-DINGIR	(16) Sîn-ēreš son of Nabû-šumu-līšir descendant of Ibni-ilī;
17. ^{m}IR$_3$-^{d}EN A-*šú šá* ^{m}*ṣil-la-a* A ^{m}MU-^{d}PAP.SUKKAL	(17) Arad-Bēl son of Ṣillaya descendant of Iddin-Papsukkal;
18. ^{md}NA$_3$-SUR-ZI.MEŠ A-*šú šá* ^{m}IR$_3$-^{d}EN A ^{m}*e-gi-bi*	(18) Nabû-ēṭir-napšāti son of Arad-Bēl descendant of Egibi;

19. ^{m}*na-di-nu* A-*šú šá* ^{m}*ap-la-a* A ^{m}ŠEŠ.MEŠ-*ú*	(19) Nādinu son of Aplaya descendant of Aḫḫûtu;
20. ^{md}AMAR.UTU-MU-URI$_3$ A-*šú šá* ^{m}EN-TIN-*iṭ* A ^{m}*pu-ú-tu*$_4$	(20) Marduk-šuma-uṣur son of Bēl-uballiṭ descendant of Pūtu;
21. ^{md}UTU-[NUMUN-DU$_3$] A-*šú šá* ^{md}*na-na-a*-MU A ^{m}*ḫa-nap*	(21) Šamaš-[zēra-ibni] son of Nanaya-iddin descendant of Ḫanap;
22. ^{m}IR$_3$-^{d}[INNIN-*na*] A-*šú šá* ^{m}DU$_3$-^{d}INNIN A ^{m}ŠU-^{d}*na-na-a*	(22) Arad-[Innin] son of Ibni-Ištar descendant of Gimil-Nanaya;
23. ^{lu_2}UMBISAG ^{m}*na-din* A-*šú šá* ^{m}[^{d}EN]-ŠEŠ.MEŠ-BA-*šá* A ^{m}*e-gi-bi*	(23) Scribe: Nādin, son of [Bēl]-aḫḫē-iqīša descendant of Egibi.
24. UNUG^{ki} ITI KIN U$_4$ 4-*kám* MU 12-*kám* ^{d}NA$_3$-I	(24–25) Uruk. 4 Ulūlu year 12 of Nabonidus, king of Babylon.
25. LUGAL TIN.TIR^{ki}	

3. Reports about Theft in High Places

Text: YBC 4176
Copy: Tremayne 1925 (YOS 7), No. 10
Translation/Discussion: Dandamaev 1984, 429–30; Joannès 2000a, 29; 2000b, No. 160 (pp. 217–18); Holtz 2009, 103–4
Place of Composition: Uruk
Date: 1.II.1 Cyr (22 April, 538 BCE)

Nabû-rēṣua, a slave of Lâbāši-Marduk, reports to the šatammu *and the royal official in charge of the Eanna that his master's son, Iddinaya, stole and hid a gem, apparently from a cultic image that was in Ištar-aḫa-iddin's care. Nabû-lū-dāri, another slave, confirms Nabû-rēṣua's testimony. Ḫašdaya, brother of the suspected thief, Iddinaya, also reports finding the stolen object on Lâbāši-Marduk's property after it had been taken from Ištar-aḫa-iddin's storehouse.*

Ištar-aḫa-iddin, the man responsible for the cultic image and the gem it contained, may have received the object, along with the gem, to make repairs (Joannès 2000a, 29). The workshop (*bīt šutummu*) from which the gem was taken may have been located on temple property and leased to Ištar-aḫa-iddin, as was typically done for artisans and administrators employed in the Eanna (Joannès 2000a, 28–29). The suspect's father, Lâbāši-Marduk son of Arad-Bēl descendant of Egibi, would have had access to this area; he held the prestigious office of "chief baker" (*šāpir nuḫatimmī*; Kümmel 1979, 152; Joannès 2000b, 217). It is not clear, however, how Iddinaya, the suspected son, could have entered the precinct without arousing suspicions.

Despite Iddinaya's reportedly suspicious behavior and the testimony against him, one should not overlook the role of the slave, Nabû-rēṣua, in connection with the crime. According to the slave's testimony, the theft took place near the end of Kislīmu, or some four months prior to the writing of the present document. This gap of time suggests that the missing object was successfully hidden for a good while. The slave's precise knowledge about the circumstances surrounding the original theft and the notice that he provides his report "without interrogation"—that is as an uncoerced confession—suggest that he may have been under some suspicion for participating in the misdeed. At the very least, if the slave witnessed the theft on the night in question, then he was probably complicit in keeping it under wraps. If so, then one may assume that the proceedings in the Eanna take place only once Ḫašdaya, the suspect's brother, has discovered the stolen object and reported it to the authorities.

The specifically religious significance of the stolen object probably added a measure of gravity to the offense and to the severity with which the case was handled. These additional aspects of the proceedings are reflected in the presence of Rīmūt-Bēl, the *šešgallu*, probably the high priest, as a witness to the proceedings (lines 14–15). He also appears among the high-ranking officers in Gimillu's trial (Document 38 below), and may have inherited the position from his father (Kümmel 1979, 134–35).

At first glance, one might imagine that this case would have cast aspersions on the careers of both Iddinaya, the suspected thief, and possibly that of his father, Lâbāši-Marduk, too. Later documents from the Eanna, however, show that this was not the case (Kümmel 1979, 114, 152). Both father and son continued to participate in the Eanna's activities well after this incident.

1. [^{m}]^{d}NA$_3$-*re-ṣu-ú-a* ^{lu_2}*qal-la šá* ^{m}*la-a-ba-ši*-^{d}AMAR.UTU 2. A-*šú šá* ^{m}IR$_3$-^{d}EN A ^{m}*e-gi-bi šá la ma-šá-a-a-al-tu*$_4$ *a-na* 3. ^{md}NA$_3$-DU-NUMUN ^{lu_2}ŠA$_3$.TAM E$_2$.AN.NA A-*šú šá* ^{m}*na-di-nu* A ^{m}*da-bi-bi* 4 *ù* ^{md}NA$_3$-ŠEŠ-MU ^{lu_2}SAG-LUGAL ^{lu_2}EN *pi-qit-tu*$_4$ E$_2$.AN.NA *iq-bi*	(1–5) Nabû-rēṣua, slave of Lâbāši-Marduk son of Arad-Bēl descendant of Egibi, without interrogation said thus to Nabû-mukīn-zēri, the *šatammu* of the Eanna, son of Nādinu descendant of Dābibī and Nabû-aḫa-iddin, the royal official in charge of the Eanna:
5. *um-ma* U$_4$ 28-*kám šá* ITI GAN NA$_4$ *mur-ḫa-ši-tu šá* ^{md}15-ŠEŠ-MU 6. A-*šú šá* ^{md}*in-nin*-MU-URI$_3$ A ^{md}NA$_3$-*šar-ḫi*-DINGIR *ul-tu muḫ-ḫi am-ma-tu* ⸢*šá*⸣ ^{d}GAŠAN *šá* UNUG^{ki} 7. *ina sa-ar-tu*$_4$ *ina mu-ši* ^{m}SUM-*na-a* A-*šú šá* ^{m}*la-a-ba-ši*-^{d}AMAR.UTU 8. A ^{m}*e-gi-bi it-ta-sa-aḫ* ⸢*ina*⸣ [*šá*]-*ad-da il-ta-kan*	(5–8) "On 28 Kislīmu, Iddinaya son of Lâbāši-Marduk descendant of Egibi unlawfully removed the precious stone from Marḫaši (in the possession) of Ištar-aḫa-iddin son of Innin-šuma-uṣur descendant of Nabû-šarḫi-ilī from the arm of the Lady of Uruk at night (and) placed (it) in a [con]tainer."
9. *ù* ^{md}NA$_3$-*lu-u-da-a-ri* ^{lu_2}*qal-la šá* ^{m}*ba-ni-ia* A-*šú* 10. *šá* ^{m}*ta-ri-bi uk-ti-in ù* ^{m}*ḫaš-da-a* ŠEŠ *šá* ^{m}SUM-*na-a*	(9–11) And Nabû-lū-dāri, slave of Bāniya son of Taribi testified, and Ḫašdaya, brother of Iddinaya, said thus in the assembly:

11. *ina* UKKIN *iq-bi um-ma* NA₄ *mur-ḫa-ši-tu šá* ⌈*ul*⌉-*tu* E₂ *šu-*⌈*tu*⌉-*um-mu*

12. *šá* ᵐᵈ15-ŠEŠ-MU *ina sa-ar-tu₄ na-šá-a-ta*

13. *ina* E₂ ᵐ*la-a-ba-ši-*ᵈAMAR.UTU AD-*ia a-ta-mar*

14. ˡᵘ²*mu-kin-nu* ᵐ*ri-mut-*ᵈEN ˡᵘ²ŠEŠ.GAL E₂.AN.NA A-*šú šá* ᵐᵈEN-TIN-*iṭ*

15. A ᵐŠU-ᵈ*na-na-a* ᵐGAR-MU A-*šú šá* ᵐDU₃-ᵈ15 A ᵐᵈ30-*tab-ni*

16. ᵐᵈ*in-nin-*MU-URI₃ A-*šú šá* ᵐMU-ᵈNA₃ A ᵐ*ki-din-*ᵈAMAR.UTU

17. ᵐᵈNA₃-TIN-*su-iq-bi* A-*šú šá* ᵐ*ib-na-a* A ᵐE₂.KUR-*za-kir*

18. ᵐ*ze-ri-ia* A-*šú šá* ᵐᵈ*na-na-a-*KAM₂ A ᵐ*ki-din-*ᵈAMAR.UTU

19. ᵐIR₃-*ia* A-*šú šá* ᵐ*ap-la-a* A ᵐᵈNA₃-*šar-ḫi-*DINGIR

20. ᵐKAR-ᵈAMAR.UTU A-*šú šá* ᵐ*kab-ti-ia* A ᵐ*ši-gu-ú-a*

21. ˡᵘ²UMBISAG ᵐ*gi-mil-lu* ⌈A-*šú šá*⌉ ᵐᵈ*in-nin-*NUMUN-MU

22. UNUGᵏⁱ ITI GU₄ U₄ 1-*kám* MU 1-*kám* ᵐ*ku-ra-áš* LUGAL KUR.KUR

(11–13) "I found the precious stone from Marḫaši which was carried away in theft from the workshop of Ištar-aḫa-iddin, in the house of Lâbāši-Marduk, my father."

(14–15) Witnesses: Rīmūt-Bēl, the *šešgallu* of Eanna, son of Bēl-uballiṭ, descendant of Gimil-Nanaya;

(15) Šākin-šumi son of Ibni-Ištar descendant of Sîn-tabni;

(16) Innin-šuma-uṣur son of Iddin-Nabû descendant of Kidin-Marduk;

(17) Nabû-balāssu-iqbi son of Ibnaya descendant of Ekur-zakir;

(18) Zēriya son of Nanaya-ēreš descendant of Kidin-Marduk;

(19) Ardiya son of Aplaya descendant of Nabû-šarḫi-ilī;

(20) Mušēzib-Marduk son of Kabtiya descendant of Šigûa;

(21) Scribe: Gimillu son of Innin-zēra-iddin.

(22) Uruk. 1 Ayaru, year 1 of Cyrus, king of the lands.

NOTES

5–8. The present reading follows Joannès 2000a, 29, and 2000b, No. 160 (p. 117), and takes the stolen item to be a precious stone from Marḫaši (NA₄ *mur-ḫa-ši-tu*). For discussion of the stone, see *CAD* M₁, 280–81. Earlier readings, recorded in various entries in *CAD* and in Dandamaev 1984, understand the missing object to be a mill for cumin (ⁿᵃ⁴ḪAR *ḫa-ši-mur*).

12. The word *na-šá-ta* can also be interpreted as a second-person verbal form and translated "you carried off" (Dandamaev 1984, 430). If this translation

is correct, then Ḫašdaya, the speaker, addresses his accusation directly to Iddi-naya, his brother, the suspected thief.

4. An Accusation of Burglary

Text: BM 74761 (83-1-18, 81)
Copy: Strassmaier 1890b (Cyr), No. 328
Translation/Discussion: Peiser 1896: No. 24 (pp. 282–85); Kohler and Peiser 1890–1898, 2:77; Oppenheim 1941, 269; Bongenaar 1997, 17 n. 38; Joannès 2002d
Place of Composition: Sippar
Date: 28.XII.8 Cyr (22 March, 530 BCE)

Nabû-aḫ̮ḫ̮ē-bulliṭ, overseer of the city of Šaḫ̮rīnu, reports the robbery of his house to the šangû *of Sippar. Nabû-aḫ̮ḫ̮ē-bulliṭ has detained his own nephew, Nanaya-iddin, along with a group of seven men who broke down the door to Nanaya-aḫ̮ḫ̮ē-bulliṭ's house and took away one mina of silver.*

Another, rather fragmentary text (Strassmaier 1890b [Cyr], No. 329) records statements made by several of the men that Nabû-aḫ̮ḫ̮ē-bulliṭ seized. It was written two days after the present text. When the two texts are taken together, they apparently document the progress of the case from the accusation, lodged in the present text, to later stages of the trial.

1.	^{md}NA$_3$-ŠEŠ.MEŠ-*bul-liṭ* A-*šú šá* ^{m}*šu*-[…]	(1–5) Nabû-aḫ̮ḫ̮ē-bulliṭ son of P[N], the overseer of the city Šaḫ̮rīnu, who on 28 Addaru, year 8 of Cyrus, king of Babylon, king of the lands, said thus to Bēl-uballiṭ, the *šangû* of Sippar:
2.	^{lu_2}*pa-qu-du šá* URU *šaḫ-ri-in-*[*ni*]	
3.	*šá* U$_4$ 28-*kám šá* ITI ŠE MU 8-*kám* ^{m}*kur-raš*	
4.	LUGAL E^{ki} LUGAL KUR.KUR *a-na* ^{md}EN-TIN-*iṭ*	
5.	^{lu_2}SANGA UD.KIB.NUN^{ki} *iq-bu-ú um-ma*	
6.	^{md}*na-na-a*-MU A-*šú šá* ^{md}KA$_2$-KAM$_2$ *ina* E$_2$-*ia*	(6–7) "I have seized Nanaya-iddin son of Bau-ēreš in my house, (saying) thus:
7.	*aṣ-ṣa-bit um-ma* ŠEŠ AD-*ka u* ^{lu_2}*pa-qu-du*	
8.	*šá* URU *a-na-ku mi-nam-ma* ŠU.2-*ka a-na muḫ-ḫi-iá*	(7–9) 'I am your father's brother and the overseer of the city. Why do you threaten me?'"

9. *ta-ad-ka* ^{md}IM-LUGAL-PAP A-*šú šá* ^{md}NA$_3$-*ú-še-zib*	(9–17) "When Adad-šarra-uṣur son of Nabû-ušēzib, Nargiya, and Erība, his brothers, Kutka-ili son of Bau-ēreš, Bēl-uballiṭ son of Bariki-ili, Bēl-aḫḫē-uṣur son of Adad-ušallim, and Iqīšaya son of Šamaš-šarra-uṣur, acted in malice (?), carried off my door and entered my house (and) turned away, they took away 1 mina of silver."
10. ^{m}*nar-gi-ia u* ^{m}*eri-ba* ŠEŠ.MEŠ-*šú*	
11. ^{m}*ku-ut-ka-*ʾ-DINGIR A-*šú šá* ^{md}KA$_2$-KAM$_2$	
12. ^{md}EN-TIN-*iṭ* A-*šú šá* ^{m}*ba-ri-ki-*DINGIR	
13. ^{md}EN-ŠEŠ.MEŠ-PAP A-*šú šá* ^{md}IM-GI	
14. *u* ^{m}BA-*šá-a* A-*šú šá* ^{md}UTU-LUGAL-PAP *ki-i*	
15. *il-lam-ma-nu* ^{giš}GAL$_2$-*a it-ta-bal-*ʾ*u*	
16. *u a-na* E$_2$-*ia ki-i ir-bu-nu it-te-ru-nu*	
17. 1 MA.NA KU$_3$.BABBAR-*a it-ta-šu-ú* ^{lú}*mu-kin-nu*	(17) Witnesses:
18. ^{md}KA$_2$-KAM$_2$ A-*šú šá* ^{m}*šu-lum-ma-du* ^{m}*ri-mut*	(18) Bau-ēreš son of Šullum-mādu;
19. A-*šú šá* ^{m}*šul-lum-ma-du* ^{m}MU-^{d}*gu-la* A-*šú šá* ^{m}DU$_3$-*ia*	(18–19) Rīmūt son of Šullum-mādu; Iddin-Gula son of Bāniya;
20. ^{md}NA$_3$-NUMUN-MU A-*šú šá* ^{m}KI$^{?}$- ^{d}EN-DUG$_3$.GA ^{m}[PN]	(20) Nabû-zēra-iddin son of Itti-Bēl-ṭābu;
21. A-*šú šá* ^{md}UTU-NUMUN-DU$_3$ ^{lú}UMBISAG ^{m}IR$_3$-^{d}EN A-*šú šá* ^{md}EN-[GI]	(20–22) [PN] son of Šamaš-zēra-ibni; Scribe: Arad-Bēl son of Bēl-[ušallim] descendant of Adad-šammê.
22. A ^{md}IM-*šam-me-e sip-par*^{ki} ITI ŠE U$_4$ 28-*kám*	(22–23) Sippar. 28 Addaru, year 8 of Cyrus, king of Babylon, king of the lands.
23. MU 8-*kám* ^{m}*kur-raš* LUGAL E^{ki} LUGAL KUR.KUR	
24. ^{md}*na-na-a-*MU *u* ^{md}IM-LUGAL-PAP	(24–25) Nanaya-iddin and Adad-šarra-uṣur at the order of Nabû-aḫḫē-bulliṭ.
25. *ina qí-bi šá* ^{md}NA$_3$-ŠEŠ.MEŠ-*bul-liṭ*	

Notes

5. *um-ma-* Both Peiser 1896, 283 and Kohler and Peiser 1890–1898, 2:77 understand this word as the beginning of a new sentence, addressed to the *šangû*. They translate the word as "*nun*" ("now"). However, the use of *umma* as an adverb in this manner is unattested (see *CAD* U, 101; *AHw*, 1413), unless a scribal error is at play. The word *umma* continues the previous sentence, indicating what was said at the time of the seizing. Therefore, the 2ms forms in the sentences are addressed directly to the seized individual.

8–9. For the idiomatic expression *qātē dekû* see *CAD* D, 127, s.v. *dekû* f2'c'2".

15. Translation of the phrase *ki-i il-lam-ma-nu* follows Kohler and Peiser 1890–1898, 2:77, who offer "um Böses anzurichten" ("in order to cause harm"), without additional comment. Their translation apparently derives the phrase from the verb *lemēnu* (see *CAD* L, 117; *AHw*, 543).

24–25. This line of the text is apparently a summary of the proceedings.

5. An Interrogation about Sheep

Text: YBC 6939
Copy: Dougherty 1920 (YOS 6), No. 137
Translation/Discussion: San Nicolò, 1933b, 289–91; Frame 1991, 74; Joannès 2000b, No. 164 (pp. 221–22)
Place of Composition: Uruk
Date: 30.IV.7 Nbn (18 August, 549 BCE)

Nabû-šarra-uṣur, the royal official in charge of the Eanna, interrogates two thieves, Marduk and Bēl-aḫḫē-iddin. During the previous night, the two men stole three ewes and one lamb from the flock of Šamaš-šuma-iddin tended by Nergal-īpuš. Nergal-īpuš, the herdsman, has found cooked meat, a pot, a hide and two live ewes and one lamb on the property of a woman. He presents the evidence in the Eanna, where Nabû-šarra-uṣur interrogates the two thieves. The two thieves confess to the crime, and incriminate a third individual, Nanaya-iddin. Nabû-šarra-uṣur returns the living sheep to Šamaš-šuma-iddin's son.

The present document is the record of a procedure called *maš'altu,* or interrogation. Other records report confessions taking place "without interrogation" (*ša lā maš'alti*) (see Documents 1 and 3 above) or that the guilty party "testified against himself" (*eli ramnīšu ukīn*) (see Document 38 below). In these other cases, the confession occurs before the Eanna authorities actively intervene in order to extract it. In contrast, the record here (and Document 6, below) reports the confession as the result of the Eanna authorities' interrogation.

As in most cases in the Eanna, the result of the procedure here is that the guilty parties confess to their crimes (San Nicolò 1933b, 301). Since admissions of guilt are so common, it has been suggested that the "interrogation" may have involved torture (San Nicolò 1933b, 302). Confirmation comes from a later text written at Uruk during the Seleucid period. This text reports that thieves were caught and convicted "by means of the rack (literally, ladder) of interrogation" (*simmiltu ša maš'alti*), which strongly suggests an implement designed to inflict physical pain (Sachs and Hunger 1989, No. 168: A15'–A20' [pp. 476–77]). A device like this, if already in use during the Neo-Babylonian period, would explain the frequency of both admissions of guilt and confessions "without interrogation."

1. *ma-šá-a-al-ti šá* ^{md}NA$_3$-LUGAL-URI$_3$ ^{lu_2}SAG-LUGAL ^{lu_2}EN *pi-*⌜*qit-tú*⌝ E$_2$.AN.NA	(1) Interrogation by Nabû-šarra-uṣur, the royal official in charge of the Eanna.

2. ^{m}*mar-duk* A-*šú šá* ^{md}NA$_3$-NUMUN-MU ^{lu_2} ^{uru}*i-pal-ti-ra-a-*[*a*]
3. *u* ^{md}EN-ŠEŠ.MEŠ-MU A-*šú šá* ^{md}*na-na-a*-KAM$_2$ ^{lu_2}*sar-ru-t*[*u*]
4. *šá* 3 U$_8$ *ù* 1 UDU *ka-lum šá* ^{md}UTU-MU-MU A-*šú šá* ^{m}*šu-la-*[*a ul-tu*]
5. *ṣe-e-nu šá* ^{md}U.GUR-DU$_3$-*uš* A-*šú šá* ^{md}NA$_3$-NUMUN-BA-*šá* ^{lu_2}NA.KAD *šá* ^{d}GAŠAN *šá* UNUG$^{⸢ki⸣}$
6. *ul-tu* ^{uru}E$_2$-^{d}LUGAL-*bàn-da mu-ši šá* U$_4$ 30-*kám šá* ITI ŠU
7. *ina sa-ar-ti i-bu-ku-ma ina* UNUG^{ki} *ina* E$_2$ ^{md}*na-na-a*-MU
8. A-*šú šá* ^{f}*at-tar-ra-mat* ^{f}*za-ki-ti* 1-*et* U$_8$ *ik-ki-su*

(2–8) Marduk son of Nabû-zēra-iddin a citizen of Ipaltira and Bēl-aḫḫē-iddin son of Nanaya-ēreš, the thieves who, in theft, led away from the city of Bīt-Lugalbanda 3 ewes and 1 lamb belonging to Šamaš-šuma-iddin son of Šulay[a, from] the flock of Nergal-īpuš son of Nabû-zēra-iqīša, a herdsman of the Lady of Uruk, on the night of 30 Dûzu, and, in Uruk, in the house of Nanaya-iddin son of Attar-ramât, a *zakītu*-woman, killed 1 ewe.

9. ^{kuš}*ši-iḫ-ṭu* UZU.HI.A *ù mu-šaḫ-ḫi-nu* ZABAR
10. *ù* 2-*ta* U$_8$ 1 UDU *ka-lum bal-ṭu-tu* ^{md}U.[GUR]-DU$_3$-*uš*
11. TA E$_2$ ^{md}*na-na-a*-MU A-*šú šá* ^{f}*at-tar-ra-mat i-*[*bu-ku-ma*]
12. *ina* E$_2$.AN.NA *ú-kal-li-mu* ^{md}NA$_3$-[LUGAL-URI$_3$ ^{lu_2}SAG-LUGAL]

(9–12) Nergal-īpuš br[ought] the hide, the meat, the bronze pot along with the 2 live ewes (and) the 1 live lamb from the house of Nanaya-iddin son of Attar-ramât and showed them in the Eanna.

13. ^{m}*mar-duk u* ^{md}EN-ŠEŠ.MEŠ-MU *iš-ʾa-al* [*ù a-na*]
14. ^{md}NA$_3$-LUGAL-URI$_3$ *iq-bu-ú um-ma mu-š*[*i* …]

(12–14) Nabû-[šarra-uṣur, the royal official] interrogated Marduk and Bēl-aḫḫē-iddin and they said thus [to] Nabû-šarra-uṣur:

15. *šá* UNUG^{ki} *ina mu-ši* 3 U$_8$ 1 UDU *ka-*[*lum ul-tu*]
16. ^{uru}E$_2$-^{d}LUGAL-*bàn-da ul-tu ṣe-e-nu* [*šá* ^{md}U.GUR-DU$_3$-*uš*]
17. *ina sa-ar-ti ki-i ni-bu-k*[*u* 1-*et* U$_8$ *ina* UNUG^{ki} *ina* E$_2$]
18. ^{md}*na-na-a*-MU *ni-it-te-*[*kis* 2 U$_8$ 1 U]DU *ka-lum*

(14–19) "[At nig]ht … of Uruk, in the night, when we, in theft, le[d away] 3 ewes and 1 la[mb from] the city of Bīt-Lugalbanda from the herd [of Nergal-īpuš], we slaughter[ed 1 ewe in Uruk in the house] of Nanaya-iddin. [The 2 living ewes (and) 1] living lamb stand (here)."

19. *bal-ṭu-tu ú-šu-uz-zu* [… *i-na*] *sa-ar-tú*

20. *a-na* IGI *ṣe-e-*⌜*nu*⌝ [*šá* ^{md}U.GUR-DU$_3$-*uš*] ^{md}*na-na-a*-MU

21. *it-ti-ni it-ta-lak* 2 [U$_8$ 1] UDU *ka-lum bal-ṭu-tu*

(19–21) "Nanaya-iddin went with us, [in] theft, to the herd [of Nergal-īpuš]."

22. ^{md}NA$_3$-LUGAL-URI$_3$ *ú-tir-ma a-na* ^{m}KI-^{d}*a-nu-um*-TIN

(21–23) Nabû-šarra-uṣur returned the 2 living [ewes and the 1] living lamb to Itti-Anum-balāṭu son of Šamaš-šuma-iddin, owner of the sheep.

23. A-*šú šá* ^{md}UTU-MU-MU EN UDU.NITA.MEŠ *id-din ù ši-iḫ-ṭu*

24. *ù mu-šaḫ-ḫi-nu* ZABAR *ina* E$_2$.AN.NA *ina* E$_2$ GUR$_7$.ME *iš-ku-un*

(23–24) He deposited the hide and the bronze pot in the Eanna, in the storehouse.

25. ^{lu_2}*mu-kin-nu* ^{md}NA$_3$-DU$_3$-ŠEŠ A-*šú šá* ^{md}NA$_3$-TIN-*su*-E A ^{md}30-TI-⌜ER$_3$⌝

(25) Witnesses: Nabû-bāni-aḫi son of Nabû-balāssu-iqbi descendant of Sîn-lēqi-unninnī;

26. ⌜^{m}NUN.ME⌝ A-*šú šá* ^{md}U.GUR-PAP A ^{lu_2}UŠ.BAR ^{md}NA$_3$-A-MU A-*šú šá* ^{m}DU$_3$-^{d}[INNIN]

(26–27) Apkallu son of Nergal-nāṣir descendant of Išparu; Nabû-apla-iddin son of Ibni-[Ištar] descendant of [E]kur-zakir;

27. A ^{m}[E$_2$]-*kur-za-kir* ^{md}AMAR.UTU-A-URI$_3$ A-*šú šá* ^{m}IDIM-*ia* A ^{m}*ši-gu-*[*ú-a*]

(27) Marduk-apla-uṣur son of Kabtiya descendant of Šig[ûa];

28. ^{m}[ZALAG$_2$-^{d}30] A-*šú šá* ^{md}NA$_3$-DU$_3$-ŠEŠ A ^{m}ZALAG$_2$-^{d}30 ^{md}NA$_3$-NUMUN-GIŠ

(28–29) [Nūr-Sîn] son of Nabû-bāni-aḫi descendant of Nūr-Sîn; Nabû-zēru-līšir [son of Nādinu] descendant of Išparu;

29. [A-*šú šá* ^{m}*na-din*] A ^{lu_2}UŠ.BAR ^{md}U.GUR-NUMUN-DU$_3$ A-*šú šá* ^{m}*šu-la-a*

30. A ^{m}[*mi-ṣir*]-*a-a*

(29–30) Nergal-zēra-ibni son of Šulaya descendant of [Miṣiraya];

31. ^{lu_2}UMBISAG ^{m}*šu-ma-a* A-*šú šá* ^{m}DU$_3$-^{d}15 A ^{lu_2}AZALAG UNUG^{ki}

(31) Scribe: Šumaya son of Ibni-Ištar descendant of Ašlaku.

32. ITI ŠU U_4 30-*kám* MU 7-*kám* $^{d}NA_3$-IM.TUK LUGAL TIN. TIR^{ki}	(32) Uruk. 30 Dûzu, year 7 of Nabonidus, king of Babylon.

NOTES

1. The text opens with the phrase "*maša'altu ša* Nabû-šarra-uṣur," which, based on lines 12–13, clearly means "interrogation by Nabû-šarra-uṣur." The same phrase—*maša'altu ša* so-and-so—occurs in other texts (see, for example, Document 6 below) with a different meaning. The named individual is the person subject to interrogation, rather than the interrogating authority.

8. In the corpus of Neo-Babylonian texts from the Eanna, the term *zakītu* refers to women who have been "cleared," or released, by their owner and dedicated to a temple (Wunsch 2006, 466–67).

28–29. Nūr-Sîn son of Nabû-bāni-aḫi descendant of Nūr-Sîn belonged to a family of jewelers in the Eanna (Kümmel 1979, 26). Nabû-zēru-līšir [son of Nādinu] descendant of Išparu belonged to a family of scribes in the Eanna (Kümmel 1979, 121–22, 131).

30. Family name completed based on Cornelia Wunsch's personal database of Neo-Babylonian names. According to her data, Miṣiraya is the only family name ending in *a-a* attested in texts from Uruk.

6. An Interrogation about Missing Gold

Text: YBC 4036
Copy: Dougherty 1920 (YOS 6), No. 223
Translation/Discussion: San Nicolò 1933b, 294–95; Holtz 2009, 286–88
Place of Composition: (Uruk)
Date: 4.XIIa.12 Nbn (22 March, 543 BCE)

The šatammu *and the scribes of the Eanna interrogate Iddin-Ištar. He declares that he handled 8 1/2 šeqels and 1 girû (1/24 of a šeqel) of gold in purchases and sales. In subsequent questioning, he is asked to name the people with whom he conducted transactions and to specify the amounts of gold involved.*

The present record is part of a broader dossier of records pertaining to investigations into the suspected mishandling of the Eanna's gold. During the month of Addaru 1 (the intercalary Addaru) of year 12 of Nabonidus, the Eanna authorities conducted an extensive "clean-up operation" of the corruption that had developed among their metalworkers (San Nicolò 1933b, 295–98; Renger 1971, 501–3). When taken together with other texts from this operation, the present record, in particular, reveals an embezzlement network of sorts. According to a document written on the day after the present interrogation took place, Anum-aḫa-iddin, whom the present document names as one of the people who purchased gold from Iddin-Ištar (line 17), also sold gold to another suspected criminal (San Nicolò 1933b, 295–96).

As with other such records, the interrogation here is a preliminary step in the adjudicatory process. Another record, dated later during the same month, 28 Addaru I, shows that the case against Iddin-Ištar continued for some time. According to this later text, two men guarantee Iddin-Ištar's presence (presumably for a hearing) before the *šatammu* and the scribes of the Eanna during the following month (San Nicolò 1933b, 297–98).

1.	*ma-šá-a-a-al-tu*$_4$ *šá* ^{m}MU-^{d}SUH A-*šú šá* ^{m}DU$_3$-^{d}INNIN	(1–2) Interrogation of Iddin-Ištar son of Ibni-Ištar who said as follows:
2.	*šá iq-bu-ú um-ma* 8 1/2 GIN$_2$ *gir*$_2$*-ú* KU$_3$.GI *ina* ŠU.2 ^{lu_2}ERIN.ME	(2–3) "8 1/2 šeqels and 1 *girû* of gold I purchased from people for silver, and I sold to people for silver."
3.	*a-na* KU$_3$.BABBAR *an-da-ḫar ù a-na* KU$_3$.BABBAR *a-na* ^{lu_2}ERIN.ME *at-ta-din*	
4.	^{lu_2}ŠA$_3$.TAM *u* ^{lu_2}UMBISAG.ME *šá* E$_2$.AN.NA *a-na* ^{m}MU-^{d}SUH	(4–5) The *šatammu* and the scribes of Eanna said thus to Iddin-Ištar:

5. *iq-bu-ú um-ma* KU$_3$.GI *ma-la ina* ŠU.2 ^{lu_2}ERIN.ME	(5–7) “Report to us, in detail, whatever (amounts of) gold you purchased from people and sold to people.”
6. *ta-am-ḫu-ru ù a-na* ^{lu_2}ERIN.ME *ta-ad-di-nu*	
7. KA$_2$.MEŠ *qí-ba-an-na-šú* ^{m}MU-^{d}SUH *iq-bi*	(7–8) Iddin-Ištar said thus:
8. *um-ma* 1/2 GIN$_2$ *mi-šil bit-qa* KU$_3$.GI *ina* ŠU.2 ^{md}NA$_3$-PAP	(8–9) “I purchased 1/2 šeqel and half of one eighth (of a šeqel) of gold from Nabû-nāṣir son of Aḫḫē-iddin.”
9. A-*šú šá* ^{m}ŠEŠ.ME-MU *an-da-ḫar* 3-*ta* 4-*tú*.ME *ina* ŠU.2	(9–10) “I purchased 3/4 (šeqel) from Ina-tēšê-ēṭir son of Ardiya.”
10. ^{m}*ina*-SUH$_3$-SUR A-*šú šá* ^{m}IR$_3$-*iá an-da-ḫar*	
11. 2 GIN$_2$ KU$_3$.GI *ina* ŠU.2 ^{md}EN-ŠEŠ-GAL$_2$-*ši* A-*šú šá* ^{md}NA$_3$-BA-*šá*	(11–12) “I purchased 2 šeqels of gold from Bēl-aḫa-šubši son of Nabû-iqīša in Babylon.”
12. *ina* TIN.TIR^{ki} *an-da-ḫar*	
13. 1 GIN$_2$ KU$_3$.GI *ina* ŠU.2 ^{md}NA$_3$-DU-NUMUN ^{lu_2}KU$_3$.DIM	(13–14) “I purchased 1 šeqel of gold from Nabû-mukīn-zēri, the goldsmith.”
14. *an-da-ḫar*	
15. KU$_3$.GI *šá* ^{m}MU-^{d}SUH *iq-bu-ú um-ma a-na* KU$_3$.BABBAR	(15–16) (The following is) the gold (about) which Iddin-Ištar said thus: “I sold it for silver to people.”
16. *a-na* ^{lu_2}ERIN.ME *at-ta-din*	
17. 3 GIN$_2$ KU$_3$.GI *a-na* ^{md}*a-num*-ŠEŠ-MU A-*šú šá* ^{m}*mu-še-zib*	(17) 3 šeqels of gold to Anum-aḫa-iddin son of Mušēzib.
18. 2 GIN$_2$ KU$_3$.GI *a-na* ^{md}NA$_3$-*mu-še-tiq*-UD.DA A-*šú*	(18–19) 2 šeqels of gold to Nabû-mušētiq-uddê son of Marduk-šuma-ibni.
19. *šá* ^{md}AMAR.UTU-MU-DU$_3$	
20. ITI DIRI ŠE.KIN.KUD U$_4$ 4-*kám* MU 12-*kám* ^{d}NA$_3$-IM.TUK	(20–21) 4 Addaru I, year 12 of Nabonidus, king of Babylon.
21. LUGAL TIN.TIR^{ki}	

NOTES

2–3. The amount of gold in Iddin-Ištar's initial statement (8 13/24 šeqels) does not agree with the sum total of the amounts of gold he enumerates in his subsequent statements (9 5/16 šeqels; San Nicolò 1933b, 295 n. 2). The text, however, does not indicate whether or not this discrepancy was significant in the case being pursued against Iddin-Ištar.

5–7. The term KA_2.MEŠ (*bābū*), literally meaning "doors," denotes specific items or sectors. In this case, the term expresses the requirement that Iddin-Ištar itemize the gold involved (*CAD* B, 26, s.v. *bābu* A, 6).

7. Testimony about a Stolen Ox

Text: YBC 3839
Copy: Dougherty 1920 (YOS 6), No. 183
Place of Composition: Uruk
Date: 23.X.10 Nbn (2 February, 545 BCE)

In the presence of 8 mār banî, *including the royal official in charge of the Eanna, Rīmūt testifies that Nanaya-... has not committed a crime. Rīmūt further testifies that he caught Iltammeš-kīni stealing an ox and immediately presented the offender in the Eanna.*

To judge from its content, the overt purpose of Rīmūt's statement before the authorities is to acquit Nanaya-... and to name the actual criminal. The statement that "Nanaya-... has not committed a crime," implies that Nanaya-... actually is under suspicion. In addition to this, however, one must also consider the possibility that, by testifying, Rīmūt intends to clear suspicions against himself, too. This would explain why he describes the circumstances surrounding his own capture of the actual thief and, most fundamentally, why Rīmūt testifies on behalf of Nanaya-... . The Eanna authorities might suspect that Rīmūt collaborated to frame Iltammeš-kīni for the theft in order to acquit Nanaya-... . Rīmūt's statement, then, reaffirms that Nanaya-... is actually innocent and that Rīmūt acted in good faith by apprehending Iltammeš-kīni and turning him over to the Eanna.

1.	^{md}NA$_3$-LUGAL-URI$_3$ ^{lu_2}SAG-LUGAL ^{lu_2}EN *pi-qit-ti* E$_2$.AN.NA	(1) Nabû-šarra-uṣur, the royal official in charge of the Eanna;
2.	^{md}DI.KU$_5$-ŠEŠ.ME-MU A-*šú šá* ^{m}*gi-mil-lu* A ^{m}*ši-gu-ú-a*	(2) Madānu-aḫḫē-iddin son of Gimillu descendant of Šigûa;
3	^{m}*na-din* A-*šú šá* ^{md}EN-ŠEŠ.ME-BA-*šá* A ^{m}*e-gi-bi*	(3) Nādin son of Bēl-aḫḫē-iqīša descendant of Egibi;
4.	^{m}*šu-ma-a* A-*šú šá* ^{m}DU$_3$-^{d}INNIN A ^{lu_2}AZALAG	(4) Šumaya son of Ibni-Ištar descendant of Ašlaku;
5.	^{m}*kal-ba-a* A-*šú šá* ^{md}BA-*šá* A ^{m}*ba-si-ia*	(5) Kalbaya son of Iqīša descendant of Basiya;
6.	^{md}*na-na-a*-MU A-*šú šá* ^{md}NA$_3$-DU$_3$-ŠEŠ A ^{m}*e*$_2$-*kur-za-kir*	(6) Nanaya-iddin son of Nabû-bāni-aḫi descendant of Ekur-zakir;
7.	^{m}DU$_3$-^{d}15 A-*šú šá* ^{md}NA$_3$-ŠEŠ.ME -GI	(7) Ibni-Ištar son of Nabû-aḫḫē-šullim;

8. ^{m}*ba-la-ṭu* A-*šú šá* ^{m}*mu-še-zib-* ^{d}EN	(8) Balāṭu son of Mušēzib-Bēl;
9. ^{lu_2}DUMU DU$_3$.MEŠ *šá ina pa-ni-šú-nu* ^{m}*ri-mut*	(9–11) The *mār banî* before whom Rīmūt son of Innin-šuma-uṣur descendant of Ḫunzû said thus:
10. A-*šú šá* ^{md}*in-nin*-MU-URI$_3$ A ^{m}*ḫu-un-zu-ú*	
11. *iq-bu-ú um-ma* ^{md}*na-na-a*-[X]	(11–13) "Nanaya-... son of Nabû-zēru-līšir has not committed a crime."
12. A-*šú šá* ^{md}NA$_3$-NUMUN-GIŠ *sa-áš-ta-a*	
13. *ul i-pu-uš* ^{m}*il-tam-meš-ki-i-ni*	(13–17) "I continually report that when Iltammeš-kīni of the Piqudu (tribe), stole the ox, as soon as I caught him red handed, I brought him (before you)."
14. ^{lu_2}*pi-qu-da-a-a sa-áš-ta-a šá* GU$_4$ *ki-i*	
15. *i-pu-uš* ŠU.2 *ṣi-bit-ti ina* ŠU.2-*šú*	
16. *ki-i aṣ-ba-ta*	
17. *ki-i a-bu-ku at-ta-na-aq-bi*	
18. ^{lu_2}UMBISAG ^{md}*a-nu*-ŠEŠ-MU A-*šú šá* ^{md}30-DU$_3$	(18–19) Scribe: Anu-aḫa-iddin son of Sîn-ibni descendant of Rēʾi-alpi.
19. A ^{lu_2}SIPA GU$_4$ UNUG^{ki} ITI AB U$_4$ 23-*kám*	(19–20) Uruk. 23 Tebēṭu year 10 of Nabonidus, king of Babylon.
20. MU 10-*kám* ^{d}NA$_3$-IM.TUK LUGAL TIN.TIR^{ki}	

NOTES

14. The Piqūdu/Puqūdu were a tribe of Arameans who lived on the edges of the Eanna's territorial holdings (Jursa 2010, 100–103).

17. According to *CAD* Q, 31–32, the form *at-ta-na-aq-bi* (an Ntn form) is actually a miswritten Gtn form (the correct form should be *aqtanabbi*), with the meaning "I testify." The translation above accepts the interpretation of the verb as a Gtn form, but retains the iterative meaning of the Gtn. Accordingly, Rīmūt has had to make a number of reports; the case against him or Nanaya-... is, apparently, a prolonged affair.

8. Examination of a Tablet as Evidence

Text: NBC 11487
Copy: Beaulieu 2000c (YOS 19), No. 92
Translation/Discussion: Beaulieu 2000c, 37–39; Dandamaev 2006, 386
Place of Composition: Uruk
Date: 22.X.13 Nbn (30 January, 542 BCE)

In the presence of eight mār banî, *and before the governor of Uruk and the* šatammu *of the Eanna, Balāṭu reads a deed pertaining to a field adjacent to the property of the Lady of Uruk. The tablet refers to Assurbanipal's twentieth year.*

The indication that the field in question is adjacent to the property of the Lady of Uruk suggests that there is some ownership dispute between Balāṭu and the Eanna authorities (Beaulieu 2000c, 38). In order to support his claim, Balāṭu presents the "mother-of-the-field tablet" (*ṭuppi ummi eqli*), which was the previous record that proves ownership (Beaulieu 2000c, 39; Charpin 2010, 67–68). Several land-related documents (e.g., Strassmaier 1890b, No. 337 and Wunsch 2000a, No. 134) indicate that the "mother-of-the-field" was transferred with the ownership of the property, as proof that the vendor of the field held legitimate title. The present document indicates that this kind of record would have been kept for a long time. The tablet that is read refers to the reign of the Neo-Assyrian king Assurbanipal, when Uruk was still governed as part of the Neo-Assyrian Empire. Assurbanipal's twentieth year corresponds to 649 BCE, more than one hundred years before the composition of the present document.

1.	^{md}AMAR.UTU-MU-MU A-*šú šá* ^{md}NA$_3$-ŠEŠ.MEŠ-TIN A ^{m}*ba-la-ṭu*	(1) Marduk-šuma-iddin son of Nabû-aḫḫē-bulliṭ descendant of Balāṭu;
2.	^{m}IR$_3$-^{d}AMAR.UTU A-*šú šá* ^{m}NUMUN-*ia* A ^{m}*e-gi-bi*	(2) Arad-Marduk son of Zēriya descendant of Egibi;
3.	^{m}*ap-la-a* A-*šú šá* ^{md}*gu-la*-NUMUN-DU$_3$ A ^{lu_2}ISIN^{ki}	(3) Aplaya son of Gula-zēra-ibni descendant of Isinaya;
4.	^{m}IR$_3$-^{d}*in-nin* A-*šú šá* ^{md}EN-MU A ^{m}*ku-ri-i*	(4) Arad-Innin son of Bēl-iddin descendant of Kurī;
5.	^{md}NA$_3$-NUMUN-GIŠ A-*šú šá* ^{m}EN-*šú-nu* A ^{m}*ku-ri-i*	(5) Nabû-zēru-līšir son of Bēlšunu descendant of Kurī;
6.	^{m}*ina*-E$_2$.SAG.IL$_2$-NUMUN A-*šú šá* ^{m}*šá-pi-i*-^{d}EN A LU$_2$-^{d}IDIM	(6) Ina-Esagil-zēri son of Ša-pî-Bēl descendant of Amēl-Ea;

7. ^{md}EN-*ka-*⸢*ṣir*⸣ A-*šú šá* ^{m}*mar-duk* A ^{m}*ki-din-*^{d}AMAR.UTU	(7) Bēl-kāṣir son of Marduk descendant of Kidin-Marduk;
8. ^{md}EN-*ib-ni* A-*šú šá* ^{m}*bul-lu-ṭu* A ^{lu_2}ŠU.KU$_6$	(8) Bēl-ibni son of Bulluṭu descendant of Bāʾiru;
9. ^{lu_2}DUMU *ba-ni-i šá ina* DU-*zu-šú-nu* ^{m}*ba-la-ṭu* A-*šú*	(9–16) The *mār banî* in whose presence, Balāṭu son of Zākir descendant of Kidin-Marduk read, in the assembly, before Nādinu, the governor of Uruk, son of Balāṭu, and Kurbanni-Marduk, the *šatammu* of the Eanna, son of Zēriya descendant of Sîn-damāqu, the "mother-of-the-field" tablet pertaining to the arable field in the town of Bīt-Šammu-il, adjacent to (the property of) the Lady of Uruk.
10. *šá* ^{m}*za-kir* A ^{m}*ki-din-*^{d}AMAR.UTU IM.DUB-*šú* AMA A.ŠA$_3$	
11. *šá* ŠE.NUMUN *šá i-na* URU E$_2$-^{m}*šá-am-mu-*DINGIR	
12. *šá* UŠ.SA.DU ^{d}GAŠAN *šá* UNUG^{ki} *ina pa-ni*	
13. ^{m}*na-di-nu* ^{lu_2}GAR.UMUŠ UNUG^{ki} A-*šú šá* ^{m}*ba-la-ṭu*	
14. *ù* ^{m}*kur-ban-ni-*^{d}AMAR.UTU ^{lu_2}ŠA$_3$.TAM E$_2$.AN.NA	
15. A-*šú šá* ^{m}NUMUN-*ia* A ^{md}30-*da-ma-qa*	
16. *i-na* UKKIN *iš-ta-as-su-ú i-na lìb-bi šaṭ-ru*	(16–17) In (it) was written thus: "Year 20 of Assurbanipal."
17. *um-ma* MU 20-*kám* ^{m}AN.ŠAR$_2$-DU$_3$-IBILA	
18. UNUG^{ki} ITI AB U$_4$ 22-*kám* MU 13-*kám* ^{d}NA$_3$-IM.TUK	(18–19) Uruk. 22 Ṭebētu, year 13 of Nabonidus, king of Babylon.
19. LUGAL TIN.TIR^{ki}	

9. A Conditional Verdict

Text: CBS 5330
Copy: Hilprecht and Clay 1898 (BE 9), No. 24
Translation/Discussion: Cardascia 1951, 184; Wells 2004, 117, 125
Place of Composition: Nippur
Date: 8.I.31 Artaxerxes I (20 April, 434 BCE)

Enlil-šuma-iddin accuses Aqubu of having taken 300 black and white sheep from his flock. Aqubu denies the charge, claiming that he only took 110 sheep, apparently legitimately. If Aqubu is caught in possession of any more than 110 sheep, he must pay Enlil-šuma-iddin 300 sheep.

The accuser quoted in the present document, Enlil-šuma-iddin, was the best-known holder of the Murašû-family archive. He apparently assumed leadership of the business after the death of his brother, who had inherited the family's holdings from their father, Murašû (Stolper 1976). Most of the documents from the Murašû archives show the family as agricultural managers and entrepreneurs who functioned as intermediaries between cultivators and landlords. Typically, people who owed monetary or service obligations because of land they possessed would turn to the Murašû family for credit to cover these duties. The "firm" would earn profit by managing these mortgaged properties (Jursa 2006, 113–14).

Extending credit required the Murašû family to have a source of silver, probably from trade of agricultural goods. The archives, however, only rarely attest to this side of the Murašû's activities (Jursa 2006, 114; van Driel 1989, 225). The present document provides one such rare glimpse. It apparently shows that, in addition to more widely attested activities, Enlil-šuma-iddin was also involved in animal husbandry.

The present document is an example of what has been called a "conditional verdict" (Wells 2004, 108–11; also see text 10 below). It reflects a quasi-final stage in the proceedings, when the case has apparently had a hearing and both sides have made arguments. When the document is issued, however, there is not sufficient evidence available to convict Aqubu. Nevertheless, Enlil-šuma-iddin's accusation has created enough of a suspicion to place Aqubu on notice and to maintain a record against him. Should additional evidence become available—from another "witness or informer"—Aqubu will be penalized, apparently without any additional process.

It is interesting to note that, according to the document, Aqubu will not have to pay more than the three hundred sheep mentioned in Enlil-šuma-iddin's accusation. In Neo-Babylonian legal texts, theft typically bears an actual penalty, either twofold in private cases, or thirtyfold in cases pertaining to temple property. One would expect the present document to stipulate a similar payment. Why the hypothetical payment is different here remains an open question.

1. ^{md}EN.LIL$_2$-MU-MU DUMU *šá* ^{m}*mu-ra-šu-ú šá a-na* ^{m}*a-qu-bu*	(1–2) Enlil-šuma-iddin son of Murašû who said thus to Aqubu son of Zabdiya:
2. A-*šá* ^{m}*za-ab-di-ia iq-bu-ú um-ma* 3 ME *ṣe-e-nu*	(2–3) “You led away 300 white and black sheep!”
3. BABBAR-*ti u ṣal-in-du ta-ta-bak ár-ku* ^{m}*a-qu-bu*	(3–4) Afterwards, Aqubu said thus:
4. *iq-bu-ú um-ma ṣe-e-nu e-lat*	(4–5) “I did not lead away more than 110 sheep!”
5. 1 ME 10-*ta ul a-bu-uk* U$_4$-*mu*	
6. *ina* ŠU.2 *ṣi-bit-ti lu-ú ba-ti-qu lu-ú mu-kin-nu*	(5–10) On the day he is later caught with more than these 110 sheep, by possession of the stolen goods, or (by) an informer or a witness, Aqubu shall pay 300 sheep to Enlil-šuma-iddin.
7. *ár-ki-šú e-lat ṣe-e-nu-a*ʾ 1 ME 10-*ta*	
8. *it-tak-šá-du* 3 ME *ṣe-e-nu*	
9. ^{m}*a-qu-bu a-na* ^{md}EN.LIL$_2$-MU-MU	
10. *i-nam-din*	
11. ^{lu_2}*mu-du* ^{m}*u$_2$-bar* A *šá* ^{md}*bu-ne-ne*-DU$_3$	(11) Witnesses: Ubar son of Bunene-ibni;
12. ^{md}MAŠ-*na-din*-MU A *šá* ^{m}*ú-bal-liṭ-su*-^{d}AMAR.UTU	(12) Ninurta-nādin-šumi son of Uballissu-Marduk;
13. ^{m}*ri-bat* A *šá* ^{m}*ni-qu-du* ^{md}EN-*na-ṣir* A *šá*	(13) Ribat son of Niqudu;
14. ^{md}EN-*ú-še-zib*	(13–14) Bēl-nāṣir son of Bēl-ušēzib;
15. ^{md}ENŠADA-MU ^{lu_2}UMBISAG DUMU *šá* ^{m}IR$_3$-^{d}ME.ME EN.LIL$_2$^{ki}	(15) Nusku-iddin, the scribe, son of Arad-Gula.
16. ITI BAR$_2$ U$_4$ 8-*kám* MU 31-*kám*	(15–17) Nippur. 8 Nisannu, year 31 of Artaxerxes, king of the lands.
17. ^{m}*ar-taḫ-šá-as-su* LUGAL KUR.KUR	
Lower edge: *ṣu-pur ša* ^{m}*a-qu-bu*	Fingernail of Aqubu

NOTES

The label on the lower edge of the document marks Aqubu's fingernail, which was impressed into the clay tablet, instead of a seal. Aqubu's mark indicates his acceptance of the document's terms, which include, potentially at least, a payment to Enlil-šuma-iddin.

10. Another Conditional Verdict

Text: NBC 4515
Copy: Beaulieu 2000c (YOS 19), No. 98
Place of Composition: Uruk
Date: 26.II.8 Nbn (6 June, 548 BCE)

If a witness or informer testifies that Nuptaya has received silver, gold, or stone from Nabû-tāriṣ, then she must repay the Lady of Uruk.

In the Eanna's efforts to protect its property, women were not above suspicion. Nuptaya has already had to account for 1 1/8 šeqels of silver; she has declared that Nabû-tāriṣ gave this amount to a man named Rīmūtu. The Eanna authorities apparently accept this statement, but suspect that Nuptaya might have received more from Nabû-tāriṣ. The present document indicates that the authorities suspect that Nabû-tāriṣ handed off misappropriated goods to Nuptaya. Should additional evidence confirm the suspicions against Nuptaya, she will be liable for the goods.

1. *ina* u_4*-mu* ^{lú_2}*mu-kin-nu lu-ú ba-ti-iq*	(1–8) On the day that a witness or an informer comes and testifies against Nuptaya daughter of Sîn-ibni (that) Nabû-tāriṣ son of Nabû-bēl-šumāti gave her silver, gold, or stone in addition to the 1 1/8 šeqels of silver about which Nuptaya said thus: "He gave them to Rīmūtu"—
2. *it-tal-kám-ma* ^{f}*nu-up-ta-a* DUMU.SAL-*su*	
3. *šá* ^{md}30-DU_3 *uk-tin-nu lu-ú* KU_3.BABBAR	
4. *lu-ú* KU_3.GI *lu-ú* NA_4 $^{md}NA_3$-LAL	
5. A-*šú šá* $^{md}NA_3$-EN-MU.MEŠ *id-da-áš-šú*	
6. *e-lat* 1 GIN_2 *bit-qa* KU_3.BABBAR *šá* ^{f}*nu-up-ta*	
7. *taq-bu-ú um-ma a-na* ^{m}*ri-mu-tú*?	
8. *id-dan-nu mim-ma id-da-áš-šú*	(8–10) Whatever he gave her she shall bring; [she] shall repay what belongs to the Lady of Uruk.
9. *ta-bal šá* ^{d}GAŠAN *šá* UNUG^{ki}	
10. [*ta*]-*at-ta-pal*	
11. ^{lú_2}*mu-kin-nu* ^{m}*gi-mil-lu* A-*šú šá* $^{m}NA_3$-MU-MU	(11–12) Witnesses: Gimillu son of Nabû-šuma-iddin descendant of Ea-ilūta-bāni;

12. A ^{md}IDIM-⸢DINGIR⸣-*tú*-DU$_3$ ^{md}EN-ŠEŠ.MEŠ-⸢SU⸣	(12–13) Bēl-aẖẖē-erība son of Nabû-bēlšunu descendant of Kurī;
13. A-*šú šá* ^{m} ⸢^{d}NA$_3$⸣-EN-*šú-nu* A ^{m}*kur-i*	
14. ^{m}NA$_3$-SUR-ZI.MEŠ A-*šú šá* ^{md}EN-BA-*šá*	(14–15) Nabû-ēṭir-napšāti son of Bēl-iqīša descendant of Bēl-apla-uṣur.
15. A ^{md}EN-A-URI$_3$ ^{lu_2}UMBISAG ^{m}KAR-^{d}AMAR.UTU	(15–16) Scribe: Mušēzib-Marduk son of Bēl-uballiṭ descendant of Amēl-Ea.
16. A-*šú šá* ^{md}EN-TIN-*iṭ* A ^{m}LU$_2$-^{d}IDIM	
17. UNUG^{ki} ITI GU$_4$ U$_4$ 26-*kám*	(17–18) Uruk. 26 Ayaru, year 8 of Nabonidus, king of Babylon.
18. MU 8-*kám* ^{md}NA$_3$-I LUGAL E^{ki}	

11. Prelude to a Trial for Manslaughter

Text: BM 46660 (81-8-30, 126)
Copy: Wunsch 2002a, 356–57
Translation/Discussion: Wunsch 2002a

Marduk-šarranu has accused Kīnaya of striking his son. They are summoned to argue their case. Two siblings, a brother and a sister, guarantee that Kīnaya will appear. If he escapes, then the two must pay Marduk-šarranu.

The designation of the guarantors' obligation to "pay compensation for the life of the victim" (*napšāti šullumu*, literally "to repay the life"), indicates beyond much doubt that a death has occurred. Thus, the present text is a rare example of a "criminal" case from what appears to be a private archival context. However, because the document cannot be situated within a known archive, the circumstances behind this case remain obscure.

According to the document, the *mār banî* will hear the parties' arguments. It is likely, then, that this group of adjudicators has already been involved in this case in some way, perhaps in establishing the presumption against Kīnaya and the imposition of the penalty upon him should he escape. It is also possible, however, that the victim's family and Kīnaya reached an agreement on their own, with the present document as a result.

1'. [*u* ^{m}*ki-na-a* DUMU-*šú šá* ^{m}BA]-*šá a-na* 2'. ⸢^{lu_2}DUMU⸣ [DU$_3$ x x x] *it-ti a-ḫa-meš*	(1'–3') [… and Kīnaya son of Iq]īšaya will go to the *mār* [*banî*] together
3'. *il-la-ku-ú-ma di-i-nu* [*šá*] 4'. ^{md}AMAR.UTU-LUGAL-*a-nu a-na* ^{m}*ki-na-*[*a*] 5'. *iq-bu-ú um-mu* DUMU-*u-*⸢*a*⸣ 6'. *ta-an-da-ḫa-aṣ ina* IGI ^{lu_2}[…]	(3'–7') They (!) /He will argue the case [in which] Marduk-šarranu said thus to Kīnaya "You struck my son!" before the …
7'. *i-dab-bu-ub* ^{md}NA$_3$-[NUMUN-MU] 8'. A-*šú šá* ^{m}ŠEŠ.MEŠ-*šá-iá u* [^{f}*iṣ-ṣur*-X] 9'. NIN-*šú pu-ut* ^{m}[*ki-na-a*]	(7'–10') Nabû-zēra-iddin son of Aḫḫūšaya and [Iṣṣur-X], his sister, assume responsibility for [Kīnaya] son of Iqīšaya.

10’. A-*šú šá* ^{m}BA-*šá-a na*-[*šu-u ki-i*] 11’. ^{m}*ki-na-a iḫ-te*-[*li-qu*] 12’. ZI.MEŠ *šá* DUMU-*šú sa*$_2$ ^{md}[AMAR.UTU-LUGAL-*a-nu*] 13’. ^{md}NA$_3$-NUMUN-MU *u* ^{f}*iṣ*-⸢*ṣur*⸣-[	(10’–14’) If Kīnaya escapes, Nabû-zēra-iddin and Iṣṣur-[X] will pay compensation for the life of the son of Marduk-šarranu.
14’. *ú-šal-lim-mu* ^{lu_2}*mu-kin-nu* ^{m}[PN	(14’–15’) Witnesses: PN son of Ibnaya descendant of Rāb-banê;
15’. A-*šú šá* ^{m}DU$_3$-*a* A ^{lu_2}GAL-DU$_3$ ^{m}*ra-šil*-[16’. ⸢A-*šú šá* ^{m}⸣^{d}EN-GI A ^{m}DU$_3$-*eš*-DINGIR	(15’–16’) Rašil-[X] son of Bēl-ušallim descendant of Eppeš-ili;
17’. […]-*ti-iq* A ^{m}*ir-a-nu*	(17’) [PN son of PN] descendant of Ir’anni;
18’. […*b*]*u-un-šu-tu*[*r*]	

1’ —NIGIN-*ir*

2’ —*si-ia*

NOTES

5’–6’. The Akkadian verb *maḫāṣu*, translated here “to strike,” can also mean “to murder.” Thus, although Kīnaya’s status as the defendant is clear, the precise relationship between his action and the death of Marduk-šarranu’s son is not specified. It is quite likely that the death occurred accidentally, in a situation in which striking or hitting was considered permissible, perhaps as part of the victim’s training (Wunsch 2002a, 359–60).

12. Requirement to Present Witnesses

Text: BM 31162 (76-11-17, 889)
Copy: Strassmaier 1889b (Nbk), No. 366
Translation/Discussion: Kohler and Peiser 1890–1898, 1:12–13; Koschaker 1966, 46–47; Wells 2004, 176–78; Holtz 2010
Place of Composition: Opis
Date: 23.VIII.40 Nbk (5 November, 565 BCE)

Gudaya, the guarantor of a grain loan to Katimu', must present witnesses to establish that he presented Katimu' to Bau-ēreš. If Gudaya successfully establishes his claim, then Gudaya is clear. If Gudaya does not establish his claim, then Gudaya must repay the barley and the interest to Bau-ēreš.

A dispute over the repayment of a loan stands behind the present document. Katimu' borrowed barley from Bau-ēreš. At the time of the loan, Gudaya had guaranteed that Katimu' would be present and available to repay the loan to Bau-ēreš, the creditor. Bau-ēreš has not been repaid, and has turned to Gudaya, the guarantor, with the claim that Katimu' never repaid the debt. For his part, Gudaya claims that he has, in fact, "presented" the debtor, that is, made him available so that the creditor can collect payment. Gudaya, however, has not yet substantiated his claim to the satisfaction of Bau-ēreš and whatever (unnamed) authorities have been involved in the proceedings. In order to avoid repaying Katimu''s debt, Gudaya must now substantiate his claim by presenting witnesses or other supporting evidence.

Apart from its value as a legal text, the present document is also important because it is one of a group written in Opis by Nabû-aḫḫē-iddin of the Egibi family (van Driel 1985–1986, 55). These texts reflect the legal early career of Nabû-aḫḫē-iddin, who, a few years later, would become one of the "royal judges" in Babylon.

1. *a-di* U$_4$ 1-*kám šá* ITI GAN ^{m}*gu-da-a* 2. A-*šú šá* ^{m}*ḫi-in-ni*-DINGIR.MEŠ 2 ^{lu_2}DUMU-DU$_3$.MEŠ 3. ^{lu_2}*mu-kin-ne-e-šú a-na* ^{uru}*ú-pi-ia ib-ba-kám-ma* 4. *a-na* ^{md}KA$_2$-KAM$_2$ A-*šú šá* ^{md}NA$_3$-DU$_3$-ŠEŠ 5. *ú-kan-ni šá* ^{m}*ka-ti-mu-ʾ* A-*šú šá* 6. ^{m}*ḫa-gu-ru šá pu-ut še-pi-šú ina* ŠU.2 7. ^{md}KA$_2$-KAM$_2$ *iš-šu-ú ina a-dan-ni-šú* 8. ^{m}*g*[*u-d*]*a-a i-bu-ka-šim*-⸢*ma*⸣ 9. ⸢*a-na* ^{m}⸣^{d}KA$_2$-KAM$_2$ *id-di-nu*	(1–9) By 1 Kislīmu, Gudaya son of Ḫinni-ilī shall bring two *mār banî* (as) his witnesses to Opis and establish, against Bau-ēreš son of Nabû-bāni-aḫi, that, at the time (of the termination of the loan), Gudaya brought Katimuʾ son of Ḫagūru—for whose presence he (Gudaya) assumed guarantee to Bau-ēreš—to him (Bau-ēreš) and handed (Katimuʾ) over to Bau-ēreš.
10. *ki-i uk-tin-nu-uš za-ki*	(10) If he (Gudaya) establishes (the case) against him (Bau-ēreš), he (Gudaya) is clear.
11. *ki-i la uk-tin-nu-uš a-ki-i ú-ìl-tim* 12. ŠE.BAR *u* HAR.RA-*šú a-na* ^{md}KA$_2$-KAM$_2$ *it-ta-din*	(11–12) If he (Gudaya) does not establish (the case) against him (Bau-ēreš), then he (Gudaya) shall pay Bau-ēreš barley and its interest according to the debt-note.
13. ^{lu_2}*mu-kin-nu* ^{m}*si-lim*-^{d}EN A-*šú šá*	(13–14) Witnesses: Silim-Bēl son of Balāṭu;
14. ^{m}*ba-la-ṭu* ^{m}MU-^{d}AMAR.UTU A-*šú šá*	(14–15) Iddin-Marduk son of Nabû-ittiya;
15. ^{md}NA$_3$-KI-*ia u* ^{lu_2}UMBISAG ^{md}NA$_3$-ŠEŠ.MEŠ-MU 16. A-*šú šá* ^{m}*šu-la-a* A ^{m}*e-gi-bi* ^{uru}*ú-pi-ia*	(15–16) and the scribe: Nabû-aḫḫē-iddin son of Šulaya descendant of Egibi.
17. ITI APIN U$_4$ 23-*kám* MU 40-*kám* 18. ^{d}NA$_3$-NIG$_2$.DU-URI$_3$ LUGAL TIN.TIR^{ki}	(16–18) Opis. 23 Araḫšamna, year 40 of Nebuchadnezzar, king of Babylon.

NOTES

Reading of this document is based on the collations of Cornelia Wunsch.

7. *ina a-dan-ni-šú-*. For the nuance of this noun in the present context see *CAD* A_1, 99, s.v. *adannu* d.

13. An Oath to Argue a Case

Text: BM 32881 (77-11-14, 10)
Copy: Strassmaier 1892 (Dar), No. 189
Translation/Discussion: Kohler and Peiser 1890–1898, 3:52; Joannès 2002d
Place of Composition: Babylon
Date: 8.XII.5 Dar (26 February, 516 BCE)

Libluṭ swears that within four months he will come before Marduk-nāṣir-apli and argue his case. If Libluṭ does not appear, then Libluṭ will have to provide a bed for Marduk-nāṣir-apli, and Marduk-nāṣir-apli will have to pay a specific amount.

The formulation of the oath and of the entire text, in general, provide important additional information on the history of this case, specifically regarding Libluṭ's obligation to Marduk-nāṣir-apli. Marduk-nāṣir-apli commissioned Libluṭ's father, Nabû-mīta-uballiṭ, to build him a bed, and the commission was recorded in a note that would have been held by Marduk-nāṣir-apli. Between that time and the time of the present document's composition, Nabû-mīta-uballiṭ has apparently died, and Libluṭ has come into possession of the note. Under normal circumstances, as the heir of the obligated party, Libluṭ would only come into possession of the debt-note once the obligation was met. Thus, Libluṭ probably relies on the note to prove that his father's obligation was fulfilled, and to justify his claim that he owes nothing to Marduk-nāṣir-apli.

Marduk-nāṣir-apli, for his part, has a substantiated claim that Libluṭ is indeed still obligated to construct the bed. One assumes that Marduk-nāṣir-apli's pursuit of the case against Libluṭ stems from a belief that a bed of the same quality can still be obtained, even though Nabû-mīta-uballiṭ, the originally commissioned craftsman, is no longer available to build it. Marduk-nāṣir-apli may know that Libluṭ was himself a craftsman of comparable skill. Alternatively, Libluṭ's father may have already built the bed, but Marduk-nāṣir-apli may have not yet received it. Under either set of circumstances, it seems that Libluṭ has been withholding delivery of the bed (either his own work of that of his father), perhaps in order to obtain a higher price.

1. ^{m}*lib*$^{!}$-*luṭ*$^{!}$ A-*šú šá* ^{md}NA$_3$-BE-TIN-*iṭ* A ^{m}SIG$_{15}$-^{d}IM 2. *i-na* ^{d}EN ^{d}NA$_3$ *u* ^{m}*da-a-ri-ia-mu-uš* 3. LUGAL TIN.TIR^{ki} LUGAL KUR.KUR *a-na* ^{md}AMAR.UTU-*na-ṣir*-IBILA 4. A-*šú šá* ^{m}KI-^{d}AMAR.UTU-TIN A ^{m}*e-gi-bi it-te-me*	(1–4) Libluṭ son of Nabû-mīta-uballiṭ descendant of Mudammiq-Adad swore by Bēl, Nabû and Darius, king of Babylon, king of the lands, to Marduk-nāṣir-apli son of Itti-Marduk-balāṭu descendant of Egibi:
5. *ki-i a-di* U$_4$ 10-*kám šá* ITI ŠU *a-na pa-ni-ku*	(5–9) "By 10 Dûzu I shall come before you (regarding) the debt-note for the bed made of *mesukkannu* wood, owed by Nabû-mīta-uballiṭ, my father, which I received as cleared of obligation but (about) which your claim that I (still) owe it has been confirmed."
6. ⸢*at*⸣-*tal-kám-ma ú-il$_3$-tim šá* ^{giš}NA$_2$ 7. *šá* ^{giš}*me-suk$_3$-kan-nu šá ina muḫ-ḫi* ^{md}NA$_3$-BE-TIN-*iṭ* 8. AD-*ia šá ina za-ku-tu$_4$ am-ḫu-ru-ma* 9. *ina muḫ-ḫi-ia tu-šá-az-za-zu ki-i*	
10. *a-di* U$_4$ 10-*kám šá* ITI ŠU ^{m}*lib-luṭ* 11. *la it-tal-kám-ma a-na muḫ-ḫi* 12. *ú-ìl-tim šá ina za-ku-tu$_4$ iš-šu-ú* 13. *it-ti* ^{md}AMAR.UTU-*na-ṣir-ap-lu* 14. *la id-dab-bu*-<*ub*> 1-*et* ^{giš}NA$_2$ *šá* ^{giš}*me-sùk-kan-nu* 15. *šá di-im-gu-ur u* ^{giš}*ti-it-tu$_4$* 16. ^{m}*lib-luṭ a-na* ^{md}AMAR.UTU-*na-ṣir*-IBILA 17 *i-nam-din-ma* 13 <GIN$_2$> KU$_3$.BABBAR ^{md}AMAR.UTU-*na-ṣir*-IBILA	(9–18) If Libluṭ does not come by 10 Dûzu, and does not argue (his case) against Marduk-nāṣir-apli regarding the debt-note which he has without obligation, Libluṭ shall give Marduk-nāṣir-apli a bed of *mesukkannu* wood, with *dimgur* and fig (ornamentation) and Marduk-nāṣir-apli shall pay Libluṭ 13 šeqels of silver.

18. *a-na* ^{m}*lib-luṭ i-nam-din* ^{lu_2}*mu-kin-nu* ^{m}*ri-mut-*^{d}EN	(18–19) Witnesses: Rīmūt-Bēl son of Ardiya descendant of Itinnu;
19. A-*šú šá* ^{m}IR$_3$-*ia* A ^{lu_2}ŠIDIM ^{m}NUMUN-*ia* A-*šú šá* ^{md}NA$_3$-DU$_3$-ŠEŠ	(19–20) Zēriya son of Nabû-bāni-aḫi descendant of Arad-Ea;
20. A ^{m}IR$_3$-^{d}BE ^{md}EN-SUR <A-*šú šá*> ^{m}DA-^{d}AMAR.UTU A ^{m}*da-bi-bi*	(20) Bēl-ēṭir son of Ile’’i-Marduk descendant of Dābibī;
21. ^{lu_2}UMBISAG ^{md}NA$_3$-MU A-*šú šá* ^{md}NA$_3$-*ga-mil*	(21–22) Scribe: Nabû-iddin son of Nabû-gāmil descendant of Suḫaya.
22. A ^{m}*su-ḫa-a-a* TIN.TIR^{ki} ITI ŠE U$_4$ 8-*kám*	(22–24) Babylon. 8 Addaru, year 5 of Darius, king of Babylon, king of the lands.
23. MU 5-*kám* ^{m}*da-ri-ia-muš* LUGAL E^{ki}	
24. LUGAL KUR.KUR	

Notes

4. Marduk-nāṣir-apli’s father, Itti-Marduk-balāṭu, is well-attested in the Egibi archive.

8. The phrase *ina zakûtu* in this context apparently indicates that the tablet was received “in the clear,” that is, on the assumption that the debt has been fulfilled. For the various translations see Kohler and Peiser 1890–1898, 3:52, *AHw*, 1507, and *CAD* Z, 33, s.v. *zakûtu* c3’. The present interpretation of the text follows Kohler and Peiser, who suggest that the term denotes that Libluṭ is in possession of the tablet because the obligation has been met.

9. In the present context, the verb *tu-šá-az-za-zu* indicates that Marduk-nāṣir-apli (subject of the verb) has a formally substantiated legal claim.

14–15. The description of the bed in these lines includes three elements: *mesukannu, dimgur*, and *tittu* (fig). A bed with exactly the same description occurs in Baker 2004, No. 12 (pp. 96–98), as part of a dowry receipt. Based on the wording of the descriptions, the precise relationship between the three elements remains unclear. The description of the bed in line 7 as “made of *mesukkannu*-wood,” suggests that this is the main component of the bed. The other two elements apparently describe ornamentation of some kind, either pictorial designs (*CAD* T, 436, s.v. *tittu*) or additional woods incorporated into the bed.

21–22. The name of the scribe follows the drawing in Strassmaier 1892, No. 189. A scribe named Nabû-aḫḫē-bulliṭ son of Nabû-gāmil descendant of Suḫaya is attested in Strassmaier 1892, No. 173, l. 19 (see Wunsch 2000a, 2:337).

14. A Counterclaim regarding Misappropriated Sheep

Text: YBC 4154
Copy: Dougherty 1920 (YOS 6), No. 123
Translation/Discussion: Holtz 2009, 173–74
Place of Composition: Uruk
Date: 5.VIII.9 Nbn (29 October, 547 BCE)

Five branded sheep were seen in the flock of Kīnaya. Zēriya testifies against Kīnaya, proving that Kīnaya stole three of the sheep. The assembly decrees that Kīnaya must repay those sheep thirtyfold. Kīnaya claims that the remaining two sheep were given to him by a shepherd. Kīnaya must present the shepherd to the administrators of the Eanna. If he does not present the shepherd, then Kīnaya must repay the Eanna thirtyfold for those two sheep, as well.

The present document illustrates the lodging of a counterclaim, a rather typical procedure in texts written at the Eanna temple in Uruk (Magdalene 2007, 69–72). Individuals who are originally the accused parties in a trial can, in an effort to clear themselves of the charges against them, name other individuals, thus becoming accusers themselves. In this case, in the wake of Zēriya's accusation, Kīnaya faces charges about two sheep (apart from the charge regarding the three sheep, for which he is found guilty). In an attempt to clear himself, Kīnaya names another shepherd as the culprit. Consequently, Kīnaya must present the man he has accused to the authorities in the Eanna.

The hearing recorded in the present document takes place "in the presence" (*ina ušuzzu*) of a panel of eight men, headed by the "deputy" (*šanû*) of Uruk. Although the names of the other men on this panel do not appear with titles, many of them are well-known as functionaries in the Eanna bureaucracy. Innin-šarra-uṣur (lines 19–20) was a member of a family of cattleherders; he, his father, several of his brothers, and his nephews held the position of "herd supervisor" (*rāb būli*) (Kümmel 1979, 79). Madānu-aḫḫē-iddin (line 21) held the prominent position of "chief brewer" (*šāpir sirāšê*; see Document 21) as did his son, Šamaš-mukīn-apli, who appears among the witnesses in Document 39 (Kümmel 1979, 133, 151). Nabû-ēṭir-napšāti (line 22) belongs to a family of prebendiaries of the Eanna (Kümmel 1979, 152). Nabû-bāni-aḫi (line 25) was himself a scribe in the Eanna, as were his sons (Kümmel 1979, 132).

1. 5 UDU.MEŠ *šá* ^{d}GAŠAN *šá* UNUG^{ki} *šá kak-kab-tu*$_{4}$ *še-en-du* 2. *šá ina ṣe-e-ni šá* ^{m}*ki-na-a* A-*šú* *šá* ^{md}U.GUR-*ina*-SUH$_{3}$-⸢SUR⸣	(1–3) 5 sheep belonging to the Lady of Uruk, branded with a star, which were seen in the flock of Kīnaya son of Nergal-ina-tēšê-ēṭir descendant of Dannea—
3. A ^{m}*dan-ne-e-a am-ra-a-ma* ^{m}NUMUN-*ia* A-*šú* 4. *šá* ^{m}TIN-*su* ^{lu_2}NA.KAD *šá* ^{d}GAŠAN *šá* UNUG^{ki} 3 *ina lìb-bi*	(3–5) about 3 of which Zēriya, son of Balāssu, the herdsman of the Lady of Uruk said thus:
5. *iq-bu-ú um-ma ina sa-ár-ti ul-tu ṣe-ni-ia*	(5–6) "They were led away from my flock in theft."
6. *ab-ka-a᾿ ina* UKKIN *a-na* ^{m}*ki-na-a ú-kin-nu*	(6) In the assembly, he testified against Kīnaya.
7. 1-*en* 30.MEŠ *ṣe-e-ni ra-bi-ti ina* UGU ^{m}*ki-na-a*	(7–8) They decided that Kīnaya must pay thirtyfold for the large sheep.
8. *par-su ù* 2-*ta ṣe-e-ni re-ḫi-it* 5-*ta ṣe-e-*[*ni*] 9. *šá kak-kab-tu*$_{4}$ *še-en-du šá* ^{m}*ki-na-a iq-bu-ú*	(8–10) And (as for) the 2 sheep, the remainder of the 5 sheep branded with a star, about which Kīnaya said thus:
10. *um-ma ul-tu* ITI ŠE MU 7-*kám* ^{m}SILA-*a-a* 11. ^{lu_2}SIPA *ina ṣe-ni-ia ip-te-qid* ^{m}SILA-*a-a*	(10–11) "Since the month of Addaru, year 7, Sūqaya, the shepherd, deposited them in my flock"—
12. *ib-ba-kám-ma a-na* ^{md}NA$_{3}$-LUGAL-URI$_{3}$ ^{lu_2}SAG-LUGAL 13. ^{lu_2}EN *pi-qit-tú* E$_{2}$.AN.NA 14. *ù* ^{lu_2}EN.MEŠ *pi-iq-ne-e-tú šá* E$_{2}$.AN.NA	(11–15) He shall bring Sūqaya and hand (him) over to Nabû-šarra-uṣur, the royal official in charge of the Eanna and (to) the administrators of the Eanna.
15. *i-nam-din ki-i* ^{m}SILA-*a-a la i-tab-kám-ma* 16. *la it-tan-nu* DIŠ-*šu ṣe-e-ni it-ti ṣe-e-ni-a᾿* 17. 1 30 *a-na* ^{d}GAŠAN *šá* UNUG^{ki} *i-nam-din*	(15–17) If he does not bring Sūqaya and does not hand (him) over, he shall pay 60 sheep together with those (other) sheep, thirtyfold (for the two sheep) to the Lady of Uruk.
18. *i-na* DU-*zu šá* ^{m}GAR-MU ^{lu_2}2-*ú šá* UNUG^{ki} A-*šú*	(18–19) In the presence of Šākin-šumi the deputy of Uruk son of Ibni-Ištar descendant of Sîn-tabni;

19. *šá* ^{m}DU$_3$-^{d}INNIN A ^{md}30-*tab-ni* ^{md}*in-nin*-LUGAL-URI$_3$ 20. A-*šú šá* ^{md}U.GUR-GI A ^{md}30-TI-ER$_2$	(19–20) Innin-šarra-uṣur son of Nergal-ušallim descendant of Sîn-lēqi-unninnī;
21. ^{md}DI.KU$_5$-ŠEŠ.MEŠ-MU A-*šú šá* ^{m}*gi-mil-lu* A ^{m}*ši-gu-ú-a*	(21) Madānu-aḫḫē-iddin son of Gimillu descendant of Šigûa;
22. ^{md}NA$_3$-SUR-ZI.MEŠ A-*šú šá* ^{m}IR$_3$-^{d}EN A ^{m}*e-gi-bi*	(22) Nabû-ēṭir-napšāti son of Arad-Bēl descendant of Egibi;
23. ^{md}EN-ŠEŠ-GAL$_2$-*ši* A-*šú šá* ^{m}*e-til-lu* A ^{m}E$_2$.KUR-*za-kir*	(23) Bēl-aḫa-šubši son of Etillu descendant of Ekur-zakir;
24. ^{md}EN-*na-din*-IBILA A-*šú šá* ^{m}NUMUN-TIN.TIR^{ki} A ^{m}DA-^{d}AMAR-UTU	(24) Bēl-nādin-apli son of Zēru-bābili descendant of Ileʾʾi-Marduk;
25. ^{md}NA$_3$-DU$_3$-ŠEŠ A-*šú šá* ^{md}NA$_3$-TIN-*su*-E A ^{md}30-TI-ER$_2$	(25) Nabû-bāni-aḫi son of Nabû-balāssu-iqbi descendant of Sîn-lēqi-unninnī;
26. ^{md}UTU-MU-DU A-*šú šá* ^{md}EN-ŠEŠ-MU A ^{lu_2}GAL-DU$_3$	(26) Šamaš-šuma-ukīn son of Bēl-aḫa-iddin descendant of Rāb-banê;
27. ^{lu_2}UMBISAG ^{m}*na-din* A-*šú šá* ^{md}EN-ŠEŠ.MEŠ-BA-*šá* A ^{m}*e-gi-bi*	(27) Scribe: Nādin son of Bēl-āḫḫē-iqīša descendant of Egibi.
28. UNUG^{ki} ITI APIN U$_4$ 5-*kám* 29. MU 9-*kám* ^{d}NA$_3$-IM.TUK 30. LUGAL TIN.TIR^{ki}	(28–30) Uruk. 5 Araḫšamna, year 9 of Nabonidus, king of Babylon.

15. A Summons to Babylon

Text: CBS 3557
Copy: Clay 1908 (BE 8/1), No. 48
Translation/Discussion: Clay 1908, 17
Place of Composition: (Nippur?)
Date: 28.VI.2 Nbn (11 October, 554 BCE)

Two brothers, Itti-Enlil-balāṭu and Bau-iqīša, have claims against each other. They are both summoned to Babylon to argue their claims. If Itti-Enlil-balāṭu fails to appear, a ruling reached earlier will apply. If Bau-iqīša does not come, Itti-Enlil-balaṭu is clear.

Documents like this one attest to a procedure in which a litigant might appeal to a higher court in Babylon (probably the court of the royal judges; compare Document 39, below). The documents themselves grant the appeals hearing and also summon the litigants to "argue their case" on a specific date (San Nicolò 1932, 339; Magdalene 2007, 64–65). The present document implies that, in the lawsuit between Bau-iqīša and Itti-Enlil-balāṭu, Itti-Enlil-balāṭu has appealed a ruling in favor of Bau-iqīša and that the appeal has been granted. The two brothers must now argue their case before the higher court in Babylon.

The present document does not provide any details about the subject of this litigation. Another document, written just two days later, fills out the picture and provides information about the case's ultimate outcome (Clay 1908, No. 42). This later document records eviction proceedings against Itti-Enlil-balāṭu. The governor, Gula-šumu-līšir (here, lines 11–12), together with Marduk-šarra-uṣur (here, lines 14–15) and Anum-šarra-uṣur (line 21), the *qīpi*-official of Nippur, "brings" Bau-iqīša (and another man named Šullumu, not mentioned in the present document) before Itti-Enlil-balāṭu, and orders Itti-Enlil-balāṭu to return Bau-iqīša's property.

Taking the two documents together, one may reconstruct the following storyline for the case. Prior to the lawsuit, Itti-Enlil-balāṭu had been holding property to which Bau-iqīša has a claim. Bau-iqīša succeeds in his initial lawsuit, but Itti-Enlil-balāṭu appeals the ruling and the present summons to Babylon is issued. In the wake of this summons, however, Itti-Enlil-balāṭu must have realized that his case against his brother's claim is quite weak. Within two days, he is ordered to forfeit the property, which apparently indicates that he has capitulated.

1. [U$_4$ X-*kám šá* ITI X ^{md}KA$_2$-BA-*ša*]	(1–5) [On X MN, Bau-iqīša and Itti]-Enlil-balāṭu sons (?) [of] Usātu shall come to Babylon and argue whatever claims they have against each other.
2. [*ù* ^{m}KI-^{d}]⸢EN.LIL$_2$-TIN A$^{?}$.MEŠ$^{?}$⸣-[*šá*]	
3. ^{m}*ú-sa-tu*$_4$ *a-na* TIN.TIR^{ki}	
4. *il-la-ku-ú-ma dib-bi-šú*-nu	
5. *šá i-ba-áš-šu-ú it-ti*	
6. *a-ḫa-meš i-dab-bu-ub*	(6–9) If Itti-Enlil-balāṭu does not come, their ruling is established.
7. *ki-i* ^{m}KI-^{d}EN.LIL$_2$-TIN	
8. *la it-tal-ka* DI.KU$_5$-*šú-nu*	
9. *šá-kin ki-i* ^{md}KA$_2$-BA-*šá*	(9–11) If Bau-iqīša does not come Itti-Enlil-balāṭu is clear.
10. ⸢*la*⸣ *it-tal-ka*	
11. ^{m}KI-^{d}EN.LIL$_2$-TIN *za-ka*	
12. *ina DU-zu šá* ^{md}*gu-la*-MU-GIŠ	(12–13) In the presence of Gula-šumu-līšir, the governor;
13. ^{lu_2}GU$_2$.EN.NA ^{md}NA$_3$-NUMUN-DU$_3$	(13) Nabû-zēra-ibni;
14. ^{md}UTU-DU-ŠEŠ ^{m}*mu-še-zib*-^{d}NA$_3$	(14) Šamaš-mukīn-aḫi; (14–15) Mušēzib-Nabû the chief of the troops;
15. ^{lu_2}GAL *ú-man-ni* ^{md}AMAR.UTU-LUGAL-URI$_3$	(15–16) Marduk-šarra-uṣur son of Mušēzibbu;
16. A-*šú šá* ^{m}*mu-še-zib-bu* ^{m}DU$_3$-*a*	(16–17) Bāniya son of Bīt-Ea-kitti;
17. A-*šú šá* ^{m}E$_2$-^{d}E$_2$-*a-kit-ti*	
18. *ù* ^{m}ŠEŠ-*ia* A-*šú šá* ^{md}EN.LIL$_2$-ŠEŠ-MU	(18) and Aḫiya son of Enlil-aḫa-iddin.
19. ⸢ITI⸣ KIN U$_4$ 28-*kám* MU ⸢2-*kám*⸣	(19–20) 28 Ulūlu, year 2 of Nabonidus, king of Babylon.
20. ⸢^{md}NA$_3$⸣-I LUGAL ⸢TIN⸣.[TIR^{ki}]	
21. ⸢^{m}⸣^{d}*a-num* LUGAL-URI$_3$	(21) Anum-šarra-uṣur.

16. Testimony and a Summons

Text: YBC 3773
Copy: Tremayne 1925 (YOS 7), No. 189
Translation/Discussion: Dandamaev 1984, 425; Kozuh 2006, 121; Holtz 2009, 121–22
Place of Composition: New Canal, *šīḫu*-property of the Lady of Uruk (Uruk)
Date: 7.II.6 Camb (22 May, 524 BCE)

In the assembly of the mār banî, *Bau-ēreš, a shepherd for the Lady of Uruk, testifies that two slaves beat him, kidnapped him, and stole sheep from the flock in his charge. Kīnaya, master of the two slaves, must present them in Uruk by 1 Simānu (in just over three weeks) and argue his case against Bau-ēreš before the judges of the king. If Kīnaya fails to present the slaves and defend himself against Bau-ēreš's claim, then Kīnaya must repay the loss of the sheep to the Lady of Uruk.*

From the point-of-view of trial procedure, the present document may be compared with Document 14, above, which also happens to pertain to misappropriated sheep. Both documents emerge in the wake of an accusation lodged before the judicial authorities in the Eanna. As a result of the accusations, both documents require the accusers to present the individuals that they have accused at a future date, when the legal proceedings will continue.

The status of the accuser in the two, however, marks an important difference between the situations in the two documents. In Document 14, it is rather clear that the accuser is also an accused individual: there, Kīnaya (different from the man with the same name in the present document) has been convicted of other thefts and will face penalties if he does not present the shepherd whom he has accused of stealing the remaining sheep. In contrast, the present document gives no indication of any suspicion against the accuser: although Bau-ēreš probably does bear some responsibility for the sheep, the text does not imply that he is lodging a counterclaim in the wake of an accusation. Instead, Bau-ēreš's accusation is probably closer to the statement of Zēriya, the herdsman who testifies against Kīnaya at the beginning of Document 14. Here, as in Document 14, the initial accusation marks the beginning of the proceedings, but here, before the proceedings can continue, the slaves' master must bring them before the authorities.

Another difference between the present document and Document 14 pertains to the penalties. In Document 14, one finds the expected thirtyfold penalty, typically imposed for misappropriation of temple property. In contrast, the present document does not impose the thirtyfold penalty, even though the sheep did belong to the temple herds. The absence of the usual penalty may stem from the fact that Kīnaya's slaves, rather than Kīnaya himself, are the ones suspected of direct involvement in the crime. Furthermore, since the litigants are to appear before the judges of the king, or outside of the Eanna's immediate jurisdiction, the thirtyfold penalty may not have applied.

1. ^{md}*ba-ú*-APIN-*eš* A-*šú šá* ^{md}NA$_3$-ŠEŠ-URI ^{lu_2}SIPA
2. *šá ṣe-e-nu* NIG$_2$.GA ^{d}GAŠAN UNUG^{ki} *u* ^{d}*na-na-a šá* ŠU.2 ^{m}IR$_3$-^{d}EN
3. A-*šú šá* ^{m}LUGAL-DU ^{lu_2}GAL *bu-ul i-na* UKKIN ^{lu_2}DUMU-DU$_3$.MEŠ

(1–4) Bau-ēreš son of Nabû-aḫa-uṣur, the shepherd of the flock of the Lady of Uruk and Nanaya, who is in the hands of Arad-Bēl son of Šarru-kīn, herd supervisor, said thus in the assembly of the *mār banî*:

4. *iq-bu-ú um-ma* ^{m}*pu-ṭi-ia u* ^{m}*šá*-^{d}NA$_3$-*ta-qu-um*
5. ^{lu_2}*la-mu-ta-nu šá* ^{m}*ki-na-a* A-*šú šá* ^{m}*ra-ḫi-im-mu*
6. *iṭ-ṭe-ru-in-ni iḫ-bi-tú-ú-in-ni ù ṣe-e-nu*
7. NIG$_2$.GA ^{d}INNIN UNUG^{ki} *šá i-na pa-ni-ia ul-tu ta-mir-tu*$_4$
8. *qaq-qar šá* ^{d}INNIN UNUG^{ki} *ik-ta-ta-mu-*ʾ

(4–8) "Puṭiya and Ša-Nabû-taqum, the slaves of Kīnaya son of Raḫimmu, beat me, kidnapped me, and stole sheep belonging to Ištar of Uruk, which were in my charge, from the irrigation district in the territory of Ištar of Uruk."

9. *a-di* U$_4$ 1-*kám šá* ITI SIG$_4$ ^{m}*ki-na-a* A-*šú*
10. *šá* ^{m}*ra-ḫi-im-mu* ^{m}*pu-ṭi-ia ù*
11. ^{m}*šá*-^{d}NA$_3$-*ta-qu-um* ^{lu_2}*la-mu-ta-ni-šú*
12. *a-na* UNUG^{ki} *ib-ba-kám-ma di-i-ni*
13. *it-ti* ^{md}KA$_2$-KAM$_2$ ^{lu_2}SIPA *šá ṣe-e-nu*
14. *šá* ^{d}INNIN UNUG^{ki} *ina* IGI ^{lu_2}DI.KU$_5$.ME *šá* LUGAL *i-dab-bu-bu*

(9–14) By 1 Simānu, Kīnaya son of Raḫimmu shall bring Puṭiya and Ša-Nabû-taqum, his slaves, to Uruk, and argue (his) case against Bau-ēreš, the shepherd of the flock of Ištar of Uruk, before the judges of the king.

15. *ki-i la i-tab-ku mi-ṭi-ti šá ṣe-e-nu šá* ^{d}INNIN UNUG^{ki} 16. *šá ina* IGI ^{md}KA$_2$-KAM$_2$ ^{lu_2}SIPA ^{m}*ki-na-a a-na* 17. ^{d}INNIN UNUG^{ki} *iṭ-ṭi-ir*	(15–17) If he does not bring them, Kīnaya shall repay to Ištar of Uruk the loss of the sheep of Ištar of Uruk which were in the charge of Bau-ēreš the shepherd.
18. ^{lu_2}*mu-kin-nu* ^{md}UTU-DU-A A-*šú šá* ^{m}*na-din* A ^{m}*e-gì-bi*	(18) Witnesses: Šamaš-mukīn-apli son of Nādin descendant of Egibi;
19. ^{m}SUM-*na-a* A-*šú šá* ^{md}*in-nin*-MU-URI$_3$ A ^{md}30-TI-ER$_2$	(19) Iddinaya son of Innin-šuma-uṣur descendant of Sîn-lēqi-unninnī;
20. ^{m}*ú-bar* A-*šú šá* ^{m}*ra-ḫi-im-mu* ^{md}EN-LUGAL-*us-su* A-*šú* 21. *šá* ^{md}UTU-MU ^{md}UTU-LUGAL-URI$_3$ A-*šú šá* ^{m}ŠEŠ-*im-me-e*	(20–21) Ubar, son of Raḫimmu; Bēl-šarrussu son of Šamaš-iddin; (21) Šamaš-šarra-uṣur son of Aḫimme;
22. ^{md}NA$_3$-GI A-*šú šá* ^{m}*ki-ṣir*-^{d}NA$_3$	(22) Nabû-ušallim son of Kiṣir-Nabû;
23. ^{lu_2}UMBISAG ^{md}AMAR.UTU-PAP A-*šú šá* ^{md}DI.KU$_5$-PAP.ME-MU A ^{m}*ši-gu-ú-*[*a*]	(23) Scribe: Marduk-nāṣir son of Madānu-aḫḫē-iddin descendant of Šigûa.
24. ID$_2$ *eš-šú ši-i-ḫu šá* ^{d}GAŠAN *šá* UNUG^{ki} ITI GU$_4$ U$_4$ 7-*kám* 25. MU 6-*kám* ^{m}*kám-bu-zi-ia* LUGAL TIN.TIR^{ki} 26. LUGAL KUR.KUR	(24–26) New Canal, *šīḫu*-property of the Lady of Uruk. 7 Ayaru, year 6 of Cambyses, king of Babylon, king of the lands.

17. A Summons to the Esagil at Babylon

Text: BM 33911 (Sp 7)
Copy: Strassmaier 1889a (Nbn), No. 102
Translation/Discussion: Kohler and Peiser 1890–1898, 4:81
Place of Composition: Babylon
Date: 25.II.3 Nbn (31 May, 553 BCE)

Amurru-nādin-... is summoned to argue his case against Aḫat-abīšu, a female oblate, in the Esagil. If he does not, he must make restitution to the god Bēl for the oblate's service.

The present document does not specify the nature of Aḫat-abīšu's claim against Amurru-nādin-.... The penalty may indicate that Amurru-nādin-... owes service to Bēl that he has not yet rendered. If this is so, then Aḫat-abīšu's role is simply as a temple functionary; her status as an oblate is only tangential to the ultimate proceedings against Amurru-nādin-.... Alternatively, the penalty may reflect a punishment against Amurru-nādin-..., rather than a pre-existing debt to the Esagil temple. If this is the correct interpretation, then Amurru-nādin-... may have already made a questionable claim to Aḫat-abīšu's services. It is in the face of this claim that the present document is issued. Amurru-nādin-... must now defend his claim or face a penalty for unrightfully using Aḫat-abīšu. For her part, Aḫat-abīšu would be arguing to maintain her status as an oblate of Bēltiya, against Amurru-nādin-...'s claim of ownership.

According to this latter interpretation, then, Aḫat-abīšu may be a former slave who was dedicated to the temple. If so, then the present document may be connected with the Egibi family archive. One document from this archive (Strassmaier 1889a [Nbn], No. 408) records the pledge of a slave named Aḫat-abīšu together with her son, named Bariki-ilī. Aḫat-abīšu's son was ultimately owned by the Egibis, so, if the connections are drawn correctly, the present document belongs to a group of records pertaining to Bariki-ilī (including Document 21 below). All of these records would have been held by Bariki-ilī's owners, the Egibi family. In addition to this overlap between the protagonists, the connection to the Egibi archive finds further support in the names of the second witness (lines 8–9) and the scribe: each is attested in other Egibi texts from nearly the same time (Strassmaier 1889b [Nbk], Nos. 368 and 403; Strassmaier 1889a [Nbn], No. 578). The surviving records, however, make it difficult to flesh out further details beyond the intriguing connections between individuals with similar names.

1. U$_4$ 15-*kám šá* ITI SIG$_4$ ^{md}KUR.GAL-MU-[X X] 2. A-*šú šá* ^{m}*mar-duk-a il-la-ak-kám-ma di-ib-*⌜*bi*⌝-[*šú*] 3. *it-ti* ^{f}*a-ḫat-*AD-*šú* ^{f}*ši-iš-ka-tu*$_4$ *šá* ^{d}GAŠAN-*ia* 4. *ina* IGI ^{lu_2}TIL.LA.MEŠ *šá* E$_2$.SAG.IL *i-dab-bu-ub*	(1–4) On 15 Simānu, Amurru-nādin-… son of Marduka shall come and argue [his] case against (the claim of) Aḫat-abīšu, the female oblate of Bēltiya, in the presence of the *qīpu*-officials (?) of the Esagil.
5. *ki-i la it-tal-ku* ^{lu_2}*dul-la* IR$_3$-*tú* 6. *a-na* ^{d}EN *i-nam-din*	(5–6) If he does not go, he shall make restitution to Bēl for (her?) slave service.
7. [^{lu_2}*mu-kin-nu* ^{m}PN$_1$] A-*šú šá* ^{m}*ap-la-a*	(7–8) [Witnesses: PN$_1$] son of Aplaya [descendant of PN$_2$];
8. [A PN$_2$] ^{m}*ri-mut-*^{d}EN A-*šú šá* ^{m}SUM.NA-ŠEŠ 9. [A ^{md}E]N-*pa-at-ta-an-ni ù* ^{lu_2}UMBISAG	(8–9) Rīmut-Bēl son of Iddina-aḫa [descendant of B]ēl-pattanni;
10. ^{md}EN-MU A-*šú šá* ^{m}DUB-NUMUN A ^{lu_2}*man-di-di*	(9–10) And the scribe: Bēl-iddin son of Šāpik-zēri descendant of Mandidi.
11. TIN.TIR^{ki} ITI GU$_4$ U$_4$ 25-*kám* MU 3-*kám* 12. [^{md}N]A$_3$-I LUGAL TIN.TIR^{ki}	(11) Babylon. 25 Ayaru, year 3 of [Na]bonidus, king of Babylon.

NOTES

1. According to a photograph (courtesy of Małgorzata Sandowicz), the tablet is broken on its right edge, where the end of the name would have been written.

4. ^{lu_2}TIL.LA.MEŠ- Apparently a scribal error based on the combination of signs ^{lu_2}TIL-(LA)-GID$_2$-DA, a common way of writing *qīpu*.

18. A Settled Case

Text: BM 30450 (76-11-16, 177)
Copy: Strassmaier 1892 (Dar), No. 260
Translation/Discussion: Kohler and Peiser 1890–1898, 3:55; Oppenheim 1940, 26; Dandamaev 1984, 382; Joannès 2002a; Holtz 2009, 79–81
Place of Composition: Šaḫrīni
Date: 25.VIII.9 Dar (1 December, 513 BCE)

Karêa and his mother, Nuptaya, argue a case against Nergal-aḫa-iddin. Nergal-aḫa-iddin is in possession of several slaves to which Karêa and Nuptaya have a claim. Fearing the impending litigation, Nergal-aḫa-iddin has returned the living slaves and sworn that he will compensate Karêa and Nuptaya for one of the slaves who has died in his possession. The present document records the ultimate settling of the case: the parties swear to each other that they will not revisit the lawsuit and Karêa and Nuptaya received the required payments from Nergal-aḫa-iddin.

The outcome recorded here resembles the results of the case following the summons issued in Document 15 above. Specifically, Nergal-aḫa-iddin's action here resembles that of Itti-Enlil-balāṭu, the man who is summoned in Document 15. Both men abandon their claims in the wake of litigation; Nergal-aḫa-iddin "fears the lawsuit" and settles, and Itti-Enlil-balāṭu apparently drops his claim to the land three days after the summons. This comparison raises the question of whether, in the present case, Nergal-aḫa-iddin's "fear" is simply the result of the initial actions by his adversaries, or prompted by a formal summons to appear in court, similar to the one recorded Document 15. The latter possibility is likely, but it is also possible that the settlement came about through negotiations between the litigants. There are, in fact, other Neo-Babylonian records of just this kind of action prior to formal litigation (see Magdalene, Wells and Wunsch 2008).

Among Neo-Babylonian lawsuit records, the present document stands out because, in addition to mentioning the defendant's "fear" of the lawsuit, the text also includes notices about the mutual oaths and receipt of payment, which mark the case's settlement. Cases that actually did come to trial before adjudicatory authorities result in similar payments or transfers of property. Nevertheless, Neo-Babylonian decision records usually do not mention the litigants' actual compliance with the ruling, which would mark the practical outcome of the lawsuit.

1. *di-i-ni šá* ^{m}*ka-re-e-a* A-*šú šá* ^{md}EN-DA A ^{m}ŠEŠ-*ú-tu*	(1–4) The suit of Karêa son of Bēl-lē'i descendant of Aḫūtu and Nuptaya daughter of Nabû-balāssu-iqbi, his mother, regarding Kuzbaya and her children and Nabû-ṣuršu, the (dependent) members of their household, which they brought against Nergal-aḫa-iddin son of Aḫḫêa.
2. *ù* ^{f}*nu-up-ta-a* DUMU.SAL-*su šá* ^{md}NA$_3$-TIN-*su-iq-bi* ⸢AMA⸣-*šú*	
3. *a-na muḫ-ḫi* ^{f}*ku-uz-ba-a ù* DUMU.MEŠ-*šú u* ^{md}NA$_3$-*ṣur-šú* UN.MEŠ E$_2$-*šú-nu*	
4. *it-ti* ^{md}U.GUR-ŠEŠ-MU A-*šú šá* ^{m}ŠEŠ.MEŠ-*e-a ir-gu-mu-'*	
5. ^{md}U.GUR-ŠEŠ-MU *di-i-ni i-dar-ma it-ti* ^{m}*ka-re-e-a*	(5–7) Nergal-aḫa-iddin feared the suit and he did not come to argue the case against Karêa and Nuptaya, his mother.
6. *u* ^{f}*nu-up-ta-a* AMA-*šú a-na da-ba-ba di-i-ni*	
7. *la il-lik* ^{f}*ku-uz-ba-a ù* DUMU. MEŠ-*šú ú-ter-ri-ma*	(7–8) He returned Kuzbaya and her children to Karêa and Nuptaya, his mother.
8. *a-na* ^{m}*ka-re-e-a ù* ^{f}*nu-up-ta-a* AMA-*šú* ⸢*id*⸣-*din*	
9. *ù* 4 MA.NA KU$_3$.BABBAR *ku-um* ^{md}NA$_3$-*ṣur-šú šá ina* E$_2$ ^{md}U.GUR-ŠEŠ-MU	(9–10) And [he paid] Karêa (and) Nuptaya, his mother, 4 mina of silver, in exchange for Nabû-ṣuršu, who died in the house of Nergal-aḫa-iddin.
10. *mi-ti a-na* ^{m}*ka-re-e-a* ^{f}*nu-up-ta-a* AMA-*šú* [*id-din*]	
11. ^{md}U.GUR-ŠEŠ-MU A-*šú šá* ^{m}ŠEŠ.MEŠ-*e-a a-mir-tu*$_4$ *it-ti* ^{m}*ka-*[*re-e-a*]	(11–12) Nergal-aḫa-iddin son of Aḫḫêa, together with Ka[rêa] and Nuptaya, daughter of Nabû-balāssu-iqbi, his mother, have settled balances.
12. *ù* ^{f}*nu-up-ta-a* DUMU.SAL-*su šá* ^{md}NA$_3$-TIN-*su*-E AMA-*šú i-*⸢*mu*⸣-[*ru*]	
13. *dib-bi šá* ^{m}*ka-re-e-a ù* ^{f}*nu-up-ta-a* AMA$^{!}$-*šú* ⸢*a-na*⸣ *muḫ-ḫi*	(13–15) The case of Karêa and Nuptaya, his mother, [regarding] the slaves and the payments against [Nergal-aḫa-iddin] is settled.
14. *a-me-lut-tu*$_4$ *ù man-da-at-tu*$_4$. MEŠ *it-ti* ^{m}[^{d}U.GUR-ŠEŠ-MU]	
15. *qa-tu-ú*	

16. ^{md}U.GUR-ŠEŠ-MU A-*šú šá* ^{m}ŠEŠ.MEŠ-*a-a* ^{m}[*ka-re-e-a*] 17. A-*šú šá* ^{md}EN-DA A ^{m}ŠEŠ-*ú-tu ù* ^{f}*nu-up-ta-a* 18. AMA-*šú* [ERASURE] «*a-na muḫ-ḫi a-ḫa-meš*» 19. *ina* ^{d}EN ^{d}NA$_3$ *u a-de-e šá* ^{m}*da-ri-ʾu-šú* LUGAL [E^{ki} *u* KUR.KUR]	(16–20) Nergal-aḫa-iddin son of Aḫḫêa, [Karêa] son of Bēl-lēʾi descendant of Aḫūtu and Nuptaya, his mother, swore to each other by Bēl, Nabû, and the oaths of Darius king [of Babylon and the lands]:
20. *a-na a-ḫa-meš it-te-mu-ú ki-i a-na* UGU [*mim-ma*]	(20–21) "We shall not reconsider regarding [anything] that we have done."
21. *šá ni-pu-uš ni-te-eḫ-si man-da-at-tu*$_4$.MEŠ [*šá* UN.MEŠ] 22. ^{m}*ka-re-e-a* A-*šú šá* ^{md}EN-DA A ^{m}ŠEŠ-*ú-tu*$_4$ ⌜*ù*⌝ [^{f}*nu-up-ta-a*]	(21–23) Karêa son of Bēl-lēʾi descendant of Aḫūtu, and [Nuptaya], his mother, have received the slave-wage [for the slaves] from Nergal-aḫa-iddin.
23. AMA-*šú ina* ŠU.2 ^{md}U.GUR-ŠEŠ-MU *eṭ-*[*ru-ʾ* ^{lú}*mu-kin-nu*] ^{m}BA-*šá*-^{d}AMAR.UTU A-*šú šá* ^{md}NA$_3$-EN-*šú-nu*	(23–24) Witnesses: Iqīša-Marduk son of Nabû-bēlšunu descendant of Nabû-naya;
24. A ^{md}NA$_3$-*bu-u-na-a-a* ^{m}[X X X] A-*šú šá* ^{m}DU-A A ^{m}*sag-di-di*	(24) [PN] son of Mukīn-apli descendant of Sagdidi;
25. ^{m}*ri-mut* A-*šú šá* ^{m}TUK$^{?}$-*ia* A ^{lú}SIPA ANŠE KUR.RA ^{md}NA$_3$-KAR-ZI.MEŠ	(25–26) Rīmut son of TUK-*ia* descendant of Rēʾi-sīsî; Nabû-ēṭir-napšāti son of Nabû-bēlšunu;
26. A-*šú šá* ^{md}NA$_3$-EN-*šú-nu* ^{md}X-X- X-X-ŠEŠ-MU A-*šú šá* ^{md}EN-*re-man-ni*	(26) DN-aḫa-iddin son of Bēl-rēmanni;
27. ^{md}NA$_3$-*bul-liṭ-su* A-*šú šá* ^{m}MU-^{d}NA$_3$ A ^{m}*da-bi-bi* ^{m}DUG$_3$.GA-*iá* A-*šú šá* ^{m}IR$_3$-*ia*	(27–28) Nabû-bulliṭsu son of Iddin-Nabû descendant of Dābibī; Ṭābiya son of Ardiya descendant of Basiya;
28. A ^{m}*ba-si-ia* ^{m}*mu-ra-šu-ú* A-*šú šá* ^{m}*na-din* A ^{m}ZALAG$_2$-^{d}30	(28) Murašû son of Nādin descendant of Nūr-Sîn;
29. ^{m}A-*a* A-*šú šá* ^{md}EN-DA A ^{m}*e-gi-bi* ^{md}AMAR.UTU-*na-ṣir*-IBILA	(29–30) Aplaya son of Bēl-lēʾi descendant of Egibi; Marduk-nāṣir-apli son of Itti-Marduk-balāṭu descendant of Egibi;
30. A-*šú šá* ^{m}KI-^{d}AMAR.UTU-TIN A ^{m}*e-gi-bi* ^{m}*mi-na-aʾ-im-bu-ka*	(30–31) Mina-imbuka descendant of Bakiya-rimiya.

31. ⸢A⸣ ^{m}*ba-ki-ia-ri-mi-a-a* ^{lu_2}UMBISAG ^{md}NA$_3$-A-MU A-*šú šá* ^{md}NA$_3$-MU-GAR-*un*	(31–32) Scribe: Nabû-apla-iddin son of Nabû-šuma-iškun descendant of Šangû-Nin-Eanna.
32. A ^{lu_2}SANGA-^{d}NIN-E$_2$.AN.NA ^{uru}*šá-aḫ-ri-ni* ITI APIN U$_4$ 25-*kám*	(32–33) Šaḫrini. 25 Araḫšamna, year 9 of Darius, king of Babylon, king of the lands.
33. MU 9-*kám* ^{m}*da-ri-muš* LUGAL E^{ki} LUGAL KUR.KUR	

Notes

Reading of this document is based on the collations of Cornelia Wunsch.

3. UN.MEŠ E$_2$-*šú-nu*- Literally translated, these words mean "the people of their house." In Neo-Babylonian legal records this phrase can refer to any dependent of the household. When used in reference to slaves, as here, the term may denote slaves born within the household, rather than purchased.

5. *i-dar-ma*- The verb as written is a durative form. The text's sense, however, requires a preterite verb, which should have been written *i-dur-ma* (with /u/, rather than /a/). This kind of fluctuation in vowels is to be expected in Neo-Babylonian orthography.

9–10. The price of 4 mina of silver is on the higher end of typical prices for male slaves (see Jursa 2010, 741–43). This suggests that the price includes some penalty.

11–12. The noun *amirtu* (literally "inspection"), here refers to the accounts that are settled. See *CAD* A$_2$, 63–64, s.v. *amirtu* A.

18. The writing at the end of this line should be deleted. It appears on the tablet because of scribal confusion with the beginning of line 20.

21. The word *mandattu* refers to payments paid to slave owners in compensation for the work of slaves.

Chapter 2
Completed Trials

19. A Dispute over the Sale of a Slave

Text: BM 41402 (81-6-25, 13)
Copy: Strassmaier 1889a (Nbn), No. 13; Wunsch 1997–98, No. 30 (p. 96; seals and legends only)
Translation/Discussion: Revillout and Revillout 1886, 387–89; Peiser 1888a, 81–86; Boissier 1890, 56–58; Peiser 1896, 206–9; Marx 1902, 53; Krecher 1970, 144; Dandamaev 1984, 189–90; Wunsch 1997–98, 96; Wells 2004, 150–51, 180–82; 2008, 240–41.
Place of Composition: Babylon
Date: 12.XI.0 Nbn (10 February, 555 BCE)

Bēlilitu presents a case before the judges of Nabonidus. She claims that Nabû-aḫḫē-iddin has not completed payment for the slave, Bazuzu, whom she sold to him some four years earlier, during the first year of Neriglissar. Nabû-aḫḫē-iddin presents evidence that he paid Bēlilitu, and Bēlilitu's sons confirm that she received payment. As a penalty, the judges require Bēlilitu to pay the full price of the slave, which she had claimed from Nabû-aḫḫē-iddin.

As the case unfolds, the plaintiff's claim seems unfounded: the defendant, the well-known Nabû-aḫḫē-iddin (see Documents 44–48), has his proofs of payment, and the plaintiff's own sons testify against her. Two additional documents from the Egibi archive shed light on the situation, but do not necessarily strengthen the plaintiff's claim. First, the actual contract recording the sale of the slave in question is preserved as Evetts 1892, Ngl No. 23, and is dated, as the present document states, to 3.V.1 Ngl (12 August, 559 BCE), about three and a half years before the lawsuit. Etillu, a son of Bēlilitu who is named in the present document as a witness against his mother, guarantees the title of the slave sold at the original transaction. Although the plaintiff claims that the defendant did not pay the full price of the slave at the time of the purchase, the contract itself does not state this. A second document, preserved as Evetts 1892, Ngl No. 42 and dated to 27.VIII.2 Ngl (22 November, 558 BCE), indicates that about two years prior to the present lawsuit, Bēlilitu's son, Zēriya (another witness in the present document), raised a claim against Nabû-aḫḫē-iddin, as a result of which Nabû-aḫḫē-iddin had to return two other slaves he had purchased from Bēlilitu. It is tempting to speculate that, in bringing a patently false claim to court, Bēlilitu is motivated by her son's earlier success.

1. ^{f}*be-li-li-tu*$_4$ DUMU.SAL-*su šá* ^{md}EN-*ú-še-zib* A ^{lu_2}*šá-[na-ši-šu]*	(1–3) Bēlilitu, daughter of Bēl-ušēzib descendant of Ša-[nāšīšu] said thus to the judges of Nabonidus, king of Babylon:
2. *a-na* ^{lu_2}DI.KU$_5$.MEŠ *šá* ^{md}NA$_3$-*na-ʾ-id* LUGAL TIN.TIR^{ki} *taq-bi*	
3. *um-ma ina* ITI NE MU 1-*kám* ^{md}U.GUR-LUGAL-URI$_3$ LUGAL TIN.TIR^{ki} ^{m}*ba-zu-zu*	(3–5) "In the month of Abu, in the first year of Neriglissar, king of Babylon, I sold my slave, Bazuzu, to Nabû-aḫḫē-iddin, son of Šulaya, descendant of Egibi for 1/2 mina 5 šeqels of silver."
4. *qal-la-a a-na* 1/2 MA.NA 5 GIN$_2$ KU$_3$.BABBAR *a-na* ^{md}NA$_3$-ŠEŠ.MEŠ-MU DUMU-*šú šá*	
5. ^{m}*šu-la-a* DUMU ^{m}*e-gi-bi ad-din-ma ú-ìl-tì i-il-ma* KU$_3$.BABBAR *la id-di-nu* ^{lu_2}DI.KU$_5$.MEŠ *šá* LUGAL	(5) "He wrote a promissory note but did not pay the silver."
6. *iš-mu-ma* ^{md}NA$_3$-ŠEŠ.MEŠ-MU *ub-lu-nim-ma ma-ḫar-šú-nu uš-ziz-zu*	(5–6) The king's judges heard and brought Nabû-aḫḫē-iddin and had him stand before them.
7. ^{md}NA$_3$-ŠEŠ.MEŠ-MU *rik-si šá* ^{f}*be-li-li-tu*$_4$	(7–8) Nabû-aḫḫē-iddin carried in the contract which he contracted (with) Bēlilitu (indicating) that he had paid her the silver of the price of Bazuzu, and showed (the contract) to the judges.
8. *ir-ku-su-ma* KU$_3$.BABBAR ŠAM$_2$ ^{m}*ba-zu-zu i-ṭi-ru-uš iš-šá-am-ma* ^{lu_2}DI.KU$_5$.ME *ú-kal-lim*	
9. *u* ^{m}NUMUN-*ia* ^{m}NA$_3$-MU-SI.SA$_2$ *u* ^{m}*e-til-lu* KU$_3$.BABBAR *šá* ^{f}*be-li-li-tu*$_4$ AMA-*šú-nu eṭ-re-tu*$_4$	(9–10) And Zērīya, Nabû-šumu-līšir and Etillu testified before the judges that Bēlilitu, their mother, was paid the silver.

10. *ina* IGI ^{lu_2}DI.KU$_5$.ME *ú-kin-nu* ^{lu_2}DI.KU$_5$.ME *im-tal-ku-ma* 1/2 MA.NA 5 GIN$_2$ KU$_3$.BABBAR *ma-la mu-qut-te-e-šú*	(10–11) The judges deliberated. They decided that Bēlilītu must pay 1/2 mina 5 šeqels of silver, whatever she had claimed to be owed, and awarded it to Nabû-aḫḫē-iddin.
11. *ina* UGU ^{f}*be-li-li-tu*$_4$ *ip-ru-su-ma a-na* ^{md}NA$_3$-ŠEŠ.MEŠ-MU *id-di-nu*	
12. *i-na* EŠ.BAR *di-i-ni šu-a-ta*	(12) At the decision of this case:
13. ^{m}E$_2$-SAG-IL$_2$-*šá-du-nu* ^{lu_2}DI.KU$_5$ DUMU ^{m}IR$_3$-^{d}*é-a*	(13) Esagil-šadûnu, the judge, descendant of Arad-Ea;
14. ^{md}AMAR.UTU-MU-URI$_3$ ^{lu_2}DI.KU$_5$ DUMU ^{md}IM-*šam-me-e*	(14) Marduk-šuma-uṣur, the judge, descendant of Adad-šammê;
15. ^{m}*mu-še-zib*-^{d}AMAR.UTU ^{lu_2}DI.KU$_5$ DUMU ^{md}KASKAL.KUR-*ú*	(15) Mušēzib-Marduk, the judge, descendant of Bālīḫû;
16. ^{md}NA$_3$-NUMUN-*kit-ti*-SI.SA$_2$ ^{lu_2}DI.KU$_5$ DUMU ^{m}*šu-ul-ma-nu*	(16) Nabû-zēr-kitti-līšir, the judge, descendant of Šulmānu;
17. ^{md}EN-*ú-bal-liṭ* ^{lu_2}DI.KU$_5$ DUMU ^{lu_2}GAL-1-*lim*	(17) Bēl-uballiṭ, the judge, descendant of Rāb-līmi;
18. ^{md}U.GUR-*ú-šal-lim* ^{lu_2}DI.KU$_5$ DUMU ^{m}*ši-gu-ú-a*	(18) Nergal-ušallim, the judge, descendant of Šigûa;
19. ^{md}U.GUR-*ba-nu-nu* DUB.SAR DUMU ^{lu_2}GAL-DU$_3$	(19) Nergal-bānûnu, the scribe, descendant of Rāb-banê.
20. TIN.TIR^{ki} ITI ZIZ$_2$ U$_4$ 12-*kám* MU SAG-NAM.LUGAL.E	(20–21) Babylon. 12 Šabāṭu, accession year of Nabonidus, king of Babylon.
21. ^{md}NA$_3$-*na-'-id* LUGAL TIN.TIR^{ki}	

Notes

1. Reading the family name based on Evetts 1892, Ngl No. 23, as collated in Sack 1994, 161.

20. A Slave's Attempt at Self-Liberation

Text: BM 33084 (79-3-1, 10)
Copy: Strassmaier 1889a (Nbn), No. 1113
Translation/Discussion: Peiser 1888b, 87–89; Peiser 1896, 254–58; Kohler and Peiser 1890–98, 1:5–7; Wallis 1964; Dandamaev 1984, 220–22, 440–42; Wells 2004, 154
Place of Composition: Bīt-šar-Bābili
Date: 17.VIII.[7+] Nbn [2 December, 549 BCE, or later]

Bariki-ilī, a slave, claims before the šangû, *the "great ones" and the judges of Nabonidus that he is a free man in the employment of Qudāšu and Šamaš-mudammiq. In reality, he had been given as part of a dowry and sold. The judges see the documents of his enslavement, including one stating that he had been pledged and one in which he had been given as part of a dowry, and demand to see his documents of manumission. This demand brings him to confess that there are no such documents and that he had attempted to escape his slavery. He also confesses that he had been sold to Itti-Marduk-balāṭu. The judges return him to slavery.*

At the time of the lawsuit, the plaintiff, Bariki-ilī, has been sold to Itti-Marduk-balāṭu, a son of Nabû-aḫḫē-iddin of the Egibi family, and has apparently attempted to escape from there, according to the slave's own confession. The decision record itself mentions events in the slave's life beginning in year 35 of Nebuchadnezzar (570/569 BCE), some twenty years before the trial takes place. Prior to his sale to his most recent master, he belonged to Gagaya, who gave him as a dowry to her daughter, Nuptaya, who gave him to her son, Zababa-iddin. Two other documents, Strassmaier 1889b, Nos. 346 and 408, afford a glimpse into the slave's earlier life as Gagaya's slave, and suggest that he has a history of escape attempts (see Dandamaev 1984, 220–22). In Strassmaier 1889b, No. 346 (dated 13.IV.39 Nbk, 11 July, 566 BCE), she, together with her husband and another kinsman, sell Bariki-ilī. About three years later, however, at the time of the composition of Strassmaier 1889b, No. 408 (14.XII.42 Nbk, 2 March 562 BCE), Bariki-ilī is back in the possession of Gagaya and her husband, who give him as a pledge in a loan, along with Aḫat-abīšu, his mother. It seems that the sale in Strassmaier 1889b, No. 346 was cancelled and the slave was returned, perhaps because he tried to get away from his new masters.

1. [^{m}*ba-ri-ki*-DINGIR].MEŠ IR$_3$ *pu-ṭu-ru* KU$_3$.BABBAR *šá* ^{f}*ga-ga-a* DUMU.SAL-*su* 2. [*šá* ^{md}E N-PAP] *šá* MU 35-*kám* ^{md}NA$_3$-NIG$_2$.DU-URI$_3$ LUGAL TIN.TIR^{ki} 3. [^{m}]ŠEŠ-*nu-ú-ri* A-*šú šá* ^{md}NA$_3$-*na-din*-ŠEŠ *a-na* 1/3 MA.NA 8 GIN$_2$ KU$_3$.BABBAR	(1–4) [Bariki-il]ī, the silver-redeemed slave of Gagaya, daughter [of Bēl-nāṣir] who, in year 35 of Nebuchadnezzar, king of Babylon, was … for 1/3 mina 8 šeqels of silver (by) Aḫu-nūri son of Nabû-nādin-aḫi, now brought suit thus:
4. [X]-*du e-nin-ni ir-gu-mu um-ma* DUMU *ba-ni-i* DIB-*nu šá* ^{md}EN-*re-man-ni* 5. [^{lu_2}]*taš-li-šú šá* ŠU.2 ^{md}UTU-SIG$_5$-*iq* A-*šú šá* ^{md}NA$_3$-*na-din*-ŠEŠ 6. *u* ^{f}*qu-da-šú* DUMU.SAL-*su šá* ^{m}ŠEŠ-*nu-ú-ru a-na-ku i-na ma-ḫar*	(4–6) "I am a free man … of Bēl-rēmanni the third charioteer under the authority of Šamaš-mudammiq son of Nabû-nādin-aḫi and Qudāšu, daughter of Aḫu-nūri."
7. ^{lu_2}SUKKAL ^{lu_2}GAL.MEŠ *ù* ^{lu_2}DI.KU$_5$.MEŠ *šá* ^{md}NA$_3$-I LUGAL TIN.TIR^{ki}	(6–8) Before the *sukkallu,* the "great ones" and the judges of Nabonidus, king of Babylon they argued (their) case.
8. *di-i-ni id-bu-bu-ma dib-bi-šú-nu iš-mu-ú ri-ka-su šá* IR$_3$-*ú-tu*	(8) They heard their case.
9. *šá* ^{m}*ba-ri-ki*-DINGIR.MEŠ *šá ul-tu* MU 35-*kám* ^{d}NA$_3$-NIG.DU-URI$_3$ LUGAL TIN.TIR^{ki} 10. *a-di* MU 7-*kám* ^{d}NA$_3$-I LUGAL E^{ki} *a-na* KU$_3$.BABBAR *na-ad-nu a-na maš-ka-nu* 11. *šak-nu a-na nu-dun-ne-e a-na* ^{f}*nu-up-ta-a* DUMU.SAL-*su šá* 12. ^{f}*ga-ga-a na-ad-nu ár-ki* ^{f}*nu-up-ta-a tak-nu-ku-šú-ma* 13. *it-ti* GIŠ.ŠUB.BA E$_2$ *ù a-me-lu-ut-ti a-na* ^{md}*za-ba$_4$-ba$_4$*-MU 14. DUMU-*šú u* ^{m}SUM.NA-*a mu-ti-šú ta-ad-di-nu-uš iš-tas-su-ú-ma*	(8–14) They read the contracts pertaining to Bariki-ilī's slave status, from year 35 of Nebuchadnezzar, king of Babylon, through year 7 of Nabonidus, king of Babylon, (in which) he was sold for silver, pledged as a pledge, given as a dowry to Nuptaya daughter of Gagaya, (and in which) afterwards Nuptaya sealed (a tablet indicating that) she gave him, together with a share of property and slaves to Zababa-iddin, her son, and Iddinaya, her husband.

15. *a-na* ^{m}*ba-ri-ki*-DINGIR.MEŠ *iq-bu-ú um-ma tar-gu-mu um-ma* DUMU *ba-ni-i*	(15) They said thus to Bariki-ilī: (15–16) "You argued thus, 'I am a free man.'"
16. *a-na-ku* DUMU *ba-nu-tú-ka kil-lim-an-na-a-šú* ^{m}*ba-ri-ki*-DINGIR *an-ni-*[*ti*]	(16) "Show us your (evidence of) your free status."
17. *i-pul um-ma* 2 ZAH$_2$ *ul-tu* E$_2$ EN-*ia ad-di-ma* U$_4$.MEŠ *ma-du-ti*	(16–17) Bariki-ilī answered this (claim) thus: "I made two escapes from the house of my master."
18. *la an-na-mar ap-laḫ-ma aq-bi um-ma* DUMU *ba-ni-i a-na-ku*	(17–18) "I was not discovered for a long time. I was afraid and I said thus: 'I am a free man.'"
19. DUMU *ba-nu-ta-a la i-ši* IR$_3$ *pu-ṭu-ru* KU$_3$.BABBAR *šá* ^{f}*ga-ga-a a-na-ku*	(19) "(Evidence of) my free status does not exist. I am a silver-redeemed slave of Gagaya."
20. ^{f}*nu-up-ta-a* DUMU.SAL-*su ta-ad-da-an-na-an-ni* ^{f}*nu-up-ta-a*	(20–22) "She gave me to Nuptaya, her daughter; Nuptaya sealed (a document) and gave me to Zababa-iddin, her son, and to Idinnaya, her husband."
21. *tak-nu-ka-an-ni ana* ^{md}*za-ba$_4$-ba$_4$*-MU DUMU-*šú u* ^{m}SUM.NA-*a* DAM-*šú*	
22. *ta-ad-di-na-an-ni ár-ki mi-tu-tu šá* ^{f}*ga-ga-a u* ^{f}*nu-up-ta-a*	(22–24) "After the death of Gagaya and Nuptaya, I have been a slave (sold) for silver (by means of a) sealed (document) to Itti-Marduk-balāṭu son of Nabû-aḫḫē-iddin descendant of Egibi. I will go and serve my master."
23. *a-na* ^{m}KI-^{d}AMAR.UTU-TIN A-*šú šá* ^{md}NA$_3$-ŠEŠ.MEŠ-MU A ^{m}*e-gi-bi a-na* KU$_3$.BABBAR	
24. *ka-na-ak* IR$_3$ *a-na-ku al-lak-ma* EN-*a a-*[*pal*]-*aḫ*	
25. [^{lu_2}SUKKAL ^{lu_2}GAL].MEŠ *ù* ^{lu_2}DI.KU$_5$.MEŠ *mu-kin-nu-*[*ut*]-*su iš-*[*mu-ma*]	(25) The *sukkallu,* the great ones and the judges heard his testimony.
26. [^{m}*ba-ri-ki*]-DINGIR *ki-i* IR$_3$-*ú-tu ú-te-ru-ma ina ú-šu-uz šá* ^{md}UTU-[SIG$_5$]	(26) They returned [Bariki]-ilī to slavery.
27. *u* ^{f}*qu-da-šú* DUMU.SAL-*su šá* ^{m}ŠEŠ-*nu-ú-ri* ^{lu_2}*na-di-na nu-dun-ne-e*	(26–27) In the presence of Šamaš-mudammiq and Qudāšu, daughter of Aḫu-Nūri, the one who gave the dowry.

28. [x x x] *a-na ša-ṭa-ri* [*ṭup-pi*] *šu-a-tim* ^{md}30-*še-zib* ^{lu_2}⌜SUKKAL⌝	(28) At the writing of this [tablet]: Sîn-šēzib, the *sukkallu*.
29. [^{m}MU-GI.NA] *u* ^{md}U.GUR-ŠEŠ-[URI$_3$] ^{lu_2}DI.KU$_5$.MEŠ	(29) [Šuma-ukīn] and Nergal-aḫa-uṣur, the judges.
30. [^{m}DA-^{d}AMAR.UTU DUB.SAR A] ^{m}DU$_3$-*eš*-DINGIR URU E$_2$ LUGAL TIN.TIR^{ki} ITI APIN U$_4$ 17-*kám*	(30–31) [Ile''i-Marduk, the scribe, descendant of] Eppeš-ili. Bīt-šar-Bābili. 17 Araḫšamna, year X of Nabonidus, king of Babylon.
31. [MU X]-*kám* ^{d}NA$_3$-IM.TUK LUGAL TIN.TIR^{ki}	
^{na_4}KIŠIB ^{md}U.GUR-ŠEŠ-URI$_3$ ^{lu_2}DI.KU$_5$	Seal of Nergal-aḫa-uṣur, the judge
^{na_4}KIŠIB ^{md}MU-GI.NA ^{lu_2}DI.KU$_5$	Seal of Šuma-ukīn, the judge
^{na_4}KIŠIB ^{m}*ki-rib-tu* ^{lu_2}*ki-zu-ú*	Seal of Kiribtu, the *kizû*

NOTES

Reading of this document is based on the collations of Cornelia Wunsch.

1. The plaintiff's name, Bariki-ilī (restored here based on the remainder of the document) is apparently the Akkadian transcription of a Hebrew name like Barakʾēl, attested in the Bible as the name of the father of Elihu, Job's interlocutor (Job 32:2, 6). Accordingly, the slave in this document has been understood to be a Judean exile (or descendant of these exiles) in Babylon (Wallis 1964). While his name is certainly not Akkadian, that he is Judean remains a matter of pure speculation.

pu-ṭu-ru KU$_3$.BABBAR- The particular nuances of the verb *paṭāru* in this context remain unclear. One might suggest that Gagaya obtained Bariki-ilī by "redeeming" him from a creditor. However, see the uncertainties expressed in San Nicolò and Ungnad 1935, 141–42.

4–6. For discussion of the ranks which Bariki-ilī claims to have, see Wallis 1964, 18 and literature cited there.

30. The reading of the place of composition follows Zadok 1985, 106. The restoration of the scribe's name is based on Contenau 1927–29 (TCL 12), No. 120, l. 25. For more on the career of this scribe, see Holtz 2008. The judges and the *kizû* also appear in Contenau 1927–29 (TCL 12), No. 120, which was also written in Bīt-šar-Bābili (Wunsch 2000b, 568 n. 33).

21. A Misappropriated Temple Slave

Text: AO 19536
Copy: Arnaud 1973; Durand 1981, No. 60
Translation/Discussion: Arnaud 1973; Joannès 2000b, No. 166 (pp. 223–25); Holtz 2009, 57–59
Place of Composition: Babylon
Date: 24.V.17 Nbn (23 August, 539 BCE)

The chief brewer of the Eanna and the scribe of the Eanna, as representatives of the temple, present their case against Nūrea for misappropriating Nanaya-ḫussini, an alleged slave of the Eanna, and her son, Tattannu. They bring Nūrea and the two alleged slaves before the judges of Nabonidus. Nūrea claims that he purchased Nanaya-ḫussinni and that she escaped from his possession and had herself branded with the mark of Nanaya to disguise herself as a temple oblate. The judges interrogate the woman, who testifies that she was dedicated to Nanaya by her previous master. The judges then call for an expert to examine the mark on the slave's hand, and he determines that she has two old marks on her hand, one for Ištar of Uruk and one for Nanaya. The judges then admonish Nūrea for not properly investigating the slave's circumstances before his purchase, effectively ending his claim. They decide that the slave belongs to the Eanna. Nūrea may seek redress from the individual who guaranteed the slave's clear title when she was purchased.

The situation in the present document makes sense in light of typical Neo-Babylonian manumission practices. During their own lifetimes, owners of slaves would free their slaves and simultaneously dedicate them as oblates to a temple. The manumitted slaves would assume oblate status, but would still reside with and serve their original owners until the owners' deaths. Then, the slaves would enter the temple's workforce (Wunsch and Magdalene in press).

One practical implication of this arrangement is that a good amount of time could elapse between the initial dedication to the temple and the slaves' actual transfer. The temple, for its part, would have to work to ensure that such slaves-turned-oblates would actually enter its service. If the temple's vigilance lapsed, an unscrupulous owner could sell the slave away to an uninformed (or equally unscrupulous) purchaser (compare Document 31 below). Similarly, an unscrupulous heir of the original master might continue to use the slave. In the present case, according to Nūrea's statement, Nanaya-ḫussini's purported escape took place during the reign of Amēl-Marduk (562–560 BCE). Since he must have purchased the slave before that time, over twenty years have passed before the lawsuit was pursued. It probably took the Eanna authorities that long to discover the misdeed and to bring their case forward.

It is quite likely, then, that Nūrea's "oversight" was not entirely innocent. But he cannot be the only guilty party in this case; the person from whom Nūrea purchased Nanaya-ḫussini was also trying to benefit illicitly from an oblate's labor. One may explain the seller's situation and motive as follows: the seller is an heir of Nanaya-ḫussini's former master. The original owner had, indeed, dedicated Nanaya-ḫussini to the temple, but had retained rights to her labor during his lifetime, as would have been customary. The heir, unhappy with the prospect of losing all profit from Nanaya-ḫussini, sold her to Nūrea (Arnaud 1973, 155).

The description of the sale suggests an alternative interpretation. The term "to lead away for silver" (*ana kaspim abāku*), which is one of the ways to describe a sale, can, when slaves are the objects "led away," indicate that the slaves were taken in payment of a debt. Thus, Nanaya-ḫussinni's original master (or his heir) may have owed a debt to Nūrea, but did not have the means (or the desire) to repay. Nūrea, the creditor, agreed to settle the debt by accepting ownership of Nanaya-ḫussinni as payment. This arrangement would have required both creditor and debtor to ignore the Eanna's claim to Nanaya-ḫussinni's service.

Whether sale or repossession, the transfer of Nanaya-ḫussinni was certainly shady. Thus, although the present document (line 41) allows Nūrea to "argue (a case) against the guarantor" to the original sale, this notice is probably more formal than practical. The guarantor, if one existed at all, would have to have been complicit in the scheme and would be long gone. It is more likely, however, that there was no such guarantor; Nūrea has either knavishly agreed to accept Nanaya-ḫussinni or foolishly agreed to purchase her without a guarantee to her clear title.

Apart from the seller and Nūrea, Nanaya-ḫusinni herself may have been complicit in the sale. After all, the purchase took place more than twenty years before the lawsuit, so Nanaya-ḫussinni has been keeping silent for a good while. At the same time, Nanaya-ḫusinni may also have played some part in bringing her situation to the attention of the authorities. Her motive for speaking out may be so that she and her son could benefit from her status as an oblate. The temple, unlike private owners, would have allowed both the mother and her son to remain together (Wunsch and Magdalene in press). Unfortunately, both oblates end up among the "basket carriers," the lowest rank of the Eanna oblates. This may or may not reflect a punitive ruling against Nanaya-ḫussinni.

Because the dispute pertains to private ownership of an alleged temple oblate, the case is heard by the royal judges in Babylon, rather than by adjudicators from within the Eanna bureaucracy (compare Document 31 below). One imagines that the case actually did begin with an internal investigation but was referred to Babylon for a final decision. Documents 15 and 39, in which appelants are summoned to Babylon to “argue their case,” reflect analogous transfers of a case to the royal courts. Although the present document does not indicate that Nūrea has appealed an original ruling, the trial here does illustrate how a case pertaining to the Eanna in Uruk could arrive before the royal judges in Babylon.

1. ^{md}DI.KU$_5$-ŠEŠ.MEŠ-MU DUMU-*šú šá* ^{m}*gi-mil-lu* A ^{m}*ši-gu-ú-a*	(1–9) Madānu-aḫḫē-iddin, son of Gimillu descendant of Šigûa, chief brewer of Ištar of Uruk, and Balāṭu, son of Sîn-ibni, scribe of Eanna, brought Nanaya-ḫussinni, a female slave whose hand was branded with a star and inscribed “(dedicated) to Nanaya,” and Tattannu, son of Nanaya-ḫussinni, with Nūrea, son of Kabtiya, before the judges of Nabonidus, king of Babylon, saying thus:
2. ^{lu_2}UGULA $^{\langle lu_2\rangle}$SIRAŠ.MEŠ *šá* ^{d}INANNA UNUG^{ki} *ù* ^{m}*ba-la-ṭu* DUMU-*šú*	
3. *šá* ^{md}30-*ib-ni* DUB.SAR E$_2$.AN.NA ^{fd}*na-na-a-ḫu-us-si-in-ni*	
4. GEME$_2$ *šá kak-kab-ti rit-ta-šú še-en-di-ti ù*	
5. *a-na* ^{d}*na-na-a šaṭ-ra-tu*$_4$ *u* ^{m}*ta-at-tan-nu* DUMU	
6. *šá* ^{fd}*na-na-a-ḫu-us-si-in-ni it-ti* ^{m}ZALAG$_2$-*e-a*	
7. DUMU-*šú šá* DUGUD-*ia a-na maḫ-ri* ^{lu_2}DI.KU$_5$.MEŠ	
8. *šá* ^{md}NA$_3$-IM.TUK LUGAL TIN.TIR^{ki} *ú-bil-lu-nim-ma*	
9. *iq-bu-ú um-ma* GEME$_2$ *an-ni-tu*$_4$ *za-ki-tu*$_4$	(9–10) “This female slave, who is dedicated to Nanaya, serves Nūrea.”
10. *šá* ^{d}*na-na-a* ^{m}ZALAG$_2$-*e-a ta-pal-làḫ* ^{m}ZALAG$_2$-*e-a i-pul*	(10–11) Nūrea answered thus:
11. *um-ma* ^{fd}*na-na-a-ḫu-us-si-in-ni a-na* KU$_3$.BABBAR	(11–12) “I led away Nanaya-ḫussinni for silver.”
12. *a-ta-bak ù ina* BAL-*e* ^{m}LU$_2$-^{d}AMAR.UTU LUGAL TIN.TIR^{ki}	(12–15) “And, during the reign of Amēl-Marduk, king of Babylon, when she escaped from my house, she had her hand branded with a star and had the inscription ‘(dedicated) to Nanaya’ written on her hand.”
13. *ul-tu* E$_2$-*ia ki-i taḫ-li-qu kak-kab-ti*	
14. *rit-ta-šú tal-te-mi-it ù šá-ṭa-ri ina* UGU	

15. *rit-ti-šú a-na* ^{d}*na-na-a-a tal-ta-ṭár* ^{lu_2}DI.KU$_5$.MEŠ 16. ^{fd}*na-na-a-ḫu-us-si-in-ni i-šá-lu-ma* 17. *taq-bi um-ma a-di la* ^{m}ZALAG$_2$-*e-a a-na* KU$_3$.BABBAR *ib-ba-kan-ni*	(15–17) The judges interrogated Nanaya-hussinni, and she said thus:
18. ^{md}DUMU-SAG.IL$_2$-*lu-mur* EN-*a maḫ-ra-a a-na*	(17–19) "Before Nūrea led me away for silver, Mār-Esagil-lūmur, my previous master, dedicated me to Nanaya."
19. ^{d}*na-na-a uz-zak-ka-an-ni* ^{lu_2}DI.KU$_5$.MEŠ	(19–20) The judges heard their statements.
20. *a-ma-a-ti-šú-nu iš-tim-mu-ma se-pi-ri ú-bil-lu-nim-ma* 21. *rit-ti šá* ^{fd}*na-na-a-ḫu-us-si-in-ni* 22. *ú-ad-di-ma iq-bi um-ma šá-ṭa-ri la-bi-ri*	(20–22) They brought an alphabet scribe before them and he informed them (regarding) Nanaya-ḫussinni's hand, saying thus:
23. *šá u$_4$-mu ru-qu-tu$_4$ a-na* ^{d}*na-na-a-a* 24. *rit-ta-šú šaṭ-ra-at*	(23–24) "Her hand is inscribed with an old inscription, from a long time ago: '(dedicated) to Nanaya.'
25. *ù šá-ṭa-ru šá-na-a ina šá-pal šá-ṭa-ri* 26. *maḫ-ra-a a-na* ^{d}INANNA UNUG^{ki} *šá-ṭi-ir*	(25–26) "And another inscription is written under this first inscription: '(dedicated) to Ištar of Uruk.'"
27. ^{lu_2}DI.KU$_5$.MEŠ *a-na* ^{m}ZALAG$_2$-*e-a iq-bu-ú um-ma mi-nam-ma*	(27) The judges said thus to Nūrea:
28. GEME$_2$ *šá a-na* ^{d}INANNA UNUG^{ki} *za-ka-a-ti kak-kab-tu$_4$* 29. *še-en-di-it-tu$_4$ ù rit-ta-šú a-na* ^{d}INANNA UNUG^{ki} 30. *u* ^{d}*na-na-a šaṭ-ra-tu$_4$ a-na* KU$_3$.BABBAR *tab-ba-ak*	(27–30) "Why did you purchase for silver a female slave dedicated to Ištar of Uruk, branded with a star, and whose hand is inscribed (as dedicated) to Ištar of Uruk and Nanaya?"

31. *ù at-ta taq-bi um-ma i-na* BAL-*e* ^{m}LU$_{2}$-^{d}AMAR.UTU
32. LUGAL TIN.TIR^{ki} GEME$_{2}$ *ul-tu* E$_{2}$-*ia taḫ-liq-ma*

(31–33) "And you said thus: 'During the reign of Amēl-Marduk, king of Babylon, the female slave escaped from my house and marked her hand with a star.'"

33. *kak-kab-tu*$_{4}$ *rit-ta-šú taš-mi-it mi-nam-ma*
34. *ina* U$_{4}$-*me-šú a-na maḫ-ri* ^{lu_2}DI.KU$_{5}$.MEŠ *ul tu-bil-šu-ma*
35. *ár-kat-su ul ip-ru-us-ma it-ti* LU$_{2}$ *šá rit-ta-šú*
36. *iš-ṭú-ru ul i-di-in-ka e-li*

(33–36) "Why did you not bring her before the judges back then? Why did they not investigate her circumstances and judge your case against the man who inscribed her wrist?"

37. ^{fd}*na-na-a-ḫu-us-si-in-ni u* ^{m}*ta-at-tan-nu* DUMU-*šú*

(36–38) "You have no claim over Nanaya-ḫussinni and Tattannu her son!"

38. *ul ra-šá-a-ti* ^{lu_2}DI.KU$_{5}$.MEŠ *im-tal-ku-ma*

(38) The judges deliberated.

39. ^{fd}*na-na-a-ḫu-us-si-in-ni u* ^{m}*ta-at-tan-nu* DUMU-*šú*
40. *it-ti um-man-ni za-bil tup-šik-ku šá* E$_{2}$.AN.NA

(39–41) They considered Nanaya-ḫussinni and Tattannu her son among the work gangs who carry the baskets of Eanna.

41. *im-nu-ú* ^{m}ZALAG$_{2}$-*e-a it-ti ár-ki-šú šá* LU$_{2}$-*ta id-di-nu-šú id-dab-bu-ub*

(41) Nūrea may argue (a case) against the guarantor of (the person) who sold him the slave.

42. *i-na ša-ṭa-ra ṭup-pi šu-a-tim*

(42) At the writing of this tablet:

43. ^{md}NA$_{3}$-TIN-*su-iq-bi* DI.KU$_{5}$ DUMU ^{m}LU$_{2}$-*ú*

(43) Nabû-balāssu-iqbi, the judge, descendant of Amēlû;

44. ^{m}*mu-še-zib*-^{d}EN DI.KU$_{5}$ DUMU ^{m}DU$_{3}$-*eš*-DINGIR

(44) Mušēzib-Bēl, the judge, descendant of Eppeš-ili;

45. ^{m}*ri-mut*-^{d}EN DI.KU$_{5}$ DUMU ^{m}*mi-ṣir-a-a*

(45) Rīmūt-Bēl, the judge, descendant of Miṣiraya;

46. ⸢^{md}⸣NA$_{3}$-NIR.GAL$_{2}$-DINGIR.MEŠ DI.KU$_{5}$ DUMU ^{md}IM-*šam-me-e*

(46) Nabû-etel-ilāni, the judge, descendant of Adad-šammê;

47. ^{md}AMAR.UTU-MU-MU DUMU E$_{2}$-<SAG>.IL$_{2}$-*a-a*

(47) Marduk-šuma-iddin, the judge, descendant of Esagilaya;

48. ^{m}*ba-laṭ-su* DI.KU$_{5}$ DUMU ^{lu_2}MA$_{2}$.LAH$_{4}$

(48) Balāssu, the judge, descendant of Malāhu;

49. ^{md}NA$_3$-MU-GAR-*un* DUB.SAR DUMU ^{lu_2}GAL-DU$_3$	(49) Nabû-šuma-iškun, the scribe, descendant of Rāb-banê;
50. ^{md}EN-*ka-ṣir* DUB.SAR DUMU ^{lu_2}AD.GUB$_x$	(50) Bēl-kāṣir, the scribe, descendant of Atkuppu;
51. ^{md}EN-SUM-*na* DUB.SAR DUMU ^{lu_2}NI.DU$_8$	(51) Bēl-iddina, the scribe, descendant of Atû.
52. TIN.TIR^{ki} ITI NE U$_4$ 24-*kám* MU 17-*kám* ^{md}NA$_3$-I LUGAL TIN.TIR^{ki}	(52) Babylon. 24 Abu, year 17 of Nabonidus, king of Babylon.
^{na_4}KIŠIB ^{md}NA$_3$-TIN-*su-iq-bu* ^{lu_2}DI.KU$_5$	Seal of Nabû-balāssu-iqbi, the judge
^{na_4}KIŠIB ^{m}*mu-še-zib*-^{d}EN ^{lu_2}DI.KU$_5$	Seal of Mušēzib-Bēl, the judge
^{na_4}KIŠIB ^{m}*ri-mut*-^{d}EN ^{lu_2}DI.KU$_5$	Seal of Rīmūt-Bēl, the judge
^{na_4}KIŠIB ^{md} NA$_3$-NIR.GAL$_2$-DINGIR.MEŠ ^{lu_2}DI.KU$_5$	Seal of Nabû-etel-ilāni, the judge
^{na_4}KIŠIB ^{md}AMAR.UTU-MU-MU ^{lu_2}DI.KU$_5$	Seal of Marduk-šuma-iddin, the judge
^{na_4}KIŠIB ^{md}*ba-laṭ-su* ^{lu_2}DI.KU$_5$	Seal of Balāssu, the judge

Notes

According to Arnaud 1973, 155 n. 6, this document is a copy of a sealed original. For this reason, the document has no seal marks on it, but does have transcribed indications of the sealings.

13–14. *tal-te-mi-it ... tal-ta-ṭár* -Nanaya-ḫussini is the subject of both of these verbs. Literally translated, then, they indicate that the slave performed both actions herself. It seems more likely, however, that she had these actions performed by another party. Also note that the text, throughout, distinguishes between the branding (*šamātu*) of the star and the writing (*šaṭāru*) of the inscription "(dedicated) to Nanaya" on the woman's hand.

20. The *sēpiru* was the scribe who wrote on parchment using the alphabet, rather than cuneiform. Marking the slave with alphabetic characters would have been an easier task than doing so with cuneiform (Arnaud 1973, 156).

35–36. *ip-ru-us-ma ... i-din-ka-* As written, both of these verbs are singular forms (of *parāsu* and *dânu*, in the G-stem). The subject of both verbs, however, is plural: the judges mentioned in line 34.

22. A Boatman's Fraud

Text: HSM 890.4.8
Copy: Beaulieu 2000c (YOS 19), No. 101
Translation/Discussion: Beaulieu 2000c, 7; Dandamaev 2001, 701
Place of Composition: Babylon
Date: 4.XII.10 Nbn (13 March, 545 BCE)

Nergal-rēṣū'a presents his case against the boatman, Amurru-natan. Nergal-rēṣū'a's master, Iddin-Marduk, arranged for the shipment of 480 kur of dates with the boatman and Nergal-rēṣū'a was to receive the shipment. When the dates arrived in Babylon, Nergal-rēṣū'a found that the amount of dates recorded by his master did not match the amount of dates unloaded. Nergal-rēṣū'a argued a case against the boatman, Amurru-natan, who falsely claimed that he did not embezzle the dates. At the conclusion of this first lawsuit, it seems that Amurru-natan agreed to pay 7 kur 1 pi of embezzled dates, but did not repay an additional 40 kur which were still in question. Now, the judges examine the transport contract and Iddin-Marduk's note to Nergal-rēṣū'a recording the amount of dates in the transport. They interrogate Amurru-natan who confesses to having embezzled the dates. They decide that Amurru-natan must pay the additional 40 kur of dates.

Nergal-rēṣū'a, the plaintiff in this case, is among the better attested slaves in the Neo-Babylonian archives, and, consequently, his career is well studied (Beljawski 1973, 139–44; Dandamaev 1984, 365–71; Wunsch 1993, 43–45). The present document demonstrates that, from the point of view of the law, slaves had equal standing as litigants. The present document is also a good illustration of the rather important role Nergal-rēṣū'a plays in the management of the affairs of his master, Iddin-Marduk. In other texts, he handles highly valuable amounts of silver and agricultural products. One undated record attests to his arrangement of shipment for a large quantity of dates on behalf of Iddin-Marduk, exactly as he does in the present document (Wunsch 1993, No. 362).

1. ^{md}U.GUR-*re-ṣu-ú-a* ^{lú}*qal-la šá* ^{m}MU-^{d}⸢AMAR.UTU⸣	(1–3) Nergal-rēṣū'a the slave of Iddin-Marduk said thus to the judges of Nabonidus, king of Babylon:
2. *a-na* ^{lú}DI.KU$_5$.MEŠ *šá* ^{md}NA$_3$-IM.TUK LUGAL TIN.TIR^{ki}	

3. *iq-bi um-ma* ^{m}MU-^{d}AMAR.UTU EN-*a* 4. 4 ME 80 GUR ZU$_2$.LUM.MA *e-pi-ru-tu* 5. *ul-tu* EDIN *a-na* ^{giš}MA$_2$.MEŠ *šá* ^{md}KUR.GAL-*na-tan* 6. ^{lu_2}MA$_2$.LAH$_5$ A-*šú šá* ^{m}*am-ma-a ú-še-li-ma*	(3–6) "Iddin-Marduk, my master, loaded (a shipment of) 480 *kur* of dates for transport (?) on the boats belonging to Amurru-natan, the boatman, son of Ammaya."
7. *pu-ut* EN.NUN-*tim šá* ZU$_2$.LUM.MA *ú-šá-áš-ši-iš*	(7) "He had him bear the responsibility for keeping the dates."
8. ^{giš}MA$_2$.MEŠ *a-na* TIN.TIR^{ki} *ú-še-la-am-ma* 9. *ši-pir-tu*$_4$ *šá* ^{m}MU-^{d}AMAR.UTU *id-di-nam-ma* 10. 4 ME 80 GUR ZU$_2$.LUM.MA *ina lìb-[bi-šú] šá-ṭi-ir*	(8–10) "He brought the boats to Babylon and he gave me Iddin-Marduk's note of authorization: 480 *kur* of dates was written i[n it]."
11. *re-eš* ZU.LUM.MA *áš-ši-ma* 47 GUR 1 PI	(11–12) "I took account of the dates, and 47 *kur* 1 *pi* were missing."
12. *ina lìb-bi* ⸢*ma*⸣-*ṭu*-⸢*ú*⸣ *a-na* UGU 13. *mi-ṭi-tu*$_4$ *šá* ZU$_2$.LUM.MA *it*-⸢*ti*⸣ ^{md}KUR.GAL-*na-tan*	(12–14) "I brought suit against Amurru-natan concerning the missing amount of the dates, but he claimed falsely (saying) thus:"
14. *ar-gum*$_2$-*ma ú-sar*-⸢*ri*⸣-*ri um-ma* ZU$_2$.⸢LUM.MA⸣-*ka*	(14–15) "'I did not take your dates.'"
15. *ul áš-ši ár*$^?$-*ki ba-ti-qu* X X X …	(15) "Afterwards, an informer …"
16. 40$^!$ GUR X X ⸢ZU$_2$.⸣[LUM.MA]	(16) "'40$^!$ *kur* of dates …"
17. *ù ku-tal-la šá* ⸢^{giš}MA$_2$-*ni*⸣ X-X *ú*	(17) "'and behind my boat …"
18. ZU$_2$.LUM.MA *šú-nu-tú i-na* X-*šú* [X X X] *am-ma*	(18) "'those dates in…"
19. *rik-su it-ti-šú ni-iš-ku-us* 20. *um-ma* 7 GUR 1 PI ZU$_2$.LUM.MA 21. [*ša*] ^{md}KUR.GAL-*na-tan ina sar-tu iš-šu-ú*	(19–21) "We contracted a contract with him stating thus: 'The 7 *kur* 1 *pi* of dates that Amurru-natan illegally took.'"
22. *ár-ki ri-ik-su šu-a-tú* ^{md}KUR.GAL-[*na-tan*] 23. *šuṭ-ur-ma a-di u*$_4$-*mu an-ni-i la* […]	(22–23) "After Amurru-[natan] wrote that contract until today … not …"

24. *i-na-an-na i-na maḫ-ri-ku-nu ub-la-áš*	(24–25) “Now, I have brought him before you. Establish our decision!”
25. EŠ.BAR-*a-ni šuk-na* ^{lú_2}DI.KU$_5$.MEŠ *dib-bi-šú-nu*	(25–29) The judges heard their case. They read before them that contract and Iddin-Marduk’s message in which 480 kur of dates was written which Nergal-rēṣūʾa brought.
26. *iš-mu-ú rik-su šu-a-tú u ši-pir-tu*$_4$	
27. *šá* ^{m}MU-^{d}AMAR.UTU *šá* 4 ME 80 GUR ZU$_2$.LUM.MA	
28. *ina lìb-bi šaṭ-ru šá* ^{md}U.GUR-*re-ṣu-ú-a ub-la*	
29. *ma-ḫar-šu-nu iš-tas-su-ú* ^{md}KUR.GAL-*na-tan*	(29–30) They interrogated Amurru-natan.
30. *i-šá-lu-ma na-šu-ú šá* ZU$_2$.LUM.MA *šá ina sar-tu*$_4$	(30–31) (Regarding) the taking of the dates, he testified about himself that they were taken illegally.
31. *na-šu-ú e-li ra-ma-ni-šú ú-kin-ma*	
32. 40 GUR ZU$_2$.LUM.MA *mi-ṭi-tu*$_4$ *šá* ZU$_2$.LUM.MA *šú-nu-šú*	(32–35) They decided that Amurru-natan (must pay) 40 *kur* of dates, the missing amount of those dates, (and) turned him over to Nergal-rēṣūʾa [slave of] Iddin-Marduk.
33. *e-li* [^{m}]^{d}KUR.GAL-*na-tan ip-ru-su-ma*	
34. *a-na* ^{md}U.GUR-*re-ṣu-ú-a* ^{lú_2}[*qal-la šá*] ^{m}MU-^{d}AMAR.UTU	
35. *id-di-nu ina* EŠ.BAR ⸢*di-i-ni*⸣ *šu-a-tim*	(35) At the decision of this case:
36. ^{md}U.GUR-[GI ^{lú_2}DI.KU$_5$] DUMU *ši-gu-ú-a*	(36) Nergal-[ušallim, the judge] descendant of Šigûa;
37. ^{md}NA$_3$-ŠEŠ.MEŠ-MU ^{lú_2}DI.KU$_5$ [DUMU]⸢*e-gi-bi*⸣	(37) Nabû-aḫḫē-iddin, the judge, [descendant of] Egibi;
38. ^{md}NA$_3$-[MU-GI].NA ^{lú_2}DI.⸢KU$_5$ DUMU *ir*⸣-*a-*[*ni*]	(38) Nabû-[šuma-ukī]n, the judge descendant of Irʾan[ni];
39. ^{md}EN-[ŠEŠ.MEŠ]-⸢MU⸣ ^{lú_2}DI.KU$_5$ DUMU ^{md}ZALAG$_2$-^{d}30	(39) Bēl-[aḫḫē]-iddin, the judge, descendant of Nūr-Sîn.
40. ^{md}EN-[KAR]-⸢*ir*⸣ ^{lú_2}DI.KU$_5$ DUMU ^{md}30-*tab-ni*	(40) Bēl-ēṭir, the judge, descendant of Sîn-tabni;
41. ^{md}NA$_3$-MU-GAR-*un* DUB.SAR DUMU ^{lú_2}GAL-DU$_3$	(41) Nabû-šuma-iškun, the scribe, descendant of Rāb-banê;
42. ^{md}EN-BA-*šá* DUB.SAR DUMU ^{md}30-*tab-ni*	(42) Bēl-iqīša, the scribe, descendant of Sîn-tabni.

43. TIN.TIR^{ki} ITI ŠE U$_4$ 4-*kám* 44. MU 10-*kám* ^{md}NA$_3$-IM.TUK LUGAL TIN.TIR^{ki}	(43–44) Babylon. 4 Addaru, year 10 of Nabonidus, king of Babylon.
Left edge:	
^{na_4}KIŠIB ^{md}U.GUR-GI ^{lu_2}DI.KU$_5$ ^{na_4}KIŠIB ^{md}NA$_3$-ŠEŠ.MEŠ-MU [^{lu_2}DI].KU$_5$ ^{na_4}KIŠIB ^{md}NA$_3$-MU-GI.NA ^{lu_2}DI.KU$_5$	Seal of Nergal-ušallim, the judge; Seal of Nabû-aḫḫē-iddin [the jud]ge; Seal of Nabû-šuma-ukīn, the judge;
Right edge:	
^{na_4}KIŠIB ^{md}EN-ŠEŠ.MEŠ-MU ^{lu_2}DI.KU$_5$ ^{na_4}[KIŠIB] ^{md}EN-KAR-[*ir*] ^{lu_2}DI.KU$_5$	Seal of Bēl-aḫḫē-iddin, the judge; [Seal] of Bēl-ēṭ[ir], the judge.

NOTES

4. *e-pi-ru-tu* (*epirūtu*). This word, which clearly describes the dates, is not known elsewhere as a qualification of dates. The suggested translation ("for transport") is based on the existence of the verb *epēru* as a variant of *ebēru,* "to cross" (*AHw*, 223, s.v. *epēru* II and *CAD* E, 191, s.v. *epēru*). This verb is used in connection with rivers and other bodies of water, which fits the present context. Therefore it seems that the word in question is an adjective meaning "for transport." Note, however, that it is the Š-stem form of the verb which usually has this meaning.

14–18. These broken lines contain the statements made during a previous suit against the boatman, as well as the accusation of an informant (*bātiqu*).

23. Inheritance

Text: BM 31672 (76-11-17, 1399)
Copy: Wunsch 2000a, No. 84 (1:229)
Translation/Discussion: Wunsch 2000a, 1:110–13; 2:108–9
Place of Composition: Babylon
Date: 29.VII.9 Nbn (24 October, 547 BCE)

*Two sons of Kurunnam-tabni present the legal history of their possessions to the judges of Nabonidus. Kurunnam-tabni received a slave as her dowry (*nudunnû*), and transferred ownership of the slave to her sons by means of a sealed document. She also received a parcel of land which she bequeathed to her children. The judges confirm her two sons' claims to the property.*

Most of the details in this lawsuit are lost to breaks in the text, but it does allude to previous litigation. In year 3 of Neriglissar, Kurunnam-tabni was awarded, presumably in a lawsuit, land and slaves by the "scribes of the king." Kurunnam-tabni, after the death of Šuma-ukīn, her husband, reserved the right to disinherit any son who would not treat her properly, in order to ensure her own support as a widow. Other documents pertaining to this case show that, in fact, she did take advantage of this right, and left the share of one son, not mentioned in the present document, to two other sons (Rutten 1947; Roth 1991–93, 14–16; Wunsch 2000a, 1:111–12).

The present document is preserved as part of the Egibi archive because soon after the present lawsuit, Nabû-aḫḫē-iddin began buying up the parcels of land that Kurunnam-tabni's sons had inherited (Wunsch 2000a, 1:113–15). Numerous documents pertaining to these plots show that the sons of Šuma-ukīn and Kurunnam-tabni, the original owners of the property, were a litigious bunch. They were also not entirely honest in their dealings with the Egibis (see Document 29 below), and various documents show that Nabû-aḫḫē-iddin took necessary precautions to protect himself (Wunsch 2000a, 1:115–16).

1. [^{m}PN$_x$ *ù*] ^{md}EN-TIN-*iṭ* DUMU.MEŠ *šá* ^{m}M[U-GI.NA]	(1–3) [PN$_x$ and] Bēl-uballiṭ sons of [Šuma-ukīn] [descendant of Sîn]-Šadûnu said thus to the judges of Nabo[nidus, king of Babylon]:
2. [DUMU ^{md}30-*šá*]-*du-nu a-na* ^{lu_2}DI.KU$_5$.MEŠ *šá* ^{md}NA$_3$-[IM.TUK]	
3. [LUGAL TIN.TIR]^{ki} *iq-bu-ú um-ma ina* MU 2-*kám* ^{md}U.[GUR-LUGAL-URI$_3$]	

4. [LUGAL TIN.TI]R^{ki} ^{fd}KAŠ. TIN-*nam-tab-ni* AMA-*a*-[*ni*...]	(3–6) "In year 2 of Ne[riglissar, king of Babylo]n, Kurunnam-tabni, ou[r] mother ..., (by means of a) sealed (document), placed [PN$_y$], the slave (which was part) of her dowry [at our] disposal."
5. [PN$_y$] IR$_3$ *šá nu-dun-né-e-šú tak-nu-uk-*[*ma*]	
6. [IGI-*ni t*]*u-šad-gil ù ár-ki* MU *3-kám* ^{md}U.GUR-[LUGAL-URI$_3$]	(6–9) "Afterwards, in year 3 of Nerig[lissar, king of Babylon], Kurunnam-tabni, our mother, of her own [will], (regarding) [2 *kur*] 2 *pi* of arable land which the scribes of the king placed [at h]er disposal as [her] dowry, declared [thus] in her tablet:"
7. [LUGAL TIN.TIR]^{ki} ^{fd}KAŠ. TIN-*nam-tab-ni* AMA-*a-ni ina mi-*[*gir lib-bi-šú*]	
8. [2 GUR] 2 PI ŠE.NUMUN *šá* DUB.SAR.MEŠ *šá* LUGAL *ku-um nu-dun-*[*ne-e-šú*]	
9. [*pa-n*]*i-šú ú-šad-gil-lu-ma ina* IM.DUB-*šú ú-še-du* [*um-ma* DUMU.MEŠ-*šú*]	
10. [*šá la i*]*-pal-la-ḫu-šú* HA.LA *ina lìb-bi ul* [*ileqqû*]	(9–10) "'[Any of her sons who do not] serve her shall not [receive] a share of it.'..."
1'. [...] ⸢ŠAM$_2$⸣	(1') price
2'. [^{fd}KAŠ.TIN]-⸢*nam-tab-ni*⸣ AMA-*šú-nu tak-nu-*[*ku*	(2') Kurunnam-tabni, their mother sealed
3'. *ú-ziz-zu* IM.DUB.MEŠ *na-*[	(3') they confirmed. The tablets ...
4'. [...] *di-i-ni* X X *im-ḫu-ru* X [	(4') ... the case they received
5'. [...] *u* ^{md}EN-TIN-*iṭ*	(5') ... and Bēl-uballiṭ
6'. [*ina* EŠ].BAR *di-i-ni* [*šu-a-tim*]	(6') [At the de]cision of [this] case:
7'. [^{md}U.GUR]-GI ^{lu_2}DI.KU$_5$ DUMU ^{m}*ši-gu-ú-a* ^{md}NA$_3$-[ŠEŠ. MEŠ-MU ^{lu_2}DI.KU$_5$ DUMU ^{m}*e-gi-bi*]	(7') [Nergal]-ušallim, the judge, descendant of Šigûa; Nabû-[aḫ̮ḫ̮ē-iddin, the judge, descendant of Egibi];
8'. [^{md}NA$_3$-MU]-GI.NA ^{lu_2}DI.KU$_5$ DUMU *ir-a-ni* ^{md}EN-[	(8') [Nabû-šuma]-ukīn, the judge, descendant of Ir'anni; Bēl-[
9'. [^{md}NA$_3$]-TIN-*su-iq-bi* ^{lu_2}DI.KU$_5$ DUMU [^{m}LU$_2$-*ú*]	(9') [Nabû]-balāssu-iqbi, the judge, descendant of [Amēlû];

10’. [^{m}*na*]-*di-nu* DUB.SAR DUMU ^{lu_2}BAHAR ^{md}NA$_3$-MU-[GAR-*un* DUB.SAR DUMU]	(10’–11’) [Nā]dinu, the scribe, descendant of Paḫāru; Nabû-šuma-[iškun, the scribe, descendant of Rāb]-banê.
11’. [^{lu_2}GAL]-DU$_3$ TIN.TIR^{ki} ITI DU$_6$ U$_4$ 29-*kám* MU 9-*kám* ^{md}NA$_3$-[IM.TUK LUGAL TIN.TIR^{ki}]	(11’) Babylon. 29 Tašrītu, year 9 of Nabonidus, king of Babylon.

24. Undivided Inheritance

Text: BM 35508 + BM 38259 (Sp 3, 14 + 80-12-11, 141)
Copy: Wunsch 2003, No. 42 (pp. 139, 141); 2012, 14–17
Translation/Discussion: Wunsch 2003, No. 42 (pp. 138–45); Holtz 2009, 228–32; Wunsch 2012, 10–28
Place of Composition: ?
Date: Nbk

The three sons of Nabû-apla-iddin and their uncle, Nabû-balāssu-iqbi, seek a resolution to their dispute over an undivided inheritance. Nabû-apla-iddin, the father of the three plaintiffs, and his brother, Nabû-balāssu-iqbi, had received shares of an inheritance, presumably from their father, and had both conducted business with their shares. After Nabû-apla-iddin's death, his sons, represented by Marduk-šuma-ibni, claim that Nabû-balāssu-iqbi should have rights to only one-sixth of the patrimony with which business was conducted. Nabû-balāssu-iqbi counters that he used his own property to conduct the business, and that he had obtained the consent of the late Nabû-apla-iddin. Furthermore, he claims that Nabû-apla-iddin invested only 10 šeqels of silver of the patrimony. Nabû-balāssu-iqbi also asserts that, with Nabû-apla-iddin's consent, he had purchased the share of another brother, Arad-Gula. The remaining arguments and the details of the decision are lost to breaks in the text. Nevertheless, it is clear that the judges confirm that Nabû-apla-iddin owned one half of the patrimony, and that the remaining three brothers, including Nabû-balāssu-iqbi, each received one sixth of it.

The specifics of this case illustrate a variant way in which primogeniture was observed in inheritance. Here (lines 12'–16') Nabû-apla-iddin, the oldest original heir, and his children, receive half of the patrimonial property. The division of the remaining property into three sixths indicates that, apart from Nabû-apla-iddin and Nabû-balāssu-iqbi, there were two other brothers: Arad-Gula (line 15') and another one who is unnamed in this document (Wunsch 2003, 144–45). More commonly, however, the expected arrangement would have given the eldest twice as much as any of his brothers. In this case, with four brothers, the expected division would have been into fifths, with two fifths going to the eldest and one fifth going to each of the remaining sons.

More generally, this legal case illustrates the problem of the undivided inheritance (Wunsch 2003, 144; 2012, 21–22). When a father died, his sons might prefer to leave the inheritance as one, undivided property, in order to make more efficient use of it. However, as might be expected, problems arise when individual heirs use the jointly-inherited propert to conduct business on their own and expect to realize profits for themselves.

1.	[^{md}AMAR.UTU-MU-*ib-ni* ^{md}NA$_3$-*mu-š*]*e-ti-iq*-UD.DA *ù* ^{md}EN-ŠEŠ.MEŠ-SUM.NA DUMU.MEŠ *šá* ^{md}NA$_3$-IBILA-S[UM.NA]	(1–3) [Marduk-šuma-ibni, Nabû-muš]ētiq-uddê and Bēl-aḫḫē-iddin sons of Nabû-apla-iddin … and Nabû-balāssu-iqbi, their father's brother, came to blows against each other concerning the division of shares; they had a legal case.
2.	[…] *ù* ^{md}NA$_3$-TIN-*su-iq-bi* ŠEŠ AD-*šú-nu a-na* UGU *za-a-zu zi-it-ti*	
3.	[… *a*]-*ḫa a-ḫa im-taḫ-ṣu-ú-ma ir-šu-ú di-i-ni*	
4.	[… *a-na*] ^{md}EN-*re-ma-an-ni* DUMU ^{lu_2}*man-di-di* ^{lu_2}GAR.UMUŠ TIN.TIR^{ki} *ik-šu-du-ni-im-ma*	(4) They arrived [before] Bēl-rēmanni descendant of Mandidi, the governor of Babylon and,
5.	[*maḫar?*] ^{lu_2}GAR.UMUŠ TIN.TIR^{ki} *ù* ^{lu_2}AB.BA.MEŠ URU DUMU.MEŠ TIN.TIR^{ki} *a-ma-ti-šu-nu*	(5–6) [before?] the governor of Babylon and the elders of the citizens of Babylon, they [recount]ed their matters.
6.	[*ú-šá-an-n*]*u-ú* ^{md}AMAR.UTU-MU-*ib-ni i-qab-bi um-ma ma-ḫi-ra-a-tú šá* ^{md}NA$_3$-TIN-*su-iq-bi*	(6) Marduk-šuma-ibni said thus:
7.	[*šá ina* KA$_2$] *šá* ^{d}EN *i-te-ep-pu-šu* KU$_3$.BABBAR *šá ma-ḫi-ra-a-ti ina lìb-bi i-te-ep-pu-šu*	(6–8) "(Regarding) the purchases which Nabû-balāssu-iqbi carried out in the Gate of Bēl: the silver with which the purchases were carried out belongs in the common property of the patrimony! There is no more than his one-sixth share (that he owns) with my father (belonging to him)!"
8.	[*i-na ka-r*]*e-*⸢*e*⸣ E$_2$ AD *šu-ú al-la ši-iš-šu zi-it-ta-šú it-ti a-bi-ia ia-a-nu*	
9.	[^{md}NA$_3$-TIN-*su-iq-bi š*]*á-ni-ti i-pu-ul-šu um-ma ma-ḫi-ra-a-ti šá i-na* KA$_2$ *šá* ^{d}EN	(9) [Nabû-balāssu-iqbi] responded to him thus:

10. [*e-te-ep-pu-šu i-n*]*a* KU$_3$.BABBAR *šá ra-ma-ni-ia e-te-pu-uš* KU$_3$.BABBAR *šá ka-re-e* E$_2$ AD-*i-ni*

(9–11) "I used my own silver in the purchases which [I carried out i]n the Gate of Bēl. [There was n]o silver from the common property of our patrimony (involved)!"

11. [*i-na lìb-bi ia-a-n*]*u ù ma-ḫi-ri šá* ^{md}NA$_3$-IBILA-MU *a-bu-ú-ka i-na* KA$_2$ *šá* ^{d}EN *i-pu-šu-ma*

12. [IM.DUB *a-na šu-mi-š*]*ú ik-nu-ku al-la* 10 GIN$_2$ KU$_3$.BABBAR *šá ka-re-e* E$_2$ AD-*ni i-na lìb-bi ia-a-ni*

(11–12) "And (regarding) the purchases which your father, Nabû-apla-iddin, carried out in the Gate of Bēl, and (for which) they sealed [a tablet in his name]: there was not more than 10 šeqels of silver from the common property of our patrimony (involved)!"

13. […] *a-na-ku ki-i ad-di-nu a-bu-ú-ka* IM.DUB *a-na šu-mi-šú ik-ta-na-ak*

(13) "When I gave … your father sealed a tablet in his name."

14. [*…m*]*a-ḫi-ra-a-ti an-na-a-ti ni-te-pu-šu*

(14) "… we carried out those purchases."

15. […] *ra-ma-ni-ia am-gu-ur-ma* ^{md}NA$_3$-IBILA-SUM.NA *ṭup-pa*

16. […] *um-ma ma-ḫi-ra-a-ti ma-la i-na* KA$_2$ *šá* ^{d}EN *ni-ip-pu-šu*

(15–16) "I agreed on my own and Nabû-apla-iddin … a tablet … thus: 'Whatever purchases we carry out in the Gate of Bēl …'"

17. [*…zi-i*]*t-ti šá* ^{m}IR$_3$-^{d}*gu-la* ŠEŠ-*ia šá a-na* KU$_3$.BABBAR-*ia am-ḫu-ru*

18. […]-*ma i-na ṭup-pa ma-ḫi-ri-ia a-na ši-bu-tu a-ši-ib*

(17–18) "(Regarding) the [sh]are of my brother, Arad-Gula, which I purchased with my own silver… and he was present as a witness on my tablet of purchase."

19. [… *a*]-*bu-ú-ka it-ti-ia ir-tak-ka-su*

(19) "… which your father contracted with me."

20. […] ŠE.NUMUN *zi-it-ti za-zu*$^{!?}$

(20) "… the cultivated property divided as a share…"

BREAK

1'. […]

2'. [… *i*]*d-da-gal*

3'. [… KU$_3$.BABBA]R *at-ru*

4'. […]-MU *te-er-din-né-e*

5'. […] *iq-bu-ú*

6'. […]-⸢MU⸣ *qí-ba-tu-šu*

(1'–6') [These lines are too fragmentary to yield any meaningful sense]

7'. [… *i-na* KA$_2$ *šá*] ^{d}EN *ir-tak-ka-su*	(7'). "… which they contracted [in the Gate of] Bēl …"
8'. […] ŠEŠ-*ú-ni ra-ba-a*ʾ	(8') "… our older brother"
9'. […^{md}N]A$_3$-TIN-*su-iq-bi ir-tak-ka-su i-ni-ma*	(9') "which [Na]bû-balāssu-iqbi contracted, he changed and"
10'. […] ⸢*e*⸣-*li* ^{md}NA$_3$-TIN-*su-iq-bi pa-ar-sa-tu*	(10') "… which is decided was owed by Nabû-balāssu-iqbi"
11'. […*a*]-*bu-ú-ni it-ti-šú ir-tak-ka-su*	(11') "which… our father contracted with him."
12'. […] ^{lu_2}GAR.UMUŠ TIN.TIR^{ki} *ù* ^{lu_2}AB.BA.MEŠ URU	(12') … the governor of Babylon and the elders of the city
13'. […] *ta-mi-ti i-na* UGU ^{md}NA$_3$-TIN-*su-iq-bi iš-ṭu-ru*	(13') … which they wrote was owed by Nabû-balāssu-iqbi
14'. […]- *bi id-di-nu ši-iš-šu zi-it-ti šá* ^{md}NA$_3$-TIN-*su-iq-bi*	(14') … and gave. One sixth share belonging to Nabû-balāssu-iqbi
15'. […] ⸢x⸣ *ù ši-iš-šu zi-it-ti šá* ^{m}IR$_3$-^{d}*gu-la*	(15') … and one sixth share belonging to Arad-Gula
16'. […*iš-ṭu*]-*ru-ú-ma a-ḫi* HA.LA *šá* ^{md}NA$_3$-DUMU.NITA-SUM.NA *i-na lìb-bi iš-ku-nu*	(16') … they [wro]te and in it established one half (as) the share of Nabû-apla-iddin.
17'. […] E$_2$ AD *šá* KA$_2$ *šá* ^{d}EN *pa-ni* ^{md}NA$_3$-TIN-*su-iq-bi ú-šad-gi-lu*	(17') … they placed the patrimony in the Gate of Bēl at the disposal of Nabû-balāssu-iqbi.
18'. […] *i-na* KA$_2$ *šá* ^{d}EN *i-na qa-ti* ^{m}*šul-lu-mu ù* ^{md}EN-ŠEŠ.MEŠ-x	(18') … in the Gate of Bēl, from the hands of Šullumu and Bēl-aḫḫē-x
19'. […*i-pu*]-*šu-ma* ^{md}NA$_3$-DUMU.NITA-SUM.NA IM.DUB *a-na šu-mi-šu ik-nu-ku*	(19') … and Nabû-apla-iddin sealed a tablet in his name.
20'. […^{md}NA$_3$-TIN-*su*]-*iq-bi i-na* KA$_2$ *šá* ^{d}EN *i-na qa-ti* ^{md}NA$_3$-MU-SI.SA	(20') [Nabû-balāssu]-iqbi in the Gate of Bēl from Nabû-šumu-līšir
21'. […] ^{m}*šu-la-a* DUMU-*šú šá* ^{m}*bal-ti-ìl* DUMU ^{md}*é-a-ṣal-mu*-DINGIR	(21') […] Šulaya son of Balti-ilī descendant of Ea-ṣalmu-ilī
22'. […*pa*]-*ni* ^{md}NA$_3$-TIN-*su-iq-bi*	(22') … to Nabû-balāssu-iqbi
23'. […] *ú-šad-gi-lu ši-iš-šu i-na* A.ŠA$_3$ E$_2$ AD *šá* E$_2$-^{m}*da-kur*	(23') … they placed at the disposal of … One sixth of the field of the patrimony at Bīt Dakkūri

24’. [...]-*šá-a šá* URU *ù* EDIN *ma-la ba-šu-ú*	(24’) ... in the city and the hinterland, whatever there is,
25’. [...] ⸢*i*⸣-*na ṭup-pa* KI.LAM *šá* ^{md}NA$_3$-TIN-*su-iq-bi ša-aṭ-ru*	(25’) ... written in a purchase tablet of Nabû-balāssu-iqbi
26’. [...] ^{md}NA$_3$-NUMUN-MU *na-ad-nu u i-na la a-šá-bi*	(26’) ... given to Nabû-zēra-ibni, and without the witness of ...
27’. [...^{md}NA$_3$-TIN-*su*]-*iq-bi ig-mu-ru* ŠU.NIGIN 7 MA.NA KU$_3$.BABBAR	(27’) [... Nabû-balāssu]-iqbi paid in full. TOTAL: 7 mina of silver
28’. [...] *šá* ^{md}NA$_3$-NUMUN-MU *šá* ^{md}NA$_3$-TIN-*su-iq-bi iš-šá-a* HA.LA 2 MA.NA KU$_3$.BABBAR *a-na*	(28’) [...] belonging to Nabû-zēra-ibni which Nabû-balāssu-iqbi received. A share of 2 mina of silver to ...
29’. [... IGI ^{md}NA$_3$]-TIN-*su-iq-bi ku-um* 5 MA.NA KU$_3$.BABBAR-*šú ú-šad-gi-lu*	(29’) they placed at the disposal of Nabû-balāssu-iqbi in exchange for his 5 mina of silver.
30’. [...] ⸢x x⸣. MEŠ *šá ka-re-e i-ti-ru-ni*	(30’) x x of the common property remained.
31’. [...] *ú pa-ni* ^{md}NA$_3$-TIN-*su-iq-bi ú-šad-gi-lu*	(31’) and placed at the disposal of Nabû-balāssu-iqbi
32’. [...^{m}*bi*]-⸢*be*⸣-*a* DUMU ^{md}EN-*e-ṭè-ru ma-aḫ-ru pa-ni*	(32’–33’) [PN son of Bi]bēa descendant of Bēl-eṭēru received and [placed] at the disposal of [...]
33’. [... *ušadgilū*] SUM.NA ^{md}NA$_3$-TIN-*su-iq-bi*	(33’) ...-iddin Nabû-balāssu-iqbi
34’. [...]-MEŠ *šu-nu-ti*	
35’. [...] *ú* [break] *ma*	
36’. ^{md}AMAR.UTU-NUMUN-[*x*]	
BREAK	

1”. […] DUMU-*šú šá* ^{md}*ba-zu-*[	(1”–15”) [The names of the witnesses and scribes are recorded. Only their fathers’ names are preserved.]
2”. […] DUMU-*šú šá* ^{m}*nad-na-a* [	
3”. […] DUMU-*šú šá* ^{m}DUG$_3$.GA-*ia*	
4”. […] DUMU-*šú šá* ^{m}*si-lim-*^{d}EN	
5”. […] DUMU-*šú šá* ^{md}EN-BA-*šá*	
6”. […] DUMU-*šú šá* ^{m}*mu-šal-li-mu*	
7”. […] ⸢x⸣ DUMU-*šú šá* ^{md}EN-*eri-ba*	
8”. […]-*ni* DUMU-*šú šá* ^{m}*pi-ir-ʾu*	
9”. […] DUMU-*šú šá* ^{md}UTU-*ú-bal-*[*liṭ*]	
10”. […]-KAR-*ir* DUMU-*šú šá* ^{md}AMAR.UTU-MU-*ú-*[*ṣur*]	
11”. […]-*a* DUMU-*šú šá* ^{md}EN-ŠEŠ.MEŠ-[…]	
12”. […]-*ši* DUMU-*šú šá* ^{m}*ṣil-la-a*	
13”. […]-*a-ni* DUMU-*šú šá* ^{m}*la-a-ba-š*[*i*…]	
14”. […]-*tú* DUMU-*šú šá* ^{md}AMAR.UTU-*ú-*[…]	
15”. […] DUMU-*šú šá* ^{md}NA$_3$-DUMU.NITA-[	
16”. [MU x]-*kám* ^{d}NA$_3$-NIG.DU-[URI$_3$ LUGAL TIN.TIR^{ki}]	(16”) [Year x] of Nebuchad[nezzar, king of Babylon].

Upper edge:

^{na_4}KIŠIB ^{md}NA$_3$-NUMUN-DU$_3$ A ^{lu_2}SU.HA	Seal of Nabû-zēra-ukīn descendant of Bāʾiru
^{na_4}KIŠIB ^{m}*tab-né-e-a* A ^{md}UTU-*ba-a-ri*	Seal of Tabnêa descendant of Šamaš-abāri

Right edge:

^{na_4}KIŠIB ^{m}*ba-la-ṭu* DUMU-*šú šá* ^{md}NA$_3$-KAR-*ir* DUMU ^{lu_2}SIPA-*si-si-i*	Seal of Balāṭu son of Nabû-ēṭir descendant of Rēʾî-sīsî

Lower edge:

^{na_4}KIŠIB ^{md}UTU-MU-URI$_3$ DUMU ^{m}*ši-gu-ú-a*	Seal of Šamaš-šuma-uṣur descendant of Šigûa
^{na_4}KIŠIB ^{m}IBILA-⸢*a* A-*šú šá*⸣ ^{m}*šu-zu-bu*	Seal of Aplaya son of Šūzubu

NOTES

Reading of this document is based on the collations in Wunsch 2012.

7’–11’. These lines contain Marduk-šuma-ibni’s response to Nabû-balāssu-iqbi, and apparently refer to a court decision against Nabû-balāssu-iqbi (see Wunsch 2012, 12).

25. A Property Dispute

Text: YBC 4161
Copy: Dougherty 1920 (YOS 6), No. 92
Translation/Discussion: Frame 1991, 78; Zadok 2003, 516
Place of Composition: Uruk
Date: 17.IX.7 Nbn (31 December, 549 BCE)

Nabû-mušētiq-uddê presents his claim to a purchased piece of property against Nabû-rēšu and Mušēzib-Bēl. In year 6 of Nabonidus, Nabû-mušētiq-uddê purchased a plot of land from Mušēzib-Bēl. Apparently, upon hearing of the sale, Nabû-rēšu raised a claim against Nabû-mušētiq-uddê by presenting a tablet that showed that he had purchased the same plot from Mušēzib-Bēl seven months earlier. Nabû-mušētiq-uddê ceded the property, only to find another, still earlier claim to the property, this time on the part of four men who claim that their grandfather, Marduk-erība, purchased that same field from Mušēzib-Bēl some 32 years before, during the reign of Nebuchadnezzar. In light of this, Nabû-mušētiq-uddê re-purchased the property from the heirs of Marduk-erība. Nevertheless, Nabû-rēšu maintains his claim and does not cede the property. The case comes before the royal official in charge of the Eanna, the governor of Uruk and the qīpu-*official together with the assembly of Babylonians and Urukians. Mušēzib-Bēl and Nabû-mušētiq-uddê present their documentary evidence. The authorities uphold Nabû-mušētiq-uddê's claim to the property and give him a tablet to record his ownership.*

In terms of its subject matter, and its external form, the present document resembles decision records from trials over which royal judges usually preside. Here, however, the adjudicators include members of the Eanna temple bureaucracy (the royal official and the *qīpu*-official) alongside the governor of Uruk. In addition, several of the men present "at the hearing of this case" (lines 54–70) are attested elsewhere in the Eanna's records. For example, Nādin son of Bēl-aḫḫē-iqīša descendant of Egibi (line 64), also held the positions of "scribe of the Eanna" and *šatammu* (Kümmel 1979, 129, 144).

In this case, the location of the property in question and the litigants' own positions explain why these members of the Eanna's administration participate in the adjudication. The property in question abuts the "territory of the Lady of Uruk" as well as property held by Nabû-apla-iddin, who is known as a scribe in other documents from the Eanna archives (Kümmel 1979, 119). Both the plaintiff, Nabû-mušētiq-uddê, and the defendant, Mušēzib-Bēl, are known as scribes in Eanna records, as well (Kümmel 1979, 118–20). The plaintiff is also known to have been involved in the management of the Eanna's cattle herds (Kümmel 1979, 67).

1.	^{md}NA$_3$-*mu-še-tiq*-UD.DA A-*šú* *šá* ^{m}TIN-*su* A ^{m}SIG$_5$-*iq* [^{md}]NA$_3$-LUGAL-URI$_3$ ^{lu_2}SAG-[LUGAL]	(1–3) Nabû-mušētiq-uddê son of Balāssu descendant of Dāmiqu approached Nabû-šarra-uṣur, the royal official in charge of the Eanna, [Ṭābi]ya, the governor of Uruk, son of Nabû-nādin-šu[mi], and Gabbi-ilī-šarra-uṣur, the *qīpu*-official of the Eanna (saying) thus:
2.	^{lu_2}EN <*pi*>-*qit-ti* E$_2$.AN.NA [^{m}DUG$_3$.GA]-*ia* ^{lu_2}GAR.UMUŠ UNUG^{ki} A-*šú* *šá* ^{md}NA$_3$-MU-M[U]	
3.	*u* ^{m}*gab-bi*-DINGIR.MEŠ-LUGAL-URI$_3$ ^{lu_2}*qí-i-pi* *šá* E$_2$.AN.NA *im-ḫur um-ma ina* [ITI] ⸢ZIZ$_2$⸣	(3–4/8–9) "In Šabāṭu of year 6 of Nabonidus, king of Babylon, I purchased the property of Mušēzib-Bēl son of Nanaya-ēreš from Mušēzib-Bēl for 2 mina 2 šeqels of silver—"
4.	*šá* MU 6-*kám* ^{md}NA$_3$-I LUGAL E^{ki} E$_2$ ^{m}KAR-^{d}EN A-*šú* *šá* ^{md}*na-na-a*-KAM$_2$	
5.	*šá* DA ^{id_2}*ḫur-ri* *šá* ^{d}URI$_3$-INIM-*su* *šá* UŠ AN-*ú* IM.MAR.TU DA E$_2$ ^{md}NA$_3$-A-MU	(5–6) Adjacent to the Ḫurri-ša-uṣur-amāssu canal—its upper side on the west adjacent to the property of Nabû-apla-iddin son of Ibni-Ištar descendant of Ekur-zakir;
6.	A-*šú* *šá* ^{m}DU$_3$-^{d}INNIN A ^{m}E$_2$.KUR-*za-kir* UŠ KI-*ú* IM KUR.RA DA E$_2$ ^{m}*na-dan*-DINGIR A ^{m}*ṣil-la-a*	(6) Its lower side on the east, adjacent to the property of Nadan-Ili son of Ṣillaya;
7.	SAG.KI AN.TA IM SI.SA$_2$ *šá* DA ^{id_2}*ḫur-ri* *šá* ^{d}URI$_3$-INIM-*su* SAG.KI KI.⸢TA⸣	(7) Its upper front on the north, adjacent to the Ḫurri-ša-uṣur-amāssu canal;
8.	IM U$_{18}$.LU DA *qaq-qar* *šá* ^{d}GAŠAN *šá* UNUG^{ki} *a-na* 2 MA.NA 2 GIN$_2$ KU$_3$.BABBAR *ina* ŠU.2 ^{m}KAR-^{d}EN	(7–8) Its lower front on the south, adjacent to the territory of the Lady of Uruk;

9. A-*šú šá* ^{md}*na-na-a*-KAM$_2$ *am-ḫur-ma ina* ITI ŠE *šá* MU 6-*kám* ^{d}NA$_3$-I LUGAL TIN.TIR^{ki}	(9–13) "In Addaru of year 6 of Nabonidus, king of Babylon, Nabû-rēšu son of Šamaš-iddin established (a case) against me (by means of) a tablet which preceded my tablet by 7 months, (indicating) that he purchased the property of Mušēzib-Bēl son of Nanaya-ēreš in Dûzu, year 6 of Nabonidus, king of Babylon for 2 mina 4 šeqels of silver, and I released the property to Nabû-rēšu."
10. ^{md}NA$_3$-*re-e-šú* A-*šú šá* ^{md}UTU-MU IM.DUB *šá* E$_2$ ^{m}KAR-^{d}EN A-*šú šá* ^{md}*na-na-a*-KAM$_2$	
11. *šá ina* ITI ŠU MU 6-*kám* ^{md}NA$_3$-I LUGAL E^{ki} *šá a-na* 2 MA.NA 4 GIN$_2$ KU$_3$.BABBAR *ina* ŠU.2 ^{m}KAR-^{d}EN	
12. A-*šú šá* ^{md}*na-na-a*-KAM$_2$ *im-ḫu-ru šá* 7 ITI *al-la* IM.DUB-*ia pa-nu-u*	
13. *a-na* UGU-*ia ú-ka-am-ma* E$_2$ *ina pa-ni* ^{md}NA$_3$-*re-e-šú ú-maš-šìr*	
14. *ár-ki ina* MU 7-*kám* ^{md}NA$_3$-I LUGAL TIN.TIR^{ki} ^{m}*ri-mut*-^{d}EN ^{md}UTU-SUR	(14–18) "Afterwards, in year 7 of Nabonidus, king of Babylon, Rīmūt-Bēl, Šamaš-ēṭir, Nanaya-aḫa-iddin and Nabû-mušētiq-uddê, [son]s of Nabû-bāni-aḫi son of Marduk-erība descendant of Ea-ṣalmu-ilāni, established (a case) against me (by means of) a tablet (indicating) that Marduk-erība son of Nergal-iddin descendant of Ea-ṣalmu-ilāni, their father's father, purchased the property of Mušēzib-Bēl son of Nanaya-ēreš in year 22 of Nebuchadnezzar, king of Babylon, from Mušēzib-Bēl son of Nanaya-ēreš."
15. ^{md}*na-na-a*-ŠEŠ-MU *u* ^{md}NA$_3$-*mu-še-tiq*-UD.DA [A].MEŠ *šá* ^{md}NA$_3$-DU$_3$-ŠEŠ A-*šú šá* ^{md}AMAR.UTU-SU A ^{md}IDIM-*ṣal-mu*-DINGIR.MEŠ	
16. IM.DUB *šá* E$_2$ ^{m}KAR-^{d}EN A-*šú šá* ^{md}*na-na-a*-KAM$_2$ *šá ina* MU 22-*kám* ^{md}NA$_3$-NIG$_2$.DU-URI$_3$ LUGAL E^{ki}	
17. *šá* ^{md}AMAR.UTU-SU A-*šú šá* ^{md}U.GUR-MU A ^{m}IDIM-*ṣal-mu*-DINGIR.MEŠ AD.AD-*šú-nu* KI.LAM *ina* ŠU.2 ^{m}KAR-^{d}EN	
18. A-*šú šá* ^{md}*na-na-a*-KAM$_2$ *i-pu-šu* [*ú-ki*]-*in-ni-ma* KI.LAM *šá* E$_2$ MU.MEŠ *ina* ŠU.2-*šú-nu*	(18–19) "I purchased that property from them, but Nabû-rēšu did not cede the property to me."
19. *e-pu-uš-ma* ^{md}NA$_3$-*re-e-šú* E$_2$ *ina pa-ni-ia la ú-maš-šìr*	

20. *i-na-an-na* ^{m}KAR-^{d}EN *ma-ḫar-ku-nu* <*ú*>*-bi-lu it-ti* ^{m}KAR-^{d}EN *u* ^{md}NA$_3$*-re-[e-šú]* ⸢*ep*$^{?}$⸣*-šú di-i-ni*	(20) "Now, I have brought Mušēzib-Bēl before you. Judge my case against Mušēzib-Bēl and Nabû-rē[šu]!"
21. ^{md}NA$_3$-LUGAL-URI$_3$ ^{lu_2}SAG-LUGAL ^{m}DUG$_3$.GA-*ia* ^{lu_2}GAR.UMUŠ UNUG^{ki} *u* ^{m}*gab-bi-*[DINGIR.MEŠ-LUGAL]-URI$_3$ ^{lu_2}*qí-i-pi*	(21–22) Nabû-šarra-uṣur, the royal official, Ṭābiya, the governor of Uruk, and Gabbi-[ili-šarra]-uṣur, the *qīpu*-official, the assembly of Babylonians and Urukians, the judges …-ed.
22. ^{lu_2}UKKIN ^{lu_2}TIN.TIR^{ki}.MEŠ ^{lu_2}UNUG^{ki}*-a-a* ^{lu_2}DI.KU$_5$.MEŠ *ú-še-*[…]	
23. ^{md}NA$_3$*-mu-še-tiq-*UD.DA *u* ^{m}KAR-^{d}EN *di-i-ni ina pa-ni-šú-nu* [*id-bu-bu*]	(23) Nabû-mušētiq-uddê and Mušēzib-Bēl [argued] (their) case before them.
24. ^{m}KAR-^{d}EN IM.DUB *šá* E$_2$ *šá ina* MU 2-*kám* ^{md}NA$_3$-⸢NIG$_2$⸣.DU-URI$_3$ LUGAL [TIN.TIR^{ki}]	(24–27) Mušēzib-Bēl [produced?] the tablet indicating that Nanaya-ēreš, his father […] the property from Nabû-zēra-ibni, son of Marduk-nāṣir descendant of [PN] in year 2 of Nebuchadnezzar, king of Babylon, and the contract of return of the property from the accession year of [Nabonidus, king of Babylo]n which Mušēzib-Bēl […] from Nabû-bāni-aḫi son of Marduk-erība—
25. *šá* ^{md}*na-na-a-*KAM$_2$ AD*-šú ina* ŠU.2 ^{md}NA$_3$-NUMUN-DU$_3$ A*-šú šá* ^{md}AMAR.UTU-PAP A [PN …]	
26. *u ri-*⸢*ik-si*⸣ *sá tur-ri šá* E$_2$ *šá ina* MU SAG.NAM.LUGAL.⸢LA⸣ [^{md}NA$_3$-I LUGAL TIN.TI]R^{ki}	
27. *šá* ^{m}KAR-^{d}EN *ina* ŠU.2 ^{md}NA$_3$-DU$_3$-ŠEŠ A*-šú šá* ^{md}AMAR.UTU-SU […]	

28. *šá* 1 2/3 MA.NA 2 GIN$_2$ KU$_3$.BABBAR *šá* ^{md}*na-na-a*-KAM$_2$ *šá* UGU [... ^{md}]U.GUR-*ú-še-zib*	(28–47) [These broken lines summarize the other evidence that is presented to the judges, including tablets that are read in court.]
29. [...] *maš-kan ṣab-ta šá ina tur-ri šá ...*	
30. [...] ⸢*ri*⸣-*ik-si a-na* UGU *e-ṭe*$_3$-[*ri*	
31. [...] *ta-a* ^{md}30-*tab-ni a-na* [...]	
32. ...^{d}]NA$_3$-NIG$_2$.DU-URI$_3$ LUGAL [TIN.TIR^{ki}	
33. ... A-*šú šá* ^{md}[	
34. ^{lu_2}TIN.TIR^{ki}.MEŠ [...] *ina* ŠU.2	
35.	
36. ...] *im-ḫu-*[*ur*	
37. ...] ^{md}NA$_3$-*mu-še-tiq*-UD.[DA	
38. ...] *ma-ḫar-šú-nu iš-tas-*[*su-u*	
39.	
40.	
41. ...] IM.DUB *šá* [	
42. ... ^{md}NA$_3$]-LUGAL-URI$_3$ ^{lu_2}GAR.UMUŠ ^{lu_2}*qi-i-*[*pi*]	
43. ...]-*su-ú* IM.DUB.MEŠ *šá* ^{m}KAR-^{d}EN A	
44. ...] *ú-ṭir-ra* ^{md}NA$_3$-*re-e-šú e-*	
45. ...^{md}NA$_3$]-*mu-še-ti-iq*-UD.DA *ma-ḫi-ir*	
46. ...^{lu_2}]GAR.UMUŠ ^{lu_2}*qí-i-pi u* ^{lu_2}[...	
47. [...] *tè-ru a-na* ^{md}NA$_3$-*re-e-*[*šú*]	
48. A [... ^{m}]KAR-^{d}EN *e-li* E$_2$ MU.MEŠ *la* [...]	(48) ... Mušēzib-Bēl shall not ... concerning that property.
49. ^{lu_2}GAR.UMUŠ [^{lu_2}*qi-i-pi u*] ^{lu_2}DI.KU$_5$.MEŠ DUB *iš-ṭu-ur-ú*	(49–50) The governor, [the *qīpu*-official and] the judges wrote a tablet and left it with[Nabû-muš]ētiq-uddê.
50. *a-na* ^{md}[NA$_3$-*mu-še*]-*tiq*-UD.DA *i-zi-*<*bu*>-*ma*! *di-in-šú-nu di-i-*[*in*]	(50) Their case is judg[ed].

51. *ina* EŠ.BAR *di-i-*[*ni* MU].MEŠ ^{md}NA$_3$-LUGAL-URI$_3$ ^{lu_2}SAG-LUGAL ^{lu_2}[EN *pi-qit-ti* E$_2$.AN.NA]	(51) At the decision of th[is ca]se: Nabû-šarra-uṣu, the royal official [in charge of the Eanna];
52. ^{m}DUG$_3$.GA-*ia* ^{lu_2}[GAR].UMUŠ UNUG^{ki} A-*šú šá* ^{m}NA$_3$-SUM-MU A [^{m}*ḫu-un-zu-ú*]	(52) Ṭābiya the [gover]nor of Uruk son of Nabû-nādin-šumi descendant of [Ḫunzû];
53. ^{m}*gab-bi*-DINGIR.⸢MEŠ⸣-LUGAL-URI$_3$ ^{lu_2}*qí-i-pi šá* E$_2$.[AN.NA]	(53) Gabbi-ilī-šarra-uṣur, the *qīpu*-official of the E[anna];
54. ^{md}KAR-^{d}EN A-*šú šá* ^{md}UTU-SIG$_{15}$ A ^{m}DU$_3$-[DINGIR]	(54) Mušēzib-Bēl son of Šamaš-muddamiq descendant of Eppeš-[ili];
55. ^{md}30-KAM$_2$ A-*šú šá* ^{md}NA$_3$-MU-GIŠ A ^{m}DU$_3$-[DINGIR]	(55) Sîn-ēreš son of Nabû-šumu-līšir descendant of Ibni-[ilī];
56. [^{md}AMAR].UTU-MU-GIŠ A-*šú šá* ^{m}*ri-mut* A ^{md}[EN-*ú-sat*]	(56) [Mar]duk-šumu-līšir son of Rīmūt descendant of Bēl-usātu;
57. [^{m}DN- *za*]-*kir* A-*šú šá* ^{m}DUG$_3$.GA-*iá* A [^{m}*ki-din*-^{d}AM]AR.UTU	(57) [DN-zā]kir son of Ṭābiya descendant of [Kidin-Marduk];
58. ^{md}EN-DU$_3$ A-*šú šá* ^{m}*bul-luṭ* [A ^{lu_2}ŠU].KU$_6$	(58) Bēl-ibni son of Bulluṭ [descendant of Bāʾi]ru;
59. [^{m}]^{d}NA$_3$-ŠEŠ.MEŠ-GI A-*šú šá* ^{m}NA$_3$-MU-DU A ^{m}[…]-^{d}MAŠ	(59) Nabû-aḫḫē-šullim son of Nabû-šuma-ukīn descendant of [X]-Ninurta;
60. ^{m}*si-lim*-^{d}EN A-*šú šá* ^{m}MU-DU A ^{m}*ḫa-nap*	(60) Silim-Bēl son of Šuma-ukīn descendant of Ḫanap;
61. ^{m}IR$_3$-^{d}*in-nin* A-*šú šá* ^{md}EN-MU A ^{m}KUR-*i*	(61) Arad-Innin son of Bēl-iddin descendant of Kurī;
62. ^{m}TIN-*su* A-*šú šá* ^{md}AMAR.UTU-MU-DU$_3$ A ^{m}*ba-bu-tu*	(62) Balāssu son of Marduk-šuma-ibni descendant of Babūtu;
63. ^{m}*ina*-E$_2$.SAG.IL$_2$-NUMUN A-*šú šá* ^{m}*šá*-KA-^{d}EN A ^{m}LU$_2$-^{d}INIM	(63) Ina-Esagil-zēri son of Ša-pî-Bēl descendant of Amēl-Ea;
64. ^{m}*na-din* A-*šú šá* ^{md}EN-ŠEŠ.MEŠ-BA-*šá* A ^{m}*e-gi-bi*	(64) Nādin son of Bēl-aḫḫē-iqīša descendant of Egibi;
65. ^{md}INNIN-MU-KAM$_2$ A-*šú šá* ^{m}TIN-*su* A ^{m}*mu-kal-lim*	(65) Ištar-šuma-ēreš son of Balāssu descendant of Mukallim;
66. ^{md}*in-nin*-MU-URI$_3$ A-*šú šá* ^{m}MU-^{d}NA$_3$ A ^{m}*ki-din*-^{d}AMAR.UTU	(66) Innin-šuma-uṣur son of Iddin-Nabû descendant of Kidin-Marduk;

67. ^{md}UTU-SU A-*šú šá* ^{md}U.GUR-MU A ^{md}30-*tab-ni*	(67) Šamaš-erība son of Nergal-iddin descendant of Sîn-tabni;
68. ^{md}AMAR.UTU-DUB-NUMUN A-*šú šá* ^{m}NIG$_2$.DU A ^{lu_2}NAGAR	(68) Marduk-šāpik-zēri son of Kudurru descendant of Nagāru;
69. ^{md}NA$_3$-NUMUN-GIŠ A-*šú šá* ^{md}EN-*šú-nu* A ^{m}*ku-ri-i*	(69) Nabû-zēru-līšir son of Bēlšunu descendant of Kurī;
70. ^{m}*na-din* ^{lu_2}UMBISAG A-*šú šá* ^{md}U.GUR-*ina*-SUH$_3$-SUR A ^{md}30-TI-ER$_2$	(70) Nādin, the scribe, son of Nergal-ina-tēšê-ēṭir descendant of Sîn-lēqi-unninnī.
71. UNUG^{ki} ITI GAN U$_4$ 17-*kám* MU 7-*kám* ^{d}NA$_3$-IM.TUK LUGAL KA$_2$.DINGIR.RA^{ki}	(71) Uruk. 17 Kislīmu year 7 of Nabonidus, king of Babylon.
72. ^{na_4}KIŠIB ^{m}DUG$_3$.GA-*iá* ^{lu_2}GAR.UMUŠ UNUG^{ki}	(72) Seal of Ṭābiya the governor of Uruk.
73. ^{na_4}KIŠIB ^{md}NA$_3$-LUGAL-URI$_3$ ^{lu_2}SAG-LUGAL ^{lu_2}EN *pi-qit-ti* E$_2$.AN.NA	(73) Seal of Nabû-šarra-uṣur, the royal official in charge of the Eanna.
74. ^{na_4}KIŠIB ^{m}*gab-bi*-DINGIR.MEŠ-LUGAL-URI$_3$ ^{lu_2}*qi-i-pi šá* E$_2$.AN.NA	(74) Seal of Gabbi-ilāni-šarra-uṣur, the *qīpu*-official of the Eanna.

Notes

13. *ú-ka-am-ma-* The translation here understands these signs as a corrupt form of the verb *kânu*. The form appears to be durative (*ukân* + *ma*) where one would expect a preterite form (*ukīn*).

20. <*ú*>-*bi-lu-* One could interpret the text as written (*bi-lu*) as a corrupt imperative form (for the expected *bi-la*) of the verb *abālu*, meaning that Nabû-mušētiq-uddê is requesting that the judges bring Mušēzib-bēl before them. This kind of request, however, is otherwise unattested. Instead, it is best to interpret the written signs *bi-lu* as a scribal error for *ú-bi-lu*, a first-person preterite form of the verb *abālu.*

26. The "contract of return" (*riksi ša turri*) apparently supports Mušēzib-Bēl's right to sell the property to Nabû-mušētiq-uddê, against the purported claim of the sons of Marduk-erība. It seems that after the property was sold to the sons of Marduk-erība, the property was returned to Mušēzib-Bēl.

50. *i-zi-*<*bu*>*-ma*$^{!}$-The actual writing on the tablet does not yield any sense. This reading follows *CAD* E, 420, s.v. *ezēbu* 2a, understanding the verb as a G-stem preterite, third-person masculine plural form of the verb *ezēbu*. Note that the use of the verb *ezēbu* with a tablet as its object is rare for Neo-Babylonian.

In the Old Babylonian period, this locution (*ṭuppam ezēbum*) has the technical sense of "to make out a legal document" (*CAD* E, 422, s.v. *ezēbum* 3d).

72–74. The present text is an unsealed copy of an originally sealed document (Frame 1991, 78). Here, these lines note the appearance of seals on the original. The fact that this text is a copy may account for the infelicitous writings noted above.

26. A Property Dispute with the Eanna Temple

Text: NBC 1207
Copy: Nies and Keiser 1920 (BIN 2), No. 134
Translation/Discussion: Joannès 2000a, 34; 2000b, No. 170 (pp. 229–30); Oelsner, Wells, and Wunsch 2003, 921–22
Place of Composition: Uruk (?)
Date: Between 2 Cyr and 5 Cyr (537–534 BCE)

*Three grandsons of Bēl-aḫḫē-iddin present their case against the authorities of the Eanna to the local governor (*šākin māti*). In year 4 of Nebuchadnezzar, Bēl-aḫḫē-iddin received a house located near the Eanna as a pledge for a debt of 5 1/2 mina of silver owed to him by another man also named Bēl-aḫḫē-iddin. The family of the creditor holds the record, and assumes that the debt was not repaid. On this assumption, the grandsons wish to gain control of the house, but are prevented from doing so because the house is under the control of former Eanna officials. The provincial governor transfers the case to the court of the governor of Uruk and the local judges. The judges read the various documents pertaining to the property's ownership history: the original debt-note, presented by two of the plaintiffs, the Eanna's contracts for the rental of the pledged property, proof that the property was recorded as belonging to the Eanna, and tablets recording the sale and subsequent repurchase of the property. Among these is a tablet in which another grandson of Bēl-aḫḫē-iddin, an heir to the property, served as a witness to a sale of the property out of the family's possession. Based on all of this evidence, the property remains in the possession of the Eanna.*

The present lawsuit contains a unique description of the progress of a lawsuit through what might best be called the Uruk court system. It begins with a complaint, lodged before a local official, against the Eanna. The local official is apparently responsible for getting the defendants to come to court and for "sending" (*šapāru*) the parties to the judges, but not for actually conducting the trial. Instead, the case is heard by the governor of Uruk (a higher-ranking official) and a group of the local official's judges.

Although neither the place of composition nor the date of this text is preserved, it is possible to reconstruct both based on the names mentioned in it and its subject matter. The proximity to the Eanna of the house in question and the consequent involvement of the Eanna administration as defendants suggest that the text was composed in Uruk. The following considerations lead to a date between years 2 and 5 of Cyrus:

- Nidinti-Bēl son of Nabû-mukīn-zēri descendant of Dābibī is the *šatammu* of the Eanna (lines 14–15). He is attested as *šatammu* from 1

Cyr to 5 Cyr (Kümmel 1979, 143).

- Nabû-aḫa-iddin, the royal official in charge of the Eanna (line 15), is attested in this position 17 Nbn to 4 Camb (Kümmel 1979, 144).
- Imbiya son of Nanaya-ēreš descendant of Kidin-Marduk is the governor of Uruk (lines 16–17), and is attested in this position from 2 Cyr to 10 Camb (Kümmel 1979, 140).

Thus, the text must date to some time between 2 Cyr (the earliest date for Imbiya) and 5 Cyr (the latest date for Nidinti-Bēl). A date of 4 Cyr (535 BCE) has been suggested (Kümmel 1979, 140; Joannès 2000b, 229).

1. [^{m}IR$_{3}$]-^{d}*in-nin* A-*šú šá* ^{m}GAR-MU ^{m}*kal-ba-a* A-*šú šá* ^{m}*si-lim*-^{d}EN
2. ^{md}UTU-MU A-*šú šá* ^{md}EN-MU DUMU.MEŠ DUMU *šá* ^{md}EN-ŠEŠ.MEŠ-MU
3. A ^{m}ŠU-^{d}*na-na-a a-na* ^{md}NA$_{3}$-ŠEŠ.MEŠ-TIN-*iṭ* ^{lu_2}GAR-KUR

(1–4) [Arad]-Innin son of Šākin-šumi, Kalbaya son of Silim-Bēl, Šamaš-iddin son of Bēl-iddin, grandsons of Bēl-aḫḫē-iddin descendant of Gimil-Nanaya said thus to Nabû-aḫḫē-bulliṭ, the provincial governor:

4. *iq-bu-ú um-ma i-na* MU 4-*kám* ^{d}NA$_{3}$-NIG$_{2}$.DU-URI$_{3}$ LUGAL TIN.TIR^{ki}
5. ^{md}EN-ŠEŠ.MEŠ-MU AD AD-*i-ni* 5 1/2 MA.NA KU$_{3}$.BABBAR
6. *a-na* ^{md}EN-ŠEŠ.MEŠ-MU A-*šú šá* ^{m}*gu-da-du-ú* A ^{md}30-TI-ER$_{2}$

(4–7) "In year 4 of Nebuchadnezzar, king of Babylon, Bēl-aḫḫē-iddin, our father's father, paid 5 1/2 mina of silver for expenses to Bēl-aḫḫē-iddin son of Gudādu descendant of Sîn-lēqi-unninnī."

7. *a-na ni-is-ḫu id-din-ma* E$_{2}$-*su šá ina* KA$_{2}$.GAL-*i*
8. *šá* E$_{2}$.AN.NA *i-na ú-ìl-tì-šú maš-ka-nu iṣ-ba-at*

(7–8) "In the debt-note, he took his house which is at the grand gate of the Eanna as pledge."

9. *a-di i-na-an-ni* ŠU.2 *šá* ^{lu_2}*qi-pa-a-nu maḫ-ru-tu*
10. *šá* E$_{2}$.AN.NA *e-li* E$_{2}$ *šu-a-tì taš-šá-da-ma*

(9–11) "Until now, the former *qīpu*-officials of the Eanna have control over that house; they have not released the house to our possession!"

11. E$_{2}$ *ina pa-ni-ni la ú-maš-ši-ru it-ti* ^{lu_2}*qi-pa-a-nu*

(11–12) "Establish our decision against the *qīpu*-officials!"

12. *šá* E$_2$.AN.NA EŠ.BAR-*a-ni šu-kun* ^{md}NA$_3$-ŠEŠ.MEŠ-TIN-*iṭ*

13. ^{lu_2}GAR-KUR ^{m}IR$_3$-^{d}*in-nin* ^{m}*kal-ba-a u* ^{md}UTU-MU

14. *it-ti* ^{m}*ni-din-tu*$_4$-^{d}EN ^{lu_2}*ša*$_3$*-tam* E$_2$.AN.NA A-*šú šá* ^{md}NA$_3$-DU-NUMUN

15. A ^{m}*da-bi-bi* ^{md}NA$_3$-ŠEŠ-MU ^{lu_2}SAG-LUGAL ^{lu_2}EN *pi-qit-tu* E$_2$.AN.NA

16. *ù* ^{lu_2}UMBISAG.MEŠ *šá* E$_2$.AN.NA *a-na ma-ḫar* ^{m}*im-bi-ia*

17. ^{lu_2}GAR.UMUŠ UNUG^{ki} A-*šú šá* ^{md}*na-na-a*-APIN-*eš* A ^{m}*ki-din*-^{d}AMAR.UTU

18. *ù* ^{lu_2}DI.KU$_5$.MEŠ *šá* ^{md}NA$_3$-ŠEŠ.MEŠ-TIN-*iṭ* ^{lu_2}GAR-KUR *a-na ša-ka-nu* EŠ.BAR-*šú-nu*

(12–19) Nabû-aḫḫē-bulliṭ, the provincial governor, sent Arad-Innin, Kalbaya, and Šamaš-iddin together with Nidintu-Bēl, the *šatammu* of the Eanna, son of Nabû-mukīn-zēri descendant of Dābibī, Nabû-aḫa-iddin, the royal official in charge of the Eanna, and the scribes of Eanna before Imbiya, the governor of Uruk, son of Nanaya-ēreš descendant of Kidin-Marduk, and the judges of Nabû-aḫḫē-bulliṭ, the provincial governor, to establish their decision.

19. *iš-pu-ur-šú-nu-tú* ^{lu_2}GAR.UMUŠ *ù* ^{lu_2}DI.KU$_5$.MEŠ *dib-bi-šú-nu*

(19–20) The governor and the judges heard their case.

20. *iš-mu-ú ú-ìl-tì šá* 5 1/2 MA.NA KU$_3$.BABBAR *šá* ^{md}EN-ŠEŠ.MEŠ-MU

21. A-*šú šá* ^{m}ŠEŠ.MEŠ-*šú šá* UGU ^{md}EN-ŠEŠ.MEŠ-MU A-*šú šá* ^{m}*gu-da-du-ú*

22. *šá i-na* MU 4-*kám* ^{d}NA$_3$-NIG$_2$.DU-URI$_3$ LUGAL TIN.TIR^{ki} *e-li-tu*$_4$

23. *ù* E$_2$ *ina ú-ìl-tì-šú maš-ka-nu ṣa-ab-tu šá* ^{m}IR$_3$-^{d}*in-nin*

24. ^{m}*kal-ba-a u* ^{md}UTU-MU *a-na ma-ḫar* ^{lu_2}DI.KU$_5$.MEŠ

(20–25) The debt-note for 5 1/2 mina of silver belonging to Bēl-aḫḫē-iddin son of Aḫḫēšu owed by Bēl-aḫḫē-iddin son of Gudādu, written in year 4 of Nebuchadnezzar, king of Babylon, and in which the house was taken as collateral, which Arad-Innin, Kalbaya and Šamaš-iddin brought before the judges—

25. *ú-bil-lu-nu ù ṭup-pi.*MEŠ *ù ri-ka-su* NIG$_2$.GA ^{d}INNIN UNUG^{ki} 26. *šá* ^{lu_2}*qi-pa-nu šá* E$_2$.AN.NA *maḫ-ru-ú-tu*$_4$ *šá* E$_2$ MU.MEŠ *a-na i-di id-di-ni* 27. *ù i-di* E$_2$ *šu-a-tì ul-tu* MU 23-*kám* ^{d}NA$_3$-NIG$_2$.DU-URI$_3$ 28. LUGAL TIN.TIR^{ki} *a-na* E$_2$.AN.NA *i-ru-bu*	(25–28) And the tablets and contracts of the property of Ištar of Uruk (indicating) that the former *qīpu*-officials of Eanna rented out that house, and the rent of that house entered the Eanna from year 23 of Nebuchadnezzar, king of Babylon—
29. ^{giš}DA NIG$_2$.GA ^{d}INNIN UNUG^{ki} *šá ina* MU 25-*kám* ^{d}NA$_3$-NIG$_2$.DU-URI$_3$ 30. LUGAL TIN.TIR^{ki} *it-ti* GI.MEŠ *šá* E$_2$.AN.NA E$_2$ *šu-a-tì*	(29–31) The writing board, property of Ištar of Uruk, of year 25 of Nebuchadnezzar, king of Babylon, in which that house was inscribed among the properties of Eanna—
31. *ina* ^{giš}DA *šá-aṭ-ru* IM.DUB *šá* ^{md}30-MU ^{lu_2}*qí-i-pi* 32. *šá* E$_2$.AN.NA *ù* ^{lu_2}UMBISAG.MEŠ *šá* E$_2$.AN.NA *ina* MU 36-*kám* 33. ^{d}NA$_3$-NIG$_2$.DU-URI$_3$ LUGAL TIN.TIR^{ki} E$_2$ *šu-a-tì ul-tu* E$_2$.AN.NA 34. *a-na* KU$_3$.BABBAR *a-na* ^{md}*in-nin*-MU-URI$_3$ A-*šú šá* ^{md}U.GUR-GI 35. A ^{md}30-TI-ER$_2$ *id-di-nu-ú-ma* ^{m}MU-^{d}NA$_3$ ŠEŠ-*šú-nu* GAL-*e* 36. ⸢A-DUMU$^{?}$⸣ [IBILA] ⸢*šá*⸣ ^{md}EN-ŠEŠ.MEŠ-MU *a-na* ^{lu_2}IGI-*ú-tu ina lìb-bi áš-bu*	(31–36) The tablet (indicating) that Sîn-iddin, *qīpu*-official of the Eanna, and the scribes of the Eanna sold that house for silver, in year 36 of Nebuchadnezzar, king of Babylon, from the property of Eanna to Innin-šuma-uṣur son of Nergal-ušallim descendant of Sîn-lēqi-unninnī, and in which Iddin-Nabû, son of the [eldest] son [of] Bēl-aḫḫē-iddin, was a witness—
37. [*ri*]-*ik-su šá ina* MU 39-*kám* ^{d}NA$_3$-NIG$_2$.DU-URI$_3$ LUGAL TIN.TIR^{ki} 38. [E$_2$ *šu-a-tì*] *ina* ŠU.2 ^{md}*in-nin*-MU-URI$_3$ *a-na* E$_2$.AN.NA	(37—39) The [con]tract (by means of) which, in year 39 of Nebuchadnezzar, king of Babylon, [that house …] to the Eanna from Innin-šuma-uṣur
39. [… E$_2$].AN.NA *a-na i-di* E$_2$	(39) … Eanna, for rent, the house
40. […] ⸢^{lu_2}RIG$_7$⸣.MEŠ *šá* E$_2$.AN.NA *na-ad-nu*	(40) … was given to oblates of the Eanna.

41. [...*il-ta*]-*as-su-ú-ma* ^{lu_2}GAR.UMUŠ	(41) ... they re[ad]. The governor
42. [...] *šá* 5 1/2 MA.NA KU$_3$.BABBAR	(42) ... of 5 1/2 mina of silver
43. [... *e*]-*li* ^{md}EN-ŠEŠ.MEŠ-MU	(43) [... ow]ed by Bēl-aḫḫē-iddin
44. [...] LUGAL TIN.TIR^{ki}	(44) ... king of Babylon
45. [...] *ú-ìl-tì a-na* NIG$_2$.GA *id-di-nu*	(45) ... the debt-note they gave to the possessions
46. .[...] TIN.TIR^{ki}	(46) ... Babylon
47. [...^{m}]^{d}UTU-MU *ù* AD.MEŠ-*šú-nu*	(47) [...]Šamaš-iddin and their fathers
48. [...*ul*]*tu*$_4$ *lìb-bi*	(48) [...] from (?)
49. [...^{m}] ^{d}UTU-MU	(49) [...]Šamaš-iddin
50. [...] UNUG^{ki}	(50) [...] Uruk
51. [...] [? ?]	
52. [...] A-*šú šá* ^{md}*na-na-a*-KAM$_2$	(52) [...] son of Nanaya-ēreš
53. [...]-^{d}*in-nin* ^{lu_2}DI.KU$_5$	(53) [...PN]-innin, the judge
54. [...] A *wu-ú-ṣu*	(54) [...], descendant of Wuṣu
55. [...] A [x x]-^{d}IDIM	(55) [...] descendant of ... -Ea

NOTES

Two seals appear on the left edge of the tablet.

9–10. ŠU.2 ... *taš-šá-da-ma-* The present reading ("to have control") follows the translation in Joannès 2000b, 230, and is based on the use of the verb *kašādu* with *qātu* as the subject to mean "to obtain possession" (*CAD* K, 279). The verb is interpreted as a corrupted form of the expected *takaššadāma,* a G-stem durative, third person dual form.

29–31. These lines describe how the property entered the Eanna's possession. It is possible that the temple gained control of the property when there was a default on a debt.

41. *il-ta*]-*as-su-ú-ma-* Following Joannès 2000b, 230, the subject of this verb (*šasû*), is understood to be the governor and the judges mentioned in lines 19–20.

45. This line apparently indicates the transfer to the Eanna, now confirmed as owner, of all of the records pertaining to the property.

27. A Dispute over a House

Text: BM 41395 (81-6-25, 6)
Copy: Strassmaier 1889b (Nbk), No. 109
Translation/Discussion: Peiser 1896, No. 12 (p. 188); Kohler and Peiser 1890–98, 2:24–25; Godbey 1905, 81; Beaulieu 2003, 329; Kleber 2008, 319–21; Holtz 2009, 261
Place of Composition: Babylon
Date: 6.I.17 Nbk (9 April, 588 BCE)

Balāṭu and Šāpik-zēri argue a case regarding a house. Zērūtu, father of Šāpik-zēri, wrote a tablet in which he gave Balāṭu the property. The judges rule in favor of Šāpik-zēri, and return the property in question to him and record their award on a tablet. The present document is the list of adjudicating officials before whom the case was heard.

Balāṭu's claim to the property is based on the tablet written by Zērūtu, while Šāpik-zēri's claim to the property stems from his rights as Zērūtu's heir. Zērūtu may have originally mortgaged the house to Balāṭu, by means of the written tablet. The return of the house and the tablet may reflect the court's ruling that the original debt has been fulfilled.

The panel of judges consists of several high-ranking officials. This is probably because of Balāṭu's important status. Balāṭu's name is followed by a feminine name, Nasikātu, which refers to his mother, rather than to his father, as would be typical. The word *nasikātu* in Akkadian means "female tribal leader." Balāṭu's mother could well have been the leader of one of the Aramean tribes that lived in the southern region of Mesopotamia known as "the Sealand" (Kleber 2008, 320–21).

1. [*an-nu-tu*] $^{\text{lú}_2}$*da-a-ne-e*
2. [*šá ina pa-ni-šú-nu* ^{m}DUB]-NUMUN A-*šú šá* ^{m}NUMUN-*tú*
3. [*it-ti* ^{m}]*ba-la-ṭu* DUMU ^{f}*na-si-ka-tu*$_4$
4. [*ina* D]U-*zu šá* $^{\text{lú}_2}$*šá-kin* KUR *tam-tim*
5. [*di*]-*i-ni šá* E$_2$ *ina pa-ni-šú-nu*

(1–6) [These are] the judges before whom Šāpik-zēri son of Zērūtu and Balāṭu son of Nasikātu, [in the pr]esence of the governor of the Sealand, argued a [ca]se regarding a house.

6. *id-bu-bu* E$_2$ *ù* IM.DUB 7. *šá* ^{m}NUMUN-*tú* AD *šá* ^{m}DUB-NUMUN 8. *ik-nu-ku-ma a-na* ^{m}*ba-la-ṭu* 9. *id-di-nu* ^{m}*ba-la-ṭu* 10. *it-ti* ^{m}DUB-NUMUN	(6–11) Balāṭu, together with Šāpik-zēri, returned the house and the tablet that Zērutu, father of Šāpik-zēri sealed and had given to Balāṭu.
11. *ú-tir-ru-nu* E$_2$ *pa-an* 12. ^{m}DUB-NUMUN *ú-šad-gi-lu* 13. *ù* IM.DUB *iš-šu-nim-ma* 14. *a-na* ^{m}DUB-NUMUN *id-di-nu*	(11–14) They placed the property at the disposal of Šāpik-zēri; and they brought the tablet and gave it to Šāpik-zēri.
15. ^{md}NA$_3$-KAR-*ir*-ZI.MEŠ 16. ^{lu_2}*qi-i-pi šá* KUR *tam-tim*	(15–16) Nabû-ēṭir-napšāti the *qīpu*-official of the Sealand;
17. ^{md}NA$_3$-*šu-uz-ziz-an-ni* 18. ^{lu_2}2-*ú šá* KUR *tam-tim*	(17–18) Nabû-šuzzizanni the *šanû* of the Sealand;
19. ^{md}AMAR.UTU-SU ^{lu_2}GAR.UMUŠ *šá* UNUG^{ki}	(19) Marduk-erība the governor of Uruk;
20. ^{m}*im-bi*-^{d}30 ^{lu_2}E$_2$.MAŠ ŠEŠ.UNUG^{ki}	(20) Imbi-Sîn the *šangû* of Ur;
21. ^{md}EN-TIN-*iṭ* A-*šú šá* ^{md}AMAR.UTU-MU-DU$_3$ 22. ^{lu_2}*qí-i-pi šá a-ḫu-ul-la-*ʾ	(21–22) Bēl-uballiṭ son of Marduk-šuma-ibni the *qīpu*-official of Aḫullaʾ;
23. ^{m}A-*a* A-*šú šá* ^{m}*šu-zu-bu* DUMU ^{m}*ba-bu-tu*	(23) Aplaya son of Šūzubu descendant of Bābūtu;
24. ^{m}*mu-še-zib*-^{d}EN A-*šú šá* ^{m}SUM.NA-ŠEŠ 25. DUMU ^{m}*ba-bu-tu*	(24–25) Mušēzib-Bēl son of Iddin-aḫa descendant of Bābūtu;
26. ^{m}*mu-še-zib*-^{d}AMAR.UTU A-*šú šá* ^{m}SUM.NA-ŠEŠ 27. DUMU ^{m}*šá-na-ši-i-šú*	(26–27) Mušēzib-Marduk son of Iddin-aḫa descendant of Ša-nāšīšu;
28. ^{m}*ba-ni-ia* A-*šú šá* ^{m}A-*a* 29. ^{lu_2}UMBISAG *šá* E$_2$ ^{d}KUR.GAL	(28–29) Bāniya son of Aplaya the scribe of the temple of Amurru;
30. ^{md}UTU-DU$_3$ ^{lu_2}E$_2$.MAŠ ^{d}KUR.GAL	(30) Šamaš-ibni the *šangû* of Amurru.

31. TIN.TIR^{ki} ITI BAR_2
32. U_4 6-*kám* MU 17-*kám*
33. [$^{md}NA_3$-NIG_2.D]U-*ú-ṣur*
34. [LUGAL TIN].TIR^{ki}

(31–34) Babylon. 6 Nisannu, year 17 of Nebuchadnezzar, king of Babylon.

NOTES

19. For other attestations of Marduk-erība, the governor of Uruk, see Kümmel 1979, 139.

28. Dispute over a Theft

Text: CBS 5418
Copy: Hilprecht and Clay 1898 (BE 9), No. 69
Translation/Discussion: Stolper 1976, 195
Place of Composition: Nippur
Date: 4.XII.39 Artaxerxes (7 March, 425 BCE)

In the assembly of Nippur, Udarnaʾ accuses members of Enlil-šuma-iddin's household of robbing Udarnaʾ's house together with Udarnaʾ's brother, Zabdiya, and Zabdiya's son, Bēl-ittannu. Enlil-šuma-iddin interrogates the members of his household, obtains the stolen items from them, and returns them to Udarnaʾ. Udarnaʾ renounces any future claims against Enlil-šuma-iddin.

This text belongs to the Murašû-family archive, which dates to a later period than most of the texts in this anthology. Unlike other "family archives," such as that of the Egibis from Babylon, the Murašû archive consists predominantly of documents pertaining to business transactions, rather than to property held by the family (Jursa 2005, 113). Thus, this text is a rare example of a record pertaining to litigation (Stolper 1976, 195).

1. ^{m}*ú-da-ar-na-ʾ* A *šá* ^{m}*ra-ḫi-mi-ìl šá ina* UKKIN EN.LIL$_{2}$$^{⸢ki⸣}$	(1–2) Udarnaʾ son of Raḫimiʾil, who spoke thus in the assembly of Nippur to Enlil-šuma-iddin son of Murašû:
2. *a-na* ^{md}EN.LIL$_{2}$-MU-MU A *šá* ^{m}*mu-ra-šu-ú iq-bu-ú um-ma* ^{lu_2}DUMU.MEŠ E$_{2}$.MEŠ-*ka*	
3. ^{lu_2}*a-lik na-áš-par-ti-ka* ^{lu_2}IR$_{3}$.MEŠ-*ka it-ti* ^{m}*zab-di-ia* ŠEŠ-*ia u* ^{md}EN-*it-tan-nu* DUMU-⸢*šú*⸣	(2–4) "When your household (members), your agent (and) your slaves, together with Zabdiya, my brother, and Bēl-ittannu, his son, entered my house, they took away my property and household items."
4. *a-na* E$_{2}$-*ia* ⸢*ki*⸣-*i i-ru-bu-ʾ* NIG$_{2}$.GA-*ia u ú-de-e* E$_{2}$-*ia it-ta-šu*-[ʾ]	
5. *ár-ki* ^{md}⸢EN⸣.LIL$_{2}$-MU-MU *a-na* ^{lu_2}DUMU.MEŠ E$_{2}$.MEŠ-*šú* ^{lu_2}*a*-⸢*lik*⸣ [*na-áš-par*]-*ti-šú* ^{lu_2}IR$_{3}$.MEŠ-⸢*šú*⸣	(5–6) Afterwards, Enlil-šuma-iddin interrogated his household (members), his a[gent], his slaves, Zab[diy]a and Bēl-ittannu.

6. ^{m}*zab-*[*di-i*]*a u* ^{md}EN-*it-tan-nu i-*⸢*šá-al*⸣*-ma* NIG$_2$.GA MU.MEŠ
7. *ina* ŠU.2-*šú*-[*nu*] *iš-šá-am-ma ú-ṭir-ma a-na* ^{m}*ú-da-ar-na-*' *id-din*

(6–7) He took that property away from them, returned it and gave it to Udarna'.

8. NIG$_2$.GA MU.MEŠ ^{m}*ú-da-ar-na-*' *ina* ŠU.2 ^{md}⸢EN.LIL$_2$⸣-MU-MU ^{lu_2}DUMU.MEŠ E$_2$.MEŠ-⸢*šú*⸣

(8–9) Udarna' has received that property from Enlil-šuma-iddin, his household, his agent and his slaves.

9. *u* ^{lu_2}*a-lik na-áš-par-ti-šú u* ^{lu_2}IR$_3$.MEŠ-*šú ma-ḫi-ir* DI.KU$_5$ *u ra-ga-*[*mu*]
10. *šá* ^{m}*ú-da-ar-na-*' *u* DUMU.MEŠ-*šú a-na muḫ-*[*ḫi* NIG$_2$].GA MU.MEŠ *it-ti* ^{md}EN.LIL$_2$-[MU-MU]
11. ^{lu_2}DUMU.MEŠ E$_2$.MEŠ-*šú* ^{lu_2}*a-lik na-áš-par-ti-*⸢*šú*⸣ [*u* ^{lu_2}]IR$_3$.MEŠ-*šú a-na* U$_4$-*mu ṣa-a-*[*tú ia-a-nu*]

(9–11) [There is no] claim or argu[ment] of Udarna' or his sons regardi[ng] that [pro]perty against Enlil-[šuma-iddin], his household, his agent or his slave, to the end of days.

12. *ul i-tur-ru-ma* ^{m}*ú-da-ar-na-*' *u* DUMU.MEŠ-*šú a-na muḫ-ḫi* NIG$_2$.GA [MU.MEŠ]
13. *it-ti* ^{md}EN.LIL$_2$-MU-MU ^{lu_2}DUMU.MEŠ E$_2$.MEŠ-*šú* ^{lu_2}*a-lik na-áš-par-ti-šú u* ^{lu_2}IR$_3$.[MEŠ-*šú*]
14. *a-na* U$_4$-*mu ṣa-a-tu ul i-*⸢*rag-gu*⸣-[*mu*]

(12–14) Udarna' and his sons shall not turn back and raise a claim concerning [that] property against Enlil-šuma-iddin, his household, his agent or his slaves to the end of days.

15. ^{lu_2}MU.DU ^{md}MAŠ-MU A *šá* ^{md}MAŠ-SU ^{md}UTU-ŠEŠ-MU A *šá* ^{md}MAŠ-[SUR]

(15) Witnesses: Ninurta-iddin son of Ninurta-erība; Šamaš-aḫa-iddin son of Ninurta-[ēṭir];

16. ^{m}I-^{d}MAŠ A *šá* ^{md}EN.LIL$_2$-MU-DU ^{m}*ap-la-a* A *šá* ^{md}EN.LIL$_2$-TIN-[*su*-E]

(16) Nā'id-Ninurta son of Enlil-šuma-ukīn; Aplaya son of Enlil-balās[su-iqbi];

17. ^{md}MAŠ-*na-ṣir* A *šá* ^{md}EN-ŠEŠ.MEŠ-MU ^{m}SU-^{d}EN.LIL$_2$ A *šá* ^{m}EN.LIL$_2$-[*ba-na*]

(17) Ninurta-nāṣir son of Bēl-aḫḫē-iddin; Erība-Enlil son of Enlil-[bana];

18. ^{m}MU-MU A *šá* ^{md}MAŠ-TIN-*iṭ* ^{m}SIG$_{15}$-*a* A *šá* ^{m}SUM.NA-*a* ^{md}UTU-TIN-*iṭ* A *šá* ^{m}*ti*[*r-ri-ia-a-ma*]	(18) Šuma-iddin son of Ninurta-uballiṭ; Damqaya son of Iddinaya; Šamaš-uballiṭ son of T[irriyama];
19. ^{m}*ú-bar* A *šá* ^{md}EN.LIL$_2$-DU-A ^{md}MAŠ-ŠEŠ-MU A *šá* ^{m}IR$_3$-E$_2$.GAL.MAH	(19) Ubar son of Enlil-mukīn-apli; Ninurta-aḫa-iddin son of Arad-Egalmaḫ;
20. ^{m}*ḫa-na-ni-ia-ma* A *šá* ^{m}*ú-da-ar-na-*ʾ ^{m}*ga-da-al-ia-a-ma* [A *šá*] 21. ^{m}*šab-ba-ta-a-a* ^{m}DINGIR.MEŠ-*id-ri-*ʾ A *šá* ^{m}*ap-pu-us-sa-a*	(20–21) Ḫananyama son of Udarnaʾ; Gadalyama son of Šabbataya; Ilī-idriʾ son of Appussa;
22. ^{md}MAŠ-*na-ṣir* A *šá* ^{m}MU-^{d}EN.LIL$_2$ ^{md}MAŠ-*ana*-E$_2$-*šú* A *šá* ^{m}*lu-ú-id-di-ia*	(22) Ninurta-nāṣir son of Iddin-Enlil; Ninurta-ana-bītīšu son of Lū-iddiya;
23. ^{m}MU-MU A *šá* ^{md}EN.LIL$_2$-PAP ^{m}A-*a* A *šá* ^{md}MAŠ-MU	(23) Šuma-iddin son of Enlil-nāṣir; Aplaya son of Ninurta-iddin;
24. ^{md}EN.LIL$_2$-*it-tan-nu* A *šá* ^{md}EN.LIL$_2$-MU ^{m}ZALAG$_2$-*šú*-^{d}EN.LIL$_2$ A *šá* ^{m}*i*-[	(24) Enlil-ittannu son of Enlil-iddin; Nūrīšu-Enlil son of I-[
25. ^{md}EN.LIL$_2$-ŠEŠ-MU A *šá* ^{md}EN.LIL$_2$-TIN-*iṭ* ^{m}IR$_3$-*ia* A *šá* ^{m}*ú*-⌜*bar*⌝	(25) Enlil-aḫa-iddin son of Enlil-uballiṭ; Ardiya son of Ubar.
26. ^{lu_2}UMBISAG ^{m}EN-*šú-nu* A *šá* ^{md}MAŠ-*na*-⌜*ṣir*⌝ EN.LIL$_2$^{ki} ITI ŠE U$_4$ 4-*kám*	(26) Scribe: Bēlšunu son of Ninurta-nāṣir.
27. MU 39-*kám* ^{m}*ar-taḫ-šá-as-su* LUGAL KUR.KUR	(26–27) Nippur. 4 Addaru, year 39 of Artaxerxes, king of the lands.
Left edge:	
^{na_4}KIŠIB ^{m}*ú-da-ar-na-*ʾ	Seal of Udarnaʾ
Upper edge:	
^{na_4}KIŠIB ^{md}UTU-ŠEŠ-MU A *šá* ^{md}MAŠ-SUR	Seal of Šamaš-aḫa-iddin son of Ninurta-ēṭir
^{na_4}KIŠIB ^{m}SU- ^{d}EN.LIL$_2$ A *šá* ^{md}EN.LIL$_2$-*ba-na*	Seal of Erība-Enlil son of Enlil-bana
Third seal legend illegible	

Lower edge:

na4KIŠIB mdMAŠ-*na-ṣir* A *šá* mdEN-ŠEŠ.MEŠ-[MU]	Seal of Ninurta-nāṣir son of Bēl-aḫḫē-[iddin]
na4KIŠIB mA-*a* A *šá* mdEN.LIL$_2$-TIN-*su*-E	Seal of Aplaya son of Enlil-balāssu-iqbi

NOTES

20–21. The name of the witness Gadalyama son of Šabbataya is Judean. Gadalyama is the equivalent of Hebrew Gedalyāhû.

29. An Attempted Fraud

Text: BM 32165 (76-11-17, 1892) + BM 32199 (76-11-17, 1926) + BM 32763 (76-11-17, 2534); MNB 1810
Copy: Strassmaier 1889a (Nbn), No. 720 (BM 32199); Wunsch 2000a, No. 90A (1:230–31); Contenau 1927–29, vol. 13, No. 219 (MNB 1810)
Translation/Discussion: Moore 1935, 223–27; San Nicolò 1939, 179–88; Joannès 2000b, No. 169 (pp. 227–28); Wunsch 2000a, 1:117–19; 2:114–16
Place of Composition: Babylon
Date: 11.VII.13 Nbn (22 October, 543 BCE)

Itti-Marduk-balāṭu presents a complaint to the judges of Nabonidus. Šāpik-zēri and Bēl-uballiṭ have claimed that they owed a debt of five mina of silver to Rīmūt, and that they have secured the debt by pledging a field which was later sold to Nabû-aḫḫē-iddin, father of Itti-Marduk-balāṭu. Šāpik-zēri and Bēl-uballiṭ have demanded that Itti-Marduk-balāṭu pay them one-half mina of silver in exchange for the debt-note. Itti-Marduk-balāṭu, with the tablet in hand, has questioned the circumstances, but Šāpik-zēri grabbed the tablet away and chewed it. Upon interrogation by the judges, Šāpik-zēri and Bēl-uballiṭ claim that the debt was paid and that Itti-Marduk-balāṭu has brought them before the judges needlessly. When the judges demand to see Rīmūt, the creditor, Šāpik-zēri and Bēl-uballiṭ cannot bring him and claim that they do not know him. The debt-note turns out to be false. The judges make Šāpik-zēri and Bēl-uballiṭ pay Itti-Marduk-balāṭu ten times the amount of the debt they had falsified. In order to apprehend the scribe who had forged the document, the judges also place the two criminals in fetters and give them over to Itti-Marduk-balāṭu.

Šāpik-zēri and Itti-Marduk-balāṭu rely on two common legal practices when they make their claim. First, when a debt was paid, the debtor would obtain possession of the note from the creditor. Thus, in presenting Itti-Marduk-balāṭu with the (ultimately false) debt-note from Rīmūt, they use their possession of the note to demonstrate that they have satisfied the debt. The two crooks also rely on a standard legal practice regarding property sales. If the sold property was, in fact, mortgaged to another creditor before the sale, then that creditor could take possession of the property from the new owners. When the two men demand payment from Itti-Marduk-balāṭu, they could claim to have done Itti-Marduk-balaṭu a service by clearing a prior lien on the propety that his father purchased.

Although the present lawsuit can be understood on its own, without reference to other archival records, it gains added significance when it is set within the context of the Egibi archives. The document belongs to the dossier pertaining to the parcel of land in Babylon described as located "near the Ḫazuzu canal" (see Wunsch 2000a, 1:110–17). This plot of land originally belonged to Šuma-ukīn, father of Šāpik-zēri and Bēl-uballiṭ, the two defendants. Upon Šuma-ukīn's death, there was extensive litigation regarding the division of the inheritance (see Document 23 above). Soon afterwards, the various heirs sold their shares of land to Nabû-aḫḫē-iddin of the Egibi family. By the time of the present lawsuit, Nabû-aḫḫē-iddin has died, and his son, Itti-Marduk-balāṭu, has assumed control of the family's affairs. In committing their fraud, it is likely that the two brothers tried to take advantage of the changed situation as a result of Nabû-aḫḫē-iddin's death. Their victim, however, would not be fooled; his suspicions lead him to bring the matter to the royal judges, some of whom were colleagues of his late father, who was also a royal judge (see Documents 22 and 23 above). In court, the fraud is brought to light and the criminals receive their punishment.

1. [^{m}*it*]-*ti*-^{d}AMAR.UTU-TIN DUMU-*šú šá* ^{md}NA$_{3}$-ŠEŠ.MEŠ-MU DUMU *e-gi-bi*
2. [*a-na*] ⸢^{lu_2}⸣DI.KU$_{5}$.MEŠ *šá* ^{md}NA$_{3}$-IM.TUK LUGAL TIN.TIR^{ki} *iq-bi*

(1–3) [It]ti-Marduk-balāṭu son of Nabû-aḫḫē-iddin descendant of Egibi said [thus to] the judges of Nabonidus:

3. [*um-ma*] ^{m}DUB-NUMUN *ù* ^{md}EN-TIN-*iṭ* DUMU.MEŠ *šá* ^{m}MU-GI.NA
4. [DUMU ^{md}]EN.ZU-*šá-du-nu ù-íl-ti šá* 5 MA.NA KU$_{3}$.BABBAR
5. [*šá*] ^{m}*ri-mut* A-*šú šá* ^{m}*ina-qí-bit*-^{d}NA$_{3}$ *šá* UGU-*šú-nu*
6. *šá* A.ŠA$_{3}$-*šú-nu šá* UGU *ḫar-ri ša ḫa-zu-zu*
7. *ina lìb-bi maš-ka-nu ṣab-tu u* A.ŠA$_{3}$ *šu-a-tu$_{4}$ a-na* ^{md}NA$_{3}$-ŠEŠ.MEŠ-MU
8. *a-bi-ia a-na* KU$_{3}$.BABBAR *in-na-ad-nu a-na pa-ni-ia iš-ku-nim-ma* 1/2 MA.NA KU$_{3}$.BABBAR
9. *bi-in-na-a-na-ši-ma ù-íl-tì ni-id-din-ka*

(3–9) "Šāpik-zēri and Bēl-uballiṭ sons of Šuma-ukīn [descendant of] Sîn-sadûnu presented me with a debt-note for 5 mina of silver, which they owe to Rīmūt son of Ina-qībit-Nabû, (and) for which their field which is near the Ḫazuzu canal is taken in pledge, and that field was sold to Nabû-aḫḫē-iddin, my father, for silver, (and they said): 'Give us 1/2 a mina of silver and we will give you the debt-note.'"

10. *ù-il-ti ú-ki-il-ma aq-bi-šú-nu-ti um-ma man-nu*	(10) "I held the tablet and said thus to them:"
11. ^{md}*ri-mut šá* A.ŠA$_3$ *maš-ka-nu ina* ŠU.2-*ku-nu ṣab-tu ú-il-tu*$_4$ *šu-a-tim*	(10–11) "'Who is Rīmūt who received the field in pledge from you?'"
12. ^{m}DUB-NUMUN *ul-tu* ŠU.2-*ia i-iḫ-bi-it-ma ina šin-ni-šú ik-su-us*	(11–12) "Šāpik-zēri grabbed that debt-note from my hands and chewed it with his teeth."
13. EŠ.BAR-*a-ni šuk-na* ^{lú_2}DI.KU$_5$.MEŠ ^{m}DUB-NUMUN	(13) "Establish our decision!"
14. *ù* ^{md}EN-TIN-*iṭ i-šá-lu-ma iq-bu-ú um-ma*	(13–14) The judges interrogated Šāpik-zēri and Bēl-uballiṭ and they said thus:
15. *ú-il-ti e-ṭir-tu*$_4$ *ši-i u mi-im-mu-ú* ^{m}*it-ti-*^{d}AMAR.UTU-TIN	(15–19) "The debt-note is paid. Whatever Itti-Marduk-balāṭu recounted before you is true. We did not bring the debt-note for claim or suit against him. *He* brought us before you!"
16. *ina-maḫ-ri-ku-nu ú-šá-an-nu-ú ki-na-a-ti-ma*	
17. *ú-il-ti a-na di-i-ni u ra-ga-mu*	
18. *a-na* UGU-*šú la nu-bi-il-la a-na maḫ-ri-ku-nu*	
19. *i-bu-ka-an-na-šú* ^{lú_2}DI.KU$_5$.MEŠ *iq-bu-šú-nu-ši*	(19–20) The judges said thus to them:
20. *um-ma* ^{m}*ri-mut* EN *ù-íl-tì a-na maḫ-ri-i-ni bi-il-la*	(20) "Bring Rīmūt, the creditor, before us!"
21. ^{m}DUB-NUMUN *u* ^{md}EN-TIN-*iṭ* ^{m}*ri-mu-tu*$_4$ EN *ù-il-tu*$_4$ *la ub-lu-ni*	(21–22) Šāpik-zēri and Bēl-uballiṭ did not bring Rīmūt, the creditor. They changed the statement they spoke and said, "We do not know Rīmūt."
22. *a-mat iq-bu-ú ik-ki-ru-ma* ^{m}*ri-mu-tu*$_4$ *la ni-i-di iq-bu-ú*	
23. ^{lú_2}DI.KU$_5$.MEŠ *a-ma-a-ti-šú-nu iš-tim-mu-ma ú-il-ti šá* ^{m}*ri-mut*	(23–27) The judges heard their statements: (That) with his teeth, Šāpik-zēri chewed Rīmūt's debt-note which was written to take Nabû-aḫḫē-iddin's purchased field in pledge and which they brought to Itti-Marduk-balāṭu, and (that) they said "We do not know Rīmūt."
24. *šá* A.ŠA$_3$ KI.LAM *šá* ^{md}NA$_3$-SEŠ.MEŠ-MU *a-na maš-ka-nu-ti a-na*	
25. ^{m}*ri-mu-tu ú-šá-áš-ṭi-ru-ma a-na* UGU ^{m}KI-^{d}AMAR.UTU-TIN	
26. *ú-bil-lu-nim-ma* ^{m}DUB-NUMUN *i-na šin-ni-šú ik-su-su*	
27. *ù* ^{m}*ri-mu-tu la ni-i-di iq-bu-ú*	

28. ^{lu_2}DI.KU$_5$.MEŠ *im-tal-ku-ma ú-il-ti šá* ^{m}DUB-NUMUN *u* ^{md}EN-[TIN-*iṭ*]	(28) The judges deliberated.
29. *ub-lu-ni a-na sur-ra-a-ti i-na pa-ni-šú-nu i-tu-ur-ra*	(28–31) In their estimation, the debt-note which Šāpik-zēri and Bēl-uballiṭ brought turned out to be false. They decided that they must pay 10 times the 5 mina of silver which was written in that debt-note and awarded (that sum) to Itti-Marduk-balāṭu.
30. 5 MA.NA KU$_3$.BABBAR *šá ina ú-il-ti šu-a-tim šaṭ-ra a-di* 10-*šú e-li-šú-nu*	
31. *ip-ru-su-ma a-na* ^{m}KI-^{d}AMAR.UTU-TIN *id-di-nu u a-na a-ba-ku šá* DUB.SAR	
32. *šá-ṭir ú-il-tì iz-qa-a-ti id-du-šu-nu-ma a-na* ^{m}KI-^{d}AMAR.UTU-TIN *ip*-[*qi-du*]	(31–32) And in order to bring forward the scribe who wrote the debt-note, they placed them in fetters and [han]ded them over to Itti-Marduk-balāṭu.
33. *ina ša-ṭa-ri ṭup-pi šu-a-ti*	(33) At the writing of this tablet
35. ^{md}U.GUR-GI ^{lu_2}DI.KU$_5$ DUMU ^{m}*ši-gu-*[*ú-a*]	(35) Nergal-ušallim, the judge, descendant of Šigûa;
36. ^{md}EN-ŠEŠ.MEŠ-MU ^{lu_2}DI.KU$_5$ DUMU ^{m}ZALAG$_2$-^{d}30	(36) Bēl-aḫḫē-iddin, the judge, descendant of Nūr-Sîn;
37. ^{md}NA$_3$-TIN-*su-iq-bi* ^{lu_2}DI.KU$_5$ DUMU ^{m}LU$_2$-*ú*	(37) Nabû-balāssu-iqbi, the judge, descendant of Amēlû;
38. ^{md}NA$_3$-MU-*li-bur* ^{lu_2}DI.KU$_5$ DUMU ^{m}*ga-ḫal*-^{d}AMAR.UTU	(38) Nabû-šumu-libūr, the judge, descendant of Gaḫal-Marduk;
39. ^{md}*mu-še-zib*-^{d}EN ^{lu_2}DI.KU$_5$ DUMU ^{m}DU$_3$-*eš*-DINGIR	(39) Mušēzib-Bēl, the judge, descendant of Eppeš-ili;
40. ^{m}[*ri*]-*mut*-^{d}EN ^{lu_2}DI.KU$_5$ DUMU ^{m}*mi-ṣir-a-a*	(40) Rīmūt-Bēl, the judge, descendant of Miṣiraya;
41. [^{md}]NA$_3$-*e-tel*-DINGIR.MEŠ ^{lu_2}DI.KU$_5$ ^{md}IM-*šam-me-e*	(41) Nabû-etel-ilāni, the judge, descendant of Adad-šammê;
42. ^{md}NA$_3$-MU-GAR-*un* DUB.SAR DUMU ^{lu_2}GAL-DU$_3$	(42) Nabû-šuma-iškun, the scribe, descendant of Rāb-bānê.
43. TIN.TIR^{ki} ITI DU$_6$-KU$_3$ U$_4$ 11-*kám*	(43–44) Babylon. 11 Tašrītu, year 13 of Nabonidus, king of Babylon.
44. MU 13-*kám* ^{md}NA$_3$-IM.TUK LUGAL TIN.TIR^{ki}	

30. A Violent Theft

Text: YBC 4136
Copy: Tremayne 1925 (YOS 7), No. 128
Translation/Discussion: Dandamaev 1984, 539; Holtz 2009, 269–70, 298–99
Place of Composition: Uruk
Date: 13.VII.2 Camb (8 October, 528 BCE)

Ištar-ālik-pāni, a herdsman of Ištar of Uruk, testifies before the assembly of mār banî. *Bēlšunu entered the flock which was at Ištar-ālik-pāni's disposal, led away a branded ewe and killed it. When Ištar-ālik-pāni ordered him not to kill the branded ewe, Bēlšunu choked him with a neck ornament and uttered imprecations against Gobryas and Pharnaces. The assembly summon and interrogate Bēlšunu, who testifies about himself. The assembly's decision is not legible, but Bēlšunu was probably ordered to make a thirtyfold payment for the sheep.*

The witness and victim of the violence, Ištar-ālik-pāni, is at the end of a rather long career in the Eanna (Ragen 2006, 72, 80–85, 128). In the present document, in addition to being described as an oblate (*širku*), he is also described as a herdsman (*nāqidu*). However, throughout most of his career, which began during the reign of Amēl-Marduk in 561 BCE, he was an overseer of the oblates (*rāb širkī*), and seems to have even risen to the rank of royal official (Ragen 2006, 84). Ištar-ālik-pāni's high status and connection to the royal government may have been what provoked his attacker, Bēlšunu, to defame the satrap and the satrap's subordinate during the violence.

1. ^{md}AMAR.UTU-MU-MU DUMU-*šú šá* ^{md}[PN.. .]	(1) Marduk-šuma-iddin son of Na[bû-];
2. ^{md}30-APIN-eš DUMU-*šú šá* ^{md}NA$_3$-[MU-GIŠ A ^{m}*ib-ni*-DINGIR]	(2) Sîn-ēreš son of Nabû-[šumu-līšir descendant of Ibni-ilī] ;
3. ^{m}*la-ba-ši*-^{d}AMAR.UTU DUMU-*šú šá* ^{md}N[A$_3$...]	(3) Lâbāši-Marduk son of Na[bû- ...];
4. ^{m}MU-GI.NA DUMU-*šú šá* ^{m}[PN...]	(4) Šuma-ukīn son of [PN...];
5. ^{m}EN-*šú-nu* A-*šú šá* ^{md}EN-ŠEŠ-GAL$_2$-*ši* A ^{m}LU$_2$-^{d}IDIM ^{md}EN-[...]	(5) Bēlšunu son of Bēl-aḫa-šubši descendant of Amēl-Ea; Bēl-[...];

6. ^{m}*ri-mut A-šú šá* ^{m}*na-din*-A DUMU ^{lu2}UŠ.BAR ^{md}INNIN.NA-MU-URI$_3$ *A-šú šá* ^{m}ŠU A ⌜m⌝[*ku-ri-i*]

(6) Rīmūt son of Nādin-apli descendant of Išparu; Innin-šuma-uṣur son of Gimillu descendant of [Kurī];

7. ^{md}NA$_3$-TIN-*iṭ* DUMU-*šú šá* ^{m}*ina*-E$_2$.SAGIIL$_2$-NUMUN DUMU ^{m}LU$_2$-^{d}⌜IDIM⌝

(7) Nabû-uballiṭ son of Ina-Esagil-zēri descendant of Amēl-Ea;

8. ^{m}IR$_3$-^{d}U.GUR A-*šú šá* ^{m}*ki-na-a* DUMU ^{m}*e-gì-bi* ^{md}*A*-⌜*nim*⌝-MU-DU$_3$ A-*šú šá* ^{md}NA$_3$-KAR A ^{md}NA$_3$-*šar-ḫi*-DINGIR.MEŠ

(8) Arad-Nergal son of Kīnaya descendant of Egibi; Anim-šuma-ibni son of Nabû-ēṭir descendant of Nabû-šarḫi-ilī;

9. ^{lu2}DUMU.DU$_3$.MEŠ *šá ina pa-ni-šú-nu* ^{md}INNIN-*a-lik-pa-ni* ^{lu2}RIG$_7$ ^{d}INNIN UNUG^{ki}

10. ^{lu2}*na-qí-du šá* ^{d}INNIN UNUG^{ki} *iq-bu-ú um-ma*

(9–10) The *mār banî* before whom Ištar-ālik-pāni, an oblate of Ištar of Uruk, a herdsman of Ištar of Uruk, said thus:

11. ^{m}EN-*šú-nu* ^{lu2}RIG$_7$ ^{d}INNIN UNUG^{ki} DUMU-*šú šá*

12. ^{m}ZALAG$_2$-*e-a a-na ši-gi-il-ti a-na* U$_8$.HI.A

13. NIG$_2$.GA ^{d}INNIN UNUG^{ki} *šá ina* IGI-*i-a ki-i ú-ri-du*

14. 1-*et-ta ina* U$_8$.HI.A *šá kak-kab-tú šen-de-e-ti*

15. *ul-tu* U$_8$.HI.A NIG$_2$.GA ^{d}INNIN UNUG^{ki} *šá ina* IGI-*i-a ki-i i-bu-uk*?

(11–16) "When Bēlšunu, an oblate of Ištar of Uruk, son of Nūrea, unlawfully went down into the (flock of) ewes, property of Ištar of Uruk, which is in my charge (and) led away 1 ewe branded with a star, from the ewes, property of Ištar of Uruk, which is in my charge, he killed (it)."

16. *it-te-kis a-na muḫ-ḫi ki-i aq-ba-áš-šú um-ma* U$_8$.HI.A

17. *šá kak-kab-tu*$_4$ AN.BAR *la ta-nak-kis qaq-qa-da-a ki-i ip-ṭu-ru*

18. *i-na ku-dúr-ra ša ti-ik-ki-šú iḫ-ta-qa-an-ni ù*

19. *i-qab-ba-*ʾ *um-ma lìb-bu-ú a-ga-a* ^{m}*gu-ba-ru*

20. *ù* ^{m}*par-nak ku-dúr-ra ti-ik-ku šá* ^{lu2}ERIM$_2$.MEŠ *i-na-ad-du-ú*

(16–20) "When I said to him thus: 'You must not kill the iron-starred ewe!' he uncovered my head, choked me with the *kudurru* on his neck, while saying thus: 'In this way, they will cast the workmen's neck-*kudurru* upon Gobryas and Pharnaces.'"

21. UKKIN ^{lu_2}DUMU TIN.TIR *u* UNUG^{ki} ^{lu_2}*ki-niš-tu*$_4$ E$_2$.AN.NA ^{m}EN-*šú-nu* 22. *i-bu-ku-nim-ma ina* UKKIN *iš-šá-al-lu-ma iq-bu-šú um-ma*	(21–22) The assembly of Babylonians and Urukians (and) the collegium of the Eanna brought Bēlšunu (before them), and interrogated him in the assembly, (saying) thus:
23. *mi-nam-ma* UDU.HI.A *šá kak-kab-tu*$_4$ AN.BAR *tab-*⌜*bu*⌝*-*[*uk tek*]*-kis*	(23) "Why did you lead away (and) kill iron-starred sheep?"
24. ^{m}EN-*šú-nu ina* [UKKIN ^{lu_2}DUMU.DU$_3$] UGU *ram-ni-šú ú-kin-*[*ni šá*] 25. UDU.HI.A *šá kak-kab-tu*$_4$ *ul-tu* UDU.HI.A *šá* ^{d}INNIN [UNUG^{ki} *šá ina* IGI] 26. ^{md}INNIN-*a-lik*-IGI *a-na* ^{lu_2}*na-qid-du-tu* [...]	(24–26) In the [assembly of the *mār banî*] Bēlšunu testifi[ed] against himself [regarding] the sheep with a star from the sheep of Ištar of [Uruk in the charge of] Ištar-ālik-pāni, for herding.
27. [...] ^{m}EN-*šú-nu a-na ši-gi-il-*[*ti u-rid* 1 U$_8$.HI.A *šá*]	(27–28) Bēlšunu, unlawfully [went down and] killed [1 ewe] of Ištar of Uruk.
28. ⌜^{d}INNIN⌝ UNUG^{ki} *ik-ki-is* UKKIN ^{lu_2}DUMU.DU$_3$ [29. *ki-i ṣi-in-da-a-tú* E$_2$.KUR [...] 30. *a-na e-ṭe-ru* UGU ^{m}EN-[*šú-nu ip-ru-su*]	(28–30) The assembly of the *mār banî* ... in accordance with the regulations of the Ekur [decided] that Bēl[šunu] must return...
31. ^{lu_2}UMBISAG ^{md}UTU-NUMUN-MU A-*šú šá* ^{m}*a-ḫu-lap-*^{d}INNIN	(31–32) Scribe: Šamaš-zēra-iddin son of Aḫulap-Ištar descendant of Ekur-zakir.
32. A ^{m}E$_2$.KUR-*za-kir* UNUG^{ki} ITI DU$_6$ U$_4$ 13-*kám* 33. MU 2-*kám* ^{m}*kám-bu-zi-iá* LUGAL TIN.TIR^{ki} 34. LUGAL KUR.KUR	(32–34) Uruk. 13 Tašrītu, year 2 of Cambyses, king of Babylon, king of the lands.

Notes

1. The first name on this tablet is probably that of Marduk-šuma-iddin son of Nabû-aḫḫē-bulliṭ descendant of Balāṭu, who often appears as a witness on documents from the Eanna (Kümmel 1979, 93). He may have been an important prebendiary (Kümmel 1979, 150).

2. Name restored based on Kümmel 1979, 143 n. 263.

11. A fisherman named Bēlšunu son of Nūrea is attested in another record from the Eanna (Kümmel 1979, 93).

16–20. Gobryas was the Persian satrap of Babylonia and the Transeuphratene territories, appointed by Cyrus the Great (ruled Babylonia 539–530), father of Cambyses (530–522). Under Cambyses, Gobryas's subordinate was Pharnaces. During the reign of Cambyses's successor, Darius I (522–486), Pharnaces held important positions in the royal palace. Although these lines describe charges of treason (against the royal officials) and violence (against the plaintiff), the implications of these charges are not manifest in the record as preserved. The assembly's decision at the end of the record apparently pertains only to the offense against the Eanna's livestock property.

23. The "iron-starred sheep" refers to sheep branded with an iron brand shaped like a star.

31. The Case of a Branded Temple Servant

Text: YBC 7428
Copy: Tremayne 1925 (YOS 7), No. 66
Translation/Discussion: Dougherty 1923, 34–35; Mendelsohn 1949, 151–52; Dandamaev 1984, 409–10, 478–79
Place of Composition: Uruk
Date: 23.III.7 Cyr (5 July, 532 BCE)

Nuptaya, a slave whose hand has been branded with a star, indicating she has been dedicated to the Lady of Uruk, testifies that her first master, Iddin-aḫa, dedicated her to the Eanna. When Iddin-aḫa died, his brother, Šamaš-zēra-šubši, inherited Nuptaya but did not give her up to the Eanna. After entering the possession of her new master, Nuptaya has given birth to three sons. The authorities in the Eanna inspect the marking on her hand and temporarily place her in Šamaš-zēra-šubši's possession. Šamaš-zēra-šubši may not marry her to a slave, and, upon his death, she and her children shall revert to the possession of the Lady of Uruk.

The proceedings recorded here probably began because the Eanna sought to gain control of Nuptaya, who was obviously marked as a slave belonging to the Lady of Uruk. Nabû-zēra-šubši, in taking possession of the slave when his brother died, seems to have acted against his brother's intent and in violation of the Eanna's claim to Nuptaya (compare Document 21 above). From this perspective, however, the outcome of the case remains a bit puzzling. Why were Nuptaya and her children allowed to remain in Šamaš-zēra-šubši's possession, even temporarily? In allowing this arrangement, the Eanna authorities gain an economic advantage: the children will be raised at Šamaš-zēra-šubši's expense, rather than the temple's.

1. ^{f}*nu-up-ta-a* GEME$_2$ *šá* ^{m}SUM.NA-ŠEŠ A-*šú šá* ^{md}NA$_3$-ŠEŠ.MEŠ-GI	(1–2) Nuptaya, female slave of Iddin-aḫa son of Nabû-aḫḫē-šullim, who said thus:
2. *šá taq-bu-ú um-ma* ^{m}SUM.NA-ŠEŠ EN-*ia kak-kab-tu*$_4$	(2–3) "When Iddin-aḫa, my master, marked me with a star he dedicated me to the [Lady] of Uruk."
3. *ki-i iš-mi-tan-ni a-na* [^{d}GAŠA]N *šá* UNUG^{ki} *uz-zak-kan-nu*	

4. ^{m}SUM.NA-ŠEŠ EN-*a šim-tu*$_4$ *u-bil-šu-ma* ^{md}UTU-NUMUN-GAL$_2$-*ši*
5. ŠEŠ *šá* ^{m}SUM.NA-ŠEŠ *šá ár-ka-tu*$_4$ ^{m}SUM.NA-ŠEŠ *il-qú-ú*
6. *ul-tu* E$_2$ ^{m}SUM-*na*-ŠEŠ *i-bu-kan-ni-ma a-na* ^{d}INNIN UNUG^{ki}

(4–7) "Iddin-aḫa, my master, died, and Šamaš-zēra-šubši, Iddin-aḫa's brother, who received Iddin-aḫa's inheritance, took me away from the house of Iddin-aḫa, but did not give me to Ištar of Uruk."

7. *la id-di-na-an-ni* ^{m}*su-qa-a-a* ^{m}SUM.NA-^{d}NA$_3$
8. *ù* ^{md}NA$_3$-ŠEŠ-*it-tan-nu* DUMU.MEŠ-*e-a ina* E$_2$ ^{md}UTU-NUMUN-GAL$_2$-*ši ú-lid*

(7–8) "I gave birth to Sūqaya, Iddin-Nabû and Nabû-aḫa-ittannu, my sons, in the house of Šamaš-zēra-šubši."

9. ^{md}*a-nu*-LUGAL-URI$_3$ ^{lu2}*qi-i-pi šá* E$_2$.AN.NA ^{md}NA$_3$-DU-A
10. ^{lu2}ŠA$_3$.TAM E$_2$.AN.NA A-*šú šá* ^{m}*na-di-nu* A ^{m}*da-bi-bi* ^{md}NA$_3$-ŠEŠ-MU
11. ^{lu2}SAG-LUGAL ^{lu2}EN *pi-qit-tu*$_4$ E$_2$.AN.NA *ù* ^{lu2}DUB.SAR.ME
12. *šá* E$_2$.AN.NA *kak-kab-tu*$_4$ *šá muḫ-ḫi ri-it-ti-šú i-mu-ru*

(9–12) Anu-šarra-uṣur, the *qīpu*-official of the Eanna, Nabû-mukīn-apli, the *šatammu* of the Eanna, son of Nādinu descendant of Dābibī, Nabû-aḫa-iddin, the royal official in charge of the Eanna and the scribes of the Eanna inspected the star on her hand.

13. ^{md}*a-nu*-LUGAL-URI$_3$ ^{lu2}*qi-i-pi šá* E$_2$.AN.NA ^{md}NA$_3$-DU-A
14. ^{lu2}ŠA$_3$.TAM E$_2$.AN.NA ^{md}NA$_3$-ŠEŠ-MU ^{lu2}SAG-LUGAL ^{lu2}EN *pi-qit* E$_2$.AN.NA
15. *ù* ^{lu2}DUB.SAR.ME *šá* E$_2$.AN.NA ^{f}*nu-up-ta-a* ^{m}*su-qa-a-a*
16. ^{m}SUM.NA-^{d}NA$_3$ *u* ^{md}NA$_3$-ŠEŠ-*it-tan-nu* DUMU.MEŠ-*šú*

(13–17) Anu-šarra-uṣur, the *qīpu*-official of the Eanna, Nabû-mukīn-apli, the *šatammu* of the Eanna, Nabû-aḫa-iddin, the royal official in charge of the Eanna, and the scribes of the Eanna deposited Nuptaya (and) Sūqaya, Iddin-Nabû and Nabû-aḫa-ittannu, her sons, in the possession of Šamaš-zēra-šubši.

17. *ina pa-ni* ^{md}UTU-NUMUN-GAL$_2$-*ši ip-qi-du* U$_4$-*mu ma-la*
18. *šá* ^{md}UTU-NUMUN-GAL$_2$-*ši bal-ṭu ta-pal-la-aḫ-šú ul i-ṣab-bi-ma*
19. ^{md}UTU-NUMUN-GAL$_2$-*ši a-na* KU$_3$.BABBAR *ul i-nam-din ù a-na* IR$_3$ *ul* [*i-ḫir-ri*]

(17–19) For as long as Šamaš-zēra-šubši lives, she shall serve him. Šamaš-zēra-šubši does not intend to sell her for silver nor [marry] her to a slave.

20. [*ár*]-*ki* ^{md}UTU-NUMUN-GAL$_2$-*ši a-na šim-tu*$_4$ *it-tal-lak*	(20–21) [Af]ter Šamaš-zēra-šubši dies, the [sl]aves shall be at the disposal of the Lady of Uruk.
21. [^{lu_2}] ⸢*a*⸣-*me-lut-tu*$_4$ *pa-ni* ^{d}GAŠAN *šá* UNUG^{ki} *ta-ad-da-gal*	
22. [^{lu_2}MU].DU ^{md}EN-*na-din*-A A-*šú šá* ^{md}AMAR.UTU-MU-MU A ^{md}EN-A-PAP	(22) [Witn]esses: Bēl-nādin-apli son of Marduk-šuma-iddin descendant of Bēl-apla-uṣur;
23. [^{m}IR$_3$]-⸢*ia*⸣ A-*šú šá* ^{m}GAR-MU A ^{m}ŠU-^{d}*na-na-a* ^{md}*a-nu*-MU-DU$_3$	(23–24) [Ardiya] son of Šākin-šumi descendant of Gimil-Nanaya; Anu-šuma-ibni [son of N]abû-ušēzib descendant of Nabû-šarḫi-ilī;
24. [A-*šú šá* ^{md}N]A$_3$-SUR A ^{md}NA$_3$-*šar-ḫi*-DINGIR ^{md}*in-nin*-MU-URI$_3$	(24–25) Innin-šuma-uṣur [son of] Gimillu descendant of Kurī;
25. [A-*šú šá* ^{m}]*gi-mil-lu* A ^{m}*kur-i* ^{md}INNIN-DU-A A-*šú šá* ^{md}NA$_3$-DU$_3$-ŠEŠ	(25–26) Ištar-mukīn-apli son of Nabû-bāni-aḫi [descendant of PN];
26. [A PN] ^{md}UTU-DU-A DUB.SAR A-*šú šá* ^{m}*na-din* A ^{m}*e-gi-bi*	(26) Šamaš-mukīn-apli, the scribe, son of Nādin descendant of Egibi.
27. [UNUG^{ki}] ITI SIG$_4$ U$_4$ 23-*kám* MU 7-*kám* ^{m}*ku-ra-áš*	(27–28) Uruk. 23 Simānu, year 7 of Cyrus, king of Babylon, king of the lands.
28. LUGAL TIN.TIR^{ki} LUGAL KUR.KUR	

32. Settling a Debt

Text: BM 41415 (81-6-25, 26)
Copy: Strassmaier 1889a (Nbn), No. 1128
Translation/Discussion: Kohler and Peiser 1890–98, 2:70–71; Wunsch 2002b, 243
Place of Composition: Babylon
Date: 11.XI.[1] Nbn (10 May, 555 BCE; for restoration of the year based on the composition of the tribunal, see Wunsch 1997–98, 98)

Nabû-gāmil argues his case against Mušēzib-Bēl before the sartennu *and the judges of Nabonidus. Mušēzib-Bēl's father, Nādin, owed a debt to Nabû-gāmil's father, Nabû-aḫḫē-bulliṭ, and property belonging to Nādin was pledged as collateral for the loan. Nabû-gāmil presents the debt-note to the judges and the* sartennu, *while Mušēzib-Bēl is unable to prove that the debt has already been repaid. After deliberation, the* sartennu *and the judges award a parcel of Mušēzib-Bēl's land to Nabû-gāmil. They also seal a tablet, including the precise dimensions of the parcel, to ensure the permanence of the land transfer.*

This case illustrates the continuation of a debt after the death of the original parties to the transaction. The plaintiff and the defendant have both inherited the debt of their fathers, respectively the creditor and the debtor.

Another fragmentary text, apparently a sale, sheds light on the subsequent history of the disputed parcel of land. This other text refers to a parcel of land "that the *sa*[*rtennu*] and the judges entrusted to Nabû-gāmil in payment of the silver of the debt owed to him" (Wunsch 1997–98, No. 36, 3'–7' [p. 98]). The text probably shows that the land was sold soon after the present lawsuit. Although the names of the parties to this apparent sale are missing, the purchaser was probably a member of the Egibi family, who would have preserved both the fragmentary sale record and the present decision record in their archives (Wunsch 1997–98, 99).

1. *[di-i-nu šá]* ^{md}NA$_3$-*ga-mil* DUMU-*šú šá* ^{md}NA$_3$-ŠEŠ.MEŠ-*bul-liṭ* 2. DUMU ^{m}*mi-ṣir-a-a a-na* UGU 2/3 MA.NA 4 GIN$_2$ KU$_3$.BABBAR 3. *ra-šu-tu šá* AD-*šú šá* UGU ^{m}*na-din* DUMU-*šú šá* ^{md}NA$_3$-MU-MU 4. DUMU ^{lu_2}GAL-DU$_3$ *it-ti* ^{m}*mu-še-zib*-^{d}EN DUMU-*šú šá* 5. ^{m}*na-di-nu* DUMU ^{lu_2}GAL-DU$_3$ *i-na ma-ḫar* ^{md}30-*eri-ba* 6. ^{lu_2}*sar-te-nu ù* ^{lu_2}DI.KU$_5$.MEŠ *šá* ^{md}NA$_3$-*na-ʾi-id* LUGAL TIN.TIR^{ki}	(1–7) [The case which] Nabû-gāmil, son of Nabû-aḫḫē-bulliṭ descendant of Miṣiraya argued against Mušēzib-Bēl son of Nādin descendant of Rāb-bānê, concerning the 2/3 mina 5 šeqels of silver, the debt to his father owed by Nādin son of Nabû-nādin-šumi descendant of Rāb-bānê, before Sîn-erība, the *sartennu,* and the judges of Nabonidus, king of Babylon.
7. *id-bu-bu ú-ìl-tì šá* ^{md}NA$_3$-ŠEŠ.MEŠ-*bul-liṭ* 8. AD *šá* ^{md}NA$_3$-*ga-mil šá* UGU ^{m}*na-di-nu* AD *šá* ^{m}*mu-še-zib*-^{d}EN 9. *šá* E$_2$-*su maš-ka-nu ṣa-ab-tu ma-ḫar-šú-nu*	(7–10) They read before them the debt-note of Nabû-aḫḫē-bulliṭ, father of Nabû-gāmil, owed by Nādinu, father of Mušēzib-Bēl, for which his house was taken as pledge.
10. *il-tas-su-ú* ^{lu_2}*sar-te-nu u* ^{lu_2}DI.KU$_5$.MEŠ 11. *rik-su u i-da-tu šá e-ṭi-ru* ^{m}*mu-še-zib*-^{d}EN	(10–12) The *sartennu* and the judges demanded from Mušēzib-Bēl the contract and the signs (proving his) repayment, but he did not bring (them).
12. *i-ri-šu-ma la ub-la im-tal-ku-ma*	(12) They deliberated.
13. 2 GI.MEŠ *ù šal-šú šá* GI *i-na* GI.MEŠ 14. *šá* ^{m}*mu-še-zib*-^{d}EN DUMU ^{lu_2}GAL-DU$_3$	(13–14) 2 1/3 reeds in the property of Mušēzib-Bēl descendant of Rab-banê—
15. 1 GAR 5$^{!}$ KUŠ$_3$ 14 ŠU.SI UŠ AN.TA 16. IM SI.SA$_2$ DA *mu-ṣu-ú*	(15–16) 1 GAR 5 cubits 14 finger-lengths on the upper side, on the north, adjacent to the exit—
17. *šá ina pu-ti-šú* AN.TA 3 KUŠ$_3$	(17) at whose upper front are 3 cubits
18. *ina* SAG-*šú* KI.TA 4 KUŠ$_3$ 3 ŠU.SI *qaq-qar*	(18) (and) at whose lower front are 4 cubits, 3 fingerlengths, the territory—

19. *a-na ma-la* E$_{2}$ ^{m}*mu-še-zib*-^{d}EN	(19) whatever (is the) house (plot) of Mušēzib-Bēl
20. 1 GAR 5 KUŠ$_{3}$ 14 ŠU.SI UŠ KI.TA IM U$_{18}$-*lu*	(20) 1 GAR 5 cubits 14 fingerlengths on the upper side, in the south
21. *ina* DA *ri-iḫ-ti* E$_{2}$ ^{m}*mu-še-zib*-^{d}EN	(21) adjacent to the remainder of Mušēzib-Bēl's house.
22. 6 KUŠ$_{3}$ 10 ŠU.SI SAG AN.TA IM MAR.TU DA SILA *rap*$^{!}$-*šu-ú*	(22) 6 cubits 10 fingerlengths on the upper front, on the west, adjacent to the wide street.
23. 5 KUŠ$_{3}$ 6 ŠU.SI SAG KI.TA IM KUR.RA DA *mu-ṣe-e* E$_{2}$.MEŠ	(23) 5 cubits 6 fingerlengths on the lower front, on the east, adjacent to the houses' exit.
24. ŠU.NIGIN 2 GI.MEŠ 2 KUŠ$_{3}$ 8 ŠU.SI ^{lu_2}*sar-te-nu u* ^{lu_2}DI.KU$_{5}$.MEŠ	(24–25) TOTAL: 2 reeds, 2 cubits, 8 fingerlengths. The *sartennu* and the judges placed at the disposal of Nabû-gāmil in payment of his silver.
25. *ku-um* [KU$_{3}$.BABBAR]-*šú ina pa-ni* ^{md}NA$_{3}$-*ga-mil ú-šad-gi-lu*	
26. <<*la e-nu šá*>> *a-na la e-ne-e* ^{lu_2}*sar-te-nu u* ^{lu_2}DI.KU$_{5}$.MEŠ	(26–28) So that (the decision) would not be changed improperly, the *sartennu* and the judges [wrote] his tablet, sealed it with their seals, and gave it to Nabû-gāmil.
27. *ṭup-pi-šu* [*išṭurū*] ^{na_4}KIŠIB.MEŠ-*šú-nu ib-ru-mu-ma*	
28. *a-na* ^{md}NA$_{3}$-*ga-mil id-di-nu*	
29. *i-na ša-ṭa-ra ṭup-pi šu-a-tim*	(29) At the writing of this tablet:
30. ^{md}30-*i-ri-ba* ^{lu_2}*sar-te-nu*	(30) Sîn-erība, the *sartennu*;
31. ^{m}E$_{2}$-SAG.IL$_{2}$-*šá-du-nu* ^{lu_2}DI.KU$_{5}$ DUMU ^{m}IR$_{3}$-^{d}*é-a*	(31) Esagil-šadûnu, the judge descendant of Arad-Ea;
32. ^{md}AMAR.UTU-MU-URI$_{3}$ ^{lu_2}DI.KU$_{5}$ DUMU ^{md}IM-*šam-me-e*	(32) Marduk-šuma-uṣur, the judge, descendant of Adad-šammê;
33. ^{m}*mu-še-zib*-^{d}AMAR.UTU ^{lu_2}DI.KU$_{5}$ DUMU ^{md}KASKAL.KUR-*ú*	(33) Mušēzib-Marduk, the judge, descendant of Bālīḫû;
34. ^{md}NA$_{3}$-NUMUN-SI.SA$_{2}$-SI.SA$_{2}$ ^{lu_2}DI.KU$_{5}$ DUMU ^{m}*šul-ma-nu*	(34) Nabû-zēr-kitti-līšir, the judge, descendant of Šulmānu;
35. ^{md}EN-TIN-*iṭ* ^{lu_2}DI.KU$_{5}$ DUMU ^{lu_2}GAL 1-*lim*	(35) Bēl-uballiṭ, the judge, descendant of Rāb-līmi;
36. ^{md}U.GUR-GI ^{lu_2}DI.KU$_{5}$ DUMU ^{m}*ši-gu-ú-a*	(36) Nergal-ušallim, the judge, descendant of Šigûa;
37. ^{m}*ri-mut*-^{d}MAŠ.MAŠ ^{lu_2}DI.KU$_{5}$ DUMU ^{m}*sag-gil-a-a*	(37) Rīmūt-Nergal, the judge, descendant of Saggilaya;

38. ^{md}U.GUR-*ba-nu-nu* DUB.SAR DUMU ^{lu_2}GAL-DU$_3$	(38) Nergal-bānûnu, the scribe, descendant of Rāb-banê;
39. ^{md}NA$_3$-ŠEŠ.MEŠ-MU DUB.SAR DUMU ^{m}*e-gi-bi*	(39) Nabû-aḫḫē-iddin, the scribe, descendant of Egibi;
40. TIN.TIR^{ki} ITI ZIZ$_2$ U$_4$ 11-*kám*	(40–41) Babylon. 11 Šabāṭu, [year 1] of Nabonidus, king of Babylon.
41. [MU 1]-*kám* ^{md}NA$_3$-*na-'i-id* LUGAL TIN.TIR^{ki}	

NOTES

For seals and inscriptions see Wunsch 1997–98, No. 35 (p. 99).
Reading of this document is based on the collations of Cornelia Wunsch.

13–14. The total area recorded in these lines is given as 2 1/3 reeds, which is the same as the total area recorded in lines 24–25: 2 reeds, 2 cubits and 8 fingerlengths.

15–16. The tablet and drawings clearly have 1 GAR 2 (instead of 5) KUŠ$_3$ 14 ŠU.SI. The reading 1 GAR 5$^!$ KUŠ$_3$ 14 ŠU.SI is required by the following calculations:

Area (A) = 2 1/3 surface reeds (lines 13–14)
Area (A) = 14 + 7/3 surface cubits (7 cubits/reed)
Area (A) = 114 + 1/3 square cubits (7 square cubits/ surface cubit)

This area measurement (A) reflects the product of the average of the length of the "sides" (L_S) and the average of the length of the "fronts" (L_F) ($A = L_S$ X L_F). Using values from lines 22 and 23,

$L_F = [6 + 10/24 + 5 + 6/24] / 2 = 5 + 20/24$ cubits.
Since $A = L_S$ X L_F , $L_S = A/L_F$, or
$L_S = (114 + 8/24)$ square cubits/ $(5 + 20/24)$
$L_S \sim 19 + 14/24$ square cubits

L_S should also equal the average of the two "sides" (lines 15 and 20). In line 20, the measurement is 19 + 14/24 square cubits: 1 GAR (= 14 square cubits) + 5 square cubits + 14/24 square cubits. Threfore, for the average of the measurement in line 15 and the measurement in line 20 to equal 19 + 14/24 square cubits, the measurement in line 15 must equal the measurement in line 20.

26. Examination of the tablet reveals traces of erasure at the beginning of this line. The scribe apparently corrected his formulation of the clause.

33. A Case from the Ebabbar at Sippar

Text: BM 74974 (83-1-18, 297)
Copy: Strassmaier 1890a (Cyr), No. 412
Translation/Discussion: Joannès 2002a; Dandamaev 2006, 390
Place of Composition: Sippar
Date: 27.XI.8 Cyr (20 February, 530 BCE)

Šamaš-iddin and Šamaš-uballiṭ settle a debt before the šangû *of Sippar, the "temple enterers" of the Ebabbar and the elders of Sippar. There are two debt-notes in question, one for 1/2 mina of silver, contracted during year 1 of Neriglissar (559–558 BCE), and one for 1 1/2 mina of silver, contracted during the reign of Nabonidus (555–538 BCE). Both debts were owed by Nergal-ēṭir, father of Šamaš-uballiṭ, to Nergal-iddin, father of Šamaš-iddin. By the time of the present document's composition, the two litigants have inherited their respective fathers' positions in the debt, with Šamaš-uballiṭ in debt to Šamaš-iddin. Šamaš-iddin presents the debt for collection. The authorities apparently arrange for Šamaš-uballiṭ to return earlier copies of the notes to Šamaš-iddin.*

The breaks in the present document make a full reconstruction of the case's narrative difficult. One main difficulty lies with the return of the documents from Šamaš-uballiṭ to Šamaš-iddin. Under normal circumstances, Šamaš-uballiṭ, as debtor, would not be in possession of the debt-notes.

Despite the broken text and the resulting uncertainties, the present document is valuable because it can be compared, from the perspective of the administration of justice, to similar documents from the Eanna at Uruk. In the present document, the *šangû* of Sippar, who stood at the head of the Ebabbar's administration, adjudicates the case together with the "temple enterers," those who held certain temple prebends (Bongenaar 1997, 149), and the "elders of Sippar." At Gimillu's trial in the Eanna (Document 38 below), the *šatammu,* whose function was similar to that of the *šangû* (Bongenaar 1997, 12), was part of the adjudicating panel, together with "the assembly of Babylonians and Urukians." Similarly, the "temple enterers" in the present document may be compared with the "collegium" (*kiništu*) at Uruk (see Document 30 above) (Bongenaar 1997, 150–53).

1. *ú-ìl-tì šá* 1/2 MA.NA KU$_3$.BABBAR *šá* KASKAL.2 *šá* MU 1-*kam* ^{md}U.GUR-[LUGAL.URI$_3$] 2. LUGAL E^{ki} *ù ú-il-tì šá* 1 1/2 MA.NA KU$_3$.BABBAR *šá* KASKAL.2 *šá* MU [X-*kam*] 3. ^{md}NA$_3$-I LUGAL E^{ki} *šá* ^{md}U.GUR-MU A-*šú šá* ^{md}NA$_3$-SU [*šá ina muḫ-ḫi*] 4. ^{md}U.GUR-SUR A-*šú šá* ^{m}*šá*-^{d}NA$_3$-*šu-ú* A ^{lu_2}NAGAR *šá* MU 8-[*kam*]	(1–4) A debt-note for 1/2 mina of silver, business capital, from year 1 of Neriglissar, king of Babylon, and a debt-note for 1 1/2 mina of silver, business capital from year [X] of Nabonidus, king of Babylon, belonging to Nergal-iddin son of Nabû-erīb [owed by] Nergal-ēṭir son of Ša-Nabû-šū descendant of Naggāru —
5. [^{m}*kur-raš*] LUGAL E^{ki} LUGAL KUR.KUR ^{md}UTU-MU A-*šú šá* ^{md}U.GUR-MU 6. *ina* UGU ^{md}UTU-TIN-*iṭ* A-*šú šá* ^{md}U.GUR-SUR *iš-ša-a-ʾ ina ma-ḫar*	(4–6) which, in year 8 of [Cyrus], king of Babylon, king of the lands, Šamaš-iddin son of Nergal-iddin brought (to court, for collection as) owed by Šamaš-uballiṭ son of Nergal-ēṭir.
7. [^{md}EN-TIN-*iṭ* ^{lu_2}SANGA *sip-par*]^{ki} ^{lu_2}KU$_4$ E$_2$ ^{d}UTU ^{lu_2}AB.BA.MEŠ URU 8. [*iš-tas-su-ú*] ^{md}UTU-TIN-*iṭ ú-ìl-tì*.MEŠ GABA.RI	(6–8) [They read] (them) before [Bēl-uballiṭ, the *šangû* of Sippar], the "temple enterers" of Šamaš (and) the elders of the city.
9. [*ú*]-⸢*íl-tì*.MEŠ⸣ […] ^{md}EN-TIN-*iṭ* ^{lu_2}SANGA *sip-par*^{ki} 10. ^{lu_2}KU$_4$ E$_2$ ^{d}UTU ^{lu_2}AB.BA.MEŠ URU *a-na* ^{md}UTU-MU A-*šú šá* ^{md}U.GUR-MU	(8–11) Šamaš-uballiṭ showed the copies of the debt-notes and the original debt- notes to Šamaš-iddin son of Nergal-iddin … Bēl-uballiṭ, the *šangû* of Sippar, the "temple enterers" of Šamaš (and) the elders of the city.
11. [*ú-kal-lim*] ^{md}EN-TIN-*iṭ* ^{lu_2}KU$_4$ E$_2$ ^{d}UTU ^{lu_2}AB.BA.MEŠ URU 12. [*ú-íl-tì*.MEŠ *ki-i*] *ú-tir-ru-ma a-na* ^{md}UTU-MU 13. [*i-din-nu* ...]	(11–13) [When] he returned [the debt-notes], Bēl-uballiṭ, the "temple enterers" of Šamaš and the elders of the city [gave (them)] to Šamaš-iddin.
1'. […]	1.'
2.' ^{md}EN-A-MU ^{lu_2}KU$_4$-E$_2$ ⸢^{d}⸣[UTU A ^{lu_2}SANGA *sip*]-*par*^{ki}	(2') Bēl-apla-iddin, the "temple enterer" of [Šamaš descendant of Šangû-Sip]par;

3'. ^{m}BA-*šá*-^{d}AMAR.UTU A-*šú šá* ^{m}*e-til-*⸢*lu* A ^{lú_2}SANGA *sip-par*^{ki}⸣	(3') Iqīša-Marduk son of Etillu descendant of Šangû-Sippar;
4'. ^{md}NA$_3$-ŠEŠ.MEŠ-GI A-*šú šá* ^{m}KAR-^{d}AMAR.UTU A ^{lú_2}SANGA-^{d}INNIN-TIN.TIR^{ki}	(4') Nabû-aḫḫē-šullim son of Mušēzib-Marduk descendant of Šangû-Ištar-Bābili;
5'. ^{m}IR$_3$-^{d}EN ^{lú_2}UMBISAG A-*šú šá* ^{md}EN-GI A ^{md}IM-*šam-me-e*	(5') Scribe: Arad-Bēl son of Bēl-ušallim descendant of Adad-šammê;
6'. UD.KIB.NUN^{ki} ITI ZIZ$_2$ U$_4$ 27-*kám* MU 8-*kám* ^{m}*kur-*⸢*ráš*⸣	(6'–7') Sippar. 27 Šabāṭu, year 8 of Cyrus, king of Babylon, king of the lands.
7'. LUGAL TIN.TIR^{ki} LUGAL KUR.KUR	

NOTES

Reading of this document is based on the collations of Cornelia Wunsch. She has detected possible traces of seals on the document.

6'–7'. Collation of these lines shows that the present document dates to the reign of Cyrus. The document's inclusion in Strassmaier 1890a (a collection of documents from the reign of Cambyses) erroneously implies that it was written during the reign of Cambyses.

34. A Case regarding Prebends

Text: BM 42299 (81-7-1, 59)
Copy: Jursa 1999, pls. 1–2
Translation/Discussion: Jursa 1999, 128–29
Place of Composition: Sippar
Date: 11.VII.? Dar (September–October, 521–486 BCE)

Šamaš-aḫḫē-lu-irši makes a claim against Šamaš-nāṣir regarding ownership of rights to income from certain prebends (the "baker's prebend" and the "red baskets"). Prior to the present lawsuit, Šamaš-nāṣir purchased the prebends from Šamaš-aḫḫē-lu-irši and his brother, Nabû-uṣuršu. Now, Šamaš-aḫḫē-lu-irši claims that they belong to his nephew, Nidintu, son of (the apparently dead) Nabû-uṣuršu, as part of an inheritance from Šamaš-kāṣir, father of Nabû-uṣuršu and Šamaš-aḫḫē-lu-irši. Before the elders of Sippar, Šamaš-nāṣir defends his rights to the prebends by presenting the document of purchase and the document indicating that he delegated the prebendary obligations (but not ownership of the prebends) to Šamaš-aḫḫē-lu-irši. On the other hand, Šamaš-aḫḫē-lu-irši is unable to produce any documentation to support his own claim. Fearing recriminations for raising a false claim, Šamaš-aḫḫē-lu-irši concedes and releases the prebends to Šamaš-nāṣir. Šamaš-nāṣir voluntarily pays Šamaš-aḫḫē-lu-irši an additional 1 mina and 5 šeqels of silver.

Prebendary income, connected to the management and operation of the temples' cultic activities, was an important component of the "wealth portfolio" of families that are attested in many of the Neo-Babylonian cuneiform archives (Jursa 2005, 31–35). The owners of the prebends received income from the temple in exchange for nominal obligations of service. The prebendary rights were treated as property; as the present document shows, they could be sold or leased for profit, and were inherited like other wealth. Apart from its economic value, prebend ownership probably had significant prestige or religious value, as well. These non-monetary considerations seem to have motivated Šamaš-nāṣir, the owner of the prebends in question here, as well as his brother, Bēl-rēmanni, the main protagonist in the archive to which the present document belongs. The archive shows that both brothers preferred prebends over other spheres of economic activity. They may have purchased prebends in order to advance their own social standing (Jursa 1999, 85).

The prebend owners themselves often did not perform the actual temple duties required by the prebend. Instead, in order to meet their obligations, they would contract with other prebendiaries. This common practice could, understandably, lead to some confusion about who properly owned any particular prebend. One may speculate that this kind of confusion, alongside more typical inheritance-related matters, led to the lawsuit in the present document.

The present document is a copy, rather than the original decision record (Jursa 1999, 11). Copyist's errors explain some of the the awkward constructions and redundancies in the version here (see lines 30–31; Jursa 1999, 11). The archive to which the present document belongs includes several other copied documents. The noticeable number of copies apparently indicates that the archive served as a tool for scribal training (Jursa 1999, 11; Jursa 2005, 127–28).

1. U_4 23-*kám* U_4 24-*kám* U_4 29-*kám* U_4 30-*kám šá* ITI BAR_2.KAM_2	(1) Day 23, 24, 29, 30 of the month of Nisannu;
2. U_4 23-*kám* U_4 24-*kám* U_4 29-*kám* U_4 30-*kám šá* ITI GU_4.KAM_2	(2) Day 23, 24, 29, 30 of the month of Ayaru;
3. U_4 23-*kám* U_4 24-*kám* U_4 29-*kám* U_4 30-*kám šá* ITI SIG_4.KAM_2	(3) Day 23, 24, 29, 30 of the month of Simānu;
4. U_4 23-*kám* U_4 24-*kám* U_4 29-*kám* U_4 30-*kám šá* ITI ŠU U_4 29-*kám* U_4 30-*kám*	(4–5) Day 23, 24, 29 of the month of Dûzu; Day 29, 30 of the month of Abu;
5. *šá* ⸢ITI NE⸣ U_4 29-*kám* U_4 30-*kám šá* ITI KIN.KAM_2 U_4 29-*kám* U_4 30-*kám*	(5) Day 29, 30 of the month of Ulūlu;
6. *šá* ITI DU_6 U_4 ⸢29⸣-*kám* U_4 30-*kám mi-šil* U_4-*mu šá* ITI APIN.KAM_2	(5–6) Day 29, 30 of the month of Tašrītu; Day 29, 30—1/2 day—of the month of Araḫšamna;
7. U_4 27-*kám* U_4 ⸢28⸣-*kám šá* ITI GAN U_4 27-*kám* U_4 28-*kám šá* ITI AB	(7) Day 27, 28 of the month of Kislīmu; Day 27, 28 of the month of Ṭebētu;
8. ⸢U_4⸣ 27-*kám* U_4 28-*kám šá* ITI ZIZ_2 U_4 27-*kám* U_4 28-*kám mi-šil* U_4-*mu šá* ITI ŠE	(8) Day 27, 28 of the month of Šabāṭu; Day 27, 28—1/2 day—of the month of Addaru.
9. [PAP 2]-*ta* U_4 15-*kám*.MEŠ ^{giš}ŠUB.BA ^{lu_2}MUHALDIM-*ú-tú i-na* U_4 15-*kám* EGIR-tu_4	(9–10) [Total: 2] 15 day periods—the baker's prebend—in the second 15-day period—by mo[nth]—in Ebabbar, the Temple of Šamaš at Sippar.
10. [ITI-*u*]*s-su ina* E_2.BABBAR.RA E_2-^{d}UTU *šá* UD.KIB.NUN^{ki}	
11. [2-*ta* U_4-*mu mi-š*]*i*[*l* U_4]-*mu sel-le-e sa-mu-tu šá* U_4 10-*kám* U_4 11-*kám* 1/2 [U_4 12-*kám*]	(11–12) [2 1/2 da]ys' "red baskets": of day 10, 11 (and) 1/2 of [12 of the month of Nisan]nu;

12. [*šá* ITI BA]R$_2$ 1-*en* U$_4$-*mu mi-šil* U$_4$-⸢*mu*⸣ *sel-le-e sa-mu-ú-tu šá* 13. [U$_4$ 10 +]-4-*kám* ⸢*ú*⸣ *mi-šil u$_4$-mu šá* U$_4$ ⸢15⸣-*kám šá še-e-ri ù*	(12–14) 1 1/2 days' "red baskets": of day [1]4 and 1/2 of 15—of the morning—and … of the month of Ayaru.
14. [x x x] ⸢U$_4$⸣-*mu šá* ITI GU$_4$ *pa*-⸢*ni*⸣ [^{d}UTU] ^{d}*a-a si-ḫi*-⸢*ir*⸣-*tu$_4$* 15. [^{d}GAŠAN *sip-par*]^{ki} *ù pa-ni* ^{d}INANNA GAŠAN *a-*[*ga-d*]*è*^{ki} *šá ina* ITI ⸢DIRI.ŠE.KIN.KUD⸣ 16. [MU SA]G.NAM.LUGAL.LA ^{m}*da-ri-ʾi-muš* LUGAL 17. [^{md}UTU-*na*]-⸢*ṣir*⸣ DUMU *šá* ^{m}*mu-šeb-ši-*^{d}AMAR.UTU A ^{lú}SANGA-^{d}UTU 18. [*ina* ŠU.2 ^{md}NA$_3$-*ú-ṣ*]*ur-šú u* ^{md}UTU.ŠEŠ.MEŠ-*lu*$^{!}$-*ir-ši* DUMU.MEŠ *šá* 19. [^{md}UTU-KAD$_2$ A] ^{lú}PA.ŠE^{ki} *a-na kàs-sap a-na* ŠAM$_2$	(14–20) (The prebends) before [Šamaš] (and) Aya of the courtyard, [Lady-of-Sippar], and before Ištar, Lady of Ak[kad]—which, in the intercalary Addaru, in the access[ion year] of Darius the king, [Šamaš]-nāṣir son of Mušebši-Marduk, descendant of Šangû-Šamaš, recei[ved from Nabû-u]ṣuršu and Šamaš-aḫḫē-lū-irši, sons of [Šamaš-kāṣir], descendant of Isinnaya, for the [full] purchase price in silver.
20. [*gam-ru-tu im-ḫu*]-*ru ár-ki* ^{md}UTU-ŠEŠ.MEŠ-*lu-ir-*<*ši*> *ina* ITI DU$_6$ 21. [MU X-*kám* ^{m}*da-ri-ʾi*]-*muš* LUGAL E^{ki} LUGAL KUR.KUR *a-na muḫ-ḫi* 22. [U$_4$-*mu*.MEŠ *u sel*]-*le-e* ^{giš}ŠUB.BA *šu-ma-tì* ^{lú}MUHALDIM-*ú-tu*	(20–23) Afterwards, Šamaš-aḫḫē-lu-irši, in Tašrītu, [year X of Dari]us, king of Babylon, king of the lands, raised a claim [against Šamaš-nā]ṣir, regarding these [days] and these baskets, the baker's prebend, saying thus:
23. [*a-na* ^{md}UTU-*na*]-*ṣir ir-gu-um um-ma* ^{giš}ŠUB.BA MU-*tì šá* 24. [^{m}*ni-din-it*]-*tú* DUMU ^{lú}ŠEŠ-*ia šá* ^{md}UTU-*ka-ṣir* AD-*ú*-<*a*> EGIR-*šu*	(23–25) "These prebends belong to [Nidin]tu, the son of my brother, which he [re]ceived from the inheritance of Šamaš-kāṣir, [my] father."

25. [*il*]-*qu-ú ši-na* ^{md}UTU-*na-*⸢*ṣir*⸣ ^{na_4}DUB KI.LAM *šá* ^{giš}ŠUB.BA ⸢MU⸣-<*tì*> 26. *ina* ŠU.2 ^{md}NA$_3$-*ú-ṣur-šú u* ^{md}UTU-ŠEŠ.⸢MEŠ⸣-*lu-ir-ši a-na kàs-sap im-ḫur-ru* 27. *ù šá-ṭa-ru šá* ^{giš}ŠUB.BA ⸢MU-*tì*⸣ *ár-ki* ^{na_4}DUB KI.LAM *a-na e-piš-*⸢*nu*⸣-[*tu*] 28. *a-na* ^{md}⸢UTU⸣-ŠEŠ.MEŠ-*lu-ir-ši* ⸢*id*⸣-*din-nu ina ma-ḫar* ^{lú_2}*ši-bu-tu* URU *a-na*	(25–29) Before the elders of the city, Šamaš-nāṣir [sh]owed Šamaš-aḫḫē-lu-irši the tablet of sale (stating) that he purchased these prebends from Nabû-uṣuršu and Šamaš-aḫḫē-lu-irši for silver and the document (stating) that, after the (issuance) of the tablet of sale, he delegated the performance of the prebendary obligations to Šamaš-aḫḫē-lu-irši.
29. ^{md}UTU-ŠEŠ.MEŠ-*lu-ir-ši* [*ú*]-*kal-lim-su* ^{na_4}DUB KI.LAM *u ša-ṭa-ru ina ma-ḫar*	(29–30) They r[e]ad the tablet of sale and the document before the elders of the city.
30. ^{lú_2}*ši-bu-ú-tu* ⸢URU⸣ *iš-ta-*[*su*]-*ú-ma* ^{md}UTU-ŠEŠ.MEŠ-*lu-ir-ši* ^{na_4}DUB KI.LAM *u ša-ṭa-ru šá e-piš-šú-nu-tu*	(30–31) But, regarding these baker's prebends, [Šamaš-aḫḫē]-lu-irši had no tablet of sale or document concerning performance of obligations.
31. [^{md}UTU-ŠEŠ].MEŠ-*lu-ir-ši ina muḫ-ḫi* ^{giš}ŠUB.BA MU-*tì* ^{lú_2}MUHALDIM-*ú-tu la ir-ši* ^{md}UTU-ŠEŠ.MEŠ-<*lu-ir-ši*> [UGU] *ram-ni-šú* 32. [*ú-kin-n*]*i i-dur-ru-ma* ^{giš}ŠUB. BA MU-*tì ina* IGI ^{md}UTU-*na-ṣir ú-maš-*⸢*šìr*⸣ [*ina mu*]*ḫ-ḫi* MU-*tì*	(31–32) Šamaš-aḫḫē-lu-irši conceded. He was frightened and released these prebends to Šamaš-nāṣir …
33. ^{md}UTU-*na-ṣir i-na mi-*[*gir*] *lìb-bi-šú re-e-mu a-na* ^{md}⸢UTU⸣-ŠEŠ.MEŠ-*lu-ir-ši ir-*[*šu*]-*ma* <<*šá* ^{md}UTU-PAP-*ir*>> 34. <<*ir-šú*>> 1 MA.NA 5 GIN$_2$ [KU$_3$].BABBAR BABBAR-*ú e-lat* KU$_3$.BABBAR [IGI]-⸢*ú*⸣ *šá* ^{na_4}DUB KI.LAM *a-na*	(33–35) Šamaš-nāṣir ha[d] mercy on Šamaš-aḫḫē-lu-irši, and, of his own will, paid Šamaš-aḫḫē-lu-irši 1 mina (and) 5 šeqels of white silver, besides the previous silver in the tablet of sale.
35. ^{md}UTU-ŠEŠ.MEŠ-*lu-ir-*[*ši*] *id-din* ^{giš}ŠUB.BA MU-*tì šá* ^{md}UTU-*na-ṣir šu-ú*	(35) This prebend belongs to Šamaš-nāṣir.

36. ^{lú_2}*mu-kin-nu* ^{m}*ni-din-it*-^{d}AMAR.UTU DUMU *šá* ^{md}⸢UTU⸣-MU-GIŠ A ^{m}DA-AMAR.UTU	(36) Witnesses: Nidinti-Marduk, son of Šamaš-šumu-līšir descendant of Ile’’i-Marduk ;
37. ^{m}*ni-din-it* DUMU *šá* ^{md}*na-din* A ^{lú_2}SIPA ⸢ANŠE-KUR-*i*⸣ ^{m}*ib-na-a* DUMU *šá* ^{m}*na-din*	(37) Nidintu, son of Nādin descendant of Rē’i-sīsî; Ibnaya son of Nādin;
38. ^{m}LU$_2$-^{d}NA$_3$ DUMU *šá* ^{md}EN-MU A ^{m}IR$_3$-GIR$_4$.KU[^{md}EN]-SUR DUMU *šá* ^{md}EN-SUM.NA	(38–39) Amēl-Nabû son of Bēl-iddin descendant of Arad-Nergal; Bēl-ēṭir son of Bēl-iddina descendant of Maštukku;
39. A ^{m}*maš-tuk-ku* ^{m}*ni-din-it* DUMU *šá* ^{md}NA$_3$-*it-tan-nu* [A ^{lú_2}] SANGA ^{d}UTU ^{m}*ḫa-ba-ṣi-ru*	(39–40) Nidintu son of Nabû-ittannu descendant of Šangû-Šamaš; Ḫabaṣīru son of Sîn-aḫa-iddin;
40. DUMU *šá* ^{md}30-ŠEŠ-MU ^{m}*na-pu-uš-tu$_4$* DUMU *šá* ^{md}EN-ŠEŠ.MEŠ-MU	(40–41) Napuštu, son of Bēl-aḫḫē-iddin, descendant of Rē’i-sīsî ;
41. A ^{lú_2}SIPA ⸢ANŠE.KUR⸣.RA ^{md}UTU-TIN-*iṭ* DUMU *šá*	(41) Šamaš-uballiṭ son of …
42. […] ^{m}*šad-din-nu* DUMU *šá* ^{md}EN-GI	(42) Šaddinu son of Bēl-ušallim …
43. [… ^{md}EN]-TIN-*iṭ* DUB.SAR DUMU *šá* ^{m}*li*-⸢*šìr*⸣ A	(43–44) [… Bēl]-uballiṭ, the scribe, son of Līšir descendant of [Šangû-Ištar-Bābili]
44. [^{lú_2}SANGA INANNA-TIN.TIR^{ki} *sip-par*^{ki} ITI] DU$_6$ U$_4$ 11-*kám*	(44) [Sippar.] 11 Tašrītu,
45. [MU X-*kam da-ri-’i*]-*muš* LUGAL TIN.TIR^{ki} LUGAL KUR.KUR	(45) [year X of Dari]us, king of Babylon, king of the lands.

Notes

14. For discussion of the group of deities, including the relatively rarely attested “Aya of the courtyard,” see Jursa 1999, 56–57.

17–18. Šamaš-nāṣir son of Mušebši-Marduk, descendant of Šangû-Šamaš is well attested as a prebendiary in the Ebabbar, as well as in another, smaller sanctuary at Sippar (Bongenaar 1997, 198).

35. A Widow and Her Husband's Creditors

Text: BM 41663+ BM 41698 + BM 41905
Copy: Wunsch 2003, No. 45 (pp. 156–57)
Translation/Discussion: Wunsch 2003, 156–62

Kuttaya and two creditors of her husband, Iddin-Marduk, settle the division of a deposit of silver before the šākin ṭēmi *and judges. The two creditors (one by proxy) provide sworn statements, in which they accept a reduced share of the silver and allow for Kuttaya's own share of the silver.*

Although Iddin-Marduk is named as the original debtor, it his wife, Kuttaya, with whom the creditors must settle matters. Iddin-Marduk's absence from the proceedings indicates that the present situation has arisen in the wake of his death. Furthermore, there do not seem to have been any adult sons or brothers, who would have otherwise assumed legal responsibility in such situations, instead of Kuttaya. What is most remarkable in the present document is that the widow apparently has a claim to the inheritance that is equally as valid as those of the other creditors (Wunsch 2003, 162).

The case itself pertains to a deposit of silver, which would have been held in a "leather purse" (13'–16'; 26'–29'). In Neo-Babylonian legal practice, this kind of deposit functioned quite like a modern-day escrow account. Then, it was used in real estate transactions for which clear title remained in question, such as in cases when the seller died before the sale was complete, without disclosing any liens on the property. The purchaser deposited a portion of the price with a third party until any questions could be resolved, after which the seller could claim the funds (Wunsch 2003, 159–60). In the present document, one must conclude that, because the inheritance of Iddin-Marduk did not cover his debts, the original sale was probably not completed.

The date of the tablet is not preserved. It may have connections to documents in the Egibi archive, and, based on these, may date to a time between the latter half of Nebuchadnezzar's reign and the beginning of Nabonidus's (Wunsch 2003, 161).

1'. [...] UGU ^{m}SUM.NA-[^{d}AMAR. UTU] *i*-⌈x⌉ [...]	1'. ... owed by Iddin-Marduk ...
2'. [...] ^{f}*ku-ut-ta-a* DAM ^{m}MU-[^{d}] AMAR.UTU *ta*-[...]	2'. ... Kuttaya, wife of Iddin-Marduk, ...
3'. [...*a*]-*na* ^{lu_2} TUK.MEŠ *šá* UGU ^{m}MU-^{d}AMAR.UTU *id*-[*di-nu*]	3'. ... which was gi[ven to] the creditors (with debts) owed by Iddin-Marduk

4’. […] ⸢*i*⸣-*na pa-an* ^{md}NA$_3$-MU-GAR-*un* ŠEŠ-*ia ul* ⸢x⸣ […]	4’. “in the possession of Nabû-šuma-iškun, my brother … not […]”
5’. […^{m}]^{d}AMAR.UTU-MU-URI$_3$ ^{lu_2}GAR.UMUŠ$_4$ *ù* ^{lu_2}⸢DI.KU$_5$⸣.MEŠ […]	5’. Marduk-šuma-uṣur, the governor, and the judges […]
6’. [… *id*]-*bu-bu-ú-ma di-in-šú-nu i*-⸢*mur*⸣-⸢*ru*⸣…	6’. … they [ar]gued and they saw to their case…
7’. [^{m}*ri-mut* A]-*šú šá* ^{md}UTU-DA A ^{m}*ár-rab-tu*$_4$ *ù* ^{m}[*ṣil-la-a* A-*šú šá*]	(7’–9’) They [ques]tioned [Rīmūt son] of Šamaš-lēʾi descendant of Arrabtu and [Ṣillaya son of X]-šuma-ibni descendant of Eppeš-ilī, the creditors (with debts) of Iddin-Marduk.
8’. [^{md}X]-MU-DU$_3$ A ^{m}DU$_3$-*eš*-DINGIR ^{lu_2}TUK.MEŠ *šá* UGU ^{m}MU-[^{d}AMAR.UTU]	
9’. [*i-šá*]-⸢*lu-ma*⸣ ^{m}*ri-mut A-šú šá* ^{md}UTU-DA A ^{m}*ár*-[*rab-tu*$_4$]	(9’–11’) Rīmūt son of Šamaš-lēʾi descendant of Arrabtu swore by Šamaš before the judges and [said] thus:
10’. *ina pa-an* ^{lu_2}DI.KU$_5$.MEŠ *niš* ^{d}UTU *iz-kur-ma an-ni*-[*tu iq-bi*]	
11’. *um-ma a-na-ku u* ^{m}*ṣil-la-a* ^{lu_2}TUK.MEŠ *šá* UGU ^{m}MU-[^{d}AMAR.UTU]	(11’) “I and Ṣillaya are the creditors (with debts) owed by Iddin-[Marduk].”
12’. *ul ni-i-du šá* ⸢KU$_3$.BABBAR⸣ *ina pa-an* ^{m}NA$_3$-MU-GAR-*un paq*-[*du*]	(12’) “We did not know that silver was depo[sited] with Nabû-šuma-iškun.”
13’. ^{m}*na-din* DAM *šá* [^{f}*i-lat*…] NIN *šá* ^{m}SUM.⸢NA⸣-[^{d}AMAR.UTU *u*]	(13’–16’) “When Nādin, husband of [Ilat] … , sister of Iddin-[Marduk] [and] Kuttaya, [wife of Iddin-Marduk] brought us before … the leather purse of [Iddin-Marduk] which was deposited with him, when he took it and, before us …”
14’. ^{f}*ku*-[*ut*]-*ta*-[*a* DAM ^{m}MU-AMAR.UTU] *a-na* ⸢*pa*⸣-*a*[*n* …]	
15’. *ki*-⸢*i*⸣ [*i-bu-ku-na*]-*a-šú* ^{kuš}*ḫi-in-du šá* [^{m}MU-^{d}AMAR.UTU]	
16’. *šá* [*ina pa-ni*]-⸢*šú paq*⸣-*da-tu ki-i iš-šá-a ina pa-ni-ni* ⸢*i*⸣-	
17’. [x MA.N]A ⸢KU$_3$.BABBAR⸣ *ina lìb-bi* ^{f}*ku-ut-ta-a* DAM ^{m}MU-^{d}AMAR.UTU *ta*-[…]	(17’) “[x mina] of silver from which Kuttaya wife of Iddin-Marduk [received?]”
18’. [*ù*] ⸢*šit*⸣-*ti a-ni-ni a-ki-i* ⸢*ra-šu*⸣-*ti-ni šá* UGU ^{m}MU-^{d}AMAR.UTU	(18’–19’) “[And] (for) the remainder, in accordance with our debt-notes owed (to us) by Iddin-Marduk, we accepted a partial payment.”

19’. [*ni-in*]-⸢*da*⸣-*ṭu ù ni*-⸢*it-ta-ši*⸣ ^{m}*ṣil-la-a* ⸢A-*šú šá*⸣ 20’. [^{md}DN-MU]-⸢DU$_3$⸣ *ma-ru-uṣ-ma* [*a-na mu-kin*]-*nu-tu la* ⸢x⸣	(19’–20’) Ṣillaya son of [X-šuma]-ibni was sick, so he did not [appear? to give testim]ony.
21’. […] ^{m}*gi-m*[*il* ^{d}*gu-la A-šú*] 22’. ⸢*šá* ^{m}⸣[KI-E$_2$-*sa*]*g-íl*-⸢NUMUN⸣ *a-na pa-ni-š*[*ú-nu*] 23’. *niš* ^{d}UTU ⸢*iz*⸣-*kur-ma ina pa-ni-šú-nu* [*an-ni-tu iq-bi*]	(21’–24’) Gimil-[Gula son] of Itti-Esagil-zēri … to them … he swore an oath of Šamaš before them and [said] thus:
24’. *um-ma a-na-ku* ⸢*u* ^{m}*ri-mut*⸣ ^{lu_2}TUK.MEŠ *šá* UGU [^{m}MU-^{d}AMAR.UTU]	(24’) “I and Rīmūt are the creditors (with debts) owed by [Iddin-Marduk].”
25’. *ul ni-i-du ki-i* [KU$_3$.BABBAR *ina pa-an* ^{m}NA$_3$-MU-GAR-*un paq-du*]	(25’) “We did not know that [silver was deposited with Nabû-šuma-iškun.]”
26’. ^{m}*na-din* DAM *šá* ^{f}*i-lat* [… NIN *šá* ^{m}SUM.NA$_3$-^{d}AMAR.UTU] 27’. *ù* ^{f}*ku-ut-ta-a* ⸢DAM ^{m}MU-^{d}AMAR.UTU *a-na*⸣ [*pa-an* …] 28’. *ki-i i-bu-ku-na-a-šú* ^{kuš}*ḫi-in-du šá* ^{m}MU-[^{d}AMAR-UTU] 29’. *šá ina* IGI-*šú paq*-[*da*]-*tu$_4$ ki-i iš-šá-a ina pa-ni-ni* […]	(26’–29’) “When Nādin, the husband of Ilat [… sister of Iddin-Marduk] and Kuttaya, wife of Iddin-Marduk, brought us before … , the leather purse of Iddin-Marduk which was handed over to him, when he took it, and, before us … “
30’. [x MA].NA KU$_3$.BABBAR *ina* [*lìb*]-*bi* ^{f}*ku-ut-ta-a* DAM ^{m}MU-^{d}[AMAR.UTU]	(30’) “[x mi]na of silver from which Kuttaya wife of Iddin-Marduk …
31’. [x x] *ta* ⸢x⸣ *ù šit-ti a-ni-ni a-ki-i ra-šu*-[*ti-ni*] 32’. [*šá* UGU ^{m}MU-^{d}AMAR.UTU *n*]*i-in-da-ṭu ù ni-it-ta*-[*ši* …]	(31’–32’) “[And] (for) the remainder, in accordance with [our] debt-notes [owed (to us) by Iddin-Marduk], we accepted a partial payment.”
33’. […] ⸢x⸣ -*ut-tu$_4$ it-te-mu an*-⸢x⸣ […]	33’. … swore…
34’. […] *šá* ^{m}MU-^{d}AMAR.UTU *ina pa-ni* […]	34’. … which Iddin-Marduk before …
35’. […] ^{lu_2}DI.KU$_5$.MEŠ *mu-kin-nu*-[*ti*] […]	35’. the judges… the testimony…
36’. [… *mi*]*m-ma šá* ^{m}MU-^{d}[AMAR.UTU]	36’. whatever, which Iddin-Marduk…

37’. […] *é-zi-da*

Left edge: ⸢^{na_4}KIŠIB⸣ ^{md}AMAR.
UTU-MU-URI$_3$ ^{lu_2}DUB.SAR

Seal of Marduk-šuma-uṣur, scribe.

NOTES

Although the seal is noted on the edge of the tablet, the seal itself does not appear.

36. Settling Dowry Obligations

Text: RSM 1909.405.22
Copy: Dalley 1979, No. 69
Translation/Discussion: Ries 1984; Joannès 2000b, No. 173 (pp. 234–36)
Place of Composition: Babylon
Date: 22.VII.1 Ngl (30 October, 559 BCE)

Bunanītu presents her claim against Bēl-apla-iddin, the son of her late husband, Nabû-šumu-līšir, most likely from another marriage. Bunanītu claims that when she married Nabû-šumu-līšir, her husband received 4 mina as the dowry. Upon Nabû-šumu-līšir's death, Bunanītu demands repayment of the dowry from Bēl-apla-iddin, her late husband's son and heir. Bēl-apla-iddin claims that although the dowry had been set at 4 mina of silver, his father actually received only 1 1/2 mina, the value of several slaves. In addition, Bēl-apla-iddin claims that he must also repay a 5-mina dowry that his father received when Bēl-apla-iddin married Etellitu. He cannot repay both women, and so instructs the judges to assess his property for the payments. The judges read both women's contracts and assess all the property. They award the two women their dowries from Bēl-apla-iddin's property, and stipulate that he is to receive support from the dowry of Etellitu.

The Neo-Babylonian dowry (*nudunnû*) was property given with the bride to the groom at the time of the marriage. The groom was responsible for maintaining the value of the dowry, which, in the event of the marriage's termination by death of the husband, would ensure the woman's maintenance and thus her financial security in the future. This is nicely illustrated in the Neo-Babylonian Laws, a fragmentary collection of of legal provisions, dating to the early seventh century BCE (Roth 1995, 143–49). Paragraphs 12–13 imagine situations quite similar to the one described in the present lawsuit (Ries 1984):

> A wife whose husband takes her dowry (*nudunnû*), and has no son or daughter, and whose husband fate carries away—from her husband's property, a dowry equivalent to the (husband's original) dowry shall be given to her …
>
> A man marries a wife, and she bears him sons. Afterwards, fate carries away that man, and that woman decides to enter the house of another man. She shall take the dowry that she brought from her father's house, as well as anything that her husband had given her (as a gift), and a husband of her choice may marry her…

In the present document, the heir of the deceased husband, the defendant Bēl-apla-iddin, is responsible for two dowries, that of his father's widow, Bunanītu, and that of his own wife, Etellitu. In an ironic twist, he ends up completely dependent on his wife's dowry for his own livelihood, because the amount of available property is sufficient only to meet these two dowry obligations. This is not entirely surprising, since, as a husband, Bēl-apla-iddin has usufruct rights to his wife's dowry during his lifetime.

The judges' ruling specifically prevents any other creditor from laying claim to the dowry property (lines 39–43). In a sense, then, the result of this lawsuit is equivalent to modern-day bankruptcy protection for an heir to a greatly diminished estate. The two women benefit here, too, since it is their livelihood that is directly protected. In fact, the women's desire for this legal insurance probably motivated their lawsuit.

1. ⌜^{f}*bu*⌝-*na-ni-tu*$_4$ DUMU.SAL-*su* *šá* ^{m}GAR-MU DUMU ^{m}DU$_3$-*eš*-DINGIR 2. *a-na* ^{md}EN-IBILA-MU DUMU-*šú šá* ^{md}NA$_3$-MU-SI.SA$_2$ DUMU ^{m}KAL-^{d}IM	(1–3) Bunanītu daughter of Šākin-šumi descendant of Eppeš-ili raised a claim against Bēl-apla-iddin son of Nabû-šumu-līšir descendant of Mudammiq-Adad.
3. *di-i-nu tag-re-e-ma a-na ma-ḫar* ^{m}*mu-še-zib*-^{d}EN ^{lu_2}GAR-UMUŠ TIN.TIR^{ki} 4. DUMU ^{m}UGU-DINGIR-GAL-^{d}AMAR.UTU ^{lu_2}DI.KU$_5$.MEŠ *u* *ši-bu-tu*$_4$ URU *ik-šu-du-ma*	(3–4) They arrived before Mušēzib-Bēl, the governor of Babylon son of Eli-ili-rabi-Marduk, the judges and the elders of the city.
5. *dib-bi-šu-nu ú-šá-an-nu-ma* ^{f}*bu-na-ni-tu*$_4$ *ki-a-am taq-bi*	(5–6) They related their case. Bunanītu said thus:
6. *um-ma* ^{md}NA$_3$-MU-SI.SA AD *šá* ^{md}EN-IBILA-MU *a-na áš-šu-tu*$_4$ *ki-i i-ḫu-za-an-nu*	(6–7) "When Nabû-šumu-līšir, father of Bēl-apla-iddin, took me as a wife, he received 4 mina of silver as my dowry."
7. 4 MA.NA KU$_3$.BABBAR *nu-dun-nu-ú-a il-te-qa* ^{md}NA$_3$-MU-SI.SA$_2$ *a-na šim-tu*$_4$ 8. *il-lik-ma* ^{md}EN-IBILA-MU DUMU-*šú* NIG$_2$.GA.MEŠ-*šú il-qe-e-ma a-di* U$_4$-*mu an-na-a*	(7–9) "Nabû-šumu-līšir died and Bēl-apla-iddin, his son, took over his property, but to this day he has not repaid my dowry to me."
9. *nu-dun-na-a-a la i-pu-la-an-nu* ^{md}EN-IBILA-MU *i-pu-ul um-ma ina ṭup-pi*	(9) Bēl-apla-iddin answered thus:

10. *nu-dun-né-e-šá* 4 MA.NA KU$_3$.BABBAR *šá* ^{f}*bu-na-ni-tu*$_4$ *it-ti* ^{md}NA$_3$-MU-SI.SA$_2$

11. AD-*ia taš-ṭur-ru al-la* 1 1/2 MA.NA KU$_3$.BABBAR *a-di* [ŠA]M$_2$ LU$_2$-*tú*

(9–12) "In her dowry tablet, Bunanītu wrote 4 mina of silver with Nabû-šumu-līšir, my father, but my father was not given more than 1 1/2 mina of silver, including the [pri]ce of slaves."

12. *a-na* AD-*ia la na-din aš-šum ri-ḫi-it* KU$_3$.BABBAR AD-*ú-a la maḫ-ri*

13. AD-*ú-a rik-sa-a-tu*$_4$ *it-ti* ^{f}*bu-na-ni-tu*$_4$ *ur-tak-kis*

(12–13) "My father wrote contracts with Bunanītu regarding the remainder of the silver (which) my father had not received."

14. *ù* 5 MA.NA KU$_3$.BABBAR *nu-dun-nu-ú šá* ^{f}*e-tel-li-tu*$_4$ *áš-šá-ti-ia*

15. ^{md}NA$_3$-MU-SI.SA$_2$ AD-*ú-a il-qe-e-ma ma-la a-pa-lu nu-dun-na-né-e*

(14–16) "Nabû-šumu-līšir, my father, also received 5 mina of silver, the dowry of Etellitu, my wife, but I am unable to repay both their dowries."

16. *šu-nu-tì la ma-ṣa-a-ku* NIG$_2$.GA.MEŠ-*ni a-mu-ra-ma nu-dun-nu-ú*

(16–17) "Investigate our possessions and provide dowries for Bunanītu (and) Etellitu from them!"

17. *a-na* ^{f}*bu-na-ni-tu*$_4$ ^{f}*e-tel-li-tu*$_4$ *ina lìb-bi a-pu-la ú-ìl-tì*

18. *šá ina* ⸢MU⸣ 31-*kám* ^{d}NA$_3$-NIG$_2$.DU-URI$_3$ LUGAL TIN.TIR^{ki} ^{md}NA$_3$-MU-SI.SA$_2$

19. *it-ti* ^{f}*bu-na-ni-tu*$_4$ *áš-šá-ti-šú i'-i-lu um-ma i-na*

20. *ú-ìl-tì šá* 4 MA.NA KU$_3$.BABBAR *al-la* 1 1/2 MA.NA KU$_3$.BABBAR *a-di* ŠIM$_2$ LU$_2$-*tú*

(17–21) The debt-note which Nabû-šumu-līšir wrote with Bunanītu in year 31 of Nebuchadnezzar, king of Babylon, stating: "In the debt-note for 4 mina of silver, Nabû-šumu-līšir has received not more than 1 1/2 mina of silver, the price of a slave from Bunanītu"—

21. ^{md}NA$_3$-MU-SI.SA$_2$ *ina qa-at* ^{f}*bu-na-ni-tu*$_4$ *la ma-ḫir ù ú-*[*ìl-tì*]

22. *šá* 5 MA.NA KU$_3$.BABBAR *nu-dun-nu-ú šá* ^{f}*bu-na-ni-tu*$_4$ *šá* ^{md}NA$_3$-MU-SI.SA$_2$

(21–23) and the de[bt-note] for 5 mina of silver, the dowry of Bunanītu (sic!) which Nabû-šumu-līšir received —

23. *il-qu-ú ú-ìl-tì*.MEŠ *ki-la-la-an ma-ḫar* ^{lu_2}GAR.UMUŠ TIN.⸢TIR⸣[^{ki}]

(23–24) they read both the debt-notes before the governor of Babylon, the judges and the elders of the city.

24. ^{lu_2}DI.KU$_5$.MEŠ *ù ši-bu-tu* URU *iš-tas-su-ma* 1 1/2 MA.[NA KU$_3$.BABBAR]
25. *nu-dun-nu-ú šá* ^{f}*bu-na-ni-tu*$_4$ *ù* 5 MA.NA KU$_3$.BABBAR *nu-dun-*[*nu-ú*]

(24–26) 1 1/2 mina of silver, the dowry of Bunanītu, and 5 mina of silver, the dowry of Etellitu, were established before them (the judges).

26. *šá* ^{f}*e-tel-li-tu*$_4$ *ma-ḫar-šu-nu i-kun re-eš* NIG$_2$.GA.MEŠ *šá* ^{md}NA$_3$-[MU-SI.SA$_2$]
27. *iš-šu-ma* ŠU.NIGIN$_2$ ŠE.NUMUN-*šú* A.ŠA$_3$ *me-ri-*⸢*šu*⸣ ⸢*ù*⸣ [*tap-tu*]-*ú* X-X- *ḫu*
28. *pi-ḫat* KIŠ^{ki} *a-di* ŠE.NUMUN *zaq-pi šá* ⸢*i*⸣-[*na x x* E$_2$] DU$_3$
29. *šá i-na* KI-*tì te-e*^{ki}*šá qé-reb* TIN.⸢TIR^{ki}⸣ [x x x] ŠAM$_2$
30. LU$_2$-*ut-tu*$_4$ *an-nu-ú* NIG$_2$.GA.MEŠ *šá* ^{md}NA$_3$-MU-SI.SA$_2$ *i-mu-*[*ru*]

(26–30) They evaluated the possessions of Nabû-[šumu-līšir]. In total: His cultivated and newly-prepared fields … in the district of Kiš, together with the cultivated lands in … a built house in the city quarter of Tē, in the midst of Babylon … the price of these slaves. Th[ey in]vestigated the property of Nabû-šumu-līšir.

31. ^{lu_2}GAR.UMUŠ TIN.TIR^{ki} DI.KU$_5$.MEŠ *ù* ⸢*ši*⸣-[*bu*]-⸢*tu*$_4$⸣ URU *im-tal-ku-ma*

(31) The governor of Babylon, the judges and the elders of the city deliberated.

32. ŠE.NUMUN *šu-a-tu*$_4$ KU$_3$.BABBAR ŠAM$_2$ E$_2$ *ù* ^{f}[x x] *ù* DUMU.SAL-*šú*
33. *a-na* 6 1/2 MA.NA KU$_3$.BABBAR *im-nu-ma a-*⸢*na*⸣[^{f}*e-tel-li-tu*$_4$] *ù* ^{f}*bu-na-ni-tu*$_4$

(32–34) That field, the silver, the price of the house, and ^{f}[PN] and her daughter they considered as the 6 1/2 mina of silver, and gave the total 6 1/2 mina of silver to Etellitu and Bunanītu as the[ir] dowries.

34. *ku-um* 6 1/2 MA.NA KU$_3$.BABBAR *nu-dun-*⸢*na-ši*⸣-[*na*] *id-di-nu* ^{f}*e-tel-li-tu*$_4$
35. *ù* ^{f}*bu-na-ni-tu*$_4$ NIG$_2$.GA.MEŠ *šu-nu-tì ku-um* 6 1/2 MA.NA KU$_3$.BABBAR
36. *i-leq-qa-a-ma ki-i* 1 *ma-*<<*na*>>*-ne-e*
37. *nu-dun-na-ši-na i-na lìb-bi i-šal-*⸢*li*⸣*-mu* ^{md}EN-IBILA-MU

(34–37) Etellitu and Bunanītu shall receive that property as the 6 1/2 mina of silver and shall be fully paid, mina for mina, (for) their dowries.

38. *it-ti* ^{f}*e-tel-li-tu*$_4$ *áš-šá-ti-šú a-na nu-dun-né-e-šú*	(37–39) Together with Etellitu, his wife, from her dowry, Bēl-apla-iddin shall receive food and clothing.
39. *a-ka-lu ù lu-bu-uš-tu*$_4$ *i-leq-qa* ^{lú}TUK-*ú*	
40. *šá* ^{md}NA$_3$-MU-SI.SA$_2$ *ù* ^{md}EN-IBILA-MU DUMU-*šú i-na* UGU *mim-ma*	(39–43) No creditor of Nabû-šumu-līšir or Bēl-apla-iddin, his son, shall have any control over anything which was giv[en] to Etellitu and Bunanītu as their dowries, and shall raise no claim against Bēl-apla-iddin regarding any part of his property.
41. *šá a-na* ^{f}*e-tel-li-tu*$_4$ *ù* ^{f}*bu-na-ni-tu*$_4$ *ku-um nu-dun-na-ši-na*	
42. *na-ad-*[*nu*] *ul i-šal-laṭ ù a-na* UGU *ra-šu-ti-šú ma-la ba-šu-ú*	
43. *it-*⸢*ti*⸣ ^{md}EN-IBILA-MU *ul i-rag-gúm di-in-šú-nu di-i-nu* EŠ.BAR-*ši-na pa-ri-is*	(43) Their case is judged; their decision is decided.
44. *a-na la e-né-e* ^{lú}GAR.UMUŠ TIN.TIR^{ki} *ù* ^{lú}DI.KU$_5$.MEŠ *ṭup-pi iš-ṭu-ru*	(44) So that (the decision) would not be changed, the governor and the judges wrote a tablet.
45. *i-na* ^{na_4}KIŠIB.MEŠ-*šú-nu ib-ru-mu-ma a-na* ^{f}*e-tel-li-tu*$_4$ *u* ^{f}*bu-na-ni-tu*$_4$ *id-di-nu*	(45) They sealed (it) with their seals and gave (it) to Etellitu and Bunanītu.
46. *i-na ša-ṭa-ri ṭup-pi šu-a-tì*	(46) At the writing of this tablet:
47. ^{m}*mu-še-zib-*^{d}EN ^{lú}GAR.UMUŠ TIN.TIR^{ki} DUMU ^{md}UGU-DINGIR.GAL-^{d}AMAR.UTU	(47) Mušēzib-Bēl, the governor of Babylon, descendant of Eli-ili-rabi-Marduk;
48. ^{md}30-DINGIR <^{lú}>ŠEŠ.GAL <^{lú}>KU$_4$-E$_2$ ^{d}AMAR.UTU DUMU ^{md}30-DINGIR	(48) Sîn-ili, the *šešgallu*, "temple enterer" of Marduk, descendant of Sîn-ili;
49. ^{m}*kal-ba-a* ^{lú}KU$_4$-E$_2$-AMAR.UTU DUMU ^{m}*ir-a-ni*	(49) Kalbaya, the "temple enterer" of Marduk, descendant of Irʾanni;
50. ^{md}U.GUR-*ina*-SUH$_3$-KAR-*ir* ^{lú}DI.KU$_5$ DUMU ^{lú}GAL.DU$_3$	(50) Nergal-ina-tēšê-ēṭir, the judge, descendant of Rāb-banê;
51. ^{md}AMAR.UTU-GAR-MU ^{lú}DI.KU$_5$ DUMU URU$_3$.DU$_3$-*ma-an-sum*	(51) Marduk-šākin-šumi, the judge, descendant of URU$_3$.DU$_3$-mansum;
52. ^{md}EN-NUMUN ^{lú}DI.KU$_5$ DUMU ^{m}*ri-mut-*^{d}IDIM	(52) Bēl-zēri, the judge, descendant of Rīmūt-Ea;
53. ^{md}EN-TIN-*iṭ* DUMU-*šú šá* ^{md}EN-DA DUMU ^{md}30-DINGIR	(53) Bēl-uballiṭ son of Bēl-lēʾi descendant of Sîn-ili;

54. ^{m}MU-^{d}AMAR.UTU DUMU-*šú šá* ^{m}BA-*šá-a* DUMU ^{m}DU$_{3}$-*eš*-DINGIR	(54) Iddin-Marduk son of Iqīšaya descendant of Eppeš-ili;
55. ^{md}AMAR.UTU-MU-DU$_{3}$ DUMU-*šú šá* ^{m}GAR-MU DUMU ^{m}*ši-gu-ú-a*	(55) Marduk-šuma-ibni son of Šākin-šumi descendant of Šigûa;
56. ^{md}EN-MU-GAR-*un* DUMU-*šú šá* ^{md}EN-GI DUMU ^{lú}NI.DU$_{8}$	(56) Bēl-šuma-iškun son of Bēl-ušallim descendant of Atû;
57. ^{m}DU-NUMUN DUMU-*šú šá* ^{m}*tab-né-e-a* DUMU ^{m}*e-gi-bi*	(57) Mukīn-zēri son of Tabnêa descendant of Egibi;
58. ^{md}AMAR.UTU-DUB-NUMUN DUB.SAR DUMU-*šú šá* ^{m}*mu-še-zib*-^{d}AMAR.UTU DUMU ^{m}*šu-ḫa-a-a*	(58) Marduk-šāpik-zēri, the scribe, son of Mušēzib-Marduk, descendant of Šuḫaya.
59. TIN.TIR^{ki} ITI DU$_{6}$ U$_{4}$ 22-*kám* MU 1-*kám* ^{md}U.GUR-LUGAL-URI$_{3}$ LUGAL TIN.TIR^{ki}	(59) Babylon. 22 Tašrītu, year 1 of Neriglissar, king of Babylon.
^{na_4}KIŠIB ^{m}*mu-še-zib*-^{d}EN ^{lú}GAR.UMUŠ TIN.TIR^{ki}	Seal of Mušēzib-Bēl, governor of Babylon.
^{na_4}KIŠIB ^{md}U.GUR-*ina*-SUH$_{3}$-KAR-*ir* ^{lú}DI.KU$_{5}$	Seal of Nergal-ina-tēšê-ēṭir, the judge.
^{na_4}KIŠIB ^{md}EN-NUMUN ^{lú}DI.KU$_{5}$	Seal of Bēl-zēri, the judge.
^{na_4}KIŠIB ^{md}AMAR.UTU-GAR-MU ^{lú}DI.KU$_{5}$	Seal of Marduk-šākin-šumi, the judge.

NOTES

18. Year 31 of Nebuchadnezzar corresponds to 574–573 BCE, which means that the debt-note was written some 15 years before the present lawsuit.

22. As has already been noted in previous editions of the text, the name Bunanītu in this line is clearly a scribal error. The dowry to which the text refers here is that of Etellitu.

36–37. The phrase *ki-i* 1 *ma-<<na>>-ne-e* (literally "as 1 mina") appears to be an idiomatic expression of the women's receipt of complete payment.

Seal inscriptions appear without the seals, indicating that the present document is a copy of the original.

Chapter 3
Four Trial Dossiers

The Infamous Gimillu (Documents 37–41)

To cuneiformists, Gimillu, son of Inni-šuma-ibni, is perhaps the best-known character from the Neo-Babylonian archives. He entered the Eanna bureaucracy towards the end of the reign of Nabonidus (539 BCE), and is first attested as the "overseer of the remainders" (*ša muḫḫi rēḫāni*) owed to the Eanna temple by its livestock farmers. Very quickly, he seems to have learned how to abuse this position; within less than a year, he was on trial for embezzling cattle and other temple property (Document 38). Despite his malfeasance, for some reason he remained in office. He continued his misdeeds but was nevertheless appointed, during the reign of Cambyses, to the position of "chief farmer" (*ša muḫḫi sūti*), where he found further opportunities for questionable activity. It was in this post that he ended his ignominious career in year 2 of Darius I (520 BCE), after nearly twenty years of (mis)serving the Eanna.

Although in several texts he is designated as an oblate (*širku*) of the Eanna (Dandamaev 1984, 533 n. 97), he was hardly a mere slave. Rather, Gimillu's positions are best characterized as "middle management," between the higher echelons of the Eanna administration, including the royal representatives, and the lower-level herders and tenant farmers. More specifically, he was personally responsible for ensuring that the Eanna received the yields that it expected from the herders and the date farmers. In other words, the Eanna relied on Gimillu to achieve its fiscal goals, even as it allowed him some measure of profit from the arrangement. Obviously, Gimillu took advantage of this arrangement, but his situation was hardly enviable. There were clear discrepancies between what the Eanna expected to receive and what agriculture could actually produce, and Gimillu would have had to negotiate these tensions (Jursa 2004a, 122–25).

Recent scholarship has returned to examine Gimillu's rather amazing survival in the Eanna despite his misdeeds (Kozuh 2006, 108–26; Ragen 2006, 479–512). If, as the texts imply, his relationship to the Eanna authorities was so bad (see Document 41 below), why did they allow him to continue his service? Gimillu, it seems, had connections to the satrapal government establishment in Babylon, and probably survived under its patronage. These same connections may also explain the particular scrutiny to which the Eanna subjected him. For, despite all appearances to the contrary, Gimillu's misappropriations almost certainly did not have a particularly great impact on the Eanna's herds (Kozuh 2006, 117–19; Ragen 2006, 506–8). Rather, the confrontations between Gimillu and the Eanna's internal bureaucracy may reflect the Eanna's resistance to imperial intervention in its affairs (Kozuh 2006, 124; Ragen 2006, 509–10). To the Eanna, Gimillu, even though he was an "oblate" (*širku*), was also an outsider.

According to one estimate, nearly one hundred texts pertaining to Gimillu's misdeeds are known today (Jursa 2004a, 109). Most remarkably, this "file" contains documents with some of the latest dates in the Neo-Babylonian corpus from the Eanna. This fact points to one possible ramification of the Gimillu affair: once the dust had settled, the Eanna probably undertook a major administrative reorganization, including, quite possibly, resetting or clearing its records (van Driel 1998, 67–68; Jursa 2004a, 132). As a result, numerous "dead files" would have been discarded, among them the Gimillu dossier, only to be rediscovered millennia later as the "Eanna archives."

37. Suspected Misappropriation

Text: YBC 3828
Copy: Dougherty 1920 (YOS 6), No. 208
Translation/Discussion: Von Bolla 1940, 140; Dandamaev 1984, 534; Wells 2004, 175–76; Holtz 2009, 146–57
Place of Composition: City of Nabû-šuma-iddin
Date: 9.III.17 Nbn (10 June, 539 BCE)

Gimillu interrogates Nabû-šuma-iddin. Nabû-šuma-iddin is under suspicion of having misappropriated a cow belonging to the temple and branded with a star. Nabû-šuma-iddin responds to Gimillu's questioning by claiming that he rented the cow from Balṭiya, alleging not to have known that Balṭiya did not have the right to rent out the cow. Nabû-šuma-iddin assumes responsibility for presenting testimony concerning Balṭiya. If he does not establish the case against Balṭiya, then Nabû-šuma-iddin will be considered guilty of misappropriating temple possessions, and must repay the temple thirtyfold for the rental fee. The cow in question is led away. Nabû-šuma-iddin must hand over his contract with Balṭiya to Gimillu.

The present document contains the earliest known attestation of Gimillu in the Eanna archives, and illustrates his role as "overseer of the remainders" (*ša muḫḫi rēḫāni*) of the livestock. In this capacity, he must account for animals that have been branded as property of the Eanna. Thus, although the document probably belongs to the Gimillu file, and may have some connection to Gimillu's malfeasance, it does not, of itself, seem to illustrate any misdeed on his part.

1. ^{m}*tab-né-e-a* A-*šú šá* ^{m}KI-^{d}EN-*tab-ni*	(1) Tabnêa son of Itti-Bēl-tabni;
2. ^{m}*gi-mil-lu* A-*šú šá* ^{m}ZALAG$_{2}$-*é-a*	(2) Gimillu son of Nūrea;
3. ^{m}*la-ba-ši* A-*šú šá* ^{md}UTU-ŠEŠ-MU	(3) Lâbāši son of Šamaš-aḫa-iddin;
4. ^{m}*i-di-ḫi*-DINGIR.MEŠ A-*šú šá* ^{m}MU-^{d}NA$_{3}$	(4) Idiḫi-ilī son of Iddin-Nabû;
5. ^{m}*nar-gi-ia* A-*šú šá* ^{m}EN-*šú-nu*	(5) Nargiya son of Bēlšunu;
6. ^{lú_2}DUMU-DU$_{3}$-*i šá ina* IGI-*šú-nu* ^{m}*gi-mil-lu*	(6–8) The *mār banî* in whose presence Gimillu son of Innin-šuma-ibni said thus to Nabû-šuma-iddin son of Aplaya:
7. A-*šú šá* ^{md}INNIN-*na*-MU-DU$_{3}$ *a-na* ^{md}NA$_{3}$-MU-MU	
8. A-*šú šá* ^{m}*ap-la-a iq-bu-ú um-ma*	
9. *mi-nam-ma* GU$_{4}$ *bu-uš-tu*$_{4}$ *šá* ^{d}GAŠAN *šá* UNUG^{ki}	(9–10) "Why did you take a cow of the Lady of Uruk which is bran[ded] with a star?"
10. *šá kak-kab-tu*$_{4}$ *še-en-*⸢*de*⸣-[*e-ti*] ⸢*tal* ⸣-*qa-ma*	
11. ^{m}NA$_{3}$-MU-MU ⸢*iq*⸣-[*bu-ú*]	(11–12) Nabû-šuma-iddin s[aid] thus:
12. *um-ma* ^{m}*bal-ṭi-ia* [A-*šú*]	(12–16) "Since Simānu, year 17 of Nabonidus, king of Babylon, Balṭiya [son of] Innina-zēra-šubši gave it to me for its rent, 4 *kur* of barley, 1 *pi* 4 *sūt* sesame, per year."
13. *šá* ^{md}INNIN-*na*- NUMUN-TIL *ul-tu* ITI SIG$_{4}$	
14. MU 17-*kám* ^{d}NA$_{3}$-I LUGAL TIN.TIR^{ki}	
15. *a-na i-di-šú a-na* MU.AN.NA 4 GUR ŠE.BAR	
16. 1 (PI) 4 (BAN$_{2}$) ŠE.GIŠ.I$_{3}$ *id-da-na-áš pu-ut*	(16–18) Nabû-šuma-iddin assumes responsibility for testimony concerning Balṭiya.
17. ^{lú_2}*mu-kin-nu-tu šá* ^{m}*bal-ṭi-ia*	
18. ^{md}NA$_{3}$-MU-MU *na-ši* U$_{4}$-*mu uk-tin-nu-uš*	(18–19) On the day he establishes (the case) against him, he is clear.

19. *za-ki ia-a-nu* 1-*en* 30 *a-na* ^{d}GAŠAN *šá* UNUG^{ki}	(19–20) If not, he shall pay thirty-fold to the Lady of Uruk.
20. *i-nam-din* GU$_4$ *bu-uš-tu*$_4$ ^{m}*gi-mil-lu*	(20–21) Gimillu has led the cow away from Nabû-šuma-iddin.
21. *ina* ŠU.2 ^{md}NA$_3$-MU-MU *i-ta-bak ú-ìl-tì*	(21–24) Nabû-šuma-iddin shall give Gimillu the debt-note which Nabû-šuma-iddin and Balṭiya drew up together.
22. *šá* ^{md}NA$_3$-MU-MU *u* ^{m}*bal-ṭi-ia it-ti a-ḫa-meš*	
23. *i-il-lu-*ʾ ^{md}NA$_3$-MU-MU *a-na*	
24. ^{m}*gi-mil-lu i-nam-din* ^{lú_2}UMBISAG	(24–25) Scribe: Nabû-bēlšunu son of Nūrea.
25. ^{md}NA$_3$-EN-*šú-nu* A-*šú šá* ^{m}ZALAG$_2$-*e-a*	
26. URU *šá* ^{md}NA$_3$-MU-MU	(26) City of Nabû-šuma-iddin.
27. ITI SIG$_4$ U$_4$ 9-*kám*	(27–29) 9 Simānu, year 17 of Nabonidus, king of Babylon.
28. MU 17-*kám* ^{d}NA$_3$-I	
29. LUGAL TIN.TIR^{ki}	

Notes

7–8. The orthography of the defendant's name, ^{md}NA$_3$-MU-MU, is ambiguous; it can be read as Nabû-šuma-iddin or Nabû-nādin-šumi. The present transliteration assumes that the *nādin* element in the latter name is usually written syllabically, rather than with the logogram MU. Note, however, that at least one man named Nabû-nādin-šumi son of Aplaya is attested as a "herdsman" (*nāqidu*) elsewhere in the Eanna material (Kümmel 1979, 68). Given the present context, it is not entirely out of the question that the same person is involved here.

38. Gimillu on Trial

Text: YBC 4188
Copy: Tremayne 1925 (YOS 7), No. 7
Translation/Discussion: Tremayne 1925, 11–12; San Nicolò 1933a; Holtz 2009, 270–72, 278–79
Place of Composition: Uruk
Date: 3.VI.1 Cyr (21 August, 538 BCE)

In the presence of twenty-one men, including the governor of Uruk, the šatammu *and the royal official in charge of the Eanna, as well as four scribes, Gimillu stands trial for twelve incidents of misappropriation of the Eanna's property. On the basis of witnesses' testimony and Gimillu's own confessions, he is convicted. The authorities impose penalties for each crime.*

The present document is one of the longest Neo-Babylonian trial records, comprising nearly 150 lines written on four columns. For convenience, the various parts of the trial are tabulated on the following chart:

Lines in Text	Subject	Date of Offense	Basis of Conviction	Penalty Imposed
1–4	Introduction			
5–29	Names of members of adjudicatory panel			
30–42	2 cows	1.VI.1 Cyr	Testimony	60 cows (30-fold penalty)
43–50	1 cow	VI.17 Nbn	Testimony and confession	30 cows (30-fold penalty)
51–59	1 ewe	—	Testimony	30 sheep (30-fold penalty)
60–76	3 sheep, illegally transferred in forced sale	25.IV.1 Cyr	Testimony	90 sheep (30-fold penalty)
77–87	1 goat, stolen by Gimillu's brother at Gimillu's orders	VI.17 Nbn	Testimony and confession	30 sheep (30-fold penalty)
88–95	1 ewe	—	Testimony	30 sheep (30-fold penalty)

96–103	1 lamb	VI.17 Nbn	Testimony and confession	30 sheep (30-fold penalty)
104–109	1 ewe	—	Confession	30 sheep (30-fold penalty)
110–116	1 ewe	IV.1 Cyr	Confession	30 sheep (30-fold penalty)
117–134	1 ram, silver, and barley (received as a bribe)	—	Testimony and confession	30 sheep 1 mina 10 šeqels of silver (30-fold penalty)
135–139	1 cow	—	Confession	2 (?) cows
140–146	1 garment	—	Confession	silver
147–148	Total fines owed by Gimillu			

The dated offenses show that this trial pertains to misdeeds that Gimillu committed during two consecutive years, year 17 of Nabonidus and year 1 of Cyrus. The earliest offense, according to the present record, occurred in the month of Dûzu of year 17 of Nabonidus (July, 539 BCE), or within a month or so of Gimillu's first appearance in the Eanna archive (Document 37).

1. GU$_4$.MEŠ *ṣe-e-nu ù mim-mu* NIG$_2$.GA ^{d}GAŠAN *šá* UNUG^{ki} 2. *u* ^{d}*na-na-a šá* ^{m}*gi-*⸢*mil-lu*⸣ A-*šú šá* ^{md}*in-nin-*MU-DU$_3$ 3. *ina* ŠU.2 ^{lu_2}GAL *bu-*[*lum ù*] ^{lu_2}SIPA.MEŠ *šá* ^{d}GAŠAN *šá* UNUG^{ki} 4. *iš-šu-ia-a-ma a-na* E$_2$.AN.NA *la id-di-in*	(1–4) The oxen, sheep and whatever property of the Lady of Uruk and Nanaya which Gimillu son of Innin-šuma-ibni received from the overseer of the he[rds and] the shepherds of the Lady of Uruk but did not give to the Eanna.
5. ^{lu_2}MU.DU.MEŠ *ú-kin-nu-šú-ma e-li ram-ni-šú ú-kin-ni*	(5) The witnesses testified against him and he testified against himself.
6. *ina* DU-*zu šá* ^{m}*na-di-nu* ^{lu_2}GAR.UMUŠ UNUG^{ki} A-*šú šá* ^{m}*ba-la-ṭu*	(6) In the presence of: Nādinu, the governor of Uruk, son of Balāṭu;
7. ^{md}*a-nu-*LUGAL-URI$_3$ ^{lu_2}*qí-i-pi šá* E$_2$.AN.NA	(7) Anu-šarra-uṣur, the *qīpu*-official of the Eanna;

8. ^{md}NA$_3$-DU-NUMUN ^{lu_2}ŠA$_3$.TAM E$_2$.AN.NA A-*šú šá* ^{m}*na-din* A ^{m}*da-bi-bi*	(8) Nabû-mukīn-zēri, the *šatammu* of the Eanna, son of Nādin descendant of Dābibī;
9. ^{md}NA$_3$-ŠEŠ-MU ^{lu_2}SAG-LUGAL ^{lu_2}EN *pi-qit-tu*$_4$ E$_2$.AN.NA	(9) Nabû-aḫa-iddin, the royal official in charge of the Eanna;
10. ^{m}*ri-mut*-^{d}EN A-*šú šá* ^{md}EN-TIN-*iṭ* A ^{m}ŠU-^{d}*na-na-a*	(10) Rīmūt-Bēl son of Bēl-uballiṭ descendant of Gimil-Nanaya;
11. ^{m}*si-lim*-DINGIR ^{lu_2}SAG-LUGAL ^{lu_2}*šá muḫ-ḫi qu-up-pu* NIG$_2$.GA E$_2$.AN.NA	(11) Silim-ili, the royal official in charge of the chest of the property of the Eanna;
12. ^{m}IR$_3$-^{d}AMAR.UTU A-*šú šá* ^{m}*ze-ri-ia* A ^{m}*e-gi-bi*	(12) Arad-Marduk son of Zēriya descendant of Egibi;
13. ^{md}30-APIN-*eš* A-*šú šá* ^{md}NA$_3$-MU-SI.SA$_2$ A ^{m}DU$_3$-DINGIR	(13) Sîn-ēreš son of Nabû-šumu-līšir descendant of Ibni-ilī;
14. ^{m}IR$_3$-^{d}EN A-*šú šá* ^{m}*ṣil-la-a* A ^{m}MU-^{d}PAP.SUKKAL	(14) Arad-Bēl son of Ṣillaya descendant of Iddin-Papsukkal;
15. ^{m}*su-qa-a-a* A-*šú šá* ^{md}AMAR.UTU-MU-MU A ^{m}ŠU-^{d}*na-na-a*	(15) Sūqaya son of Marduk-šuma-iddin descendant of Gimil-Nanaya;
16. ^{md}*in-nin*-MU-URI$_3$ A-*šú šá* ^{m}MU-^{d}NA$_3$ A ^{m}*ki-din*-^{d}AMAR.UTU	(16) Innin-šuma-uṣur son of Iddin-Nabû descendant of Kidin-Marduk;
17. ^{m}IR$_3$-^{d}*in-nin* A-*šú šá* ^{md}EN-MU A ^{m}*ku-ri-i*	(17) Arad-Innin son of Bēl-iddin descendant of Kurī;
18. ^{m}GAR-MU A-*šú šá* ^{m}DU$_3$-^{d}15 A ^{md}30-*tab-ni*	(18) Šākin-šumi son of Ibni-Ištar descendant of Sîn-tabni;
19. ^{m}*ki-rib*-⸢*tu*$_4$⸣ A-*šú šá* ^{m}*na-di-nu* A ^{m}*ba-bu-tu*	(19) Kiribtu son of Nādinu descendant of Babūtu;
20. ^{md}EN-*ka-ṣir* A-*šú šá* ^{m}*mar-duk* A ^{m}*ki-din*-^{d}AMAR.UTU	(20) Bēl-kāṣir son of Marduk descendant of Kidin-Marduk;
21. ^{md}NA$_3$-TIN-*su*-E A-*šú šá* ^{m}*ib-na-a* A ^{m}E$_2$-*kur-za-kir*	(21) Nabû-balāssu-iqbi son of Ibnaya descendant of Ekur-zakir;
22. ^{m}IR$_3$-^{d}*in-nin* A-*šú šá* ^{m}DU$_3$-^{d}15 A ^{m}ŠU-^{d}*na-na-a*	(22) Arad-Innin son of Ibni-Ištar descendant of Gimil-Nanaya;
23. ^{md}*in-nin*-NUMUN-DU$_3$ A-*šú šá* ^{md}NA$_3$-ŠEŠ.MEŠ-GI A ^{lu_2}SANGA-^{d}MAŠ	(23) Innin-zēra-ibni son of Nabû-aḫḫē-šullim descendant of Šangû-Ninurta;

24. ^{md}UTU-TIN-*iṭ* A-*šú šá* ^{m}*na-di-nu* A ^{m}LU$_{2}$-*u*	(24) Šamaš-uballiṭ son of Nādinu descendant of Amēlû;
25. ^{m}*gi-mil-lu* A-*šú šá* ^{md}NA$_{3}$-MU-MU A ^{m}ŠU-^{d}*na-na-a*	(25) Gimillu son of Nabû-šuma-iddin descendant of Gimil-Nanaya;
26. [^{m}*ḫaš*]-*di-ia* A-*šú šá* ^{md}15-MU-KAM$_{2}$ A ^{md}IM-GAL	(26) [Ḫaš]diya son of Ištar-šuma-ēreš descendant of Adad-rabû;
27. [^{m}]*na-di-nu* ^{m}*ki-na-a* ^{m}*mu-ra-nu* *ù* ^{m}*ba-la-ṭu*	(27–28) Nādinu, Kīnaya, Mūrānu and Balāṭu, the scribes of the Eanna.
28. ^{lu2}UMBISAG.MEŠ *šá* E$_{2}$.AN.NA UNUG^{ki} ITI KIN ⸢U$_{4}$ 3⸣-*kám*	(28–29) Uruk. 3 Ulūlu year 1 of Cyrus, king of the lands.
29. MU 1-*kám* ^{m}*ku-ra-áš* LUGAL [KUR.KU]R	
30. 2 AB$_{2}$.GAL.MEŠ *šá kak-kab-tu$_{4}$* [*še-en*]-⸢*du*⸣ *šá* U$_{4}$ 1-*kám šá* ITI KIN	(30–36) 2 cows, [brand]ed with a star, (regarding) which, on 1 Ulūlu, [year 1] of Cyrus, king of the lands, Nabû-bāni-aḫi son of [X]-iqbi descendant of Kurī reported to Anu-šarra-uṣur [the *qīpu*-official of] the Eanna, Nabû-mukīn-zēri, the *šatammu* of the Eanna, [son of Nādinu] descendant of Dābibī, Nabû-aḫa-iddin, the royal official, [admin]istrator of the Eanna and the scribes of the Eanna:
31. [MU 1-*kám* ^{m}]*ku-ra-as$_{2}$* LUGAL KUR.KUR *šá* ^{md}NA$_{3}$-DU$_{3}$-ŠEŠ A-*šú šá*	
32. [^{m}PN]-*iq-bi* A ^{m}*ku-ri-i a-na* ^{md}*a-nu*-LUGAL-URI$_{3}$	
33. [^{lu2}*qí-pi šá*] E$_{2}$.AN.NA ^{md}NA$_{3}$-DU-NUMUN ^{lu2}ŠA$_{3}$.TAM E$_{2}$.AN.NA	
34. [A-*šú šá* ^{m}*na-di*]-*nu* A ^{m}*da-bi-bi* ^{md}NA$_{3}$-ŠEŠ-MU ^{lu2}SAG-LUGAL	
35. [^{lu2}EN *pi*]-*qit-tu$_{4}$* E$_{2}$.AN.NA *ù* ^{lu2}UMBISAG.MEŠ *šá* E$_{2}$.AN.NA	
36. *iq-bu-ú* ^{lu2}*qi-i-pi* ^{lu2}ŠA$_{3}$.TAM ^{md}NA$_{3}$-ŠEŠ-MU *ù* ^{lu2}UMBISAG.ME	(36–37) The *qīpu,* the *šatammu*, Nabû-aḫa-iddin and the scribes sent (word) concerning those cows and

37. *a-na muḫ-ḫi* AB$_2$.GAL.MEŠ *šu-a-tim iš-pu-ru-ú-ma* 2 AB$_2$.GAL.ME	(37–40) They brought two cows branded with a star out of Gimillu's house and presented them before Nādinu, the governor of Uruk, and the assembly of the Babylonians and the Urukians, and
38. *šá kak-*⸢*kab*⸣*-tu$_4$ še-en-du ul-tu* E$_2$ ^{m}*gi-mil-lu*	
39. *i-bu-ku-nim-ma ma-ḫar* ^{m}*na-di-nu* ^{lu_2}GAR.UMUŠ UNUG^{ki}	
40. UKKIN ^{lu_2}TIN.TIR^{ki}.MEŠ *ù* ^{lu_2}UNUG^{ki}*-a-a uš-šu-zi-zu-ma*	
41. 60-*šu* AB.GAL.MEŠ *ku-mu* 2 AB$_2$.GAL.MEŠ *šá kak-kab-tu$_4$*	(41–42) They decided that [Gi]millu must pay 60 cows for the 2 cows [branded] with a star.
42. ⸢*še*⸣-[*en-du e*]-*l*[*i* ^{m}*gi*]-*mil-lu ip-ru-su*	
43. 1 AB$_2$.GAL *šá ina re-e-ḫu šá ṣe-e-nu i-na* ŠU.2	(43–46) 1 cow from the remainder of the flock, led away from Nanaya-iddin son of Arad-Innin, and branded in the Eanna and deposited with Ibnaya son of Nabû-aḫḫē-šullim:
44. ^{md}*na-na-a*-MU A ^{m}IR$_3$-^{d}*in-nin ab-ka-ta-am-ma*	
45. *ina* E$_2$.AN.NA *še-en-de-ti ù a-na* ^{m}*ib-na-a*	
46. A-*šú šá* ^{md}NA$_3$-ŠEŠ.MEŠ-GI *paq-ad-da-ti ù* ^{m}*ib-na-a*	
47. *iq-bu-ú um-ma ina* ITI KIN MU 17-*kám* AB$_2$.GAL *šu-a-tim*	(46–47) And Ibnaya said thus:
48. *ina* ŠU.2 ^{lu_2}SIPA-*ia* ^{m}*gi-mil-lu i-ta-ba-ak*	(47–48) "In Ulūlu, year 17 (of Nabonidus), Gimillu led that cow away from my shepherd."
49. *ù* ^{m}*gi-mil-lu* AB$_2$.GAL *šu-a-tim e-li ram-ni-šú ú-kin*	(49) And Gimillu testified against himself (regarding) that cow.
50. 30 AB$_2$.GAL.MEŠ *ku-mu* 1 AB$_2$.GAL *e-li* ^{m}*gi-mil-lu ip-ru-su*	(50) They decided that Gimillu must pay 30 cows for the 1 cow.
51. *qa-pu-ut-tu$_4$ šá ṣe-e-nu šá* ^{d}GAŠAN *šá* UNUG^{ki} *šá ina pa-ni*	(51–52) The herd of sheep of the Lady of Uruk, which is in the care of Šumaya son of Marduk-aḫa-iddin.

52. ^{m}*šu-ma-a* A-*šú šá* ^{md}AMAR.UTU-ŠEŠ-MU *il-la* DU-*zu* 53. *šá* ^{m}*šu-ma-a* ^{m}*gi-mil-lu ul-tu* EDIN *šá la* ^{lu_2}*qí-pa-a-nu* 54. *ù* ^{lu_2}UMBISAG.MEŠ *šá* E_2.AN.NA *a-na* E_2.AN.NA *i-bu-ku ina lìb-bi* U_8 55. *šá kak-kab-tu*$_4$ *še-en-de-ti* 1 *par-rat* 1 SAL.ÁŠ.GAR *ta-mi-me-e*	(52–56) Without Šumaya being present, Gimillu brought it to the Eanna from the pasture without (informing) the *qīpu*-officials or the scribes of the Eanna. Of the ewes branded with a star, Gimillu led away 1 lamb and 1 unmarked female goat.
56. ^{m}*gi-mil-lu i-ta-ba-ak ù* ^{m}SUM-*na-a* A-*šú šá* ^{m}ŠEŠ-DUG.GA 57. ^{lu_2}SIPA *šá ṣe-e-nu i-bu-ku ina* UKKIN *ú-kin-nu-uš*	(56–57) And Iddinaya son of Aḫu-ṭāb, the shepherd who brought the sheep, testified against him in the assembly.
58. 30 *ṣe-e-nu ku-mu* 1 U_8 *šá kak-kab-tu*$_4$ 59. *še-en-de-ti e-li* ^{m}*gi-mil-lu ip-ru-su*	(58–59) They decided that Gimillu must pay 30 sheep for the 1 ewe branded with a star.

---

60. 5 U_8.ME *šá kak-kab-tu*$_4$ *še-en-du šá qa-pu-ut-tu*$_4$ 61. *šá* ^{m}*ḫaš-di-ia* A-*šú šá* ^{md}NA_3-DIB-UD.DA ^{lu_2}NA.KAD *šá* ^{d}GAŠAN *šá* UNUG^{ki} 62. *šá* ^{md}*dan-nu*-ŠEŠ.MEŠ-*šu*-DU_3 A-*šú šá* ^{m}LUGAL-DU ^{lu_2}SIPA *šá* ^{m}*ḫaš-di-ia* 63. *ul-tu qa-pu-tu*$_4$ *šá* ^{m}*ḫaš-di-ia i-bu-ku-ú-ma*	(60–63) 5 ewes, branded with a star, from the herd of Ḫašdiya son of Nabû-mušētiq-uddê, the herdsman of the Lady of Uruk, which Dannu-aḫḫēšu-ibni son of Šarru-kīn, Ḫašdiya's shepherd, led away from the herd of Ḫašdiya and
64. *ina* UNUG^{ki} ^{m}*gi-mil-lu* U_4 27-*kám šá* ITI ŠU MU 1-*kám* 65. ^{m}*ku-ra-áš* LUGAL KUR.KUR *ṣe-e-nu ù* ^{lu_2}SIPA 66. *ina* DU-*zu šá* ^{md}UTU-NUMUN-BA-*šá* A-*šú šá* ^{m}[^{d}*in-nin*-MU]-URI_3 67. *ú-ki-il a-na* ^{m}*ni-din-tu*$_4$ A-*šú šá* ^{m}*ki*-[X ^{lu_2}NA.KAD *šá*] ^{d}GAŠAN *šá* UNUG^{ki}	(64–68) In Uruk, on 27 Dûzu, year 1 of Cyrus, king of the lands, Gimillu detained the sheep and the shepherd in the presence of Šamaš-zēra-iqīša son of [Innin-šuma]-uṣur (and) said thus to Nidintu son of [PN the herdsman of] the Lady of Uruk:

68. *iq-bu-ú* ⌜*um*⌝*-ma ṣe-e-nu a-bu-ku-ma* KU$_3$.BABBAR-*ši-na*	(68–69) "Take the sheep! Bring me and give me their silver!"
69. *i-šá-ʾ i-bi-ʾ* ^{m}*ni-din-tu*$_4$ *ina* UKKIN *ú-kin-ni-šú*	(69–70) In the assembly, Nidintu testified against him thus:
70. *um-ma* 3 *ṣe-e-nu ina lìb-bi ki-i a-bu-ku* 3 GIN$_2$ KU$_3$.BABBAR	(70–71) "When I led away 3 sheep from the lot, (and) when I received the 3 šeqels of silver, I gave (them) to him."
71. *ki-i áš-šá-ʾ at-ta-na-áš-šu ú-ìl-tim šá* ^{m}*ki-na-a*	(71–74) In the assembly, they read the document of Kīnaya which he contracted with Dannu-aḫḫēšu-ibni, (and which stated) thus: "The silver is given to Gimillu."
72. *šá it-ti* ^{md}*dan-nu*-ŠEŠ.MEŠ-*šú*-DU$_3$ *i-il-li*	
73. *ù ina lìb-bi šaṭ-ru um-ma* KU$_3$.BABBAR *šá a-na* ^{m}*gi-mil-lu* SUM-*na*	
74. *ina* UKKIN *iš-ta-as-su-ú*	
75. *ṣe-e-nu-aʾ* 3 1-*en* 30 90 *ṣe-e-nu*	(75–76) They decided that Gimillu must pay thirtyfold for those 3 sheep: 90 sheep.
76. *e-li* ^{m}*gi-mil-lu ip-ru-su*	

---

77. 1 UD$_5$ *šá kak-kab-tu*$_4$ *še-en-de-ti sá qa-pu-ut-tu*$_4$	(77–81) 1 goat branded with a star, from the flock of Nabû-mušētiq-uddê, son of Nanaya-iddin, which, in Ulūlu, year 17 (of Nabonidus), Nabû-mušētiq-uddê brought to the Eanna together with his flock and about which Nabû-mušētiq-uddê said:
78. *šá* ^{md}NA$_3$-DIB-UD.DA A-*šú šá* ^{md}*na-na-a*-MU *šá* ^{md}NA$_3$-DIB-UD.DA	
79. *ina* ITI KIN MU 17-*kám it-ti ṣe-e-ni-šú*	
80. *a-na* E$_2$.AN.NA *i-bu-ku ù* ^{md}NA$_3$-DIB-UD.DA	
81. *iq-bu-ú ina* KA$_2$ *ṭi-li-mu* ^{m}SUM-*na-a* ŠEŠ *šá* ^{m}ŠU	(81–82) "At the Ṭilimu-gate, Iddinaya, Gimillu's brother, led (it) away."
82. *i-ta-ba-ak ù* ^{md}NA$_3$-ŠEŠ.MEŠ-MU A-*šú šá* ^{md}EN-KAM$_2$	(82–83) In the assembly, Nabû-aḫḫē-iddin son of Bēl-ēreš said thus:
83. *ina* UKKIN *iq-bi um-ma* UD$_5$ *šu-a-tim ina pa-ni-ia*	(83–84) "Iddinaya led that goat away in my presence."
84. ^{m}SUM-*na-a i-ta-ba-ak ù* ^{m}*gi-mil-lu iq-bi*	(84–85) And Gimillu said thus: "It was I who sent Iddinaya my brother."
85. *um-ma a-na-ku* ^{m}SUM-*na* ŠEŠ-*ú-a al-tap-ra*	

86. UD$_5$-*a*ʾ 1 1-*en* 30 30 *ṣe-e-nu* 87. *e-li* ^{m}*gi-mil-lu ip-ru-su*	(86–87) They decided that Gimillu must pay thirtyfold for that 1 goat: 30 sheep.
88. 1 U$_8$ *šá kak-kab-tu še-en-de-ti šá qa-pu-ut-tu*$_4$ 89. [*šá* ^{m}]*la-qi-pi* A-*šú šá* ^{md}NA$_3$-MU-DU ^{lu_2}NA.KAD *šá* ^{d}GAŠAN *šá* UNUG^{ki} 90. [*šá ina* IM.DUB] *šá-ṭi-ru ina* E$_2$ ^{md}NA$_3$-*na-din*-ŠEŠ ^{m}*gi-mil-lu*	(88–91) 1 ewe branded with a star, from the flock [of] Lāqīpi son of Nabû-šuma-ukīn, the herdsman of the Lady of Uruk, recorded [in the tablet]. In the house of Nabû-nādin-aḫi, Gimillu [sl] aughtered (it):
91. [*it*]-⸢*te*⸣-*ki-is* ^{m}*mu-še-zib*-^{d}EN A-*šú šá* ^{m}GI-^{d}AMAR.UTU 92. [^{m}]^{d}*na-na-a*-ŠEŠ-MU A-*šú šá* ^{md}U.GUR-*ina*-SUH$_3$-KAR-*ir* 93. ^{md}30-DU$_3$ A-*šú šá* ^{md}*na-na-a*-KAM$_2$ *ù* ^{md}NA$_3$-MU-MU A-*šú šá* ^{md}*na-na-a*-KAM$_2$	(91–94) In the assembly, Mušēzib-Bēl son of Mušallim-Marduk, Nanaya-aḫa-iddin son of Nergal-ina-tēšê-ēṭir, Sîn-ibni son of Nanaya-ēreš and Nabû-šuma-iddin son of Nanaya-ēreš testified against Gimillu.
94. *ina* UKKIN ^{m}*gi-mil-lu ú-kin-nu* U$_8$-*a*ʾ 1 1-*en* 30 95. 30 *ṣe-e-nu e-li* ^{m}*gi-mil-lu ip-ru-su*	(94–95) They decided that Gimillu must pay thirtyfold for that 1 ewe: 30 sheep.
96. 1 *ka-lum šá* ^{md}NA$_3$-DIB-UD.DA A-*šú šá* ^{md}*na-na-a*-MU	(96–97) 1 lamb (about) which Nabû-mušētiq-uddê son of Nanaya-iddin, the herdsman of the Lady of Uruk said thus:
97. ^{lu_2}NA.KAD *šá* ^{d}GAŠAN *šá* UNUG^{ki} *iq-bu-ú um-ma ina* ITI KIN MU 17-*kám* 98. *it-ti ṣe-e-nu ina re-e-ḫu šá ina muḫ-ḫi-ia* 99. *a-na* E$_2$.AN.NA *áš-pu-ru* ^{m}*gi-mil-lu ina* ŠU.2 ^{md}INNIN-ŠEŠ.MEŠ-SU	(97–100) "In Ulūlu, year 17 (of Nabonidus), I sent (this sheep) together with the remainder (of the sheep) which I owed to the Eanna. Gimillu led away (this sheep) from Innin-aḫḫē-erība, my brother."
100. ŠEŠ-*ia i-ta-ba-ak ù* ^{m}*gi-mil-lu e-li*	(100–101) Gimillu testified against himself thus:

101. *ram-ni-šú ú-kin-ni um-ma ka-lum šu-a-tim a-ta-bak*	(101–102) "I led away that lamb apart from the 2 rams which I received as a gift."
102. *e-lat* 2 UDU.NITA.MEŠ *šá a-na nu-up*$^{!}$*-tu*$_4$ *a-na-ku at-ta-áš-šú*	
103. *ka-lum-a*ʾ 1 1-*en* 30 30 *ṣe-en* UGU ^{m}ŠU *ip-ru-su*	(103) They decided that Gimillu must pay thirtyfold for that 1 lamb: 30 sheep.

104. 1 *par-rat šá qa-pu-ut-tu*$_4$ *šá* ^{m}*zu-um-bu* A-*šú šá* ^{md}*na-na-a*-KAM$_2$	(104–105) 1 lamb from the flock of Zumbu son of Nanaya-ēreš, the herdsman of the Lady of Uruk, (about) which [Zumbu] said thus:
105. ^{lu_2}NA.KAD *šá* ^{d}GAŠAN *šá* UNUG^{ki} *šá* ^{m}[*zu-um-bu*] *iq-bu-ú um-ma ul-tu*	(105–106) "Gimillu led (it) away from my flock."
106. *ṣe-e-ni-ia* ^{m}*gi-mil-lu i-ta-ba-ak ù*	
107. ^{m}*gi-mil-lu e-li ram-ni-šú u-kin-ni*	(106–107) And Gimillu testified against himself:
108. *e-lat* 2 GIN$_2$ KU$_3$.BABBAR *ù* MAŠ.TUR *šá a-na nu-up-tu*$_4$ *at-ta-áš-šú*	(108) "(This is) apart from 2 šeqels of silver and 1 he-goat that I received as a gift."
109. *par-rat-a*ʾ 1 1-*en* 30 30 *ṣe-e-nu* UGU ^{m}ŠU *ip-ru-su*	(109) They decided that Gimillu must pay thirtyfold for that 1 lamb: 30 sheep.

110. 1 *par-rat šá kak-kab-tu*$_4$ *še-en-de-ti šá ina* ITI ŠU MU 1-*kám*	(110–112) 1 lamb, branded with a star which Gimillu sold to Nidintu son of Ardiya for silver in Dûzu, year 1 of Cyrus, king of the lands, and
111. ^{m}*ku-ra-áš* LUGAL KUR.KUR *šá* ^{m}*gi-mil-lu a-na* KU$_3$.BABBAR	
112. *a-na* ^{m}*ni-din-tu*$_4$ A-*šú šá* ^{m}IR$_3$-*ia id-di-nu-ma par-rat*	(112–113) The lamb was led to the Eanna.
113. *a-na* E$_2$.AN.NA *ab-ka-ta ù* ^{m}*gi-mil-lu ina* UKKIN	(113–114) And in the assembly, Gimillu testified against himself thus:
114. *e-li ram-ni-šú u-kin-ni um-ma a-na-ku par-rat*	(114–115) "It was I who gave the lamb to Nidintu."
115. *a-na* ^{m}*ni-din-tu*$_4$ *at-ta-din par-rat-a*ʾ 1 1-*en* 30	(115–116) They decided that Gimillu must pay thirtyfold for that 1 lamb: 30 sheep.
116. 30 *ṣe-e-nu e-li* ^{m}*gi-mil-lu ip-ru-su*	

117. ^{md}UTU-ŠEŠ-MU A-*šú šá* ^{md}NA$_3$-MU-DU ^{lu_2}NA.KAD *šá* ^{d}GAŠAN *šá* UNUG^{ki} 118. *šá* 10 MU.AN.NA.MEŠ *it-ti ṣe-e-ni-šú a-na* E$_2$.AN.NA 119. *la i-ru-bu šá* ^{lu_2}*qi-pa-a-nu ù* ^{lu_2}UMBISAG.MEŠ *šá* E$_2$.AN.NA 120. ^{m}*gi-mil-lu a-na muḫ-ḫi* ^{md}UTU-ŠEŠ-MU *iš-pu-ru-ú-ma*	(117–120) Šamaš-aḫa-iddin son of Nabû-šuma-ukīn, the herdsman of the Lady of Uruk, who did not come with his sheep to the Eanna for ten years. The *qīpu*-officials and the scribes of the Eanna sent Gimillu to Šamaš-aḫa-iddin and
121. ^{m}*gi-mil-lu* ^{md}UTU-ŠEŠ-MU *i-mu-ru-ma a-na* E$_2$.AN.NA	(121–122) Gimillu inspected (the herd of) Šamaš-aḫa-iddin but did not bring him to the Eanna.
122. *la i-bu-ku* ^{m}*la-qí-pi* ^{lu_2}*qal-la šá* ^{md}UTU-ŠEŠ-MU	(122–123) Lāqīpi, the slave of Šamaš-aḫa-iddin, said thus:
123. *iq-bu-ú um-ma* 4 GUR ŠE.BAR 2 GIN$_2$ KU$_3$.BABBAR 1 UDU.NITA 124. ^{m}*gi-mil-lu ina* ŠU.2 ^{md}UTU-ŠEŠ-MU *ù* ^{m}*ṣil-la-a* A-*šú* 125. *it-ta-ši ù* ^{m}*ṣil-la-a* A-*šú šá* ^{md}UTU-ŠEŠ-MU *iṣ-qát* AN.BAR.MEŠ	(123–126) "Gimillu received 4 *kur* of barley, 2 šeqels of silver and one ram from Šamaš-aḫa-iddin and Ṣillaya his son. And he released Ṣillaya son of Šamaš-aḫa-iddin who was placed in iron fetters."
126. *ki-i id-du-ú un-da-šìr* ^{m}*gi-mil-lu iq-bi*	(126–127) Gimillu said thus:
127. *um-ma al-la* 1 UDU.NITA *ina* ŠU.2-*šú ul a-bu-uk*	(127) "I did not lead away more than 1 ram from him."
128. ^{md}30-DU$_3$ A-*šú šá* ^{md}*na-na-a*-KAM$_2$ *ina* UKKIN *a-na* ^{m}*gi-mil-lu*	(128–129) In the assembly, Sîn-ibni son of Nanaya-ēreš testified against Gimillu thus:
129. *ú-kin um-ma ina* DU-*zu-iá* 2 GIN$_2$ KU$_3$.BABBAR 130. ^{m}NA$_3$-SIG$_5$-*an-ni a-na muḫ-ḫi* ^{m}*ṣil-la-a*	(129–130) "In my presence, Nabû-udammiqanni … 2 šeqels of silver for Ṣillaya."
131. [KU$_3$.BABBAR-*a*ʾ 2 GIN$_2$] 132. 1-*en* 30 *ù* UDU-*a*ʾ 1 1-*en* 30 133. 1 MA.NA 10 GIN$_2$ KU$_3$.BABBAR *ù* 30 *ṣe-e-nu* 134. *e-li* ^{m}*gi-mil-lu ip-ru-su*	(131–134) They decided that Gimillu must pay thirtyfold [for the 2 šeqels of silver] and thirtyfold for the 1 sheep: 1 mina 10 šeqel of silver and 30 sheep.

135. 1 AB₂.GAL šar-ḫi-tu₄ šá ᵐᵈU. GUR-MU-DU₃ A-šú šá ᵐŠEŠ-šá-a
136. ˡᵘ²NA.KAD šá ᵈGAŠAN šá UNUGᵏⁱ šá ᵐgi-mil-lu [ina] ŠU.2
137. ᵐᵈU.GUR-MU-DU₃ i-bu-ku ù ᵐgi-mil-lu ina UKKIN
138. [e-li] ram-ni-šú ú-kin-ni AB₂.GAL-a' 1
139. [1-en x AB₂ e]-li ᵐgi-mil-lu ip-ru-su
140. 1 [ᵗᵘᵍ²šir]-a-am šá in-za-ḫu-ru-e-ti šá ul-tu
141. E₂.AN.NA ˡᵘ²qí-pa-a-nu ù ˡᵘ²UMBISAG.ME šá E₂.AN.NA
142. a-na ᵐMU-MU A-šú šá ᵐᵈU.GUR-GI šá muḫ-ḫi ˡᵘ²GAN.MEŠ
143. šá ˡᵘ²SIPA.MEŠ šá it-ti LUGAL id-di-nu-ma
144. ᵐgi-mil-lu ina ŠU.2 ᵐMU-MU iš-šu-ú
145. ù ᵐgi-mil-lu ina UKKIN e-li ram-ni-šú ú-kin-ni
146. ù KU₃.BABBAR ku-mu ᵗᵘᵍ²šir-a-am e-li ᵐgi-mil-lu ip-ru-su
147. NIGIN 92 AB₂.GAL.MEŠ 302 ṣe-e-nu
148. ù 1 MA.NA 10 GIN₂ KU₃.BABBAR

(135–137) 1 beautiful branded cow, belonging to Nergal-šuma-ibni son of Aḫišaya, the herdsman of the Lady of Uruk, which Gimillu led away [fr]om Nergal-šuma-ibni.

(137–138) And, in the assembly, Gimillu testified [against] himself.

(138–139) They decided that Gimillu shall pay [x cows] for that 1 cow.

(140–143) 1 tunic of inzaḫurētu wool which the qīpu-officials and the scribes of the Eanna gave from the Eanna to Šuma-iddin son of Nergal-ušallim who is in charge of the archers of the shepherds with the king.

(144) Gimillu received it from Šuma-iddin.

(145) And, in the assembly, Gimillu testified against himself.

(146) They decided that Gimillu must pay silver for the tunic.

(147–148) Total: 92 cows, 302 sheep and 1 mina 10 šeqel of silver.

Notes

11. The "chest of the property of the Eanna" denotes the Eanna's treasury.

71–74. The document mentioned here may be a deposition in which the whereabouts of the silver are recorded.

123–126. Ṣillaya was held in distraint for the debts owed by his father, Šamaš-aḫa-iddin.

132–134. The 1 mina of silver and the 30 sheep correspond exactly to the thirtyfold penalty for 2 šeqels of silver and 1 sheep. The additional 10 šeqels of silver may reflect a payment for the barley mentioned in line 123. San Nicolò (1933a, 70 n. 4) argues against this possibility, but revised price data may, in fact, support it (see Jursa 2010, 443–51).

138–139. It would seem natural to restore the thirtyfold penalty in this line. However, this restoration cannot be reconciled with the total of 92 cows in line 147. Therefore, San Nicolò suggests that in this case only the double penalty was imposed (1933a, 71 n. 4). This restoration yields the desired 92 cows: 60 (lines 41–42) + 30 (line 50) + 2.

147. The total of 302 sheep does not accord with the amounts enumerated following each judgment. According to these enumerations, Gimillu owes only 300 sheep, rather than 302. San Nicolò accounts for the remaining two sheep as follows: one is owed for the unmarked goat (line 55) and one for the fifth of the five ewes mentioned in line 60. The remaining four ewes are accounted for in lines 75–76 and 115 (1933a, 71 n. 4).

39. The King's Court of Law

Text: YBC 3865
Copy: Tremayne 1925 (YOS 7), No. 31
Translation/Discussion: San Nicolò 1932, 337–38; Magdalene 2007, 64–65, 91; Kleber 2008, 57; Holtz 2009, 118–20
Place of Composition: Uruk
Date: 11.VIII. 4 Cyr (22 November, 535 BCE)

Marduk-dīna-īpuš is responsible for two branded sheep that belong to the Eanna's flock and that were led away by Gimillu. Marduk-dīna-īpuš is summoned to the king's court of law in Babylon to argue his case against the šatammu, *the royal official and the scribes of the Eanna. If Marduk-dīna-īpuš does not appear, he must pay thirtyfold for the two sheep.*

As San Nicolò suggests, the present text originates in an appeal against an earlier ruling by the Eanna authorities (San Nicolò 1932, 339; Magdalene 2007, 64–65). Accordingly, one may assume that a trial, similar to the one described in Document 38, has taken place prior to the promulgation of the present document. In the earlier trial, Marduk-dīna-īpuš was found to be responsible for the two sheep in question. He has appealed the ruling, probably with the claim that he delivered the sheep to Gimillu, who "led them away" on behalf of the Eanna. One may speculate that although Gimillu received the sheep, the sheep never reached the Eanna. Another text (Contenau 1927–29, No. 134) describes just such a situation: a herdsman reports that Gimillu received a ewe from him but did not give it to the Eanna.

The present document demonstrates that the litigation of the Gimillu affair was hardly a matter limited to the internal affairs of the temple at Uruk. If Marduk-dīna-īpuš indeed complied with its terms, then the case reached the royal court of law in Babylon.

1. U_4 20-*kám šá* ITI GAN MU 4-*kám* ᵐ*ku-ra-áš*	(1–3) On 20 Kislīmu, year 4 of Cyrus, king of Babylon, king of the lands, Marduk-dīna-īpuš son of Ḫiraḫḫa shall come to Babylon.
2. LUGAL TIN.TIR^{ki} LUGAL KUR.KUR ^{md}ASAR.LU_2.HI-DI. KU_5-DU_3-*uš*	
3. A-*šú šá* ᵐ*ḫi-ra-aḫ-ḫa a-na* TIN. TIR^{ki} *il-la-ka-ma*	

4. *di-i-ni šá* 2 UDU.NITA.MEŠ *šá kak-kab-*tu_4 *še-en-du*	(4–10) He shall argue the case regarding 2 sheep branded with a star, which Gimillu son of Innin-šuma-ibni led away from the flock of Marduk-dīna-īpuš, against Nidintu-Bēl, the *šatammu* of the Eanna, Nabû-aḫa-iddin, the royal official in charge of the Eanna, and the scribes of the Eanna, in the king's court of law.
5. *šá* ^{m}*gi-mil-lu* A-*šú šá* ^{md}*in-nin-*MU-*ib-ni*	
6. *ul-tu ṣe-e-ni šá* ^{md}ASAR.LU_2.HI-DI.KU_5-DU_3-*uš*	
7. *i-bu-ku it-ti* ^{m}*ni-din-*tu_4-^{d}EN ^{lu_2}$ŠA_3$.TAM E_2.AN.NA	
8. ^{md}NA_3-ŠEŠ-MU ^{lu_2}SAG-LUGAL ^{lu_2}EN *pi-qit-*tu_4 E_2.AN.NA	
9. *ù* ^{lu_2}UMBISAG.MEŠ *šá* E_2.AN.NA *ina* E_2 *di-i-ni*	
10. *šá* LUGAL *i-dab-ub-bu ki-i*	(10–12) If he does not come, he shall pay thirtyfold for these 2 sheep to the Lady of Uruk.
11. *la it-tal-ku* UDU.NITA-*a*ʾ 2	
12. 1-*en* 30 *a-na* ^{d}GAŠAN *šá* UNUG^{ki} *i-nam-din*	
13. ^{lu_2}*mu-kin-nu* ^{md}UTU-DU-IBILA A-*šú šá* ^{md}DI.KU_5-ŠEŠ.MEŠ-MU	(13–14) Witnesses: Šamaš-mukīn-apli son of Madānu-aḫḫē-iddin descendant of Šigûa;
14. A ^{m}*ši-gu-ú-a* ^{m}GI-^{d}AMAR.UTU A-*šú šá*	(14–15) Mušallim-Marduk son of Arad-Nabû descendant of Šangû-Nabû;
15. ^{m}IR_3-^{d}NA_3 A ^{lu_2}E_2.MAŠ-^{d}NA_3 ^{md}AMAR.UTU-SUR	(15–16) Marduk-ēṭir son of Bēl-uballiṭ descendant of Amēl-Ea;
16. A-*šú šá* ^{md}EN-TIN-*iṭ* A ^{m}LU_2-^{d}IDIM	
17. ^{md}EN-A-MU A-*šú šá* ^{md}EN-*re-man-ni* A ^{lu_2}*šá*-MUN.HI.A-*šú*	(17) Bēl-apla-iddin son of Bēl-rēmanni descendant of Ša-ṭabti-šu
18. ^{lu_2}UMBISAG ^{m}*gi-mil-lu* A-*šú šá* ^{md}*in-nin-*NUMUN-MU	(18) Scribe: Gimillu son of Innin-zēra-iddin.
19. UNUG^{ki} ITI APIN U_4 11-*kám* MU 4-*kám*	(19–20) Uruk. 11 Araḫšamna, year 4 of Cyrus, king of Babylon, king of the lands.
20. ^{m}*kur-áš* LUGAL TIN.TIR^{ki} LUGAL KUR.KUR	

NOTES

13–14. Šamaš-mukīn-apli son of Madānu-aḫḫē-iddin descendant of Šigûa held a "brewer's prebend" and eventually functioned in the prominent position of "chief brewer" (*šāpir sirāšê*) (Kümmel 1979, 151). His father is attested in the same position in Document 21.

40. Oral and Written Evidence

Text: YBC 3921
Copy: Tremayne 1925 (YOS 7), No. 102
Translation/Discussion: Dougherty, 1923, 61; San Nicolò, 1933a, 73–74; Dandamaev 1984, 494–95; Joannès 2000b, No. 167 (pp. 225–26)
Place of Composition: (Uruk)
Date: 27.IX.0 Camb (11 January, 529 BCE)

Riḫētu testifies to the šatammu *and the royal official in charge of the Eanna that in year 8 of Cyrus, he escaped from the service of Šamaš-mukīn-apli. In the accession year of Cambyses, Gimillu saw Riḫētu and entrusted him to Sîn-ibni, and instructed Sîn-ibni to send the wages for Riḫētu's work directly to Gimillu. Sîn-ibni then testifies that Gimillu entrusted Riḫētu to him with a contract for the wages of 5 šeqels per year. After the contract, however, Gimillu also sent a letter offering Riḫētu to Nabû-nādin. Sîn-ibni and Riḫētu submit the letter that Gimillu sent to Nabû-nādin, and the letter corroborates the testimony of Sîn-ibni. The assembly binds and seals the letter and places it in the Eanna, probably to be used as evidence against Gimillu.*

The present document provides a superb depiction of Gimillu's wheeling and dealing. Instead of properly addressing the problem of the escaped plowman (perhaps by returning him, for example), Gimillu seized the opportunity to make money by arranging for Riḫētu's rental and pocketing the rent. Apparently not satisfied with the first arrangement with Sîn-ibni, Gimillu pursued a second deal, this time with Nabû-nādin. But in doing so, it seems that he made the fateful mistake of leaving a written record, even if this record was not on clay but on less durable materials. Riḫētu and Sîn-ibni got hold of Gimillu's letter to Nabû-nādin, which would now serve as incriminating evidence.

1. ^{m}*ri-ḫe-e-tu*$_4$ DUMU-*šú šá* ^{m}IR$_3$-^{d}*in-nin* ^{lu_2}APIN ^{lu_2}RIG$_7$ ^{d}INNIN UNUG^{ki} 2. *a-na* ^{md}NA$_3$-DU-IBILA ^{lu_2}ŠA$_3$.TAM E$_2$.AN.NA *ù* ^{md}NA$_3$-ŠEŠ-MU	(1–3) Riḫētu son of Arad-Innin, the plowman, an oblate of Ištar of Uruk, said thus to Nabû-mukīn-apli, the *šatammu* of the Eanna, and Nabû-aḫa-iddin, the royal official in charge of the Eanna:
3. ^{lu_2}SAG-LUGAL ^{lu_2}EN *pi-qit-tu*$_4$ E$_2$.AN.NA *iq-bi um-ma ul-tu* 4. MU 8-*kám* ^{m}*ku-ra-áš* LUGAL TIN.TIR^{ki} LUGAL KUR.KUR *ul-tu* UGU ^{giš}APIN	(3–6) "From year 8 of Cyrus, king of Babylon, king of the lands, I escaped from the plow of Šamaš-mukīn-apli son of Sîn-nādin-šumi, the plowman of the Lady of Uruk, owner of my plow."

5. *šá* ^{md}UTU-DU-IBILA DUMU-*šú* *šá* ^{md}30-*na-din*-MU ^{lu_2}APIN *šá* ^{d}GAŠAN *šá* UNUG^{ki} EN ^{giš}APIN-*iá*	
6. *aḫ-li-iq-ma i-na* ITI KIN MU SAG.NAM.LUGAL.LA ^{m}*kam-bu-zi-ia*	(6–8) "In Ulūlu of the accesion year of Cambyses, king of Babylon, king of the lands, Gimillu son of Innin-šuma-ibni saw me and entrusted me to Sîn-ibni son of Nabû-zabādu (saying) thus:"
7. LUGAL TIN.TIR^{ki} LUGAL KUR. KUR ^{m}*gi-mil-lu* DUMU-*šú šá* ^{md}*in-nin*-MU-DU$_3$	
8. *i-mu-ra-an-ni-ma ina* IGI ^{md}30-*ib-ni* DUMU-*šú šá* ^{md}NA$_3$-*za-ba-du*	
9. *ip-qí-da-an-na um-ma* KU$_3$. BABBAR *i-di-šú i-šá-am-ma i-bi-in-nu*	(9) "'Bring the silver of his wages and give it (to me)!'"
10. *ù* ^{md}30-DU$_3$ *iq-bu-ú um-ma* ^{m}ŠU ^{m}*ri-ḫe-e-tu*$_4$ *ina* IGI-*iá*	(10) And Sîn-ibni said thus:
11. *ip-te-qid ù rik-su a-na* MU.AN. NA 5 GIN$_2$ KU$_3$.[BABBAR]	(10–12) "Gimillu entrusted Riḫētu to me and contracted a contract for 5 šeqels of silver per year as his (Riḫētu's) wage."
12. *a-na i-di-šú it-ti-ia iš-ta-ka-as*	
13. *ár-ki rik-su šá* ^{m}*gi-mil-lu it-ti-iá iš-ku-su*	(13–15) "After Gimillu contracted the contract with me, he sent a letter to Nabû-nādin son of Erībaya, the administrator of the city of Kî-Nabû, (stating) thus:
14. *ši-pir-ti a-na* ^{md}NA$_3$-*na-din* DUMU-*šú šá* ^{m}*eri-ba-a* ^{lu_2}EN *pi-qit-tu*$_4$	
15. *šá* URU *šá* ^{m}*ki-i*-^{d}NA$_3$ *il-tap-ru um-ma i-na pa-ni-ka li-iz-ziz-ma*	(15–17) "'Let him serve you. If he pleases you, send 5 šeqels of silver per year as his wage. If not, let him be at the disposal of Sîn-ibni.'"
16. *ki-i pa-ni-ka ma-ḫir i-na* MU.AN. NA 5 GIN$_2$ KU.BABBAR	
17. *i-di-šú šu-bi-lu ù ia-a-nu-ú lu-ú ina* IGI ^{md}30-*ib-ni iš-šu-ú*	
18. *a-di i-na-an-na* ^{m}*ri-ḫe-e-tu*$_4$ *ina* IGI ^{md}NA$_3$-*na-din ú-šu-uz*	(18) "Until now, Riḫētu remains at the disposal of Nabû-nādin."
19. *ši-pir-tu*$_4$ *šá* ^{m}ŠU *a-na* UGU ^{m}*ri-ḫe-e-tu*$_4$ *a-na* ^{md}NA$_3$-*na-din iš-pu-ru*	(19–20) Sîn-ibni and Riḫētu gave the *šatammu* and Nabû-aḫa-iddin the letter that Gimillu sent to Nabû-nādin concerning Riḫētu.

20. ^{md}30-DU$_3$ *ù* ^{m}*ri-ḫe-e-tu*$_4$ *a-na* ^{lu_2}ŠA$_3$.TAM *u* ^{md}NA$_3$-SEŠ-MU *id-di-nu-ma*	
21. *ki-i pi-i* ^{lu_2}*mu-kin-nu-tu šá* ^{md}30-DU$_3$ *ina* ŠA$_3$ *šá-ṭir um-ma ki-i*	(21) Corroborating the testimony of Sîn-ibni, therein was written thus:
22. *pa-ni-ka ma-ḫir* ^{m}*ri-ḫe-e-tu*$_4$ *ina* IGI-*ka li-iz-ziz-ma* MU.AN.NA	(21–24) "If he pleases you, let Riḫētu serve you and send me 5 šeqels of silver per year as his wage. If not, give him to Sîn-ibni. Let my letter be witness to you."
23. 5 GIN$_2$ KU$_3$.BABBAR *i-di-šú šu-bi-lu ù ia-a-nu-ú a-na* ^{md}30-DU$_3$	
24. *i-din-su ši-pir-ta-a lu-ú* ^{lu_2}*mu-kin-nu ina muḫ-ḫi-ka ši-pir-tu*$_4$	(24–27) The letter of the parchment-scribe which Gimillu sent to Nabû-nādin concerning Riḫētu, and which was seen in the assembly—they tied, sealed and placed in the Eanna.
25. *šá* ^{lu_2}*si-pi-ri šá* ^{m}ŠU *a-na* UGU <m>*ri-ḫe-e-tu*$_4$ *a-na*	
26. ^{md}NA$_3$-*na-din iš-pu-ru-ma ina* UKKIN *ta-nam-ru*	
27. *iš-ku-su ik-nu-ku u ina* E$_2$.AN.NA *iš-ku-nu*	
28. ITI GAN U$_4$ 27-*kám* MU SAG. NAM.LUGAL.⸢LA⸣	(28–29) 27 Kislīmu, accession year of Cambyses, king of Babylon.
29. ^{m}*ka-am-bu-zi-iá* LUGAL TIN. TIR^{ki}	
30. LUGAL KUR.KUR	

NOTES

1–6. The escaped plowman, Riḫētu, and the man from whom he escaped, Šamaš-mukīn-apli, both belonged to families that included other plowmen (Kümmel 1979, 102–3).

10-12. Comparison with the available data shows that the rate of hire here (5 šeqels per year) would have been extremely low, and thus very attractive to the potential employer (Jursa 2010, 676–77, 731).

41. A Suspicion of Contract for Murder

Text: YBC 6932
Copy: Jursa 2004a, No. 5 (pp. 126–27)
Translation/Discussion: Jursa 2004a, No. 5 (pp. 125–30); Ragen 2006, 492–94
Place of Composition: Bitqa-ša-Bēl-ēṭir, district of the Lady of Uruk
Date: 18.I.1 Dar (1 May, 521 BCE)

Zumbu, an oblate of the Eanna, reports to the assembly, including the qīpu-*official and the* šatammu *of the Eanna, that, on the previous day, Anu-zēra-šubši, another oblate, has informed him that Gimillu has contracted to murder the royal official in charge of the Eanna. The assembly summons Anu-zēra-šubši, who swears that he has neither heard anything about Gimillu's purported contract nor reported anything to Zumbu.*

At the time of the present text's composition, Gimillu holds the position of "chief farmer" (*ša muḫḫi sūti*) and his career is nearing its end. The relationship between Gimillu and the institution he represents has clearly soured, so that a rumor of his murderous intentions could emerge and at least seem plausible, even if the plot never came to fruition (Jursa 2004a, 129).

1. ^{m}*im-bi-ia* ^{lu_2}TIL.LA.GID$_2$.DA *šá* E$_2$.AN.NA DUMU-*šú*	(1–2) Imbiya, *qīpu*-official of the Eanna, son of Nanaya-ēreš descendant of Kidin-Marduk;
2. *šá* ^{md}*na-na-a*-KAM$_2$ DUMU ^{m}*ki-din*-^{d}AMAR.UTU	
3. ^{md}UTU-DU-A ^{lu_2}ŠA$_3$.TAM E$_2$.AN.NA DUMU-*šú šá* ^{m}*na-di-nu* DUMU ^{m}⸢*e-gi-bi*⸣	(3) Šamaš-mukīn-apli, the *šatammu* of the Eanna, son of Nādinu descendant of Egibi;
4. ^{md}30-ŠEŠ.MEŠ.TIN-*iṭ* DUMU-*šú šá* ^{md}NA$_3$-MU-MU DUMU ^{m}*su-pe-e*-^{d}EN	(4) Sîn-aḫḫē-bulliṭ son of Nabû-šuma-iddin descendant of Supê-Bēl;
5. ^{m}NUMUN-*ia* DUMU-*šú šá* ^{md}*na-na-a*-KAM$_2$ DUMU ^{m}*ki-din*-⸢^{d}⸣[AMAR.UT]U	(5) Zēriya son of Nanaya-ēreš descendant of Kidin-[Mardu]k;
6. ^{md}EN-SUM-⸢IBILA⸣ DUMU-*šú šá* ^{m}*ki-din*-^{d}AMAR.UTU DUMU ^{m}*e-ṭe-ru*	(6) Bēl-nādin-apli son of Kidin-Marduk descendant of Ēṭeru;
7. ^{md}INNIN-ŠEŠ-MU A-$_2$ *šá* ^{md}NA$_3$-*šu*-⸢*um*⸣-URI$_3$ DUMU ^{m}E$_2$.KUR-*za-kir*	(7) Ištar-aḫa-iddin son of Nabû-šuma-uṣur descendant of Ekur-zakir;

8. ^{md}*a-nu*-ŠEŠ-TIN DUMU-*šú šá* ^{md}INNIN-SUM-MU DUMU ^{m}*ku-ri-i*	(8) Anu-aḫa-bulliṭ son of Ištar-nādin-šumi descendant of Kurī;
9. ^{md}UTU-NUMUN-GAL$_2$-*ši* A-*šú šá* ^{m}DU$_3$-*ia* DUMU ^{m}*an-da-ḫar*	(9) Šamaš-zēra-šubši son of Bāniya descendant of Andaḫar.
10. UKKIN ^{lu_2}TIL.LA.GID$_2$.DA.ME *ù* ^{lu_2}DUMU DU$_3$.MEŠ	(10–13) (These are) the assembly of *qīpu*-officials and *mār banî* in whose presence Zumbu son of Rīmūtu, an oblate of Ištar of Uruk, said thus:
11. *šá i-na ú-šu-uz-zi-šú-nu* ^{m}*zu-um-bu* DUMU-*šú*	
12. *šá* ^{m}*ri-mu-tu* ^{lu_2}RIG$_7$ ^{d}INNIN UNUG^{ki}	
13. *iq-bu-ú um-ma ina* ITI BAR$_2$ U$_4$ 17-*kám* MU 1-*kám*	(13–16) "On 17 Nisannu, year 1 of Darius, king of Babylon, king of the lands, Anu-zēra-šubši son of Lâbāši, an oblate of Ištar of Uruk, said thus to me:"
14. ^{m}*da-a-ri-ia-a-mu-uš* LUGAL TIN.TIR^{ki} LUGAL KUR.KUR	
15. ^{md}*a-nu*-NUMUN-GAL$_2$-*ši* A-*šú šá* ^{m}*la-ba-ši* ^{lu_2}RIG$_7$ ^{d}INNIN UNUG^{ki}	
16. *iq-ta-ba-a um-ma* ^{m}ŠU ^{lu_2}*šá muḫ-ḫi* ^{giš}BAN$_2$ *šá* ^{d}GAŠAN *šá* UNUG^{ki}	(16–18) "'Gimillu, the chief farmer of the Lady of Uruk, contracted a contract for the killing of Sîn-šarra-uṣur, the royal official in charge of the Eanna.'"
17. *rik-su a-na da-a-ku šá* ^{md}30-LUGAL-URI$_3$ ^{lu_2}SAG-LUGAL	
18. ^{lu_2}EN *pi-qit-tu*$_4$ E$_2$.AN.NA *iš-ta-ka-as*	
19. ^{lu_2}TIL.LA$_2$.GID$_2$.DA.ME *ù* ^{lu_2}DUMU DU$_3$-*ia iš-pu-ru-ma*	(19–21) The *qīpu*-officials and the *mār banî* sent and brought Anu-zēra-šubši to them and, in the assembly, he swore (thus) by the gods:
20. ^{md}*a-nu*-NUMUN-GAL$_2$-*ši i-bu-ku-nim-ma i-na* UKKIN	
21. *ni-iš* DINGIR.MEŠ *iz-ku-ur ki-i ul-tu muḫ-ḫi*	(21–26) "Indeed, as long as I live, I have not heard anything regarding any document concerning Sîn-šarra-uṣur from Gimillu, the chief farmer, or anyone belonging to him, or his staff, and I have not said (anything) to Zumbu, the oblate."
22. *šá ba-al-ṭa-ka mim-ma šá si-pi-ri*	
23. *šá* ^{md}30-LUGAL-URI$_3$ *i-na pi-i šá* ^{m}ŠU	
24. ^{lu_2}*šá* UGU ^{giš}BAN$_2$ *mam-ma-ne-e-šú ma-la*	
25. *ba-šu-ú ù* ^{lu_2}ERIN$_2$.ME ŠU.2-*šú áš-mu-ú*	

26. *ù a-na* ^{m}*zu-um-bu* ^{lu_2}RIG$_7$ *aq-bu-u*	
27. ^{m}IR$_3$-^{d}AMAR.UTU ^{lu_2}DUB.SAR DUMU ^{md}EN-IBILA-URI$_3$	(27) Arad-Marduk, the scribe, son of Bēl-apla-uṣur.
28. ^{uru}*bit-qa šá* ^{md}EN-SUR 29. *ši-i-ḫu šá* ^{d}GAŠAN UNUG^{ki} 30. ITI BAR$_2$ U$_4$ 18-*kám* MU 1-*kám* 31. ^{m}*da-a-ri-ia-mu-uš* LUGAL TIN.TIR^{ki} 32. LUGAL KUR.KUR	(28–32) Bitqa-ša-Bēl-ēṭir, district of the Lady of Uruk. 18 Nisannu, year 1 of Darius, king of Babylon, king of the lands.

NOTES

1–2. During the reign of Cyrus and Cambyses, Imbiya served as the governor (*šākin ṭēmi*) of Uruk (Kümmel 1979, 139–40).

5. Zēriya and his brothers belonged to a well-attested family of cattle-herders. Zēriya held the position of herdsman (*nāqidu*) and "overseer of the herds" (*rāb būli*) (Kümmel 1979, 78–79).

9. Šamaš-zēra-šubši is attested as a jeweler (*kabšarru*) who was designated as a "temple enterer" (*ērib bīti*), which is the term used for someone who had entrance privileges in the Eanna (Kümmel 1979, 26).

The Case of Anu-šarra-uṣur's Branded Sheep (Documents 42–43)

The Eanna records rarely provide multiple documents pertaining to the various stages of the same legal case. Documents 42 and 43, both of which stem from one trial, are an important illustration of how the different stages in a trial are documented. One can trace the progress of the trial from the gathering of evidence, by recording the parties' statements (Document 42), through the sentencing (Document 43). Over the course of about one month, the case progresses from investigation by the Eanna authorities to a ruling by two royal judges.

This is another rather "high profile" case; it involves members of the upper levels of the Eanna's herd management as well as other higher-ups in the Eanna bureaucracy. In Document 42, Anu-šarra-uṣur, owner of the pen where the sheep in question were held, bears the title "herdsman of Ištar of Uruk," a position just below the chief herdsman. Bēl-šarra-uṣur, the man who testifies first in Document 42, held the title of "herdsman of Ištar of Uruk," too, and his brother was also a herdsman (Kümmel 1979, 58). On the adjudicatory side, the initial inquiries (Document 42) are conducted by the royal official of the Eanna, and when the two royal judges deliver the sentence (Document 43), the record is written in his presence, as well as in the presence of the *šatammu*. The witnesses to the initial investigation (Document 42) include Silim-ili (line 25), identified as the royal official in "charge of the chest" (*ša muḫḫi quppi*) (Kümmel 1979, 145–46), Bēl-eṭēri-Nabû (line 28), identified as a "royal official" (^{lu_2}SAG-LUGAL), Šamaš-mukīn-apli (line 27), a prominent member of the Eanna bureaucracy, who ultimately became "chief brewer" (Kümmel 1979, 151), Nabû-mukīn-apli (line 26), Nabû-nādin-aḫi (lines 26–27) and Lūṣi-ana-nūri-Marduk (lines 28–29), who are all elsewhere attested as scribes in the Eanna (Kümmel 1979, 116, 128, 131), and Kīnaya son of Innin-līpi-uṣur, who is known as a herdsman (Kümmel 1979, 64). The witnesses on Document 43 are Arad-Marduk (line 19) and Sîn-ēreš (line 20), who both appear in prominent positions as witnesses in many Eanna texts, and were probably prebendiaries of the Eanna (Kümmel 1979, 152), and Bēl-nādin-apli (line 21), who is well-attested as a scribe in the Eanna records with several family connections to other people named in the Eanna records (Kümmel 1979, 113, 128).

42. Testimony Regarding Five Branded Sheep

Text: YBC 4006
Copy: Tremayne 1925 (YOS 7), No. 140
Translation/Discussion: San Nicolò 1932b, 341; Holtz 2009, 86–89; Kleber 2012, 186–89; Sandowicz 2012, 284–87

Place of Composition: Uruk
Date: 3.XI.3 Camb (12 February, 526 BCE)

Five sheep from the pen of Anu-šarra-uṣur, branded for Ištar of Uruk, have been found in the possession of Bēl-šarra-uṣur. The royal official of the Eanna questions Bēl-šarra-uṣur, who states that Bēl-iqīša gave him the sheep. Bēl-iqīša is brought to the assembly for interrogation, where he claims that he received the five branded sheep directly from Anu-šarra-uṣur, the original owner, along with five other unbranded sheep, all in payment for a debt Anu-šarra-uṣur owed Bēl-iqīša. He swears that he deposited only the five branded sheep in question with Bēl-šarra-uṣur. Bēl-šarra-uṣur then swears that Bēl-iqīša deposited the five branded sheep with him, and that the branded ewes gave birth.

Bēl-iqīša testifies that Anu-šarra-uṣur has given him one branded ram, four branded ewes and five unbranded lambs, for a total of ten sheep. In the eyes of the law, there would have been nothing wrong with the transfer of the five unbranded lambs in payment of a debt. The main legal issue here is that Bēl-iqīša, according to his own testimony, has accepted five branded sheep in payment of a debt owed to him by Anu-šarra-uṣur. Branded sheep are marked as the Eanna's property, so Anu-šarra-uṣur should not have used them to pay off a personal debt and Bēl-iqīša should not have accepted them in payment (see Kleber 2012, 190–91).

Because of this illegality, Bēl-iqīša cannot keep the branded sheep in his possession without raising suspicions. So, perhaps in collusion with Anu-šarra-uṣur—who would have every interest in seeing his debt to Bēl-iqīša paid from the Eanna's herds instead of from his own—Bēl-iqīša has transferred the sheep to Bēl-šarra-uṣur, a temple herdsman. There, the branded sheep would appear "innocent" and the two men might avoid the consequences of their shady deal.

The timeline of this case casts suspicions on all of the parties involved. Anu-šarra-uṣur's initial illegal payment of the branded sheep to Bēl-iqīša occurs in Dûzu of year 2 of Cambyses. Bēl-iqīša waits four months, until Araḫšamna, to pass the sheep on to the Eanna's herdsman; he seems to have avoided suspicion until that point. Did fear of an impending investigation already then lead Bēl-iqīša (with or without Anu-šarru-uṣur) to take this action? Be that as it may, the dates on the records themselves indicate that over a year passes before the Eanna takes action. Did Bēl-šarra-uṣur, the herdsman, accept the sheep into his herd innocently, or, was he, too, part of the scheme by knowingly covering for Bēl-iqīša? In the end, it seems likely that someone, perhaps the herdsman Bēl-šarra-uṣur himself, has informed the Eanna about what has occurred. The result is the investigation and the judgment, one month later.

1.	1-*en* UDU *pu-ḫal ù* 4-*ta* UDU U$_8$.⸢ME⸣ [NIGIN 5-*ta*] ⸢*ṣe-e*⸣-*nu šá kak-kab-tu*$_4$	(1–4) 1 ram, 4 ewes, [a total of 5] sheep, branded with a star, property of Ištar of Uruk [and] Nanay[a from the pen] of Anu-šarra-uṣur son of Šarru-kīn, a herdsman of Ištar [of Uruk …], [led away] from the pen of Bēl-šarra-uṣur son of Aḫiya-a[lidu]:
2.	*še-en-du* NIG$_2$.GA [^{d}]INNIN UNUG⸢^{ki}⸣ [*ù*] ⸢^{d}*na-na*⸣-[*a šá qa-pu-ut-tu*$_4$] *šá* ^{md}*a-nu*-LUGAL-URI$_3$	
3.	A-*šú šá* ^{m}LUGAL-DU ^{lu2}NA.GAD *šá* ^{d}⸢INNIN⸣ [UNUG^{ki} …] *šá* <*ul-tu*> *qa-pu-ut-tu*$_4$	
4.	*šá* ^{md}EN-LUGAL-URI$_3$ A-*šú šá* ^{m}⸢ŠEŠ⸣-*ia-a*-[*li-du ab-ku* ^{md}NA$_3$-ŠEŠ-MU ^{lu2}SAG]-LUGAL	(4–6) [Nabû-aḫa-iddin, the royal] official in charge of the Eanna and [PN] said thus [to Bēl-šarra-uṣur]:
5.	^{lu2}EN *pi-qit-tu*$_4$ E$_2$.AN.NA *ù* [^{m}PN *a-na* ^{md}EN-LUGAL-URI$_3$] *iq-bu-ú*	
6.	*um-ma man-na ṣe-e-nu-aʾ šá*! [*kak-kab-tu*$_4$ *še-en-du ina* ŠU.2]-⸢*ka*⸣ *ip-qid*	(6) "Who deposited these sheep [branded with a star with you]?"
7.	^{md}EN-LUGAL-URI$_3$ *ina* UKKIN *iq-bi* ⸢*um-ma ina* MU 2⸣-[*kám* ^{m}*kam-bu-zi*]-⸢*ia* LUGAL TIN.TIR⸣^{ki} LUGAL KUR.KUR	(7) In the assembly, Bēl-šarra-uṣur said thus:
8.	1-*en* UDU *pu-ḫal ù* 4-*ta* UDU [U$_8$].ME [NIGIN] 5-[*ta ṣe-e-nu šá kak-kab-tu*$_4$] ⸢*še-en-du*⸣	(7–9) "In year 2 of [Camby]ses, king of Babylon, king of the lands, Bēl-iqīša son of Ṣillaya [deposited] 1 ram and 4 [ewe]s, [total] 5 [sheep branded with a star] with me."
9.	^{md}EN-BA-*šá* A-*šú šá* ^{m}*ṣil-la-a ina* ⸢ŠU.2⸣-*ia* ⸢*ip-qid*⸣ [^{md}EN-BA-*šá*]	(9–11) They brought [Bēl-iqīša] and interrogat[ed him … he said] thus:
10.	*i-bu-ku-nim-ma iš-šá-al*-[*lu-šu*… *iq-bi*]	

11. *um-ma* 1-*en* UDU *pu-ḫal* 4-*ta* [UDU U$_8$.ME *šá kak-kab-tu še-en-du*] *ù* 12. 5-*ta* UDU *par-rat*.ME *ta-mi-*⸢*im-ma-ta* NIGIN 10-ta *ṣe*⸣-[*e-nu ul-tu*] ⸢*ṣe-e-nu*⸣ 13. NIG$_2$.GA ^{d}INNIN UNUG^{ki} ⸢*šá qa-pu-ut-tu*$_4$⸣ *šá* ^{md}*a-nu*-LUGAL-URI$_3$ A-*šú šá* ^{m}[LUGAL]-*ki-i-ni* 14. ^{lu_2}NA.GAD *šá* ^{d}INNIN UNUG^{ki} ^{md}*a-nu*-LUGAL-URI$_3$ ⸢*ku-um*⸣ *ra-*⸢*šu-ti-ia*⸣	(11–15) "In Dûzu, year 2, Anu-šarra-uṣur gave me, as (payment for) my claim, 1 ram, 4 [ewes branded with a star] and 5 unblemished lambs, a total of 10 sh[eep from the] sheep, property of Ištar of Uruk, from the pen of Anu-šarra-uṣur son of Šarru-kīni, herdsman of Ištar of Uruk."
15. *ina* ITI ŠU MU 2-*kám it-tan-ni* ^{m}[^{d}EN-BA]-*šá* [*ina* ^{d}E]N *u* ^{d}NA$_3$] 16. *u* [*a-de-e šá* ^{m}*kám-bu-zi-ia* LUGAL TIN.TIR^{ki} LUGAL KUR.KUR] *ina* UKKIN *it-te-*⸢*me*⸣	(15–16) Bēl-iqīša swore [by Be]l [and Nabu] and [the oaths of Cambyses, king of Babylon], in the assembly:
17. *ki-i e-lat* 1-*en* UDU *pu-ḫal* 4 UDU *laḫ-rat*.ME *šá kak-kab-tu*$_4$ *še-en-du* 18. *ù* 5-*ta* UDU *par-rat*.ME *ta-mi-im-ma-a-ta* NIGIN 10-*ta ṣe-e-nu* 19. *ku-um ra-šu-ti-ia* ^{md}*a-nu*-LUGAL-URI$_3$ *id-di-ni šá ina lìb-bi* 1-*en* UDU *pu-ḫal ù* 20. 4-*ta* UDU *laḫ-rat*.ME NIGIN 5-*ta ṣe-e-nu šá kak-kab-tu*$_4$ *še-en-du ina pa-ni* ^{md}EN-LUGAL-URI$_3$	(17–21) "Indeed, Anu-šarra-uṣur did not give me anything as (payment for) my claim, apart from the 1 ram, 4 ewes branded with a star and 5 unbranded lambs, a total of 10 sheep. Of these, I deposited 1 ram and 4 lambs, a total of 5 sheep branded with a star, with Bēl-šarra-uṣur son of Aḫiya-alidu, the shepherd of Ištar of Uruk."
21. A-*šú šá* ^{m}ŠES-*ia-a-li-du* ^{lu_2}NA.GAD *šá* ^{d}INNIN UNUG^{ki} *ap-te-qid* ^{md}EN-LUGAL-URI$_3$ 22. *ina* UKKIN *niš* DINGIR.MEŠ *u* LUGAL *iz-kur ù a-na* ^{md}EN-BA-*šá u-ki-in um-ma* 1-*en* UDU *pu-ḫal*	(21–22) In the assembly, Bēl-šarra-uṣur took an oath by the gods and the king. And he testified thus against Bēl-iqīša:

23. *ù* 4$^{!}$ UDU U$_{8}$.ME *šá kak-kab-tu*$_{4}$ *ina* ITI APIN MU 2-*kám ina pa-ni-ia ta-ap-te-qid*	(22–24) "In Araḫšamna, year 2, you deposited with me 1 ram and 4$^{!}$ ewes branded with a star. In Šabāṭu, year 2, these 4$^{!}$ ewes gave birth."
24. *ina* ITI ZIZ$_{2}$ MU 2-*kám* UDU U$_{8}$.ME-*a*ʾ 4$^{!}$-*ta ina pa-ni-ia it-tal-da-*ʾ	
25. ^{lu_2}*mu-kin-nu* ^{m}*si-lim*-DINGIR ^{lu_2}SAG-LUGAL ^{lu_2}*šá muḫ-ḫi qu-up-pu šá* E$_{2}$.AN.NA	(25) Witnesses: Silim-ili, the royal official in charge of the chest of the Eanna;
26. ^{md}NA$_{3}$-DU-IBILA A-*šú šá* ^{md}AMAR.UTU-MU-MU A ^{m}*ba-la-ṭu* ^{md}NA$_{3}$-*na-din*-ŠEŠ A-*šú*	(26–27) Nabû-mukīn-apli son of Marduk-šuma-iddin descendant of Balāṭu; Nabû-nādin-aḫi son of Arad-Bēl descendant of Iddin-Papsukkal;
27. *šá* ^{m}IR$_{3}$-^{d}EN A ^{m}MU-^{d}PAP. SUKKAL ^{md}UTU-DU-A A-*šú šá* ^{md}DI.KU$_{5}$-ŠEŠ.MEŠ-MU A ^{m}*ši-gu-ú-a*	(27) Šamaš-mukīn-apli son of Madānu-aḫḫē-iddin descendant of Šigûa;
28. ^{md}EN-KAR-^{d}NA$_{3}$ ^{lu_2}SAG-LUGAL ^{m}*lu-uṣ-a-na*-ZALAG$_{2}$-^{d}AMAR.UTU A-*šú šá* ^{md}NA$_{3}$-ŠEŠ.MEŠ-TIN-*iṭ*	(28–29) Bēl-eṭēri-Nabû, the royal official; Lūṣi-ana-nūri-Marduk son of Nabû-aḫḫē-bulliṭ descendant of Dābibī;
29. A ^{m}*da-bi-bi* ^{m}*ki-na-a* A-*šú šá* ^{md}*in-nin-li-pi-ú-ṣur*	(29) Kīnaya son of Innin-līpī-uṣur;
30. ^{m}*na-di-nu* ^{m}IR$_{3}$-^{d}AMAR.UTU *u* ^{m}KI-^{d}AMAR.UTU-TIN ^{lu_2}DUB. SAR.ME *šá* E$_{2}$.AN.NA	(30) Nādinu, Arad-Marduk and Itti-Marduk-balāṭu, scribes of the Eanna.
31. UNUG^{ki} ITI ZIZ$_{2}$ U$_{4}$ 3-*kám* MU 3-*kám* ^{m}*kám-bu-zi-ia*	(31–32) Uruk. 3 Šabāṭu, year 3 of Cambyses, king of Babylon, king of the lands.
32. LUGAL TIN.TIR^{ki} LUGAL KUR.KUR	

Notes

23–24. On the tablet, the number 5, rather than 4, appears in the indication of the number of ewes. The emendation to 4 in the present reading yields the reading most consistent with the rest of the known parts of the case. For the emendation of the numeral in line 23, see Sandowicz 2012, 285. The emendation of the numeral in line 24 follows naturally: the same four ewes gave birth. The scribal confusion here is easy to explain: two groups of five sheep (branded and unbranded) have been mentioned in the proceedings up to this point. Moreover, as the following text shows, when the four ewes gave birth, it was to five lambs.

43. A Decision Regarding Branded Sheep

Text: YBC 3771
Copy: Tremayne 1925 (YOS 7), No. 161
Translation/Discussion: San Nicolò 1932b, 341–43; Kleber 2012, 189–91
Place of Composition: Uruk
Date: 12.XII.3 Camb (22 March, 526 BCE)

Two judges determine that Bēl-iqīša, who led away sheep belonging to the Eanna from the pen of Anu-šarra-uṣur, must repay 155 sheep to the property of the Eanna. This payment represents the thirtyfold penalty for five branded sheep (one ram and four ewes), as well as the replacement of five unbranded lambs. Bēl-iqīša must make this payment on 25 Addaru. Arad-Nergal guarantees that Bēl-iqīša will make the payment.

Approximately one month after the earlier proceedings (Document 42), two royal judges reach their decision regarding Anu-šarra-uṣur's sheep. It seems that in the intervening month, the case has become complicated. Although Document 42 is admittedly broken in some places, the royal judges were probably not involved in the initial proceedings. As far as one can tell from the earlier record, the Eanna bureaucracy intended to address the problem within its own adjudicatory framework. For some reason, perhaps because of the suspects' status, it was unable to do so (see Kleber 2012, 192). Ultimately, the situation required the royal judges to intervene and settle the matter.

In the end, Bēl-šarra-uṣur's accusation against Bēl-iqīša has proven successful; it is Bēl-iqīša, rather than Bēl-šarra-uṣur, who is held liable for paying the penalties. Anu-šarra-uṣur, who must have participated in the illegal payment, apparently avoids punishment. This suggests that rather than being complicit, Anu-šarra-uṣur may have been coerced by Bēl-iqīša, and that the court considered this in their ultimate decision.

The payment that the judges impose requires some clarification. As expected, and as the present document indicates (lines 8–9), Bēl-iqīsa must pay the thirtyfold penalty for the five branded sheep that he has received in payment from Anu-šarru-uṣur. This accounts for 150 sheep. In addition to this, he must also repay five unblemished lambs. In all likelihood, these five unblemished lambs are the offspring to which the four branded ewes gave birth while in the care of Bēl-šarra-uṣur. Bēl-šarra-uṣur, in his own testimony against Bēl-iqīša in Document 42, has mentioned this birth, without specifying how many lambs were actually born. The present document clarifies why Bēl-šarra-uṣur mentions the birth. By doing so, he informs the Eanna that Bēl-iqīša actually owes them more than just the five embezzled sheep.

1. [1-*en* UDU *pu-ḫal* 4 UDU U$_8$.MEŠ] NIGIN 5 *ṣe-e-nu šá* MUL-*tu*$_4$ *še-en-du* 2. ⸢*ù*⸣ [5 *par*]-*rat*.ME *ta-mi-ma-a-ta* NIGIN 10 *ṣe-e-nu* 3. NIG$_2$.GA ^{d}INNIN UNUG^{ki} *u* ^{d}*na-na-a šá qa-pu-ut-tu*$_4$ 4. *šá* ^{md}*a-nu*-LUGAL-URI$_3$ DUMU-*šú šá* ^{m}LUGAL-DU *šá ina* ITI APIN MU 2-*kám* 5. ^{m}*ka-am-bu-zi-ia* LUGAL TIN.TIR^{ki} LUGAL KUR.KUR ^{md}EN-BA-*šá* 6. DUMU-*šú šá* ^{m}*ṣil-la-a ina* ŠU.2 ^{md}*a-nu*-LUGAL-URI$_3$ A-*šú šá* ^{m}LUGAL-DU *i-bu-ku-ma*	(1–6) [1 ram 4 ewes] total 5 sheep branded with a star and 5 unblemished lambs, a total of 10 sheep, property of Ištar of Uruk and Nanaya, from the pen of Anu-šarra-uṣur son of Šarru-kīn, which in Araḫšamna, year 2 of Cambyses, king of Babylon, king of the lands, Bēl-iqīša son of Ṣillaya led away (in payment) from Anu-šarra-uṣur son of Šarru-kīn.
7. *ina* ITI ŠE MU 3-*kám* ^{m}*ri-mut u* ^{md}*ba-ú*-APIN-*eš* 8. $^{\text{lú}_2}$DI.KU$_5$.ME 150 *ṣe-e-nu ku-um ṣe-e-nu šá* ^{d}15 9. *šen-de-e-ti* 1-*en a-di* 30 *ù* 5 *par-rat ta-mi-ma-a-ta* 10. NIGIN 155 *ṣe-e-nu a-na e-ṭe*$_3$*-ru šá* ^{d}INNIN UNUG^{ki} 11. *i-na ṭup-pi iš-ṭu-ru-ma e-li* ^{md}EN-BA-*šá ú-kin-nu*	(7–11) In Addaru, year 3, Rīmūt and Bau-ēreš, the judges, wrote in a tablet and determined for Bēl-iqīša to pay 150 sheep, thirtyfold for the sheep branded for Ištar and 5 unbranded lambs, a total of 155 sheep, for repayment to Ištar of Uruk.
12. U$_4$ 25-*kám šá* ITI ŠE MU 3-*kám ṣe-e-nu a*ʾ 155 ^{md}EN-BA-*šá* 13. DUMU-*šú šá* ^{m}*ṣil-la-a ib-ba-kám-ma ina* E$_2$.AN.NA *i-šim-mi-it-ma*	(12–14) On 25 Addaru, year 3, Bēl-iqīša son of Ṣillaya shall bring these 155 sheep, brand them in the Eanna and give them to the property of the Eanna.
14. *a-na* NIG$_2$.GA E$_2$.AN.NA *i-nam-din* ^{m}IR$_3$-^{d}U.GUR DUMU-*šú šá* ^{m}DU-A 15. DUMU ^{m}*e-gi-bi pu-ut e-ṭe*$_3$*-ru šá ṣe-e-nu-a*ʾ	(14–16) Arad-Nergal son of Mukīn-apli descendant of Egibi assumes responsibility for the repayment of these 155 sheep.

16. 155 *na-ši-i i-na ú-šu-uz-zu šá* ^{md}NA$_3$-DU-⸢IBILA⸣	(16–17) In the presence of Nabû-mukīn-apli, the *šatammu* of the Eanna, son of Nādinu descendant of Dābibī;
17. ^{lu_2}ŠA$_3$.TAM E$_2$.AN.NA DUMU-*šú šá* ^{m}*na-di-nu* DUMU ^{m}*da-bi-bi*	
18. ^{md}NA$_3$-ŠEŠ-MU ^{lu_2}SAG-LUGAL ^{lu_2}EN *pi-qit-ti* E$_2$.AN.NA	(18) Nabû-aḫa-iddin, the royal official in charge of the Eanna.
19. ^{lu_2}*mu-kin-nu* ^{m}IR$_3$-^{d}AMAR.UTU DUMU-*šú šá* ^{m}NUMUN-*ia* DUMU ^{m}*e-gi-bi*	(19) Witnesses: Arad-Marduk, son of Zēriya descendant of Egibi;
20. ^{md}30-APIN-*eš* DUMU-*šú šá* ^{md}NA$_3$-MU-SI.SA$_2$ DUMU ^{m}DU$_3$-DINGIR	(20) Sîn-ēreš son of Nabû-šumu-līšir descendant of Ibni-ili;
21. ^{md}EN-SUM-IBILA DUMU-*šú šá* ^{md}AMAR.UTU-MU-MU DUMU ^{md}EN-IBILA-URI$_3$	(21) Bēl-nādin-apli son of Marduk-šuma-iddin descendant of Bēl-apla-uṣur;
22. ^{m}*na-di-nu* DUB.SAR DUMU ^{m}*e-gi-bi*	(22) Nādinu, the scribe, descendant of Egibi;
23. ^{m}IR$_3$-^{d}[AMAR.UTU] DUB.SAR DUMU ^{md}EN-IBILA-URI$_3$	(23) Arad-Marduk, the scribe, descendant of Bēl-apla-uṣur.
24. UNUG^{ki} ITI ŠE U$_4$ 12-*kám* MU 3-*kám* ^{m}*kám-bu-zi-ia*	(24–25) Uruk. 12 Addaru, year 3 of Cambyses, king of Babylon, king of the lands.
25. LUGAL TIN.TIR^{ki} LUGAL KUR.KUR	

Notes

1–6. According to the opening lines of the present document, Bēl-iqīša has received the unbranded lambs from the pen of Anu-šarra-uṣur, together with the branded sheep. This seems to correspond to Bēl-iqīša's own statement in Document 42 (lines 17–21) that he received a total of ten sheep from Anu-šarra-uṣur. From the legal perspective, however, there is nothing wrong with receipt of unbranded livestock as payment, so it is difficult to understand why, in the end, Bēl-iqīša must repay five additional unbranded lambs to the Eanna. Instead, as has been suggested in the introduction to the present document, the five additional lambs that Bēl-iqīša owes are those that were born to the four branded ewes he deposited with Bēl-šarra-uṣur, but were never actually from the herd of Anu-šarra-uṣur. The Eanna has a claim to the lambs, as the offspring of its branded property, but it cannot impose the thirtyfold penalty on Bēl-iqīša, who did not actually embezzle these lambs. Thus, the original transaction between

Anu-šarra-uṣur and Bēl-iqīša and the penalty Bēl-iqīša has to pay both involve groups of ten sheep, five branded and five unbranded. But only the branded sheep are the same. There are actually two separate sets of unbranded sheep in this case: one set paid to Bēl-iqīša, for which he owes nothing, and another set born to the branded sheep, which Bēl-iqīša must restore to the Eanna. It is easy to see how this coincidence might have confused the scribes who composed the present document and mistakenly attributed the five unbranded lambs to Anu-šarru-uṣur's herd.

4. According to this tablet, the illegal transfer from Anu-šarra-uṣur's herd to Bēl-iqīša occurred in Araḫšamna. According to Document 42 (line 15), this transfer occurred four months earlier, in Dûzu. It was the transfer of the sheep to Bēl-šarra-uṣur, the Eanna herdsman, that took place in Araḫšamna (line 23). One should probably attribute the discrepancy between the two documents to scribal oversight in the present document. Note, however, that both of the scribes in the present document were involved in writing Document 42.

7. Rīmūt and Bau-ēreš are designated as "judges," which, in the Neo-Babylonian legal texts, is the term commonly used to refer to royal judges, or "judges of the king" (Wunsch 2000b, 572–74). Their status as royal judges is confirmed by several other texts that refer to them using more complete designations (Holtz 2009, 257–58).

THE CASE OF LĀ-TUBĀŠINNI AND HER CHILDREN (DOCUMENTS 44–48)

The dossier of this case consists of five documents, written over the course of some thirty-three years, from year 13 of Nebuchadnezzar II (592 BCE), at least through the accession year of Neriglissar (560 BCE). The case itself is narrated in Document 48, in which Lā-tubāšinni, a manumitted female slave, confronts Bēl-aḫḫē-iddin, her previous master, in court, with the claim that her children were born after she had been freed. Were she to win the case, her children would also be free. She does not, however, and the judges award ownership of five of the children to Bēl-aḫḫē-iddin. Lā-tubāšinni is awarded custody of only one son, Ardiya, who was actually born after her manumission.

Cornelia Wunsch, who first published the decision record itself, also identified the other four relevant documents (Documents 44–47; Wunsch 1997–98, 62–67). They furnish details about Lā-tubāšinni's own biography, as well as about the stories of some of her children, and thus afford insight into the history behind the lawsuit. Taken together, then, these five documents not only shed light on particulars of this case, but also offer glimpses into Neo-Babylonian social history.

According to her marriage contract (Document 44), Lā-tubāšinni was married to Dāgil-ilī by her mother, Ḫammaya, who received a brideprice totaling one mina of silver from the groom. The marriage, however, is best characterized as a purchase; unlike typical Neo-Babylonian grooms, Dāgil-ilī did not receive a dowry from the bride's family in return. It was probably through this marriage-by-purchase that Lā-tubāšinni originally became a slave (Wunsch 1997–98, 65). Although Dāgil-ilī himself is never called a slave in the extant texts, his atypical marriage and the fact that his children were slaves indicate that he was probably not of high social standing. A clue about Dāgil-ilī's circumstances comes from the notice at the end of Document 44 (lines 13–14). Here, the text indicates that a member of the Sîn-damāqu family was present as an interested party to the marriage transaction. Bēl-aḫḫē-iddin, the defendant against whom Lā-tubāšinni brings suit, and Esagil-šuma-ibni, the defendant's father who owned some of the children, are also members of this family. This suggests that the Sîn-damāqu family may have financed the marriage for Dāgil-ilī, and thus may have acquired rights to the children (Wunsch 1997–98, 66).

Together, Lā-tubāšinni and Dāgil-ilī have six children, four sons and two daughters. Documents 45, 46 and 47 all attest to the status of the children as slaves belonging to Esagil-šuma-ibni and later (probably upon his death), to his wife and sons, including Bēl-aḫḫē-iddin, the defendant. In Document 46, the family sells three of Lā-tubāšinni's children (and her daughter-in-law) to Nabû-aḫḫē-iddin, a prominent member of the Egibi family (see van Driel 1985–1986). Lā-tubāšinni's lawsuit is probably an attempt to prevent this transaction (Wunsch

1997–98, 63). When Bēl-aḫḫē-iddin prevails in court, the sale to the Egibi family is deemed valid. All the relevant documentation, including a copy of the record of the decision in Bēl-aḫḫē-iddin's favor, would have been kept in the Egibi archive as proof of their rightful title to the slaves.

44. Lā-tubāšinni's Marriage Contract

Text: BM 30571 (76-11-17, 298)
Copy: Strassmaier 1889b (Nbk), No. 101
Translation/Discussion: Kohler and Peiser 1890–98, 1:7; Peiser 1896, 186–89; Boissier 1890, 40–42; Marx 1902, 4–6; Roth 1989a, 42–44; Wunsch 1997–98, No. 1 (p. 73), 62–67.
Place of Composition: Babylon
Date: 9.VIII.13 Nbk (19 November, 592 BCE)

Lā-tubāšinni is given in marriage to Dāgil-ilī by her mother, Ḫammaya. The brideprice that Dāgil-ilī pays to Ḫammaya for her daughter's hand consists of a slave, valued at one-half a mina, and an additional one-half mina of silver.

Although this document follows the basic conventions of Neo-Babylonian marriage agreements (Roth 1989a; Wunsch 2003, 1–31), anomalous details suggest that the marriage is not typical of the urban elite, whose marriage contracts are most widely attested. Neither the bride nor the groom has a family name, unlike the other people named in the text, including the bride's mother, who gives her in marriage. When taken together with the absence of the bride's dowry (see introductory discussion above), this suggests that both the bride and groom are of low social rank. Furthermore, the bride's father is not named, either; her mother's role in the transaction suggests that there is no other living male relative who can legally give Lā-tubāšinni as a bride. Is Lā-tubāšinni an adopted child that Ḫammaya has raised and is now marrying off (Wunsch 1997–98, 65)? Or is Ḫammaya, herself a descendant of a Babylonian family, facing more dire circumstances (with the death or absence of a husband) that force her to assent to her daughter's atypical marriage? The terms of the transaction, in which the one mina brideprice is composed of a slave and one-half mina of silver, rather than a full mina of silver, suggest that Ḫammaya is interested in quickly obtaining ready cash.

1. ^{m}*da-gi-il*-DINGIR.MEŠ A-*šú šá* ^{m}*za-am-bu-bu a-na* ^{f}*ḫa-am-*[*ma*]*-a* 2. DUMU.SAL-*su šá* ^{md}U.GUR-MU A ^{m}*ba-bu-tu* << *a* >> *ki-a-am iq-bi*	(1–3) Dāgil-ilī son of Zambubu said thus to Ḫammaya, daughter of Nergal-iddin, descendant of Bābūtu:
3. *um-ma* ^{f}*la-tu-ba-ši-in-ni* DUMU.SAL-*ka bi-in-nim-ma*	(3–4) "Give me Lā-tubāšinni, your daughter, and let her be (my) wife!"
4. *lu-ú* DAM *ši-i* ^{f}*ḫa-am-ma-a ta-*<*aš*>*-me-e-šu-ma* 5. ^{f}*la-tu-ba-ši-in-ni* DUMU.SAL.A.NI *a-na* DAM-*ú-tu*	(4–5) Ḫammaya heard him and gave him Lā-tubāšinni, her daughter, as a wife.
6. *ta-ad-da-áš-šú ù* ^{m}*da-gi-il*-DINGIR.MEŠ *ina ḫu-ud lìb-bi* 7. ^{m}*a-na-muḫ-ḫi*-EN-*a-mur* ^{lu_2}*qal-la šá a-na* 1/2 MA.NA KU$_3$.BABBAR *ab-ka* 8. *ù* 1/2 MA.NA KU$_3$.BABBAR *it-ti-i a-na* ^{f}*ḫa-am-ma-a* 9. *ku-mu* ^{f}*la-tu-ba-ši-in-ni* DUMU.SAL-*šú id-din*	(6–9) And Dāgil-ilī, with the joy of (his) heart, gave Ana-muḫḫī-Bēl-āmur, his slave purchased for 1/2 mina of silver, and an additional 1/2 mina of silver to Hammaya for Lā-tubāšinni, her daughter.
10. *u*$_4$*-mu* ^{m}*da-gi-il*-DINGIR.MEŠ DAM *ša-ni-tam* 11. *iš-ta-áš-šu-ú* 1 MA.NA KU$_3$.BABBAR ^{m}*da-gi-il*-DINGIR.MEŠ 12. *a-na* ^{f}*la-tu-ba-ši-in-ni i-nam-din-ma a-šar*	(10–13) The day that Dāgil-ilī takes another wife, Dāgil-ilī shall pay Lā-tubāšinni 1 mina of silver, and she shall go wherever she pleases.
13. *maḫ-ri tal-la-ka ina a-ša-bi šá* ^{m}MU-MU 14. A-*šú šá* ^{m}SUH$_3$ -SUR A ^{md}30-*da-ma-qu*	(13–14) In the presence of Šuma-iddin son of Tēšê-ēṭir descendant of Sîn-damāqu.
15. ^{lu_2}*mu-kin-nu* ^{md}EN-ŠEŠ.MEŠ-MU A-*šú šá* ^{md}NA$_3$-EN-MU.MEŠ	(15–16) Witnesses: Bēl-aḫḫē-iddin son of Nabû-bēl-šīmāti descendant of Šangû-Ištar-Bābili;
16. A ^{lu_2}E$_2$.MAŠ-^{d}INNIN-TIN.TIR^{ki} ^{md}AMAR.UTU-LUGAL-*a-ni*	(16–17) Marduk-šarrani son of Balāṭu descendant of Paḫāru;

17. A-*šú šá* ^{m}*ba-la-ṭu* A ^{lu_2}BAHAR$_2$ ^{m}AMAR.UTU-KAR-*ir*	(17–18) Marduk-ēṭir son of Nergal-iddin descendant of Bābūtu;
18. DUMU *šá* ^{md}U.GUR-MU A ^{m}*ba-bu-tu u* ^{lu_2}UMBISAG ^{md}NA-DU-NUMUN	(18–19) Scribe: Nabû-mukīn-zēri son of Marduk-zēra-ibni descendant of Šangû-Ištar-Bābili.
19. A-*šú šá* ^{md}AMAR.UTU-NUMUN-DU$_3$ A ^{lu_2}E$_2$.MAŠ-INNIN-TIN.TIR^{ki}	
20. TIN.TIR^{ki} ITI APIN U$_4$ 9-*kám* MU 13-*kám*	(20–21) Babylon. 9 Araḫšamna, year 13 of Nebuchadnezzar, king of Babylon.
21. ^{d}NA$_3$-NIG$_2$.DU-URI$_3$ LUGAL KA$_2$.DINGIR.RA^{ki}	

NOTES

10–13. This clause governs divorce (here referred to as the husband's marriage to another woman) by stipulating a payment of 1 mina for the wife's support. In effect, this payment is a penalty intended to prevent divorce, since Dāgil-ili is probably of little means himself, and has not received any dowry by which he might otherwise offset this high cost.

13–14. The person named in this clause is not designated as a "witness" (*mukinnu*), but rather as someone in whose presence (*ina ašābi*) the contract was concluded. In Neo-Babylonian documents, this designation introduces the names of relatives of the main parties, often women (see *CAD* A$_2$, 391), whose assent to the transaction was required in order to preclude any subsequent opposition on their part.

17–18. The witness Marduk-ēṭir is Lā-tubāšinni's uncle, brother of Ḫammaya, mother of the bride. For a complete genealogy of the main parties in this dossier, see figure 1.

45. Nabû-ēda-uṣur's Slave Wages

Text: BM 30342 (76-11-17, 62)
Copy: Strassmaier 1889b (Nbk), No 193
Translation/Discussion: Peiser 1896, 190–91; Wunsch 1997–98, No. 2 (p. 74), 62–67
Place of Composition: Babylon
Date: 6.X.28 Nbk (30 December, 577 BCE)

Ubar agrees to pay Ina-Esagil-šuma-ibni the daily wage of a slave named Nabû-ēda-uṣur, set at 2 BAN_2 per day, should Ubar be found in possession of Nabû-ēda-uṣur.

Nabû-ēda-uṣur, the slave who is the subject of this document, is named in the decision record (Document 48) as one of the children that Lā-tubāšinni attempts to free. Here, some seventeen years before his sale to the Egibi family (Document 46) and his mother's failed court case (Document 48), he is already designated as a slave who belongs to the head of the family that ultimately sold him to the Egibis. Assuming that Nabû-ēda-uṣur was born to Dāgil-ilī and Lā-tubāšinni early in the marriage (in Document 48 he is the first child named), then he would have been in his early teens, at most, when the present document was drawn up. By the time of his subsequent sale (Document 46), he was married, and probably around thirty years old.

Documents such as the present one would have been drawn up when there was reason to suspect that slaves would "turn up" in the possession of someone other than their owner, probably because the slaves escaped on their own or were hired out but not returned (Dandamaev 1984, 118–19). Those in unlawful possession of the slaves must pay their slave-wages (*mandattu*) to the slaves' rightful owners. It is interesting to note that in this case, Ubar, the person who must pay, is probably Nabû-ēda-uṣur's own paternal uncle (Wunsch 1997–98, 64): Ubar's father, Zambubu, is probably also the father of Dāgil-ilī mentioned in Document 44. Does this connection indicate that Nabû-ēda-uṣur's family has already been trying to attain his freedom? Whatever the background story, the familial connection is legally significant: it shows that a member of the slave's own family acknowledged the man's status as slave. Thus, with this evidence in hand, Bēl-aḫḫē-iddin, the defendant, could prove his rights to sell Nabû-ēda-uṣur, since it is an official record that the slave belonged to Bēl-aḫḫē-iddin's father, Ina-Esagil-šuma-ibni.

1. *u_4-mu šá* ^{md}NA$_3$-1-URI$_3$ ^{lu_2}*qal-la* 2. *šá* ^{m}*ina*-E$_2$.SAG.IL-MU-DU$_3$ 3. *ina* IGI ^{m}*u_2-bar* A-*šú šá* ^{m}*za-am-bu-bu* 4. *i-te-la-*ʾ U$_4$-*mu* 2 (BAN$_2$) ŠE.BAR 5. *man-da-at-ta-šú a-na* 6. ^{m}*ina*-E$_2$.SAG.IL-MU-DU$_3$ *i-nam-din*	(1–6) On the day that Nabû-ēda-uṣur, slave of Ina-Esagil-šuma-ibni, turns up in the possession of Ubar son of Zambubu, he (Ubar) shall pay Ina-Esagil-šuma-ibni 2 BAN$_2$ of barley per day (as) his (Nabû-ēda-uṣur's) slave-wage.
7. ^{lu_2}*mu-kin-nu* ^{m}*a-ḫu-nu* 8. A-*šú šá* ^{md}IM-NUMUN-MU	(7–8) Witness: Aḫūnu son of Adad-zēra-iddin.
9. *u* ^{lu_2}UMBISAG ^{md}EN-ŠEŠ.MEŠ-SU 10. A-*šú šá* ^{md}EN-*ú-še-zib* A ^{m}*da-bi-bi*	(9–10) and the scribe: Bēl-aḫḫē-erība son of Bēl-ušēzib descendant of Dābibī.
11. TIN.TIR^{ki} ITI AB U$_4$ 6-*kám* 12. MU 28 ^{md}NA$_3$-NIG$_2$.DU-URI$_3$ 13. LUGAL TIN.TIR^{ki}	(11–13) Babylon. 6 Ṭebētu, year 28 of Nebuchadnezzar, king of Babylon.

NOTES

2. In the rest of the dossier, Ina-Esagil-šuma-ibni is known as Esagil-šuma-ibni.

46. Sale of Four Slaves

Text: BM 30228 (75-6-9, 1)
Copy: Evetts 1892 (Ngl), No. 2
Translation/Discussion: Dandamaev 1984, 188–89, 667 (No. 11); Sack 1994, 140–42; Wunsch 1997–98, No. 4 (p. 75), 62–67
Place of Composition: Babylon
Date: 16.VI.0 Ngl (5 September, 560 BCE)

Bēl-āhhē-iddin and Nabû-aḫḫē-bulliṭ, together with their mother, Rēšat, sell four slaves, a man, his wife and his two sisters, to Nabû-aḫḫē-iddin for 2 mina of silver. The sellers assume responsibility against any claim that may stand in the way of the sale.

The sale of three of Lā-tubāšinni's children—her son, Nabû-ēda-uṣur (see Document 45), and two daughters, Kišrinni and Gimillinni—recorded in this document is probably the direct cause of Lā-tubāšinni's lawsuit, which takes place about two months later (Document 48). In addition to these three children, who are also named in the decision record, the sale includes Nabû-ēda-uṣur's wife, Banītumma. The sellers in this document are the wife and two sons of Esagil-šuma-ibni, who, according to Document 45, was Nabû-ēda-uṣur's master. The absence of the former master from the present transaction indicates beyond much doubt that he has died at some point during the seventeen years since the writing of Document 45. It is for this reason that his widow and her sons, the male heirs, are the ones who sell the slaves.

1. ^{md}EN-ŠEŠ.MEŠ-MU *u* ^{md}NA$_3$-ŠEŠ.MEŠ-*bul-liṭ* DUMU.MEŠ [*šá* ^{m}E$_2$.SAG.IL-MU-DU$_3$]
2. A ^{md}30-*da-ma-qu ù* ^{f}*re-šat* AMA-[*šú-nu* DUMU.SAL-*su*]
3. *šá* ^{m}*šu-zu-bu* A ^{lu_2}SANGA-BAR$_2$ *ina ḫu-ud lìb-bi-*[*šú-nu*]
4. ^{md}NA$_3$-*e-du*-URI$_3$ ^{fd}DU$_3$-*ni-tu$_4$-um-ma* DAM-[*šú*]
5. ^{f}*ki-iš-ri-in-ni u* ^{f}*gi-mil-in-ni* NIN.⌜MEŠ-*šú*⌝
6. PAP 4 *a-me-lut-tu$_4$ a-na* 2 MA.NA KU$_3$.BABBAR *a-na* ŠAM$_2$

(1–8) Bēl-aḫḫē-iddin and Nabû-aḫḫē-bulliṭ sons [of Esagil-šuma-ibni] descendant of Sîn-damāqu and Rēšat [their] mother [daughter] of Šūzubu descendant of Šangû-parakki, with the joy of [their] heart, sold Nabû-ēda-uṣur, Banītumma [his] wife, Kišrinni and Gimillinni, his sisters—a total of 4 slaves—to Nabû-aḫḫē-iddin son of Šulaya descendant of Egibi, for the complete price of 2 mina of silver.

7. *gam-ru-tu a-na* ^{md}NA$_3$-ŠEŠ.MEŠ-MU A-*šú šá* ^{m}*šu-la-a*	
8. A ^{m}*e-gi-bi id-di-nu pu-ut se-ḫi-i pa-qir-ra-nu* 9. *u* DUMU DU$_3$-*ú-tu šá a-me-lut-tu*$_4$ ^{md}EN-ŠEŠ.MEŠ-MU 10. *u* ^{md}NA$_3$-ŠEŠ-MEŠ-*bul-liṭ* DUMU.MEŠ *šá* ^{m}E$_2$-SAG.IL$_2$-MU-DU$_3$ 11. A ^{md}30-SIG$_5$ *u* ^{f}*re-šat* AMA-*šú-nu na-šu-ú*	(8–11) Bēl-aḫḫē-iddin, Nabû-aḫḫē-bulliṭ sons of Esagil-šuma-ibni descendant of Sîn-damāqu and Rēšat, their mother, assume responsibility against any false claimant, contester, or (claim regarding) the slaves' free status.
12. 1-*en pu-ut* 2-*ú na-šu-u*	(12) Each assumes responsibility for the other.
13. ^{lu_2}*mu-kin-nu* ^{md}NA$_3$-DU$_3$-ŠEŠ A-*šú šá* ^{m}*šu-zu-bu* A ^{lu_2}SANGA-BAR$_2$	(13) Witnesses: Nabû-bāni-aḫi son of Šūzubu descendant of Šangû-parakki;
14. [^{m}*a-ša*]-*ri-du* A-*šú šá* ^{md}AMAR.UTU-*na-ṣir* A ^{lu_2}SANGA-DINGIR	(14) [Aša]ridu son of Marduk-nāṣir descendant of Šangû-ili;
15. ^{md}AMAR.UTU-BA-*šá-an-ni* A-*šú šá* ^{m}*ba-ni-ia* A ^{m}DINGIR-*til-lat-i*	(15) Marduk-iqīšanni son of Bāniya descendant of Ilu-tillatī;
16. ^{m}DUB-NUMUN A-*šú šá* ^{md}U.GUR-GI A ^{md}30-*ka-ra-bi-iš-me*	(16) Šāpik-zēri son of Nergal-ušallim descendant of Sîn-karābi-išme;
17. ^{md}EN-MU A-*šú šá* ^{md}EN-*ú-šeb-ši* A ^{lu_2}SANGA-*za-ri-qu*	(17) Bēl-iddin son of Bēl-ušebši descendant of Šangû-Zariqu;
18. ^{md}IM-*ib-ni* A-*šú šá* ^{md}*za-ri-qu*-NUMUN-DU$_3$ A ^{lu_2}SANGA-^{d}*za-ri-qu*	(18) Adad-ibni son of Zariqu-zēra-ibni descendant of Šangû-Zariqu;
19. *u* ^{lu_2}UMBISAG ^{m}*ri-mut* A-*šú šá* ^{md}NA$_3$-MU-GAR-*un* A ^{m}*ga-ḫul*	(19) and the scribe: Rīmūt son of Nabû-šuma-iškun descendant of Gaḫul;
20. TIN.TIR^{ki} ITI KIN U$_4$ 16-*kám* MU SAG.NAM.LUGAL 21. ^{md}U.GUR-LUGAL-URI$_3$ LUGAL TIN.TIR^{ki}	(20–21) Babylon. 16 Ulūlu, accession year of Neriglissar, king of Babylon.

NOTES

8–11. This clause enumerates possible factors that might prevent the sale. By assuming responsibility against them, the sellers guarantee clear title to the slave (Dandamaev 1984, 182–86).

47. Sale of a Slave

Text: BM 31285 (76-11-17, 1012)
Copy: Wunsch 1997–98, No. 3 (p. 74)
Translation/Discussion: Wunsch 1997–98, No. 3 (p. 74), 62–67
Place of Composition: (Babylon?)
Date: 10.X.1 (Ngl?) (14 January, 558 BCE?)

Bēl-āhhē-iddin and Nabû-aḫḫē-bulliṭ, together with their mother, Rēšat, sell one male slave for 5/6 mina and 8 šeqels (58 šeqels) of silver to Šāpik-zēri. The sellers assume responsibility against any claim that may stand in the way of the sale.

As in Document 46, the sellers in this document are also the widow and two male heirs of Esagil-šuma-ibni. The slave they sell, at least as he is named in the document, is Nabû-ēda-uṣur, the same slave who is sold in Document 46. This fact, together with the broken date on Document 47 (see note below), present complications to the otherwise straightforward narrative of events that can be reconstructed based on the other documents in the dossier. How can the same owners sell the same slave twice to different people? Wunsch (1997–98, 66–67) suggests a number of solutions, of which the more likely two are summarized here:

1) It is possible that this text predates the sale recorded in Document 46 and the subsequent lawsuit in Document 48. Nabû-ēda-uṣur was sold twice by the same owners, first to Šāpik-zēri (the present document) and again to Nabû-aḫḫē-iddin (Document 46). If so, then the sale recorded here must have been invalidated by the time of the writing of Document 46 and Document 48. A document, now lost, would have indicated that the first sale was invalid, and would have been transferred to the Egibi archive with the ultimate sale of Nabû-ēda-uṣur.
2) Alternatively, the present document was, in fact, written after Document 46 and the subsequent lawsuit in Document 48. The sale here, however, is not of Nabû-ēda-uṣur, but rather of his brother, Bēl-aḫa-uṣur, who is named as one of the children of Lā-tubāšinni in Document 48, but is not included in the sale in Document 46. Thus, the heirs of Esagil-šuma-ibni still owned this slave, and could, therefore, sell him. The fact that the present document probably belongs to the Egibi archive may indicate that the Egibi family was somehow involved in the sale, albeit only tangentially.

Although the second possibility requires emending personal names in the operative section of the document, this option should not be discounted out of hand. For one thing, the first possibility also requires a "suspicious" reading of the present document as invalid. Moreover, in the present document, the price of the one slave here (58 šeqels) is nearly equal to the price of all four slaves sold in Document 46 (60 šeqels). If the present document was written before Document 46, then one would have to imagine that Nabû-ēda-uṣur's value decreased dramatically between the sales. It may be simpler to imagine that a different slave, who might have always had a higher value, is sold here.

1. ^{md}EN-ŠEŠ.MEŠ-MU *ù* ^{md}NA$_3$-ŠEŠ.MEŠ-*bul-liṭ* 2. DUMU.MEŠ *šá* ^{m}E$_2$-SAG.IL-MU-DU$_3$ A ^{md}30-SIG$_5$ 3. *u* ^{f}*re-šat* AMA-*šú-nu ina ḫu-ud lìb-bi-šú-nu* 4. ^{md}NA$_3$-AŠ-URI$_3$ ^{lu_2}*qal-la-šú-nu a-na* 5/6 MA.NA 8 GIN$_2$ KU$_3$.BABBAR 5. *a-na* ŠAM *ḫa-ri-iṣ a-na* ^{m}DUB-NUMUN A-*šú šá* 6. ^{m}MU-^{d}AMAR.UTU A ^{m}*ši-gu-ú-a id-di-nu-ʾ*	(1–6) Bēl-aḫḫē-iddin and Nabû-aḫḫē-bulliṭ sons of Esagil-šuma-ibni descendant of Sîn-damāqu and Rēšat, their mother, with the joy of their heart, sold Nabû-ēda-uṣur, their slave, for the exact price of 5/6 mina 8 šeqels of silver to Šāpik-zēri son of Iddin-Marduk descendant of Šigûa.
7. *pu-ut* ^{lu_2}*se-ḫi-i* ^{lu_2}*pa-qir-a-nu* ^{lu_2}ERIN$_2$.MEŠ LUGAL-*ú-tu* 8. *u* DUMU-DU$_3$-*ú-tu ša* $^{m⸢d}$NA$_3$-AŠ-URI$_3$⸣ 9. ^{md}EN-ŠEŠ.MEŠ-MU ^{md}N[A$_3$-ŠEŠ.MEŠ-*bul-liṭ*] 10. *u* ^{f}*re-šat* AMA-⸢*šú*⸣-[*nu našû*]	(7–10) Bēl-aḫḫē-iddin, N[abû-aḫḫē-bulliṭ] and Rēšat, thei[r] mother, [assume] responsibility against any false claimant, contester, corvée duties of the king or (claim regarding) Nabû-ēda-uṣur's free status.
11. 1-*en pu-ut šá-ni-i na-š*[*u-ú*]	(11) Each assu[mes] responsibility for the other.
12. ^{lu_2}*mu-kin-nu* ^{md}NA$_3$-DU$_3$-ŠEŠ A-*šú šá* ^{m}*šu-zu-bu*	(12–13) Witnesses: Nabû-bāni-aḫi son of Šūzubu descendant of Šangû-parakki;
13. A ^{lu_2}SANGA-BAR$_2$ ^{md}NA$_3$-ŠEŠ.MEŠ-MU A-*šú šá*	(13–14) Nabû-aḫḫē-iddin son of Zākir descendant of Amēl-Isin;
14. ^{m}*za-kir* A LU$_2$-ISIN^{ki} ^{m}*ṣil-la-a* A-*šú*	(14–15) Ṣillaya son of Lâbāši descendant of Šigûa;
15. *šá* ^{m}*la-a-ba-ši* A ^{m}*ši-gu-u-a*	

16. *u* ^{lu_2}DUB.SAR ^{m}*kab-ti-iá* A-*šú* *šá* ^{md}AMAR.UTU-MU-DU$_3$	(16–17) and the scribe: Kabtiya son of Marduk-šuma-ibni descendant of Amēl-[Ea].
17. A LU$_2$-^{d}[E$_2$-a X X X] ⸢ITI⸣ ZIZ$_2$ U$_4$ 10-*kám*	(17–18) [X X X] 10 Šabāṭu, year 1 of [Neriglissar, king] of Babylon.
18. MU 1-*kám* [^{d}U.GUR-LUGAL-URI$_3$ LUGAL] TIN.TIR^{ki}	

NOTES

17–18. The legible part of the date states that it was composed in year 1 of a king, but the name of this king is lost. Logically, two reconstructions are possible: Amēl-Marduk and Neriglissar. If the king was Amēl-Marduk, then this document was composed on 6 January, 560 BCE, some nine months before the sale recorded in Document 46 and eleven months before the lawsuit. If the king was Neriglissar, then this document was written about two years later on 14 January, 558 BCE. For the implications of these dates, see the introductory discussion to the present document.

48. The Status of Lā-tubāšinni's Children

Text: BM 31797 (76-11-17, 1524)
Copy: Wunsch 1997–98, No. 5 (p. 77)
Translation/Discussion: Wunsch 1997–98, No. 5 (pp. 75–77), 62–67
Place of Composition: Babylon
Date: 10.VIII.0 Ngl (29 October, 560 BCE)

Lā-tubāšinni, a manumitted slave, argues a case regarding the status of her children against Bēl-aḫḫē-iddin before the sukkallu *and the judges. Lā-tubāšinni claims that five of her children, three sons and two daughters, were born after she received her tablet of manumission (*ṭuppi mār banûti*), and that, therefore, Bēl-aḫḫē-iddin has no rights to them. Bēl-aḫḫē-iddin is able to prove that the five children in question were born before Lā-tubāšinni's manumission. The* sukkallu *and the judges confirm that the children in question are the property of Bēl-aḫḫē-iddin. One of Lā-tubāšinni's sons, Ardiya, was born after the manumission and is, therefore, under her control.*

As narrated, the lawsuit is between Lā-tubāšinni and Bēl-aḫḫē-iddin, each of whom claims some right to the children. Thus, the judges' ruling is formulated as "giving" (*nadānu*) specifically named children either to Bēl-aḫḫē-iddin or to Lā-tubāšinni, which implies that the prevailing litigant may now deal with the children as he or she sees fit. As noted above, the existence of related documents allows the reconstruction of the events surrounding the lawsuit itself and, in turn, the practical implications of the ruling. Bēl-aḫḫē-iddin has sold some of Lā-tubāšinni's children (Document 45), and her claim against him is intended to prevent the final sale. Because Lā-tubāšinni cannot prove her claim to the children sold by Bēl-aḫḫē-iddin, the ruling implies that the sale is valid.

1.	[^{f}*la-t*]*u-ba-šin-ni* DAM ^{m}*da-gil*-DINGIR.M[EŠ *u... ana*]	(1–3) Lā-tubāšinni, wife of Dāgil-ilī [and …] [c]ame [before Nabû-mukīn]-apli, the *sukkallu,* and the judges of [Neriglissar, king of Babylon].
2.	[^{md}NA$_3$-GIN]-DUMU.NITA ^{lu_2}U$_2$ *u* ^{lu_2}DI.KU$_5$.MEŠ *šá* ^{md}U.[GUR-LUGAL URI$_3$ LUGAL E^{ki}]	
3.	[*il-l*]*i-ku-nim-ma it-ti* ^{md}EN-ŠEŠ.MEŠ-MU DUMU-⸢*šú*⸣ [*šá* ^{m}E$_2$-SAG-IL$_2$-MU-DU$_3$]	(3–4) They argued a case against Bēl-aḫḫē-iddin son of [Esagil-šuma-ibni descendant of] Sîn-damāqu.

4. [DUMU ^{md}]30-SIG$_5$ *di-i-ni id-bu-bu-ma* ^{f}*la-tu-ba-*[*šin-ni taqbi umma*]	(4) Lā-tubāšinni [said thus]:
5. [^{md}NA$_3$]-AŠ-URI$_3$ ^{md}EN-ŠEŠ-URI$_3$ ^{m}E$_2$-SAG-IL$_2$-*re-ṣu-*⌜*ú*⌝-[*a* ^{f}*kiš-ri-in-ni*]	(5–7) "[Nabû]-ēda-uṣur, Bēl-aḫa-uṣur, Esagil-rēṣua, [Kišrinni], and Gimilinni, are my children to whom [I gave bi]rth in your house after the writ[ing of my tablet of manumission]."
6. [*u* ^{f}*gi*]-*mil-in-ni* DUMU.MEŠ-*e-a šá ina* E$_2$-*ku-nu ár-ki šá-ṭa-*[*ri* DUB DUMU *ba-nu-tú*]	
7. [*ú-li*]-*du* ^{lu_2}U$_2$ *u* ^{lu_2}DI.KU$_5$.MEŠ *ar-kát-su-nu iš-ta-lu-*[*ma* ^{m}EN-ŠEŠ.MEŠ-MU]	(7) The *sukkallu* and the judges investigated the circumstances of their case.
8. [*ri-k*]*a-si-šú šá a-di la ṭup-pi* DUMU *ba-nu-tú šá* ^{f}*la-tu-*[*ba-šin-ni*]	(7–12) [Bēl-aḫḫē-iddin bro]ught his [co]ntract (stating) that Nabû-ēda-uṣur, Bēl-aḫa-uṣur, Esagil-[rēṣua], Kišrinni and Gimilinni were born before Lā-tubāšinni's tablet of manumission [was] written and the not[e (stating) that... Nabû]-ēda-uṣur and Bēl-aḫa-uṣur ... for slave-wage and showed it to the *sukkallu* and to the judges.
9. [*iš*]-*šaṭ-ṭa-ru* ^{md}NA$_3$-AŠ-URI$_3$ ^{md}EN-ŠEŠ-URI$_3$ ^{m}E$_2$-SAG-IL$_2$-[*re-ṣu-ú-a*]	
10. [^{f}*k*]*iš-ri-in-ni u* ^{f}*gi-mil-in-ni ma-al-du ú-ìl-*[*tì šá*...]	
11. [^{md}NA$_3$]-*e-du-*URI$_3$ *u* ^{md}EN-ŠEŠ-URI$_3$ *a-na man-da-at-ti ú-*[…]	
12. [*ub-la*]-*am-ma a-na* ^{lu_2}SUKKAL *u* ^{lu_2}DI.KU$_5$.MEŠ *ú-kal-lim*	
13. [^{m}E$_2$-SAG]-IL$_2$-MU-DU$_3$ AD *šá* ^{md}EN-Š[EŠ.MEŠ]-⌜SUM⌝.[NA]	(13–15) [Esagil]-šuma-ibni, the father of Bēl-aḫḫē-iddin ... his de[dication ...] to Bēl ... they saw, [and heard their ca]se.
14. […]-*li-šú a-na* ^{d}EN *ú z*[*ak-*...]	
15. […]-*nu i-mu-ru u dib-*[*bi-šu-nu išmû*]	
16. [^{md}NA$_3$-*e-da*-URI$_3$] ^{md}EN-ŠEŠ-URI$_3$ ^{f}*kiš-ri-*[*in-ni u* ^{f}*gi-mil-in-ni*]	(16–18) They gave [Nabû-ēda-uṣur], Bēl-aḫa-uṣur, Kišr[inni and Gimilinni], [who were born before] Lā-t[ubāšinni]'s tablet of manumission, to [Bē]l-aḫḫē-iddin.
17. [*šá a-di la*] DUB DUMU *ba-nu-tu šá* ^{f}*la-t*[*u-ba-ši-in-ni aldū ana*]	
18. [^{md}E]N-ŠEŠ.MEŠ-MU *id-di-nu u* ^{m}IR$_3$-*ia* [*šá arki šaṭār ṭuppi*]	(18–19) And they [gave] Ardiya, who was born [after the writing of] Lā-tubāšinni's [tablet] to [Lā-tubāšinni].
19. [*šá* ^{f}]*la-tu-ba-šin-ni mál-du a-na* ^{f}[*la-tu-ba-šin-ni iddinū*]	

20. [*ma*]-*ti-ma* ^{f}*la-tu-ba-šin-ni u* ^{m}IR$_3$-*ia* DUMU-*šú a-na* [UGU ^{md}NA$_3$-AŠ-URI$_3$]	(20–21) [In] the future, Lā-tubāšinni and Ardiya, her son, shall not [raise a claim concerning Nabû-ēda-uṣur], Bēl-aḫa-uṣur, Kašrinni and Gimilinni.
21. [^{m}]^{d}EN-ŠEŠ-URI$_3$ ^{f}*kaš-ri-in-ni u* ^{f}*gi-mil-in-ni la* [*iraggumū*]	
22. ^{lu_2}U$_2$ *u* ^{lu_2}DI.KU$_5$.MEŠ *ṭup-pi iš-ṭu-ru ina* ^{na4}[KIŠIB-*šu-nu*]	(22–23) The *sukkallu* and the judges wrote a tablet and sealed (it) with [their seals] and ga[ve] (it) to Bēl-aḫḫē-iddin.
23. *ib-ru-mu-ma a-na* ^{md}EN-ŠEŠ.MEŠ-MU *id*-[*di-nu*]	
24. *ina* EŠ.BAR *di-i-ni šu-a-ta* ^{md}EN-DU-IBILA [^{lu_2}U$_2$]	(24) At the decision of this case: Nabû-mukīn-apli, [the *sukkallu*]
25. ^{md}AMAR.UTU-GAR-MU ^{lu_2}DI.KU$_5$ DUMU ^{md}URU$_3$-[DU$_3$-*mansum*]	(25) Marduk-šākin-šumi, the judge, descendant of URU$_3$.[DU$_3$-mansum];
26. [^{md}]NA$_3$-SUM.NA ^{lu_2}DI.KU$_5$ DUMU ^{m}SIG$_5$-[^{d}IM]	(26) Nabû-iddin, the judge, descendant of Mudammiq-[Adad];
27. [^{m}]^{d}NA$_3$-*mu-tir*-ŠU ^{lu_2}UMBISAG DUMU ^{m}[*gaḫal-Marduk*]	(27) Nabû-mutīr-gimilli, the scribe, descendant of [Gaḫal-Marduk].
28. E^{ki} ITI APIN U$_4$ 10-*kám* MU SAG-NAM.LUGAL.LA [^{d}U.GUR-LUGAL-URI$_3$]	(28) Babylon. 10 Araḫšamna, accession year of [Neriglissar].

NOTES

5–7. Lā-tubāšinni names Esagil-rēṣua as one of her five children here, and he is also mentioned when the document describes how Bēl-aḫḫē-iddin proves his case (lines 7–12). When the judges reach their decision (lines 16–19), however, Esagil-rēṣua's name is not included: only four, rather than five, children go to Bēl-aḫḫē-iddin, and a fifth, named Ardiya, goes to Lā-tubāšinni. One may conclude from the absence of Esagil-rēṣua's name that he probably died earlier (Wunsch 1997–98, 63 n. 16).

13–15. These lines, although broken, seem to mention one person's dedication of another person (*zukkû*) to the god Bēl. The lines may refer to the fate of Dāgil-ilī, the man who married Lā-tubāšinni (Wunsch 1997–98, 63).

22–23. Although these lines mention the sealing of a document, the present document is not sealed. Therefore, this is not the original document to which these lines refer, but is, instead, a copy of that original (Wunsch 1997–98, 64).

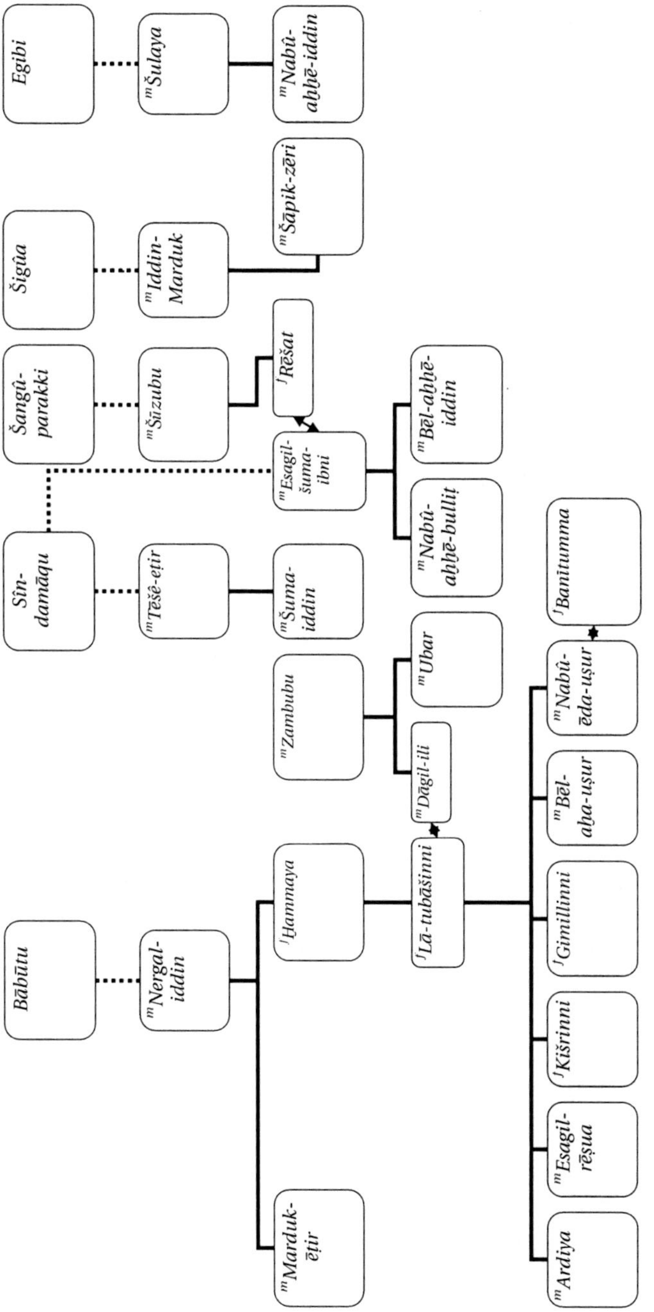

Figure 1- Lā-tubāšinni's Family Tree

KEY: ······ *Descent from Family* —— *Descent from Parent* ↔ *Marriage*

An Unauthorized Marriage (Documents 49–50)

Documents 49 and 50 pertain to an illicit marriage that takes place between a female slave and Nabû-aḫḫē-bulliṭ, son of a royal official (*ša rēš šarri*) named Nargiya. The marriage is arranged by the servants of Amurru-šarra-uṣur, the royal official in charge of the inner residence (*ša muḫḫi bītānu*), but meets the opposition of the groom's father, Nargiya, the plaintiff in the lawsuit (Document 50). Ultimately, this arrangement is overturned in court. Thus, these two documents are a good illustration of the strength of paternal authority, even over the marriage of a son (Joannès 2000b, 206).

49. A Guarantee for Testimony

Text: BM 30975 (76-11-17, 702)
Copy: Strassmaier 1890b (Cyr), No. 311
Translation/Discussion: Peiser 1896, No. 23 (pp. 280–84); Marx 1902, 11–12; Dougherty 1923–24, 41–42; Koschaker 1966, 159–60; Dandamaev 1984, 105–6, 432–34; Joannès 1994; 2000b, No. 150 (pp. 207–8); Holtz 2009, 148
Place of Composition: Babylon
Date: 8.V.8 Cyr (7 August, 531 BCE)

Nabû-ēṭir and his son, Rīmūt-Nabû, guarantee testimony regarding Mušēzib-Bēl, a slave in the household of a high-ranking official. Mušēzib-Bēl, acting as if on behalf of his master, ordered a document to be drawn up for the marriage between Kupputtu and Nabû-aḫḫe-iddin son of Nargiya. Rīmūt-Nabû was the scribe who wrote the document and Nabû-ēṭir was a witness on it. However, Nargiya, the groom's father, does not approve of this marriage, so Nabû-ēṭir and Rīmut-Nabû face a penalty for writing the document against his wishes. In order to clear themselves, the two men guarantee testimony regarding Mušēzib-Bēl's role in the situation. Presumably, they (or Mušēzib-Bēl himself) will testify that they were only acting on the assumption that Mušēzib-Bēl's master, the high-ranking official, had ordered the marriage document to be written. If they do not provide this testimony then they must compensate Nargiya.

Although some of the protagonists in the present document are different from those in Document 50, a number of factors suggest that the two documents are related:

1) In both documents the groom is named Nabû-aḫḫē-bulliṭ son of Nargiya and, in both, Nargiya is the son of Ḫanunu.

2) Both documents involve members of the household of the official in charge of the inner residence (*ša muḫḫi bītānu*).
3) The two documents are written within three days of each other.

Therefore, the slave, who is named Kuputtu in the present document, is probably the same as the slave named Tabluṭu in Document 50 (Koschaker 1966, 159 n. 43; Joannès 2000b, 206). Thus, the present document is a record of the preliminary legal proceedings leading up to the trial itself, three days later.

1. *pu-ut* ^{lu_2}*mu-kin-nu-ú-tu šá* ^{m}*mu-še-zib-*^{d}EN 2. ^{lu_2}*qal-la šá* ^{lu_2}*šá* UGU E$_2$*-a-nu šá ina na-áš-pir-tu*$_4$ 3. *šá* ^{lu_2}*šá* UGU E$_2$*-a-nu il-li-ku-ma iq-bu-ú um-ma* 4. <<*um-ma*>> ^{lu_2}*šá* UGU E$_2$*-a-nu il-tap-ra-an-ni um-ma* 5. IM.DUB *šá* ^{f}*kup-pu-ut-tu*$_4$ *ku-nu-uk*$^{!}$*-ma a-na* 6. DAM-*ú-tu a-na* ^{md}NA$_3$-ŠEŠ.MEŠ-*bul-liṭ* A-*šú šá* ^{m}*nar-gi-iá* 7. *i-din* ^{md}NA$_3$-SUR A-*šú šá* ^{m}IR$_3$-^{d}EN A ^{m}*ár-rab-tu*$_4$ 8. ^{lu_2}*mu-kin-nu* IM.DUB *ù* ^{m}*ri-mut-*^{d}NA$_3$ DUMU-*šú*	(1–9) Nabû-ēṭir son of Arad-Bēl descendant of Arrabtu, the witness on the tablet, and Rīmūt-Nabû, his son, the scribe who wrote the tablet, assume responsibility for testimony regarding Mušēzib-Bēl, slave of the official in charge of the inner residence, who went, at the orders of the official in charge of the inner residence, and said thus: "The official in charge of the inner residence has sent me, and ordered, 'Seal the tablet of Kuputtu and give her as a wife to Nabû-aḫḫē-bulliṭ son of Nargiya.'"
9. DUB.SAR *šá-ṭir* IM.DUB *na-šu-ú ina* E$_2$ DI.KU$_5$ 10. *ú-kan-nu-ma a-na* ^{m}*nar-gi-ia* A-*šú šá*	(9–11) They shall testify in the courthouse and present (the document) to Nargiya son of Ḫanunu.
11. ^{m}*ḫa-nu-nu i-nam-din-nu-ʾ ki-i la ú-*[*kan-nu*] 12. 1/2 GU.UN KU$_3$.BABBAR *mi-ṭi-tu*$_4$ 13. *šá* UGU ^{m}*nar-gi-ia šak-na-tu*$_4$	(11–14) If they do not t[estify], they shall pay 1/2 talent of silver, (for) the loss inflicted upon Nargiya.
14. *ú-šal-lam-uʾ* ^{lu_2}*mu-kin-nu* 15. ^{md}NA$_3$-ŠEŠ-MU A-*šú šá* ^{m}NA$_3$-TIN-*su*-E	(14–15) Witnesses: Nabû-aḫa-iddin son of Nabû-balāssu-iqbi;

16. ^{m}IR$_3$-*ia* A-*šú šá* ^{m}NA$_3$-GAL$_2$-*ši*	(16) Ardiya son of Nabû-ušabši;
17. ^{m}A-*a* A-*šú šá* ^{m}*lib-luṭ* ^{m}NU-MUN-*ia* A-*šú šá* ^{m}*ú-bar*	(17) Aplaya son of Libluṭ; Zēriya son of Ubar;
18. *ù* ^{md}NA$_3$-DU-NUMUN ^{lu_2}UMBISAG DUMU-*šú šá*	(18–19) and Nabû-mukīn-zēri, the scribe, son of Nabû-šuma-ēreš descendant of Ēreb-bīti.
19. ^{md}NA$_3$-MU-KAM$_2$ DUMU ^{lu_2}AD E$_2$ TIN.TIR^{ki}	(19–21) Babylon. 8 Abu, year 8 of Cyrus, king of Babylon, king of the lands.
20. ITI NE U$_4$ 8-*kám* MU 8 ^{m}*kur-ra-áš*	
21. LUGAL TIN.TIR^{ki} LUGAL KUR.KUR	

Notes

1. The Akkadian relative particle *ša* may indicate that the two men assume responsibility for the testimony *of* Mušēzib-Bēl, rather than testimony *regarding* him. However, the apparently plural verbs in lines 10–11 suggest that it is the testimony of the two guarantors, rather than of Mušēzib-Bēl, that is required.

50. An Unauthorized Marriage

Text: BM 33065 (78-11-7, 3)
Copy: Strassmaier 1890b (Cyr), No. 312
Translation/Discussion: Kohler and Peiser 1890–98, 2:7–8; Marx 1902, 11; Oppenheim 1944, 14; Joannès 2000b, No. 149 (p. 207); Joannès 2002c
Place of Composition: Babylon
Date: 11.V.8 Cyr (10 August, 531 BCE)

Nargiya, a royal official, presents his case against Amurru-šarra-uṣur, the royal official in charge of the inner residence, before a court consisting of "Great Ones" and judges of Cyrus. Nargiya claims that, without his permission, Amurru-šarra-uṣur and Nabû-uballiṭ, one of Amurru-šarra-uṣur's servants, had a tablet drawn up attesting to the marriage between Nargiya's son, Nabû-aḫḫē-bulliṭ, and Tabluṭu, sister of the servant Nabû-uballiṭ. The judges interrogate Amurru-šarra-uṣur, who denies participating in this scheme. Nabû-uballiṭ, his servant, confesses to having had the tablet of marriage drawn up. The judges invalidate this tablet and rule that Tabluṭu will be branded as a slave if she is seen with Nabû-aḫḫē-bulliṭ.

This trial takes place three days after the scribe who wrote the marriage document and his father, one of the witnesses, guaranteed the testimony pertaining to the involvement of another suspect (Document 50). The present document makes it clear that the scheme to illicitly marry Kupputu/Tabluṭu to Nabû-aḫḫē-bulliṭ was not simply a plan hatched among highly-placed household servants. As the son of Nargiya, a royal official according to the present document, Nabû-aḫḫē-bulliṭ is probably of significant social standing, which suggests that the schemers may have had less than pure motives. Furthermore, Amurru-šarra-uṣur, a royal official himself, is brought to court as one of the defendants. There must have been some suspicion that the scheme originated not with the servants, but with their master. This suspicion was strong enough to require Amurru-šarra-uṣur to come to court, face interrogation, and clear himself by taking an oath. Ultimately, however, it is the slave's brother, the servant Nabû-uballiṭ, who accepts responsibility for the scheme.

1. ^{m}*nar-gi-ia* ^{lu2}SAG-LUGAL DUMU-*šú šá* ^{m}*ḫa-nu-nu* 2. ^{md}KUR.GAL-LUGAL-URI$_3$ ^{lu2}SAG-LUGAL ^{lu2}*šá* UGU E$_2$-*a-ni* 3. *a-na maḫ-ri* ^{lu2}GAL.MEŠ LUGAL *ù* ^{lu2}DI.KU$_5$.MEŠ 4. *šá ku-ra-áš* LUGAL TIN.TIR^{ki} LUGAL KUR.KUR	(1–5) Nargiya, the royal official, son of Ḫanunu, brought Amurru-šarra-uṣur, the royal official in charge of the inner residence, before the "Great Ones" of the king and the judges of Cyrus, king of Babylon, king of the lands, and said thus:
5. *ú-bil-lam-ma iq-bi um-ma* ^{md}KUR.GAL-LUGAL-URI$_3$ 6. ^{lu2}*šá* UGU E$_2$-*a-ni u* ^{md}NA$_3$-TIN-*iṭ* DUMU-*šú šá* ^{md}NA$_3$-*šá-ma-ʾ* 7. *šá* E$_2$ ^{lu2}*šá* UGU E$_2$-*a-ni* IM.DUB *áš-šu-tu* 8. *šá* ^{f}*tab-lu-ṭu* NIN *šá* ^{md}NA$_3$-TIN-*iṭ ba-lu-ú-a* 9. *ik-nu-uk-ma a-na* ^{md}NA$_3$-ŠEŠ.MEŠ-*bul-liṭ* DUMU-*ia id-di-nu*	(5–9) "Amurru-šarra-uṣur, the official in charge of the inner residence, and Nabû-uballiṭ son of Nabû-šamaʾ, a member of the household of the official in charge of the inner residence, sealed a tablet of wifehood for Tabluṭu, sister of Nabû-uballiṭ, without my permission, and gave (her in marriage) to Nabû-aḫḫē-bulliṭ, my son."
10. ^{lu2}GAL.MEŠ *u* DI.KU$_5$.MEŠ *šá* UGU E$_2$-*a-ni i-šá-lu-ma*	(10) The "Great Ones" and the judges interrogated the official in charge of the inner residence and
11. *niš* DINGIR.[MEŠ *iz-kur*]-⸢*ma*⸣ *iq-bi um-ma* [IM.DUB] *šu-a-tú*	(11) He [took an oath] of the god[s] and said thus:
12. *ul ak-nu-uk u a-na ši* -[*bu-ti ina*] *lib-bi ul ú-šib*	(11–12) "I did not seal that [tablet] and did not serve as a wit[ness] on it."
13. *ul-tu . . ú-kin-ni...* ^{f}*tab-lu-ṭu*	(13–14) After he testified … they interrogated Tabluṭu
14. *i-šá-lu-ma... ú-kin-nu-ma*	(14) … testified and …
15. ^{md}NA$_3$-TIN-*iṭ iq-*[*bi um-ma...*] IM.DUB *áš-šu-*⸢*tu*⸣	(15) Nabû-uballiṭ sa[id thus]:

16. *šá* ^{f}*tab-lu-ṭu* NIN-*i*[*a ak-nu*]-*uk a-na* 17. [^{md}NA$_3$-ŠEŠ].MEŠ-*bul-liṭ* DUMU-*šú šá* [^{m}*nar-gi*]-*ia ad-din*	(15–17) "I [seal]ed a tablet of wifehood for Tabluṭu, [my] sister, and gave it to [Nabû-aḫḫē]-bulliṭ son of [Narg]iya."
18. [*ù* ^{f}*tab-lu-ṭu taq-bi um-ma* ^{md}NA$_3$]-TIN-*iṭ* ŠEŠ-*ú-a*	(18) [And Tabluṭu said thus "Nabû]-uballiṭ, my brother
19. […] *ši-ḫa* ŠEŠ-*šú*	(19) …
20. […] E$_2$ *i-šu*	(20) …
21. […] IM.DUB *áš-šu-tu* 22. *šá* ^{f}*tab-lu-ṭu šá* ^{md}NA$_3$-TIN-*iṭ ik-nu-uk-ma* 23. *a-na* ^{md}NA$_3$-ŠEŠ.MEŠ-*bul-liṭ ba-lu* ^{m}*nar-gi-iá* 24. AD-*šú id-din a-šar in-nam-ma-ru ḫe-pi*	(21–24) … The tablet of wifehood of Tabluṭu, which Nabû-uballiṭ sealed and gave to Nabû-aḫḫē-bulliṭ without the permission of Nargiya, his father—wherever it is found, it shall be broken.
25. [*ki-i ul*]-*tu an-na-a* ^{f}*tab-lu-ṭu it-ti* 26. ^{md}NA$_3$-ŠEŠ.MEŠ-*bul-liṭ ta-at-ta-nam-mar* 27. [*šen*]-*da-tu* GEME$_2$-*ú-tu tam-maḫ-ḫar*	(25–26) If, after this, Tabluṭu is seen with Nabû-aḫḫē-bulliṭ, she shall receive the [br]and of the female slave.
28. [*ina*] *maḫ-ri* ^{md}[PN] ^{lu_2}*sar-te-nu* 29. [^{md}AMAR.UTU]-*za-kir-šu-um* ^{lu_2}GAR.UMUŠ TIN.TIR^{ki} 30. ^{md}NA$_3$-LUGAL-URI$_3$ ^{lu_2}SUKKAL 31. ^{md}NA$_3$-A-MU ^{md}NA$_3$-TIN-*su-iq-bi* ^{m}DUGUD-^{d}AMAR.UTU 32. ^{md}NA$_3$-*ú-ša-lim* ^{m}*ri-mut*-^{d}EN *u* ^{md}NA$_3$-NIR.GAL$_2$-DINGIR.MEŠ	(28–33) The document was written before [PN], the *sartennu*, Marduk-zākir-šum(i) the governor of Babylon, Nabû-šarra-uṣur the *sukkallu*, Nabû-apla-iddin, Nabû-balāssu-iqbi, Kabti-Marduk, Nabû-ušallim, Rīmūt-Bēl and Nabû-etel-ilāni, the judge(s).

33. ^{lú}DI.KU$_5$ *šá-ṭa-ri ša-ṭi-ir* ^{md}AMAR.UTU-*na-ṣir* DUB.SAR	(33–34) Marduk-nāṣir, the scribe, descendant of Bāne-ša-iliya.
34. DUMU ^{m}DU$_3$-*a-šá*-DINGIR-*ia* TIN.TIR^{ki}	
35. ITI NE U$_4$ 11-*kám* MU 8-*kám*	(35–36) Babylon. 11 Abu, year 8 of Cyrus, king of Babylon, king of the lands.
36. ^{m}*ku-ra-áš* LUGAL TIN.TIR^{ki} LUGAL KUR.KUR	

NOTES

3. The "Great Ones" mentioned in this line are probably the *sartennu,* the governor and the *sukkallu* in whose presence the document was written (lines 29–34).

18–21. Transcription of these lines follows Joannès 2000b. The drawing in Strassmaier 1890b, No. 312 shows an additional illegible line of text.

29–34. Nabû-balāssu-iqbi, Rīmūt-Bēl and Nabû-etel-ilāni, who are named as "judges of Cyrus" in the present document, are also named as "judges of Nabonidus" in earlier documents (Wunsch 2000b, 574). This attests to the continuity of the office of "royal judge" even after Babylon was incorporated into the Achaemenid Empire.

Normalized Texts

Reading and translating any Akkadian text begin with two basic steps of interpretation: transcription and normalization. Transcription, also known as transliteration, is the representation of the cuneiform signs on the tablet in Latin characters, based on readers' understandings of what appears. From a transcription, a trained Assyriologist should be able to draw (or imagine) the cuneiform writing on the original text. At times this step requires little more than a quick glance at the tablet, but a scribe's poor handwriting or millenia of wear and tear can present some serious challenges.

Normalization, the second interpretive step, brings the syllabic transcription into conformity with a grammar and a lexicon. To some extent, it is hard to separate this step from transcription, since grammatical considerations often govern reading choices, including the basic determination of where one word ends and another begins. Apart from separating the words, however, a transcription does not represent other linguistic features, such as vowel length and, most crucially, the Akkadian that stands behind the ubiquitous Sumerograms (signs representing whole words instead of syllables). In contrast, normalization shows the reader's judgment as to the words that the signs represent. Put otherwise, if somewhat simply, normalizations attempt to render what the native audience "heard" when they read the text.

Most scholarly editions of Neo-Babylonian legal texts provide transliterations and translations, but not normalizations. This is mostly because there are many grammatical inconsistencies within the corpus, which confound (or at least complicate) transforming the cuneiform syllables into a coherent language (see Jursa 2005, 3 n. 15). For example, the evidence points to the loss of word-final short vowels, which leads to somewhat unpredictable use of vowel-final (CV) cuneiform signs. This, in turn, creates difficulties for anyone familiar with the more consistent use of the Akkadian case system (a system based on distinctions between word-final short vowels) from earlier periods. Normalization assumes a basic similarity between the writing on the tablet and the language of the scribe and the audience. In the Neo-Babylonian period, the gaps between writing and language are so great that any attempt at normalization will probably require overriding some evidence on the tablet itself.

Despite these serious considerations, this book provides normalizations, presented here. The series editor and others felt that this information would benefit readers who might otherwise struggle to understand the relationship between the transliterated texts and the translations. It allows these readers to see the words as words, rather than as groups of syllables or Sumerograms, which will certainly improve their access to the texts.

Nevertheless, it is important to remember that the normalizations below are no more than a fair guess at the actual language. Every effort was made to be as consistent as possible. In all personal names, and in many other situations, too, the normalizations rely on the conventions of Old Babylonian, which is the base dialect on which standard Akkadian grammars are based. This allows meaningful normalizations, but sometimes requires ignoring what is written on the tablets. Thus, normalization comes at the expense of a potentially more accurate rendering of the language of the Neo-Babylonian period.

Document 1

(1–4) *Lū-dānu māršu ša Ibni-Ištar mār ... ša Iltammeš-baraku māršu ša Nabû-zēra-X ina šašti iṣbatâššim-ma ana Nergal-nāṣir mārīšu ša Nanaya-ibni iddinuš*

(4–5) *ša lā maš'alti iqbi umma*

(5–14) *anāku Murašû māršu ša Zēra-ibni Ištar-aḫa-iddin māršu ša ... Basiya u Innin-aḫḫē-iddin mārū ša Ibni-Ištar ina mūši niksu ana bīt Nergal-nāṣir mārīšu ša Nanaya-ibni ša ina muḫḫi Takkiru kî nikkisu kî nīrubu 1 nasḫiptu appat parzilli kalabbāt parzilli 3 mar parzilli u muṣipetu 1 še 1 kur suluppū kî niššû ana Zēra-ibni abi ša Murašû bā'iri ša ittīni niptaqid*

(15–18) *1 nasḫiptu ša kakkabtu šendet ša ultu bīt Nergal-nāṣir iššû ša Iltameš-baraku ina qātēšu iššâ qāt ṣibbitīšu ina Eanna iškunū*

Document 2

(1–5) *ūm 4 ša Ulūli šanat 12 Nabû-na'id šar Bābili rāb-banûtu maḫar Bēlti ša Uruk Nanaya u Bēlti ša rēši ša Anum-šumu-līšir māršu ša Nabû-apla-iddin suluppū u lurindu ana naptani ša Bēlti ša Uruk ušēlâm-ma*

(6) *kūm bēšû ana Bēlti ša Uruk la iqrubū*

(7) *baṭlu iškunū-ma*

(7–10) *Zēriya šatam Eanna māršu ša Ibnaya mār Egibi u ṭupšarrū ša Eanna suluppū u lurindu ultu Eanna ana Bēlti ša Uruk uqarribū*

(10–11) *Anum-šumu-līšir simerē ša ina Eanna iddi*

(11–14) *u suluppī u lurindu ša ana naptani ušēlâm-ma kūm bēšû lā iqrubū ina Eanna iknuk*

Document 3

(1–5) *Nabû-rēṣua qallu ša Lâbāši-Marduk mārīšu ša Arad-Bēl mār Egibi ša lā maš'alti ana Nabû-mukīn-zēri šatam Eanna mārīšu ša Nādinu mār Dābibī u Nabû-aḫa-iddin ša rēš šarri bēl piqitti Eanna iqbi umma*

(5–8) *ūm 28 ša Kislīmi abnu murḫašītu ša Ištar-aḫa-iddin mārīšu ša Innin-šuma-uṣur mār Nabû-šarḫi-ilī ultu muḫḫi ammati ša Bēlti ša Uruk ina sarti ina mūši Iddinaya māršu ša Lâbāši-Marduk mār Egibi ittasaḫ ina šaddi iltakan*

(9–11) *u Nabû-lū-dāri qallu ša Bāniya mārīšu ša Taribi uktīn u Ḫašdaya aḫu ša Iddinaya ina puḫri iqbi umma*

(11–12) *abnu murḫašītu ša ultu bīt šutummi ša Ištar-aḫa-iddin ina sarti našât ina bīt Lâbāši-Marduk abīya ātamar*

Document 4

(1–5) *Nabû-aḫḫē-bulliṭ māršu ša PN paqūdu ša Šaḫrinni ša ūm 28 ša Addari šanat 8 Kuraš šar Bābili šar mātāti ana Bēl-uballiṭ šangā Sippar iqbû umma*

(6–7) *Nanaya-iddin māršu ša Bau-ēreš ina bītīya aṣṣabit umma*

(7–9) *aḫi abīka u paqūdu ša āli anāku mīnamma qātēka ana muḫḫīya tadkâ*

(9–17) *Adad-šarra-uṣur māršu ša Nabû-ušēzib Nargiya u Erība aḫḫūšu Kutka-ili māršu ša Bau-ēreš Bēl-uballiṭ māršu ša Bariki-ili Bēl-aḫḫē-uṣur māršu ša Adad-ušallim u Iqīšaya māršu ša Šamaš-šarra-uṣur kî illammanū daltu'a ittabalū u ana bītīya kî īrbūni iterrūni 1 manā kaspu ittašû*

Document 5

(1) *maš'altu ša Nabû-šarra-uṣur ša rēš šarri bēl piqitti Eanna*

(2–9) *Marduk māršu ša Nabû-zēra-iddin Ipaltiraya u Bēl-aḫḫē-iddin māršu ša Nanaya-ēreš sarrūtu ša 3 laḫrāti u 1 kalūmu ša Šamaš-šuma-iddin mārīšu ša Šulaya ultu ṣēni ša Nergal-īpuš mārīšu ša Nabû-zēra-iqīša nāqidi ša Bēlti ša Uruk ultu Bīt Lugalbanda mūši ša ūmi 30 ša Dûzi ina sarti ībukū-ma ina Uruk ina bīt Nanaya-iddin mārīšu ša Attar-ramât zakīti 1 laḫru ikkisū*

(9–12) *šiḫṭu šīru u mušaḫḫin siparri u 2 laḫrāti 1 kalūmu balṭūti Nergal-īpuš ultu bīt Nanaya-iddin mārīšu ša Attar-ramât ībukū-ma ina Eanna ukallimū*

(12–14) *Nabû-šarra-uṣur ša rēš šarri Marduk u Bēl-aḫḫē-iddin išāl u ana Nabû-šarra-uṣur iqbû umma*

(14–19) *mūši ... ša Uruk ina mūši 3 laḫrāti 1 kalūmu ultu Bīt Lugalbanda ultu ṣēni ša Nergal-īpuš ina sarti kî nībuku 1 laḫru ina Uruk ina bīt Nanaya-iddin nittekis 2 laḫrātu 1 kalūmu balṭūti ušuzzū ... .*

(19–21) *ina sarti ana pāni ṣēni ša Nergal-īpuš Nanaya-iddin ittīni ittalak*

(21–23) *2 laḫrāti 1 kalūmu balṭūti Nabû-šarra-uṣur utīr-ma ana Itti-Anum-balāṭu mārīšu ša Šamaš-šuma-iddin bēl immerī iddin*

(23–24) *u šiḫṭu u mušaḫḫin siparri ina Eanna ina bīt karê iškun*

Document 6

(1–2) *maš'altu ša Iddin-Ištar mārīšu ša Ibni-Ištar ša iqbû umma*

(2–3) *8 1/2 šiqil girû ḫurāṣu ina qātē ṣābi ana kaspi andaḫar*

(4–5) *šatammu u ṭupšarrū ša Eanna ana Iddin-Ištar iqbû umma*

(5–7) *ḫurāṣu ina qātē ṣābi tamḫuru u ana ṣābi taddinu bābu qibannâši*

(7–8) *Iddin-Ištar iqbi umma*

(8–9) *1/2 šiqil mišil bitqi ḫurāṣu ina qātē Nabû-nāṣir mārīšu ša Aḫḫē-iddin andaḫar*

(9–10) *3/4 ina qātē Ina-tēšê-ēṭir mārīšu ša Ardiya andaḫar*

(11–12) *2 šiqil ḫurāṣu ina qātē Bēl-aḫa-šubši mārīšu ša Nabû-iqīša ina Bābili andaḫar*

(13–14) *1 šiqil ḫurāṣu ina qātē Nabû-mukīn-zēri kutīmi andaḫar*

(15–16) *ḫurāṣu ša Iddin-Ištar iqbû umma ana kaspi ana ṣābi attadin*

(17) *3 šiqil ḫurāṣu ana Anum-aḫa-iddin mārīšu ša Mušēzib*

(18–19) *2 šiqil ḫurāṣu ana Nabû-mušētiq-uddê mārīšu ša Marduk-šuma-ibni*

Document 7

(1–8) Personal names

(9–11) *mār banî ša ina pānīšunu Rīmūt māršu ša Innin-šuma-uṣur mār Ḫunzû iqbû umma*

(11–13) *Nanaya-X māršu ša Nabû-zēru-līšir sašta ul īpuš*

(13–17) *Iltammeš-kīni Piqudaya sašta ša alpi kî ābuku aqtanabbi*

Document 8

(1–8) Personal names

(9–16) *mār banî ša ina ušuzzīšunu Balāṭu māršu ša Zākir mār Kidin-Marduk tuppašu ummi eqli ša zēri ša ina āl Bīt-Šammu-il ša iti Bēlti ša Uruk ina pāni Nādinu šākin ṭēmi Uruk mārīšu ša Balāṭu u Kurbanni-Marduk šatam Eanna mārīšu ša Zēriya mār Sîn-damāqu ina puḫri ištasû*

(16–17) *ina libbi šaṭru umma šanat 20 Aššur-bāni-apli*

Document 9

(1–2) *Enlil-šuma-iddin māršu ša Murašû ša ana Aqubu mār Zabdiya iqbû umma*

(2–3) *300 ṣēnu peṣūti u ṣalindu tātabak*

(3–4) *arku Aqubu iqbû umma*

(4–5) *ṣēnu elat 110 ul ābuk*

(5–10) *ūmu ina qāt ṣibitti lū bātiqu lū mukinnu arkīšu elat ṣēnu-aʾ 110 ittakšadu 300 ṣēnu Aqubu ana Enlil-šuma-iddin inamdin*

Document 10

(1–8) *ina ūmi mukinnu lū bātiqu ittalkam-ma Nuptaya mārassu ša Sîn-ibni uktinnu lū kaspu lū ḫurāṣu lū abnu Nabû-tāriṣ māršu ša Nabû-bēl-šumāti iddaššu elat 1 šiqil bitqa kaspu ša Nuptaya taqbû umma ana Rīmūtu iddanu*

(8–10) *mimma iddaššu tabbal ša Bēlti ša Uruk tātappal*

Document 11

(1'–3') … *u Kīnaya māršu ša Iqīšaya ana mār banî itti aḫāmeš illakū-ma*

(3'–7') *dīnu ša Marduk-šarranu ana Kīnaya iqbû ummu mārūʾa tandaḫaṣ idabbub*

(7'–10') *Nabû-zēra-iddin māršu ša Aḫḫūšaya u Iṣṣur-X aḫāssu pūt Kīnaya mārīšu ša Iqīšaya našû*

(10'–14') *kî Kīnaya iḫteliqu napšātu ša mārīšu ša Marduk-šarranu Nabû-zēra-iddin u Iṣṣur-X ušallamū*

Document 12

(1–9) *adi ūmi 1 ša Kislīmi Gudaya māršu ša Ḫinni-ilī 2 mār bānî mukinnēšu ana Upiya ibbakam-ma ana Bau-ēreš mārīšu ša Nabû-mukīn-apli ukân ša Katimuʾ māršu ša Ḫaguru ša pūt šēpīšu ina qātē Bau-ēreš iššû ina adānīšu Gudaya ībukašim-ma ana Bau-ēreš iddinu*

(10) *kî uktinnuš zaki*

(11–12) *kî lā uktinnuš akî uʾilti šeʾu u ḫubullašu ana Bau-ēreš ittaddin*

Document 13

(1–4) *Libluṭ māršu ša Nabû-mīta-uballiṭ mār Mudammiq-Adad ina Bēl Nabû u Dariamuš šar Bābili šar mātāti ana Marduk-nāṣir-apli mārīšu ša Itti-Marduk-balāṭu mār Egibi itteme*

(5–9) *kî adi ūmi 10 ša Dûzi ana pānika attalkam-ma u᾽iltu ša erši ša mesukkanni ša ina muḫḫi Nabû-mīta-uballiṭ abīya ša ina zakûti amḫuru-ma ina muḫḫīya tušazzazu*

(9–18) *kî adi ūmi 10 ša Dûzi Libluṭ lā ittalkam-ma ana muḫḫi u᾽ilti ša ina zakûti iššû itti Marduk-nāṣir-apli lā idabbub 1 eršu ša mesukkanni ša dimgur u titti Libluṭ ana Marduk-nāṣir-apli inamdin-ma 13 šiqil kaspu Marduk-nāṣi-apli ana Libluṭ inamdin*

Document 14

(1–3) *5 immerū ša Bēlti ša Uruk ša kakkabtu šendû ša ina ṣēni ša Kīnaya mārīšu ša Nergal-ina-tēšê-ēṭir mār Dannea amrā-ma*

(3–5) *Zēriya māršu ša Balāssu nāqidu ša Bēlti ša Uruk 3 ina libbi iqbû umma*

(5–6) *ina sarti ultu ṣēnīya abkā*

(6) *ina puḫri ana Kīnaya ukinnu*

(7–8) *1 30 ṣēni rabīti ina muḫḫi Kīnaya parsū*

(8–10) *u 2 ṣēni rēḫit 5 ṣēni ša kakkabtu šendû ša Kīnaya iqbû umma*

(10–11) *ultu Addari šanat 7 Sūqaya rē᾽û ina ṣēnīya ipteqid*

(11–15) *Sūqaya ibbakam-ma ana Nabû-šarra-uṣur ša rēš šarri bēl piqitti Eanna u bēlē piqnēti ša Eanna inamdin*

(15–17) *kî Sūqaya lā ītabkam-ma lā ittannu 60 ṣēnu itti šēni-a᾽ 1 30 ana Bēlti ša Uruk inamdin*

Document 15

(1–5) *ūm X ... Bau-iqīša u Itti-Enli-balāṭu mārū ša Usātu ana Bābili illakū-ma dibbīšunu ša ibaššû itti aḫāmeš idabbubū*

(6–9) *kî Itti-Enlil-balāṭu lā ittalkam dīnšunu šakin*

(9–11) *kî Bau-iqīša lā ittalkam Itti-Enlil-balāṭu zaki*

Document 16

(1–4) *Bau-ēreš māršu ša Nabû-aḫa-uṣur rē᾽û ša ṣēni makkūr Bēlet Uruk u Nanaya ša qātē Arad-Bēl mārīšu ša Šarru-kīn rāb būli ina puḫur mār banî iqbû umma*

(4–8) *Puṭiya u Ša-Nabû-taqum lamutānu ša Kīnaya mārīšu ša Raḫimmu iṭṭerûnni iḫbitūnni u ṣēnu makkūr Ištar Uruk ša ina pānīya ultu tamirti qaqqar ša Ištar Uruk iktamū*

(9–14) *adi ūmi 1 ša Simāni Kīnaya māršu ša Raḫimmu Puṭiya u Ša-Nabû-taqum lamutānīšu ana Uruk ibbakam-ma*

(15–17) *kî lā ītabku miṭītu ša ṣēni ša Ištar Uruk ša ina pāni Bau-ēreš Kīnaya ana Ištar Uruk iṭṭir*

Document 17

(1–4) *ūm 15 ša Simāni Amurru-nādin-X māršu ša Marduka illakam-ma dibbīšu itti Aḫat-abīšu šiškati ša Bēltiya ina pāni qīpāni ša Esagil idabbub*

(5–6) *kî lā ittalku dullu ardūtu ana Bēl inamdin*

Document 18

(1–4) *dīnu ša Karêa mārīšu ša Bēl-lē᾽i mār Aḫūtu u Nuptaya mārassu ša Nabû-balāssu-iqbi ummīšu ana muḫḫi Kuzbaya u mārīšu u Nabû-uṣuršu nīšī bītīšunu itti Nergal-aḫa-iddin mārīšu ša Aḫḫêa irgumū*

(5–7) *Nergal-aḫa-iddin dīnu īdar-ma itti Karêa u Nuptaya ummīšu ana dabāb dīni lā illik*

(7–8) *Kuzbaya u mārīšu utīr-ma ana Karêa u Nuptaya ummīšu iddin*

(9–10) *u 4 manā kaspu kūm Nabû-ṣuršu ša ina bīt Nergal-aḫa-iddin mītu ana Karêa Nuptaya ummīšu iddin*

(11–12) *Nergal-aḫa-iddin māršu ša Aḫḫêa amirtu itti Karêa u Nuptaya mārassu ša Nabû-balāssu-iqbi ummīšu īmurū*

(13–15) *dibbu ša Karêa u Nuptaya ummīšu ana muḫḫi amēlūutti u mandattiī itti Nergal-aḫa-iddin qatû*

(16–20) *Nergal-aḫa-iddin māršu ša Aḫḫêa Karêa māršu ša Bēl-lē'i mār Aḫūtu u Nuptaya ummašu ina Bēl Nabû u adê ša Dari'ušu šar Bābili u mātāti ana aḫāmeš ittemû*

(20–21) *kî ana muḫḫi mimma ša nīpušu niteḫsi*

(21–23) *Karêa māršu ša Bēl-lē'i mār Aḫūtu u Nuptaya ummašu ina qātē Nergal-aḫa-iddin eṭrû*

Document 19

(1–3) *Bēlilitu mārassu ša Bēl-ušēzib mār Ša-nāšīšu ana dayyānī ša Nabû-na'id taqbi umma*

(3–5) *ina Abi šanat 1 Nergal-šarra-uṣur šar Bābili Bazuzu qallū'a ana 1/2 manā 5 šiqil kaspi ana Nabû-aḫḫē-iddin mārīšu ša Šulaya mār Egibi addin-ma*

(5) *u'iltu ī'il-ma kaspu lā iddin*

(5–6) *dayyānū ša šarri išmû-ma Nabû-aḫḫē-iddin ublūnim-ma maḫaršunu ušzizzū*

(7–8) *Nabû-aḫḫē-iddin riksu ša Bēlilitu irkusu-ma kasap šīm Bazuzu īṭiruš iššâm-ma dayyānū ukallim*

(9–10) *u Zēriya Nabû-šumu-līšir u Etillu kaspu ša Bēlilitu ummīšunu eṭrat ina pāni dayyānī ukinnū*

(10–11) *dayyānū imtalkū-ma 1/2 manā 5 šiqil kaspu mala muquttêšu ina muḫḫi Bēlilitu iprusū-ma ana Nabû-aḫḫē-iddin iddinū*

(12) *ina parās dīni šuāti*

Document 20

(1–4) *Bariki-ilī ardu puṭur kaspi ša Gagaya mārassu ša Bēl-nāṣir ša šanat 35 Nabû-kudurra-uṣur šar Bābili Aḫu-nūri māršu ša Nabû-nādin-aḫi ana 1/3 manā kaspi ... eninni irgum umma*

(4–6) *mār banî ... ša Bēl-rēmanni tašlīšu ša qātē Šamaš-mudammiq mārīšu ša Nabû-nādin-aḫi u Qudāšu mārassu ša Aḫu-nūri anāku*

(6–8) *ina maḫar sukkalli rabî u dayyānī ša Nabû-na᾿id šar Bābili dīni idbubū-ma*

(8) *dibbīšunu išmû*

(8–14) *rikasī ša ardūti ša Bariki-ilī ša ultu šanat 35 Nabû-kudurra-uṣur šar Bābili adi šanat 7 Nabû-na᾿id šar Bābili ana kaspi nadnu ana maškani šaknu ana nudunnê ana Nuptaya mārassu ša Gagaya nadnu arki Nuptaya taknukūšu-ma itti isiq bīti u amēlutti ana Zababa-iddin mārīšu u Iddinaya mutīšu taddinuš ištasû-ma*

(15) *ana Bariki-ilī iqbû umma*

(15–16) *targum umma mār banî anāku*

(16) *mār banûtūka kulilim annâšu*

(16–17) *Bariki-ilī annīti īpul umma 2 ḫalāqī ultu bīt bēlīya addi-ma*

(17–18) *ūmī mādūti lā annamar aplaḫ-ma aqbi umma mār banî anāku*

(19) *mār banûtīya lā iši ardu puṭur kaspi ša Gagaya anāku*

(20–22) *Nuptaya mārassu taddananni Nuptaya taknukanni ana Zababa-iddin mārīšu u Iddinaya mutīšu taddinanni*

(22–24) *arki mītūti ša Gagaya u Nuptaya ana Itti-Marduk-balāṭu mārīšu ša Nabû-aḫḫē-iddin mār Egibi ana kaspi kanāk ardu anāku allak-ma bēlū᾿a apallaḫ*

(25) *sukkallu rabû u dayyānū mukinnūssu išmû-ma*

(26) *Bariki-ilī kî ardūti uterrū-ma*

(26–27) *ina ušuzzi ša Šamaš-mudammiq u Qudāšu mārassu ša Aḫu-Nūri nādin nudunnê*

(28) *ana šaṭār ṭuppi šuāti*

Document 21

(1–9) *Madānu-aḫḫē-iddin māršu ša Gimillu mār Šigûa šāpir sirāšê ša Ištar Uruk u Balāṭu māršu ša Sîn-ibni ṭupšar Eanna Nanaya-ḫussinni amtu ša kakkabtu rittašu šendet u ana Nanaya šaṭrat u Tattannu māru ša Nanaya-ḫussinni itti Nūrea mārīšu ša Kabtiya ana maḫri dayyānī ša Nabû-na᾿id šar Bābili ubbilūnim-ma iqbû umma*

(9–10) *amtu annītu zakītu ša Nanaya Nūrea tapallaḫ*

(10–11) *Nūrea īpul umma*

(11–12) *Nanaya-ḫussinni ana kaspi ātabak*

(12–15) *u ina palê Amēl-Marduk šar Bābili ultu bītīya kî taḫliqu kakkabtu rittašu taltemit u šaṭāri ina muḫḫi rittīšu ana Nanaya taltaṭar*

(15–17) *dayyānū Nanaya-ḫussinni išālū-ma taqbi umma*

(17–19) *adi lā Nūrea ana kaspi ibbakanni Mār-Esagil-lūmur bēlū'a maḫrû ana Nanaya uzakkânni*

(19–20) *dayyānū amātīšunu ištimû-ma*

(20–22) *sepīru ubilūnim-ma rittu ša Nanaya-ḫussinni u'addi-ma iqbi umma*

(22–24) *šaṭāru labīru ša ūmī rūqūti ana Nanaya rittašu šaṭrat*

(25–26) *u šaṭāru šanû ina šapal šaṭāri maḫrî ana Ištar Uruk šaṭir*

(27) *dayyānū ana Nūrea iqbû umma*

(27–30) *mīnamma amtu ša ana Ištar Uruk zakât kakkabtu šendet u rittašu ana Ištar Uruk u Nanaya šaṭrat ana kaspi tābak*

(31–33) *u atta taqbi umma ina palê Amēl-Marduk šar Bābili amtu ultu bītīya taḫliq-ma kakkabtu rittašu tašmit*

(33–36) *mīnamma ina ūmīšu ana maḫri dayyānī ul tūbilšu-ma arkassu ul iprus-ma itti amēli ša rittašu išṭuru ul idīnka*

(36–38) *eli Nanaya-ḫussinni u Tattannu mārīšu ul rašâta*

(38) *dayyānū imtalkū-ma*

(39–41) *Nanaya-ḫussinni u Tattannu mārūšu itti ummānni zābil tupsikkī ša Eanna imnû*

(41) *Nūrea itti arkīšu ša amēlūti iddinūšu idabbub*

(42) *ina šaṭār ṭuppi šuāti*

Document 22

(1–3) *Nergal-rēṣūʾa qallu ša Iddin-Marduk ana dayyānī ša Nabû-naʾid šar Bābili iqbi umma*

(3–6) *Iddin-Marduk bēlūʾa 480 kur suluppū epirūtu ultu ṣēri ana eleppēti ša Amurru-natan malāḫi mārīšu ša Ammaya ušēli-ma*

(7) *pūt maṣṣarūti ša suluppī ušaššīšu*

(8–10) *eleppēti ana Bābili ušēlâm-ma šipirtu ša Iddin-Marduk iddinnam-ma 480 kur suluppū ina libbīšu šaṭir*

(11–12) *rēš suluppī ašši-ma 47 kur 1 pi ina libbi maṭû*

(12–14) *ana muḫḫi miṭīti ša suluppī itti Amurru-natan argum-ma usarrir umma*

(14–15) *suluppūka ul ašši*

(15) *arki bātiqu ...*

(16) *40 kur ... suluppū*

(17) *u kutalla ša eleppāni ...*

(18) *suluppū šunūti ina ...*

(19–21) *riksu ittīšu niškus umma 7 kur 1 pi suluppū ša Amurru-natan ina sarti iššû*

(22–23) *arki riksu šuātu Amurru-natan ... šuṭur-ma adi ūmi annî lā ...*

(24–25) *inanna ina maḫrīkunu ublâš purussâni šuknā*

(25–29) *dayyānū dibbīšunu išmû riksu šuātu u šipirtu ša Iddin-Marduk ša 480 kur suluppī ina libbi šaṭru ša Nergal-rēṣūʾa ubla maḫaršunu ištasû*

(29–30) *Amurru-natan išālū-ma*

(30–31) *našû ša suluppī ša ina sarti našû eli ramānīšu ukīn-ma*

(32–35) *40 kur suluppī miṭītu ša suluppī šunūti eli Amurru-natan iprusū-ma ana Nergal-rēṣūʾa qalli ša Iddin-Marduk iddinū*

(35) *ina parās dīni šuāti*

Document 23

(1–3) *PN_x u Bēl-uballiṭ mārū ša Šuma-ukīn mār Sîn-šadûnu ana dayyānī ša Nabû-na'id šar Bābili iqbû umma*

(3–6) *ina šanat 2 Nergal-šarra-uṣur šar Bābili Kurunnam-tabni ummani ... PN_y ardu ša nudunnêša taknuk-ma pānīni tušadgil*

(6–9) *u arki šanat 3 Nergal-šarra-uṣur šar Bābili Kurunnam-tabni ummani ina migir libbīšu 2 kur 2 pi zēru ša ṭupšarrū ša šarri kūm nudunnêšu pānīšu ušadgilû-ma ina ṭuppīšu ušēdu umma*

(9–10) *mārūšu ša lā ipallaḫšu zittu ina libbi ul ileqqû*

...

(6') *ina parās dīni šuāti*

Document 24

(1–3) *Marduk-šuma-ibni Nabû-mušētiq-uddê u Bēl-aḫḫē-iddin mārū ša Nabû-apla-iddin ... u Nabû-balāssu-iqbi aḫi abīšunu ana muḫḫi zâz zitti ... aḫa aḫa imtaḫṣūma iršû dīnu*

(4) ... *ana Bēl-rēmanni mār Mandidi šākin ṭēmi Bābili ikšudūnim-ma*

(5–6) *maḫar šākin ṭēmi u šībūt āli mārī Bābili amātīšunu ušannû*

(6) *Marduk-šuma-ibni iqbi umma*

(6–8) *maḫīrātu ša Nabû-balāssu-iqbi ša ina bābi ša Bēl ītepušu kaspu ša maḫīrāti ina libbi ītepušu ina karê bīt abi šū alla šiššu zittašu itti abīya yānu*

(9) *Nabû-balāssu-iqbi šanīti īpulšu umma*

(9–11) *maḫīrāti ša ina bābi ša Bēl ētepušu ina kaspi ša ramānīya ētepuš kaspu ša karê bīt abīni ina libbi yānu*

(11–12) *u maḫīrī ša Nabû-apla-iddin abūka ina bābi ša Bēl īpušu-ma ṭuppu ana šumīšu iknukū alla 10 šiqil kaspi ša karê bīt abīni ina libbi yāni*

(13) ... *anāku kî addinu abūka ṭuppu ana šumīšu iktanak*

(14) ... *maḫīrāti annâti nītepušu*

(15–16) ... *ramānīya amgur-ma* ... *Nabû-apla-iddin ṭuppa* ... *umma maḫirāti mala ina bābi ša Bēl nippušu* ...

(17–18) *zitti ša Arad-Gula aḫīya ša ana kaspi amḫuru* ... *ina ṭuppi maḫīrīya ana šībūti ašib*

(19) ... *abūka ittīya irtakasu*

(20) ... *zēru zitti zâzu*

...

(7') ... *ina bābi ša Bēl irtakasū*

(8') ... *aḫūni rabû*

(9') ... *Nabû-balāssu-iqbi irtakasu īni-ma*

(10') ... *eli Nabû-balāssu-iqbi parsatu*

(11') ... *abūni ittīšu irtakasu*

(12') ... *šākin ṭēmi Bābili u šībūt āli*

(13') ... *tamīti ina muḫḫi Nabû-balāssu-iqbi išṭurū*

(14') ... *iddinū šiššu zitti ša Nabû-balāssu-iqbi*

(15') ... *u šiššu zitti ša Arad-Gula*

(16') ... *išṭurū-ma aḫi zitti ša Nabû-apla-iddin ina libbi iškunū*

(17') ... *bīt abi ša bābi ša Bēl pāni Nabû-balāssu-iqbi ušadgilū*

(18') ... *ina bābi ša Bēl ina qātē Šullumu u Bēl-aḫḫē-X*

(19') ... *īpušū-ma Nabû-apla-iddin ana šumīšu iknuku*

(20') *Nabû-balāssu-iqbi ina bābi ša Bēl ina qātē Nabû-šumu-līšir*

(21') ... *Šulaya māršu ša Balt-ilī mār Ea-ṣalmu-ilī*

(22') ... *pāni Nabû-balāssu-iqbi*

(23') ... *ušadgilū šiššu ina eqel bīt abī ša Bīt Dakkūri*

(24') ... *ša āli u ṣēri mala bašû*

(25') ... *ina ṭuppi maḫīri ša Nabû-balāssu-iqbi šaṭru*

(26') ... *Nabû-zēra-iddin nadnu ina lā ašābi*

(27') ... *Nabû-balāssu-iqbi igmuru napḫar 7 manā kaspu*

(28') ... *ša Nabû-zēra-ibni ša Nabû-balāssu-iqbi iššâ zitti 2 manā kaspi ana*

(29') ... *pāni Nabû-balāssu-iqbi kūm 5 manā kaspīšu ušadgilū*

(30') ... *ša karê ītirūni*

(31') *u pāni Nabû-balāssu-iqbi ušadgilū*

(32'–33') *PN māršu ša Bibēa mār Bēl-eṭēru maḫru pāni ... ušadgilū*

Document 25

(1–3) *Nabû-mušētiq-uddê māršu ša Balāssu mār Dāmiqu Nabû-šarra-uṣur ša rēš šarri bēl piqitti Eanna Ṭābiya šākin ṭemi Uruk māršu ša Nabû-nādin-šumi u Gabbi-ilī-šarra-uṣur qīpu ša Eanna imḫur umma*

(3–4) *ina Šabāṭi šanat 6 Nabû-na'id šar Bābili bīt Mušēzib-Bēl mārīšu ša Nanaya-ēreš*

(5–6) *ša ṭāḫ Ḫurri-ša-uṣur-amāssu šiddu elû amurru ṭāḫ bīt Nabû-apla-iddin mārīšu ša Ibni-Ištar mār Ekur-zakir*

(6) *šiddu šaplû šadû ṭāḫ bīt Nadan-Ili mār Ṣillaya*

(7) *qaqqadu elû itānu ša ṭāḫ Ḫurri-ša-uṣur-amāssu*

(7–8) *qaqqadu šaplû sūtu ṭāḫ qaqqari ša Bēlti ša Uruk*

(8–9) *ana 2 manā 2 šiqil kaspi ina qātē Mušēzib-Bēl amḫur-ma*

(9–13) *ina Addari ša šanat 6 Nabû-na'id šar Bābili Nabû-rēšu māršu ša Šamaš-iddin ṭuppu ša bīt Mušēzib-Bēl mārīšu ša Nanaya-ēreš ša ina Dûzi šanat 6 Nabû-na'id šar Bābili ša ana 2 manā 4 šiqil kaspi ina qātē Mušēzib-Bēl mārīšu ša Nanaya-ēreš imḫuru ša 7 arḫū alla ṭuppīya panû ana muḫḫīya ukâm-ma bītu ina pāni Nabû-rēšu umaššir*

(14–18) *arki ina šanat 7 Nabû-na'id šar Bābili Rīmūt-Bēl Šamaš-ēṭir Nanaya-aḫa-iddin u Nabû-mušētiq-uddê mārū ša Nabû-bāni-aḫi mārīšu ša Marduk-erība mar Ea-ṣalmu-ilāni ṭuppu ša bīt Mušēzib-Bēl mārīšu ša Nanaya-ēreš ša ina šanat 22 Nabû-kudurra-uṣur šar Bābili ša Marduk-erība māršu ša Nergal-iddin mār Ea-ṣalmu-ilāni ab abīšunu maḫīru ina qātē Mušēzib-Bēl mārīšu ša Nanaya-ēreš īpušu ukinnūnim-ma*

(18–19) *maḫīru ina qātēšunu ēpuš-ma Nabû-rēšu bītu ina pānīya lā umaššir*

(20) *inanna Mušēzib-Bēl maḫarkunu ubil itti Mušēzib-Bēl u Nabû-rēšu epšā dīnī*

(21–22) *Nabû-šarra-uṣur ša rēš šarri Ṭābiya šākin ṭēmi Uruk u Gabbi-ilāni-šarra-uṣur qīpu puḫur Bābilaya Urukaya dayyānū ...*

(23) *Nabû-mušētiq-uddê u Mušēzib-Bēl dīnu ina pānīšunu idbubū*

...

Document 26

(1–4) *Arad-Innin māršu ša Šākin-šumi Kalbaya māršu ša Silim-Bēl Šamaš-iddin māršu ša Bēl-iddin mārū māri ša Bēl-aḫḫē-iddin mār Gimil-Nanaya ana Nabû-aḫḫē-bulliṭ šākin māti iqbû umma*

(4–7) *ina šanat 4 Nabû-kudurra-uṣur šar Bābili Bēl-aḫḫē-iddin ab abīni 5 1/2 manā kaspu ana Bēl-aḫḫē-iddin mārīšu ša Gudādu mār Sîn-lēqi-unninnī ana nisḫi iddin-ma*

(7–8) *bīssu ša ina abulli ša Eanna ina u'iltīšu maškanu iṣbat*

(9–11) *adi inanni qātū ša qīpāni maḫrûti ša Eanna eli bīti šuāti takaššadā-ma bītu ina pānīni lā umašširū*

(11–12) *itti qīpāni ša Eanna purussâni šukun*

(12–19) *Nabû-aḫḫē-bulliṭ šākin-māti Arad-Innin Kalbaya u Šamaš-iddin itti Nidintu-Bēl šatam Eanna mārīšu ša Nabû-mukīn-zēri mār Dābibī Nabû-aḫa-iddin ša rēš šarri bēl piqitti Eanna u ṭupšarrī ša Eanna ana maḫar Imbiya šākin ṭēmi Uruk mārīšu ša Nanaya-ēreš mār Kidin-Marduk u dayyānī ša Nabû-aḫḫē-bulliṭ šākin māti ana šakān purussîšunu išpuršunūti*

(19–20) *šākin ṭēmi u dayyānū dibbīšunu išmû*

(20–25) *u'iltu ša 5 1/2 manā kaspi ša Bēl-aḫḫē-iddin mārīšu ša Aḫḫēšu ša muḫḫi Bēl-aḫḫē-iddin mārīšu ša Gudādu ša ina šanat 4 Nabû-kudurra-uṣur šar Bābili e'iltu u bītu ina u'iltīšu maškanu ṣabtu ša Arad-Innin Kalbaya u Šamaš-iddin ana maḫar dayyanī ublūnim*

(25–28) *u ṭuppāti u riksāti makkūr Ištar Uruk ša qipānu ša Eanna maḫrûtu ša bītu ana idi iddinû u idi bīti šuāti ultu šanat 23 Nabû-kudurra-uṣur šar Bābili ana Eanna īrubu*

(29–31) *lē'u makkūr Ištar Uruk ša ina šanat 25 Nabû-kudurra-uṣur šar Bābili itti qanâti ša Eanna bītu šuāti ina lē'i šaṭru*

(31–36) *ṭuppu ša Sîn-iddin qīpu ša Eanna u ṭupšarrū ša Eanna ina šanat 36 Nabû-kudurra-uṣur šar Bābili bītu šuāti ultu Eanna ana kaspi ana Innin-šuma-uṣur mārīšu ša Nergal-ušallim mār Sîn-lēqi-unninnī iddinû-ma Iddin-Nabû mār apli ša Bēl-aḫḫē-iddin ana mukinnūti ina libbi ašbu*

(37–40) *riksu ša ina šanat 39 Nabû-kudurra-uṣur šar Bābili bītu šuāti ina qātē Innin-šuma-uṣur ana Eanna ... ana idi bītu ... širkī ša Eanna nadnu*

(41) *iltasû-ma*

...

(45) ... *u'iltu ana makkūri iddinū*

Document 27

(1–6) *annūtu dayyanū ša ina pānīšunu Šāpik-zēri māršu ša Zērūtu itti Balāṭu mār Nasikātu ina ušuzzi ša šākin māt Tâmti dīnu ša bīti ina pānīšunu idbubū*

(6–11) *bītu u ṭuppu ša Zērūtu abu ša Šāpik-zēri iknuku-ma ana Balāṭu iddinu Balāṭu itti Šāpik-zēri utirrū*

(11–14) *bītu pān Šāpik-zēri ušadgilū u ṭuppu iššûnim-ma ana Šāpik-zēri iddinū*

Document 28

(1–2) *Udarna' māru ša Raḫim'il ša ina puḫur Nippur ana Enlil-šuma-iddin māri ša Murašû iqbû umma*

(2–4) *mārū bītātīka ālik našpartīka ardūka itti Zabdiya aḫīya u Bēl-ittannu mārīšu ana bītīya kî īrubû makkūrū'a u udê bītīya ittašû*

(5–6) *arki Enlil-šuma-iddin ana mārī bītātīšu ālik našpartīšu ardīšu Zabdiya u Bēl-ittannu išāl-ma*

(6–7) *makkūru šuāti ina qātēšunu iššâm-ma uṭṭir-ma ana Udarnaʾ iddin*

(8–9) *makkūru šuāti Udarnaʾ ina qāti Enlil-šuma-iddin mārī bītātīšu u ālik našpartīšu u ardīšu maḫir*

(9–11) *dīnu u ragāmu ša Udarnaʾ u mārīšu ana muḫḫi makkūri šuāti itti Enlil-šuma-iddin mārī bītātīšu ālik našpartīšu u ardīšu ana ūmī ṣâtī yānu*

(12–14) *ul iturrū-ma Udarnaʾ u mārīšu ana muḫḫi makkūri šuāti itti Enlil-šuma-iddin mārī bītātīšu ālik našpartīšu u ardīšu ana ūmī ṣâtī ul iraggumū*

Document 29

(1–3) *Itti-Marduk-balāṭu māršu ša Nabû-aḫḫē-iddin mār Egibi ana dayyānī ša Nabû-naʾid šar Bābili iqbi umma*

(3–9) *Šāpik-zēri u Bēl-uballiṭ mārū ša Šuma-ukīn mār Sîn-šadûnu uʾiltu ša 5 manā kaspi ša Rīmūt mārīšu ša Ina-qībit-Nabû ša muḫḫīšunu ša eqelšunu ša muḫḫi ḫarri ša Ḫazuzu ina libbi maškanu ṣabtu u eqlu šuātu ana Nabû-aḫḫē-iddin abīya ana kaspi innadnu ana pānīya iškunūnim-ma 1/2 manā binnanâši-ma uʾilti ninaddinka*

(10) *uʾiltu ukīl-ma aqbīšunūti umma*

(10–11) *mannu Rīmūt ša eqlu maškanu ina qātēkunu ṣabtu*

(11–12) *uʾiltu šuāti Šāpik-zēri ultu qātēya iḫbit-ma ina šinnīšu iksus*

(13) *purussâni šuknā*

(13–14) *dayyānū Šāpik-zēri išālū-ma iqbû umma*

(15–19) *uʾiltu eṭirtu šī u mimmû Itti-Marduk-balāṭu ina maḫrīkunu ušannû kīnāti-ma uʾiltu ana dīni u ragāmi ana muḫḫīšu lā nubila ana maḫrīkunu ībukannâši*

(19–20) *dayyānū iqbûšunūši umma*

(20) *Rīmūt bēl uʾilti ana maḫrīni bilā*

(21–22) *Šāpik-zēri u Bēl-uballiṭ Rīmūt bēl u'ilti lā ublūni amat iqbû ikkirū-ma Rīmūt lā nīde iqbû*

(23–27) *dayyānū amātīšunu ištemû-ma u'iltu ša Rīmūt ša eqel maḫīri ša Nabû-aḫḫē-iddin ana maškanūti ana Rīmūt ušašṭiru-ma ana muḫḫi Itti-Marduk-balāṭu ublūnim-ma Šāpik-zēri ina šinnīšu iksusu u Rīmūt lā nīde iqbû*

(28) *dayyānū imtalkū-ma*

(28–31) *u'iltu ša Šāpik-zēri u Bēl-uballiṭ ublûni ana surrāti ina pānīšunu itūra 5 manā kaspu ša ina u'ilti šuāti šaṭrā adi 10–šu elīšunu iprusū-ma ana Itti-Marduk-balāṭu iddinū*

(31–32) *u ana abāki ša ṭupšarri šāṭir u'ilti izqātē iddûšunu-ma ana Itti-Marduk-balāṭu ipqidū*

(33) *ina šaṭār ṭuppi šuāti*

Document 30

(1–8) Personal names and titles

(9–10) *mār banî ša ina pānīšunu Ištar-ālik-pāni širik Ištar Uruk nāqidu ša Ištar Uruk iqbi umma*

(11–16) *Bēlšunu širik Ištar Uruk māršu ša Nūrea ana šigilti ana laḫrāti makkūr Ištar Uruk ša ina pānīya kî uridu 1 ina laḫrāti ša kakkabtu šendet ultu laḫrāti makkūr Ištar Uruk ša ina pānīya kî ībuku ittekis*

(16–20) *ana muḫḫi kî aqbâššu umma laḫrātu ša kakkabti parzilli lā tanakkis qaqqadâ kî ipṭuru ina kudurri ša tikkīšu iḫtaqqanni u iqbâm umma libbû agâ Gubāru u Parnakku kudurru tikki ša ṣābī inaddû*

(21–22) *puḫur mār Babili u Uruk kinišat Eanna Bēlšunu ībukūnim-ma ina puḫri išallū-ma iqbûšu umma*

(23) *mīnamma ṣēnu ša kakkabti parzilli tābuk tekkis*

(24–26) *Bēlšunu ina puḫur mār banî eli ramnīšu ukīn ša ṣēnu ša kakkabti ultu ṣēni ša Ištar Uruk ša ina pāni Ištar-ālik-pāni ana nāqidūti ...*

(27–28) *Bēlšunu ana šigilti urid 1 laḫru ša Ištar Uruk ikkis*

(28–30) *puḫur mār banî ... kî ṣindat Ekur ana eṭēri eli Bēlšunu iprusū*

Document 31

(1–2) *Nuptaya amtu ša Iddin-aḫa māršu ša Nabû-aḫḫē-šullim ša taqbû umma*

(2–3) *Iddin-aḫa bēlū'a kakkabtu kî išmitanni ana Bēlti ša Uruk uzakkanni*

(4–7) *Iddin-aḫa bēlū'a šīmtu ubilšu-ma Šamaš-zēra-šubši aḫu ša Iddin-aḫa ša arkat Iddin-aḫa ilqû ultu bīt Iddin-aḫa ībukanni-ma ana Ištar Uruk lā iddinanni*

(7–8) *Sūqaya Iddin-Nabû u Nabû-aḫa-ittannu mārêya ina bīt Šamaš-zēra-šubši ulid*

(9–12) *Anu-šarra-uṣur qīpu ša Eanna Nabû-mukīn-apli šatam Eanna māršu ša Nādinu mār Dābibī Nabû-aḫa-iddin ša rēš šarri bēl piqitti Eanna kakkabtu ša muḫḫi rittīšu īmurū*

(13–17) *Anu-šarra-uṣur qīpu ša Eanna Nabû-mukīn-apli šatam Eanna Nabû-aḫa-iddin ša rēš šarri bēl piqitti Eanna u ṭupšarrū ša Eanna Nuptaya Suqaya Iddin-Nabû u Nabû-aḫa-ittannu mārêša ina pāni Šamaš-zēra-šubši ipqidū*

(17–19) *ūmu mala ša Šamaš-zēra-šubši balṭu tapallaḫšu ul iṣabbi-ma Šamaš-zēra-šubši ana kaspi ul inamdin u ana ardi ul iḫâr*

(20–21) *arki Šamaš-zēra-šubši ana šīmti ītalak amēlūtu pāni Bēlti ša Uruk tad-dagal*

Document 32

(1–7) *dīnu ša Nabû-gāmil māršu ša Nabû-aḫḫē-bulliṭ mar Miṣiraya ana muḫḫi 2/3 manā 4 šiqil kaspi rašūti ša abīšu ša eli Nādin mārīšu ša Nabû-nādin-šumi mār Rab-bānê itti Mušēzib-Bēl mārīšu ša Nādin mār Rab-bānê ina maḫar Sîn-erība sartenni u dayyāni ša Nabû-na'id šar Bābili idbubu*

(7–10) *u'iltu ša Nabû-aḫḫē-bulliṭ abi ša Nabû-gāmil ša eli Nādin abi ša Mušēzib-Bēl ša bīssu maškanu ṣabtu maḫaršunu iltasû*

(10–12) *sartennu u dayyānū riksu u idātu ša eṭēri Mušēzib-Bēl īrišū-ma lā ubla*

(12) *imtalkū-ma*

(13–14) *2 qanâtu u šalšu ša qanî ina qanāti ša Mušēzib-Bēl mār Rāb-banê*

(15–16) *1 pān 5 ammat 14 ubān šiddu elû iltānu ṭāḫ mūṣî*

(17) *ša ina pūtīšu elīti 3 ammātu*

(18) *ina qaqqadīšu šaplî 4 ammat 3 ubān qaqqar*

(19) *ana mala bīt Mušēzib-Bēl*

(20) *1 pān 5 ammat 14 ubān šiddu šaplû šūtu*

(21) *ina ṭāḫ rīḫti bīt Mušēzib-Bēl*

(22) *6 ammat 10 ubān qaqqadu elû amurru ṭāḫ sūqi rapši*

(23) *5 ammat 6 ubān qaqqadu šaplû šadû ṭāḫ muṣê bītī*

(24–25) *napḫar 2 qanâtu 2 ammat 8 ubān*

sartennu u dayyānū kūm kaspīšu ina pāni Nabû-gāmil ušadgilū

(26–28) *ana lā enê sartennu u dayyānū ṭuppašu išṭurū kunukkīšunu ibrumū-ma ana Nabû-gāmil iddinū*

(29) *ina šaṭār ṭuppi šuāti*

Document 33

(1–4) *u'iltu ša 1/2 manā kaspi ša ḫarrāni ša šanat 1 Nergal-šarra-uṣur šar Bābili u u'iltu ša 1 1/2 manā kaspi ša ḫarrāni ša šanat X Nabû-na'id šar Bābili ša Nergal-iddin mārīšu ša Nabû-erīb ša ina muḫḫi Nergal-ēṭir mārīšu ša Ša-Nabû-šū mār Naggāru*

(4–6) *ša šanat 8 Kuraš šar Bābili šar mātāti Šamaš-iddin māršu ša Nergal-iddin ina muḫḫi Šamaš-uballiṭ mārīšu ša Nergal-ēṭir iššâm*

(6–8) *ina maḫar Bēl-uballiṭ šangā Sippar ērib bīti Šamaš šībūt āli ištasû*

(8–11) *Šamaš-uballiṭ u'ilēti gabrāti u'ilēti ... Bēl-uballiṭ šangā Sippar ērib bīti Šamaš šībūt āli ana Šamaš-iddin mārīšu ša Nergal-iddin ukallim*

(11–13) *Bēl-uballiṭ ērib bīti Šamaš šībūt āli u'ilēti kî utirru-ma ana Šamaš-iddin iddinū*

Document 34

(1) *ūmu 23 ūmu 24 ūmu 29 ūmu 30 ša Nisanni*

(2) *ūmu 23 ūmu 24 ūmu 29 ūmu 30 ša Ayari*

(3) *ūmu 23 ūmu 24 ūmu 29 ūmu 30 ša Simāni*

(4–5) *ūmu 23 ūmu 24 ūmu 29 ūmu 30 ša Dûzi ūmu 29 ūmu 30 ša Abi*

(5) *ūmu 20 ūmu 30 ša Ulūli*

(5–6) *ūmu 29 ūmu 30 ša Tašrīti ūmu 29 ūmu 30 mišil ūmi ša Araḫšamni*

(7) *ūmu 27 ūmu 28 ša Kislīmi ūmu 27 ūmu 28 ša Ṭebēti*

(8) *ūmu 27 ūmu 28 ša Šabāṭi ūmu 27 ūmu 28 mišil ūmi ša Addari*

(9–10) *napḫar 2 ūmī 15 isiq nuḫatimmūti ina ūmi 15 arkīti arḫussu ina Ebabbar bīt Šamaš ša Sippar*

(11–12) *2 ūmū mišil ūmi sellū sāmūtu ša ūmi 10 ūmi 11 1/2 ūmi 12 ša Nisanni*

(12–14) *1 ūmu mišil ūmi sellū sāmūtu ša ūmi 14 u mišil ūmi ša ūmi 15 ša šēri u ... ša Ayyari*

(14–20) *pāni Šamaš Aya siḫirti bēlet Sippar u Ištar bēlet Agade ša ina Addari arkî šanat rēš šarrūti Dari᾽muš šarri Šamaš-nāṣir māru ša Mušebši-Marduk mār Šangû-Šamaš ina qātē Nabû-uṣuršu u Šamaš-aḫḫē-lū-irši mārī ša Šamaš-kāṣir mār Isinnaya ana kaspi ana šīmī gamrūti imḫuru*

(20–23) *arki Šamaš-aḫḫē-lū-irši ina Tašrīti šanat X Dari᾽muš šar Bābili šar mātāti ana muḫḫi ūmī u sellî isqi šuāti nuḫatimmūti ana Šamaš-nāṣir irgum umma*

(23–25) *isqu šuāti ša Nidintu mār aḫīya ša Šamaš-kāṣir abū᾽a arkatīšu ilqû šīna*

(25–29) *Šamaš-nāṣir ṭuppi maḫīri ša isqi šuāti ina qātē Nabû-uṣuršu u Šamaš-aḫḫē-lū-irši ana kaspi imḫuru u šāṭaru ša isqu šuāti arki ṭuppi maḫīri ana epišānūti ana Šamaš-aḫḫē-lū-irši iddinu ina maḫar šībūt āli ana Šamaš-aḫḫē-lū-irši ukallimšu*

(29–30) *ṭuppi maḫīri u šaṭāru ina maḫar šībūt āli ištasû-ma*

(30–31) *Šamaš-aḫḫē-lū-irši ṭuppi maḫīri u šaṭāru ša epišānūti Šamaš-aḫḫē-lū-irši ina muḫḫi isqi šuāti nuḫatimmūti lā irši*

(31–32) *Šamaš-aḫḫē-lū-irši eli ramnīšu ukīn īdur-ma isqu šuāti ina pāni Šamaš-nāṣir umaššir ...*

(33–35) *Šamaš-nāṣir ina migir libbīšu rēmu ana Šamaš-aḫḫē-lū-irši iršu-ma 1 manā 5 šiqil kaspu peṣû elat kaspi maḫri ša ṭuppi maḫīri ana Šamaš-aḫḫē-lū-irši iddin*

(35) *isqu šuāti ša Šamaš-nāṣir šū*

Document 35

(1') … *muḫḫi Iddin-Marduk*

(2') *Kuttaya aššat Iddin-Marduk*

(3') … *ana rašūti ša muḫḫi Iddin-Marduk iddinu*

(4') … *ina pān Nabû šuma-iškun aḫīya ul ...*

(5') … *Marduk-šuma-uṣur šākin ṭēmi u dayyānū ...*

(6') ... *idbubū-ma dīnšunu īmurū*

(7'–9') *Rīmūt māršu ša Šamaš-lē'i mār Arrabtu u Ṣillaya māršu ša X-šuma-ibni mār Eppeš-ilī rāšūtāni ša muḫḫi Iddin-Marduk išālū-ma*

(9'–11') *Rīmūt māršu ša Šamaš-lē'i mār Arrabtu ina pān dayyānī nīs Šamaš izkur-ma annīta iqbi umma*

(11') *anāku u Ṣillaya rāšūtānu ša muḫḫi Iddin-Marduk*

(12') *ul nīde ša kaspu ina pān Nabû-šuma-iškun paqdu*

(13'–16') *Nādin mutu ša PN aḫāti ša Iddin-Marduk u Kuttaya aššat Iddin-Marduk ana pān ... kî ībukūniāši ḫindu ša Iddin-Marduk ša ina pānīšu paqdat kî iššâm ina pānīni ...*

(17') X *manā kaspi ina libbi Kuttaya aššat Iddin-Marduk ...*

(18'–19') *u šitti annî akî rašūtīni ša muḫḫi Iddin-Marduk nimtaṭi u nittaši*

(19'–20') *Ṣillaya māršu ša* PN *maruṣ-ma ana mukinnūti lā ...*

(21'–24') … *Gimil-Gula māršu ša Itti-Esagil-zēri ana pānīšunu nīš Šamaš izkur-ma ina pānīšunu annītu iqbi umma*

(24’) *anāku u Rīmūt rāšūtānu ša muḫḫi Iddin-Marduk*

(25’) *ul nīdi ša kaspu ina pān Nabû-šuma-iškun paqdu*

(26’–29’) *Nādin mutu ša PN aḫāti ša Iddin-Marduk u Kuttaya aššat Iddin-Marduk ana pān ... kî ībukūniāši ḫindu ša Iddin-Marduk ša ina pānīšu paqdat kî iššâm ina pānīni ...*

(30’) X *manā kaspi ina libbi Kuttaya aššat Iddin-Marduk ...*

(31’–32’) *u šitti annî akî rašūtīni ša muḫḫi Iddin-Marduk nimtaṭi u nittaši*

(33’) ... *ittemû*

(34’) ... *ša Iddin-Marduk*

(35’) ... *dayyānū mukinnūti*

(36’) ... *mimma ša Iddin-Marduk*

Document 36

(1–3) *Bunanītu mārassu ša Šākin-šumi mār Eppeš-ili ana Bēl-apla-iddin mārīšu ša Nabû-šumu-līšir mār Mudammiq-Adad dīnu tagre-ma*

(3–4) *ana maḫar Mušēzib-Bēl šākin ṭēmi Bābili mār Eli-ili-rabi-Marduk dayyānī u šībūt āli ikšudū-ma*

(5–6) *dibbīšunu ušannû-ma Bunanītu kiam taqbi umma*

(6–7) *Nabû-šumu-līšir abu ša Bēl-apla-iddin ana aššūti kî īḫuzanni 4 manā kaspu nudunnû᾿a ilteqa*

(7–9) *Nabû-šumu-līšir ana šīmti illik-ma Bēl-apla-iddin māršu nikkasīšu ilqe-ma adi ūmi annî nudunnû᾿a lā īpulanni*

(9) *Bēl-apla-iddin īpul umma*

(9–12) *ina ṭuppi nudunnêša 4 manā kaspu ša Bunanītu itti Nabû-šumu-līšir abīya tašṭuru alla 1 1/2 manā kaspi adi šīm amēlūti ana abīya lā nadin*

(12–13) *aššum rīḫit kaspi abū᾿a la maḫru abū᾿a riksāti itti Bunanītu urtakkis*

(14–16) *u 5 manā kaspu nudunnû ša Etellitu aššatīya Nabû-šumu-līšir abū᾿a ilqe-ma mala apālu nudunnanê šunūti lā maṣâku*

(16–17) *nikkassīni amrā-ma nudunnû ana Bunanītu Etellitu ina libbi apulā*

(17–21) *u'iltu ša ina šanat 31 Nabû-kudurrī-uṣur šar Bābili Nabû-šumu-līšir itti Bunanītu aššatīšu ī'ilu umma ina u'ilti ša 4 manā kaspi alla 1 1/2 manā kaspi adi šīm amēlūti Nabû-šumu-līšir ina qāt Bunanītu lā maḫir*

(21–23) *u u'iltu ša 5 manā kaspi nudunnû ša Bunanītu ša Nabû-šumu-līšir ilqû*

(23–24) *u'ilēti kilallān maḫar šākin ṭēmi Bābili dayyānī u šībūt āli ištasû-ma*

(24–26) *1 1/2 manā kaspu nudunnû ša Etellitu maḫršunu ikūn*

(26–30) *rēš nikkassī ša Nabû-šumu-līšir iššû-ma napḫar zērīšu eqel mērīšu u taptû ... pīḫāt Kiš adi zēri zaqpi ša ina ... bīti banî ša ina erṣeti Tē ša qereb Bābili ... šīm amēlūti annî nikkāsī ša Nabû-šumu-līšir īmurū*

(31) *šākin ṭēmi Bābili dayyānu u šībūt āli imtalkū-ma*

(32–34) *zēru šuāti kaspu šīm bīti u* PN *u mārtīša ana 6 1/2 manā kaspi imnû-ma ana Etellitu u Bunanītu kūm 6 1/2 manā kaspi nudunnâšina iddinū*

(34–37) *Etellitu u Bunanītu nikkasī šunūti kūm 6 1/2 manā kaspi ileqqâ-ma kî 1 manā nudunnâšina ina libbi išallimā*

(37–39) *Bēl-apla-iddin itti Etellitu aššatīšu ana nudunnêša akalu u lubuštu ileqqâ*

(39–43) *rašû ša Nabû-šumu-līšir u Bēl-apla-iddin mārīšu ina muḫḫi mimma ša ana Etellitu u Bunanītu kūm nuddunêšina nadnu ul išallaṭ u ana muḫḫi rašūtīšu mala bašû itti Bēl-apla-iddin ul iraggam*

(43) *dīnšunu dīn purussûšina paris*

(44) *ana lā enê šākin ṭēmi Bābili u dayyānū ṭuppu išṭurū*

(45) *ina kunukkīšunu ibrumū-ma ana Etellitu u Bunanītu iddinū*

(46) *ina šaṭār ṭuppi šuāti*

Document 37

(1–5) Names

(6–8) *mār banî ša ina pānīšunu Gimillu māršu ša Innin-šuma-ibni ana Nabû-šuma-iddin mārīšu ša Aplaya iqbû umma*

(9–10) *mīnamma būštu ša Bēlti ša Uruk ša kakkabtu šendet talqâm-ma*

(11–12) *Nabû-šuma-iddin iqbi umma*

(12–16) *Balṭiya māršu ša Innina-zēra-šubši ultu Simāni šanat 17 Nabû-na'id šar Bābili ana idīšu ana šatti 4 kur šêu 1 pi 4 sūt šamaššammu iddinaššu*

(16–18) *pūt mukinnūti ša Balṭiya Nabû-šuma-iddin naši*

(18–19) *ūmu uktīnūšu zaki*

(19–20) *yānu 1 30 ana Bēlti ša Uruk inamdin*

(20–21) *būštu Gimillu ina qātē Nabû-šuma-iddin ītabak*

(21–22) *u'iltu ša Nabû-šuma-iddin u Balṭiya itti aḫāmeš ī'ilû Nabû-šuma-iddin ana Gimillu inamdin*

Document 38

(1–4) *alpū ṣēnu u mimma makkūr Bēlti ša Uruk u Nanaya ša Gimillu māršu ša Innin-šuma-ibni ina qātē rāb buli u rē'î ša Bēlti ša Uruk iššâm-ma ana Eanna lā iddinu*

(5) *mukinnū ukinnūšu-ma eli ramnīšu ukīn*

(6–29) Names and date

(30–36) *2 liātu ša kakkabtu šendû ša ūm 1 ša Ulūli šanat 1 Kuraš šar mātāti ša Nabû-bāni-aḫi māršu ša PN mār Kurī ana Anu-šarra-uṣur qīpi ša Eanna Nabû-mukīn-zēri šatam Eanna mārīšu ša Nādinu mār Dābibi Nabû-aḫa-iddin ša rēš šarri bēl piqitti Eanna u ṭupšarrī ša Eanna iqbû*

(36–37) *qīpu šatammu Nabû-aḫa-iddin u ṭupšarrū ana muḫḫi liāti šuāti išpurū-ma*

(37–40) *2 liāti ša kakkabtu šendû ultu bīt Gimillu ībukūnim-ma maḫar Nādinu šākin ṭēmi Uruk puḫur Bābilāya u Urukāya ušzizzū-ma*

(41–42) *60 liāti kūm 2 liāti ša kakkabtu šendû eli Gimillu iprusū*

—

(43–46) *1 lītu ša ina rēḫi ša ṣēni ina qātē Nanaya-iddin mār Arad-Innin abkatam-ma ina Eanna šendet u ana Ibnaya mārīšu ša Nabû-aḫḫē-šullim paqdat*

(46–47) *u Ibnaya iqbû umma*

(47–48) *ina Ulūli šanat 17 lītu šuāti ina qātē rē'īya Gimillu ītabak*

(49) *u Gimillu lītu šuāti eli ramnīšu ukīn*

(50) *30 liāti kūm 1 līti eli Gimillu iprusū*

—

(51–52) *qaputtu ša ṣēni ša Bēlti ša Uruk ša ina pāni Šumaya mārīšu ša Marduk-aḫa-iddin*

(52–56) *illā ušuzzi ša Šumaya Gimillu ultu ṣēri ša lā qīpānu u ṭupšarrū ša Eanna ana Eanna ībuku ina libbi laḫri ša kakkabtu šendet 1 parratu 1 unīqu tamīmāti Gimillu ītabak*

(56–57) *u Iddinaya māršu ša Aḫu-ṭāb rē'û ša ṣēnu ībuku ina puḫri ukīnaššu*

(58–59) *30 ṣēnu kūm 1 laḫri ša kakkabtu šendet eli Gimillu iprusū*

—

(60–63) *5 laḫrātu ša kakkabtu šendû ša qaputti ša Ḫašdiya mārīšu ša Nabû-mušētiq-uddê nāqidi ša Bēlti ša Uruk ša Dannu-āḫḫēšu-ibni māršu ša Šarru-kīn rē'û ša Ḫašdiya ultu qaputti ša Ḫasdiya ībuku-ma*

(64–68) *ina Uruk Gimillu ūmu 27 ša Dûzi šanat 1 Kuraš šar mātāti ṣēnu u rē'û ina ušuzzi ša Šamaš-zēra-iqīša mārīšu ša Innin-šuma-uṣur ikla ana Nidintu mārīšu ša* PN *nāqidi ša Bēlti ša Uruk iqbi umma*

(68–69) *ṣēnu abuk-ma kasapšina išâ ibi*

(69–70) *Nidintu ina puḫri ukīnaššu umma*

(70–71) *3 ṣēni ina libbi kî ābuku 3 šiqil kaspu kî aššâm attadinaššu*

(71–74) *u'iltu ša Kīnaya itti Dannu-aḫḫēšu-ibni ī'ilu u ina libbi šaṭru umma kaspu ša ana Gimillu nadin ina puḫri ištasû*

(75–76) *ṣēnu-a' 3 1 30 90 ṣēnu eli Gimillu iprusū*

—

(77–81) 1 *enzu ša kakkabtu šendet ša qaputti ša Nabû-mušētiq-uddê mārīšu ša Nanaya-iddin ša Nabû-mušētiq-uddê ina Ulūli šanat 17 itti ṣēnīšu ana Eanna ībuku u Nabû-mušētiq-uddê iqbû*

(81–82) *ina bāb Ṭilimu Iddinaya aḫu ša Gimillu ītabak*

(82–83) *u Nabû-aḫḫē-iddin māršu ša Bēl-ēreš ina puḫri iqbi umma*

(83–84) *enzu šuāti ina pānīya Iddinaya ītabak*

(84–85) *u Gimillu iqbi umma anāku Iddinaya aḫū'a altapram*

(86–87) *enzu-a' 1 1 30 30 ṣēnu eli Gimillu iprusū*

—

(88–91) *1 laḫru ša kakkabtu šendet ša qaputti ša Lāqīpi mārīšu ša Nabû-šuma-ukīn nāqidi ša Bēlti ša Uruk ša ina ṭuppi šaṭru ina bīt Nabû-nādin-aḫi Gimillu ittakis*

(91–94) *Mušēzib-Bēl māršu ša Mušallim-Marduk Nanaya-aḫa-iddin māršu ša Nergal-ina-tēšê-ēṭir Sîn-ibni māršu ša Nanaya-ēreš u Nabû-šuma-iddin māršu ša Nanaya-ēreš ina puḫri Gimillu ukinnū*

(94–95) *laḫru-a' 1 1 30 30 ṣēnu eli Gimillu iprusū*

—

(96–97) *1 kalūmu ša Nabû-mušētiq-uddê māršu ša Nanaya-iddin nāqidu ša Bēlti ša Uruk iqbû umma*

(97–100) *ina Ulūli šanat 17 itti ṣēni ina rēḫi ša ina muḫḫīya ana Eanna ašpur Gimillu ina qātē Innin-aḫḫē-erība aḫīya ītabak*

(100–101) *u Gimillu eli ramnīšu ukīn umma*

(101–102) *kalūmu šuāti ātabak elat 2 immerī ša ana nupti anāku attašû*

(103) *kalūmu-a'* 1 1 30 30 *ṣēnu eli Gimillu iprusū*

—

(104–105) *1 parratu ša qaputti ša Zumbu mārīšu ša Nanaya-ēreš nāqidi ša Bēlti ša Uruk ša Zumbu iqbû umma*

(105–106) *ultu ṣēnīya Gimillu ītabak*

(106–107) *u Gimillu eli ramnīšu ukīn*

(108) *elat 2 šiqil kaspi u urīṣi ša ana nupti attašû*

(109) *parratu-aʾ 1 1 30 30 ṣēnu eli Gimillu iprusū*

—

(110–112) *1 parratu ša kakkabtu šendet ša ina Dûzi šanat 1 Kuraš šar mātāti ša Gimillu ana kaspi ana Nidintu mārīšu ša Ardiya iddinu-ma*

(112–113) *parratu ana Eanna abkat*

(113–114) *u Gimillu ina puḫri eli ramnīšu ukīn umma*

(114–115) *anāku parratu ana Nidintu attadin*

(115–116) *parratu-aʾ 1 1 30 30 ṣēnu eli Gimillu iprusū*

—

(117–120) *Šamaš-aḫa-iddin māršu ša Nabû-šuma-ukīn nāqidu ša Bēlti ša Uruk ša 10 šanātu itti ṣēnīšu ana Eanna lā īrubu ša qīpānu u ṭupšarrū ša Eanna Gimillu ana muḫḫi Šamaš-aḫa-iddin išpurû-ma*

(121–122) *Gimillu Šamaš-aḫa-iddin īmuru-ma ana Eanna lā ībuku*

(122–123) *Lāqīpi qallu ša Šamaš-aḫa-iddin iqbû umma*

(123–126) 4 *kur šê 2 šiqil kaspu 1 immēru Gimillu ina qātē Šamaš-aḫa-iddin u Ṣillaya mārīšu ittaši u Ṣillaya māršu ša Šamaš-aḫa-iddin iṣ qāt parzilli kî iddû ūtaššir*

(126–127) *Gimillu iqbi umma*

(127) *alla 1 immēri ina qātēšu ul ābuk*

(128–129) *Sîn-ibni māršu ša Nanaya-ēreš ina puḫri ana Gimillu ukīn umma*

(129–131) *ina ušuzzīya 2 šiqil kaspu Nabû-udammiqanni ana muḫḫi Ṣillaya ...*

(131–134) *kaspu-aʾ 2 šiqlū 1 30 u immēru-aʾ 1 1 30 1 manā kaspu u 30 ṣēnu eli Gimillu iprusū*

—

(135–137) *1 lītu šarḫītu ša Nergal-šuma-ibni māršu ša Aḫišaya nāqidi ša Bēlti ša Uruk ša Gimillu ina qātē Nergal-šuma-ibni ībuku*

(137–138) *u Gimillu ina puḫri eli ramnīšu ukīn*

(138–139) *lītu-aʾ 1 1 ... lītu eli Gimillu iprusū*

(140–143) *1 širʾam ša inzaḫurēti ša ultu Eanna qīpānu u ṭupšarrū ša Eanna ana Šuma-iddin mārīšu ša Nergal-ušallim ša muḫḫi qašti ša rēʾî ša itti šarri iddinū-ma*

(144) *Gimillu ina qātē Šuma-iddin iššû*

(145) *u Gimillu ina puḫri eli ramnīšu ukīn*

(146) *u kaspu kūm širʾam eli Gimillu iprusū*

(147–148) *napḫaru 92 liātu 302 ṣēnu u 1 manā 10 šiqil kaspu*

Document 39

(1–3) *ūmu* 20 *ša Kislīmi šanat 4 Kuraš šar Bābili šar mātāti Marduk-dīna-īpuš māršu ša Hiraḫḫa ana Bābili illakam-ma*

(4–10) *dīnu ša 2 immerī ša kakkabtu šendû ša Gimillu māršu ša Innin-šuma-ibni ultu ṣēni ša Marduk-dīna-īpuš ībuku itti Nidintu-Bēl šatam Eanna Nabû-aḫa-iddin ša rēš šarri bēl piqitti Eanna u ṭupšarrī ša Eanna ina bīt dīni ša šarri idabbub*

(10–12) *kî lā ittalku immerū-aʾ* 2 *istēn* 30 *ana Bēlti ša Uruk inamdin*

Document 40

(1–3) *Riḫētu māršu ša Arad-Innin ikkaru širik Ištar Uruk ana Nabû-mukīn-apli šatam Eanna u Nabû-aḫa-iddin ša rēš šarri bēl piqitti Eanna iqbi umma*

(3–6) *ultu šanat 8 Kuraš šar Bābili šar mātāti ultu muḫḫi mayyāri ša Šamaš-mukīn-apli mārīšu ša Sîn-nādin-šumi ikkari ša Bēlti ša Uruk bēl mayyārīya aḫliq-ma*

(6–8) *ina Ulūli šanat rēš šarrūt Kambuziya šar Bābili šar mātāti Gimillu māršu ša Innin-šuma-ibni īmuranni-ma ina pāni Sîn-ibni mārīšu ša Nabû-zabādu ipqidanni umma*

(9) *kasap idīšu išâm-ma ibinna*

(10) *u Sîn-ibni iqbi umma*

(10–12) *Gimillu Riḫētu ina pānīya iptaqid u riksu ana 5 šiqil kaspi ana idīšu ittīya ištakas*

(13–15) *arki riksu ša Gimillu ittīya iškusu šipirtu ana Nabû-nādin mārīšu ša Erībaya bēl piqitti ša āli ša Kî-Nabû iltapar umma*

(15–17) *ina pānīka lizzizma kî pānīka maḫir ina šatti 5 šiqil kaspu idīšu šūbil u yānû lū ina pāni Sîn-ibni iššû*

(18) *adi inanna Riḫētu ina pāni Nabû-nādin izziz*

(19–20) *šipirtu ša Gimillu ana muḫḫi Riḫētu ana Nabû-nādin išpuru Sîn-ibni u Rīḫētu ana šatammi u Nabû-aḫa-iddin iddinū-ma*

(21) *kî pî mukinnūti ša Sîn-ibni ina libbi šaṭir umma*

(21–24) *kî pānīka maḫir Riḫētu ina pānīka lizzizma šattu 5 šiqil kaspu idīšu šūbil u yānû ana Sîn-ibni idissu šipirtī lū mukinnu ina muḫḫīka*

(24–27) *šipirtu ša sipīri ša Gimillu ana muḫḫi Riḫētu ana Nabû-nādin išpuru-ma ina puḫri tannamru iškusū iknukū u ina Eanna iškunū*

Document 41

(1–9) Personal names

(10–13) *puḫur qīpāni u mār banî ša ina ušuzzīšunu Zumbu māršu ša Rīmūtu širik Ištar Uruk iqbi umma*

(13–16) *ina Nisanni šanat 1 Dariamuš šar Bābili šar mātāti Anu-zēra-šubši māršu ša Lâbāši širik Ištar Uruk iqtabâm umma*

(16–18) *Gimillu ša muḫḫi sūti ša Bēlti ša Uruk riksu ana dâki ša Sîn-šarra-uṣur ša rēš šarri bēl piqitti Eanna ištakas*

(19–21) *qīpāni u mār banî išpurū-ma Anu-zēra-šubši ībukūnim-ma ina puḫri nīš ilī izkur*

(21–26) *kî ultu muḫḫi ša balṭāku mimma ša sipri ša Sîn-šarra-uṣur ina pî ša Gimillu ša muḫḫi sūti mammanīšu mala bašû u ṣāb qātēšu ašmû*

Document 42

(1–4) *1 puḫālu u 4 laḫrātu napḫar 5 ṣēnu ša kakkabtu šendû makkūr Ištar Uruk u Nanaya ša qaputti ša Anu-šarra-uṣur mārīšu ša Šarru-kīn nāqidi ša Ištar Uruk … ša ultu qaputti Bēl-šarra-uṣur mārīšu ša Aḫiya-alidu abkū*

(4–6) *Nabû-aḫa-iddin ša rēš šarri bēl piqitti Eanna u PN ana Bēl-šarra-uṣur iqbû umma*

(6) *mannu ṣēnu-aʾ ša kakkabtu šendû ina qātēka ipqid*

(7) *Bēl-šarra-uṣur ina puḫri iqbi umma*

(7–9) *ina šanat 2 Kambuziya šar Bābili šar mātāti 1 puḫālu u 4 laḫrāti ša kakkabtu šendû Bēl-iqīša māršu ša Ṣillaya ina qātēya ipqid*

(9–11) *Bēl-iqīša ībukūnim-ma išālūšu ... iqbi umma*

(11–15) *1 pūḫālu 4 laḫrāti ša kakkabtu šendû u 5 parrāti tamīmāti napḫar 10 ṣēnu ultu ṣēni makkūr Ištar Uruk ša qaputti ša Anu-šarra-uṣur mārīšu ša Šarru-kīn nāqidi ša Ištar Uruk Anu-šarra-uṣur kūm rašûtīya ina Dûzi ittaddinam*

(15–16) *Bēl-iqīša ina Bēl u Nabû u adê ša Kambuziya šar Bābili šar mātāti ina puḫri itteme*

(17–21) *kî elat 1 puḫāli 4 laḫrāti ša kakkabtu šendû u 5 parrāti tamīmāti napḫar 10 ṣēnu kūm rašûtīya Anu-šarra-uṣur iddinam ša ina libbi 1 puḫālu u 4 laḫrāti napḫar 5 ṣēnu ša kakkabtu šendû ina pāni Bēl-šarra-uṣur mārīšu ša Aḫiya-alidu nāqidi ša Ištar Uruk aptaqid*

(21–22) *Bēl-šarra-uṣur ina puḫri nīs ilī u šarri izkur u ana Bēl-iqīša ukīn umma*

(22–24) *1 puḫālu u 4 laḫrāti ša kakkabti ina Araḫšamni šanat 2 ina pānīya taptaqid ina Šabāṭi šanat 2 laḫrātu-aʾ 4 ina pānīya ittaldā*

Document 43

(1–6) *1 puḫālu 4 laḫrātu napḫar 5 ṣēnu ša kakkabtu šendû u 5 parrātu tamīmātu napḫar 10 ṣēnu makkūr Ištar Uruk u Nanaya ša qaputti ša Anu-šarra-uṣur mārīšu ša Šarru-kīn ša ina Araḫšamni šanat 2 Kambuziya šar Bābili šar mātāti Bēl-iqīša māršu ša Ṣillaya ina qātē Anu-šarra-uṣur mārīšu ša Šarru-kīn ībuku-ma*

(7–11) *ina Addari šanat 3 Rīmūt u Bau-ēreš dayyānū 150 ṣēnu kūm ṣēni ša Ištar šendēti 1 adi 30 u 5 parrāti tamīmāti napḫar 155 ṣēnu ana eṭēri ša Ištar Uruk ina ṭuppi išturū-ma eli Bēl-iqīša ukinnū*

(12–15) *ūm 25 ša Addari šanat 3 ṣēnu-aʾ 155 Bēl-iqīša māršu ša Ṣillaya ibbakam-ma ina Eanna išammit-ma ana makkūr Eanna inamdin*

(14–16) *Arad-Nergal māršu ša Mukīn-apli mār Egibi pūt eṭēri ša ṣēnu-aʾ 155 naši*

Document 44

(1–3) *Dāgil-ilī māršu ša Zambubu ana Ḫammaya mārtīšu ša Nergal-iddin mār Bābūtu kiam iqbi umma*

(3–4) *Lā-tubāšinni māratka binnimma lū aššatu šî*

(4–5) *Ḫammaya tašmēšu-ma Lā-tubāšinni mārassa ana aššūti taddinaššu*

(6–9) *u Dāgil-ilī ina ḫūd libbi Ana-muḫḫi-Bēl-āmur qallu ša ana 1/2 manā kaspi abka u 1/2 manā kaspi ittî ana Ḫammaya kūm Lā-tubāšinni mārtīša iddin*

(10–13) *ūm Dāgil-ilī aššātu šanītu ittašû 1 manā kaspu Dāgil-ilī ana Lā-tubāšinni inamdin-ma ašar maḫri tallaka*

(13–14) *ina ašābi ša Šuma-iddin mārīšu ša Tēšê-ēṭir mār Sîn-damāqu*

Document 45

(1–6) *ūmu ša Nabû-ēda-uṣur qallu ša Ina-Esagil-šuma-ibni ina pāni Ubar mārīšu ša Zambubu ītelâ ūmu 2 sūt šeʾu mandattušu ana Ina-Esagil-šuma-ibni inamdin*

Document 46

(1–8) *Bēl-aḫḫē-iddin u Nabû-aḫḫē-bulliṭ mārū ša Esagil-šuma-ibni mār Sîn-damāqu u Rēšat ummašunu mārassu ša Šūzubu mār Šangû-parakki ina ḫūd libbīšunu Nabû-ēda-uṣur Banītumma aššassu Kišrinni u Gimillinni aḫḫātīšu napḫar 4 amēlūti ana 2 manā kaspi ana šīmi gamrūti ana Nabû-aḫḫē-iddin mārīšu ša Šulaya mār Egibi iddinū*

(8–11) *pūt sēḫî pāqirāni u mār banûti ša amēlūti Bēl-aḫḫē-iddin Nabû-aḫḫē-bulliṭ mārū ša Esagil-šuma-ibni mār Sîn-damāqu u Rēšat ummašunu našû*

(12) *1 pūt šanî našû*

Document 47

(1–6) *Bēl-aḫḫē-iddin u Nabû-aḫḫē-bulliṭ mārū ša Esagil-šuma-ibni mār Sîn-damāqu u Rēšat ummašunu ina ḫūd libbīšunu Nabû-ēda-uṣur qallašunu ana 5/6 manā 8 šiqil kaspi ana sīmi ḫarṣi ana Šāpik-zēri mārīšu ša Iddin-Marduk mār Šigûa iddinū*

(7–10) *pūt sēḫî pāqirāni arad šarrūti u mār banûti ša Nabû-ēda-uṣur Bēl-aḫḫē-iddin Nabû-aḫḫē-bulliṭ u Rēšat ummašunu našû*

(11) *1 pūt šanî našû*

Document 48

(1–3) *Lā- tubāšinni aššat Dāgil-ilī u ... ana Nabû-mukīn-apli sukalli u dayyānī ša Nergal-šarra-uṣur šar Bābili illikūnim-ma*

(3–4) *itti Bēl-aḫḫē-iddin mārīšu ša Esagil-šuma-ibnn mar Sîn-damāqu dīnu idbubū-ma*

(4) *Lā-tubāšinni taqbi umma*

(5–7) *Nabû-ēda-uṣur Bēl-aḫa-uṣur Esagil-rēṣua Kišrinni u Gimilinni mārīya ša ina bītīkunu arki šaṭār ṭuppi mār banūti uldu*

(7) *sukkallu u dayyānū arkassunu ištālū-ma*

(7–12) *Bēl-aḫḫē-iddin riksātīšu ša adi lā ṭuppi mār bānūti ša Lā-tubāšinni iššāṭru Nabû-ēda-uṣur Bēl-aḫa-uṣur Esagil-rēṣua Kišrinni u Gimilinni maldū u'iltu ša ... Nabû-ēda-uṣur u Bēl-aḫa-uṣur ana mandatti ... ublam-ma ana sukkalli u dayyānī ukallim*

(13–15) *Esagil-šuma-ibni abu ša Bēl-aḫḫē-iddin ... īmurū u dibbīšunu išmû*

(16–18) *Nabû-eda-uṣur Bēl-aḫa-uṣur Kišrinni u Gimilinni ša adi lā ṭuppi mār banūti ša Lā-tubāšinni maldū ana Bēl-āḫḫē-iddin iddinū*

(18–19) *u Ardiya ša arki šaṭār ṭuppi ša Lā-tubāšinni maldu ana Lā-tubāšinni iddinū*

(20–21) *matīma Lā-tubāšinni u Ardiya māršu ana muḫḫi Nabû-ēda-uṣur Bēl-aḫa-uṣur Kašrinni u Gimilinni lā iraggumū*

(22–23) *sukkallu u dayyānū ṭuppu išṭurū ina kunukkīšunu ibrumū-ma ana Bēl-aḫḫē-iddin iddinū*

(24) *ina parās dīni šuāti*

Document 49

(1–9) *pūt mukinnūti ša Mušēzib-Bēl qalli ša ša muḫḫi bītāni ša ina našparti ša ša muḫḫi bītāni illiku-ma iqbû umma ša muḫḫi bītāni iltapranni umma ṭuppu ša Kuputtu kunuk-ma ana aššūti ana Nabû-aḫḫē-bulliṭ mārīšu ša Nargiya idin Nabû-ēṭir mārīšu ša Arad-Bēl mār Arrabtu mukīn ṭuppi u Rīmūt-Nabû mārīšu ṭupšarru šāṭir ṭuppi našû*

(9–11) *ina bīt dīni ukannū-ma ana Nargiya mārīšu ša Ḫanunu inaddinū*

(11–14) *kî lā ukannū 1/2 bilat kaspu miṭītu ša eli Nargiya šaknat ušallamū*

Document 50

(1–5) *Nargiya ša rēš šarri māršu ša Ḫanunu Amurru-šarra-uṣur ša rēš šarri ša muḫḫi bītāni ana maḫar rabūt šarri u dayyānī ša Kuraš šar Bābili šar mātāti ublam-ma iqbi umma*

(5–9) *Amurru-šarra-uṣur ša muḫḫi bītāni u Nabû-uballiṭ māršu ša Nabû-šama' ša bīti ša muḫḫi bītani ṭuppi aššūti ša Tabluṭu aḫāti ša Nabû-uballiṭ balū'a iknuk-ma ana Nabû-aḫḫē-bulliṭ mārīya iddinū*

(10) *rabūt šarri u dayyānū ša muḫḫi bītāni išālū-ma*

(11) *nīš ilī izkur-ma iqbi umma*

(11–12) *ṭuppu šuātu ul aknuk u ana šībūti ina libbi ul āšib*

(13–14) *ultu ... ukīn ... Tabluṭu išālū-ma ... ukinnū-ma*

(15) *Nabû-uballiṭ iqbi umma*

(15–17) *ṭuppi aššūti ša Tabluṭu aḫātīya aknuk ana Nabû-aḫḫē-bulliṭ mārīšu ša Nargiya addin*

(18) *u Tabluṭu taqbi umma Nabû-uballiṭ aḫū᾿a ...*

(21–24) *ṭuppi aššūti ša Tabluṭu ša Nabû-uballiṭ iknuku-ma ana Nabû-aḫḫē-bulliṭ balu Nargiya abīšu iddinu ašar innammaru ḫepi*

(25–26) *kî ultu annî Tabluṭu itti Nabû-aḫḫē-bulliṭ tattanammaru šimat ammāti tammaḫḫar*

(28–33) *ina maḫar ... šaṭāru šaṭir*

Bibliography

Arnaud, Daniel. 1973. "Un document juridique concernant les oblats." *RA* 67: 147–56.

Baker, Heather D. 2001. "Degrees of Freedom: Slavery in Mid-First Millennium BC Babylonia." *World Archaeology* 33: 18–26.

———. 2004. *The Archive of the Nappāḫu Family.* AfO Beiheft 30. Vienna: Institut für Orientalistik der Universität Wien.

Beaulieu, Paul-Alain. 2000a. "A Finger in Every Pie: The Institutional Connections of a Family of Entrepreneurs in Neo-Babylonian Larsa." Pages 43–72 in *Interdependency of Institutions and Private Entrepreneurs*. Edited by A. C. V. M. Bongenaar. MOS Studies 2. Istanbul: Nederlands Historisch-Archaeologisch Instituut te Istanbul.

———. 2000b. "A Land Grant on a Cylinder Seal and Assurbanipal's Babylonian Policy." Pages 25–45 in *Studi sul vicino oriente antico dedicate alla memoria di Luigi Cagni*. Edited by Simonetta Graziani. Istitut Universitario Orientale Dipartimento di Studi Asiatici Series Minor 61. Naples: Istituto Universitario Orientale.

———. 2000c. *Legal and Administrative Texts from the Reign of Nabonidus.* YOS 19. New Haven: Yale University Press.

———. 2003. *The Pantheon of Uruk during the Neo-Babylonian Period.* Cuneiform Monographs 23. Leiden: Brill.

Beljawski, Vitali A. 1973. "Die Sklavenelite des Hauses Egibi." *Jahrbuch für Wirtschaftsgeschichte* 1: 133–58.

Boissier, Alfred. 1890. *Recherches sur quelques contrats babyloniens*. Paris: Leroux.

Bolla, Sibylle von. 1940. *Untersuchungen zur Tiermiete und Viehpacht im Altertum.* MBPF 30. Munich: Beck.

Bongenaar, A. C. V. M. 1997. *The Neo-Babylonian Ebabbar Temple at Sippar: Its Administration and Its Prosopography.* Istanbul: Nederlands Historisch-Archaeologisch Instituut te Istanbul.

———. 2000. "Private Archives in Neo-Babylonian Sippar and Their Institutional Connections." Pages 73–94 in *Interdependency of Institutions and Private Entrepreneurs*. Edited by A.C.V.M. Bongenaar. MOS Studies 2. Istanbul: Nederlands Historisch-Archaeologisch Instituut te Istanbul.

Borger, Riekele. 1967–73. *Handbuch der Keilschriftliteratur*. Berlin: de Gruyter.

Cardascia, Guillaume. 1951. *Les archives des Murašû: une famille d'hommes d'affaires babyloniens à l'époque perse (455–403 av. J.–C.)*. Paris: Imprimerie Nationale.

Charpin, Dominique. 2010. *Writing, Law, and Kingship in Old Babylonian Mesopotamia.*

Translated by Jane Marie Todd. Chicago: University of Chicago Press, 2010.

Clay, Albert T. 1908. *Legal and Commercial Transactions Dated in the Assyrian, Neo-Babylonian and Persian Periods, Chiefly from Nippur*. BE 8/1. Philadelphia: Department of Archaeology, University of Pennsylvania.

Cocquerillat, Denise. 1968. *Palmeraies et cultures de l'Eanna d'Uruk (559–520)*. Ausgrabungen der Deutschen Forschungsgemeinschaft in Uruk-Warka 8. Berlin: Gebr. Mann.

———. 1973–74. "Recherches sur le verger du temple campagnard de l'Akītu ($KIRI_6$ ḫallat)." *WO* 7: 96–134.

Contenau, Georges. 1926. *Contrats et lettres d'Assyrie et de Babylonie*. TCL 9. Paris: Geuthner.

———. 1927–29. *Contrats néo-babyloniens*. TCL 12–13. Paris: Geuthner.

Cuq, Édouard. 1929. *Études sur le droit babylonien, les lois assyriens et les lois Hittites*. Paris: Geuthner.

Dalley, Stephanie. 1979. *A Catalogue of the Akkadian Cuneiform Tablets in the Collections of the Royal Scottish Museum, Edinburgh, with Copies of the Texts*. Art and Archaelogy 2. Edinburgh: Royal Scottish Museum.

Dandamaev, Muhammad A. 1984. *Slavery in Babylonia: From Nabopolassar to Alexander the Great* (626–331 B.C.). Translated by Victoria M. Powell. DeKalb, IL: Northern Illinois University Press.

———. 2001. Review of *Legal and Administrative Documents Texts from the Reign of Nabonidus*, by Paul-Alain Beaulieu. *JAOS* 121:700–702.

———. 2006. "Neo-Babylonian and Achaemenid State Administration in Mesopotamia." Pages 373–98 in *Judah and the Judeans in the Persian Period.* Edited by Oded Lipschitz and Manfred Oeming. Winona Lake, IN: Eisenbrauns.

Dougherty, Raymond Philip. 1920. *Records from Erech, Time of Nabonidus (555–538 B.C.)*. YOS 6. New Haven: Yale University Press.

———. 1923. *The Shirkûtu of Babylonian Deities.* YOSR 5.2. New Haven: Yale University Press.

———. 1923–24. "Cuneiform Parallels to Solomon's Provisioning System." *AASOR* 5: 23–65.

Driel, G. van. 1985–86. "The Rise of the House of Egibi: Nabû-aḫḫē-iddina." *JEOL* 29: 50–67.

———. 1989. "The Murašûs in Context." *JESHO* 32: 203–29.

———. 1998. "The 'Eanna Archive.'" *BiOr* 55: 59–80.

———. 2000. "Institutional and Non-Institutional Economy in Ancient Mesopotamia." Pages 5–23 in *Interdependency of Institutions and Private Entrepreneurs*. Edited by A. C. V. M. Bongenaar. MOS Studies 2. Istanbul: Nederlands Historisch-Archaeologisch Instituut te Istanbul.

Durand, Jean-Marie. 1981. *Textes babyloniens d'époque récente.* Recherche sur les grandes civilisations 6. Paris: A.D.P.F.

Ebeling, Erich. 1952–53. "Kriminalfälle aus Uruk." *AfO* 16: 67–69.

Evetts, Basil Thomas Alfred. 1892. *Inscriptions of the Reigns of Evil-Merodach (BC 562–559); Neriglissar (BC 559–555) and Loborosoarchod (BC 555).* Babylonische Texte 6B. Leipzig: Pfeiffer.

Finley, M. I. 1964. "Between Slavery and Freedom."*Comparative Studies in Society and History* 6: 233–49.

Frame, Grant. 1991. "Nabonidus, Nabû-šarra-uṣur, and the Eanna Temple." *ZA* 81: 37–86.

Godbey, A. H. 1905. "The Ḳêpu." *AJSL* 22: 81–88.

Hilprecht, Hermann Vollrat and Albert T. Clay. 1898. *Business Documents of Murashû Sons of Nippur Dated in the Reign of Artaxerxes I (464–424 B. C.)*. BE 9. Philadelphia: Department of Archaeology and Palaeontology of the University of Pennsylvania.

Holtz, Shalom E. 2008. "The Career of a Neo-Babylonian Court Scribe." *JCS* 60: 81–85.

———. 2009. *Neo-Babylonian Court Procedure*. Cuneiform Monographs 38. Leiden: Brill.

———. 2010. "A Comparative Note on the Demand for Witnesses in Isaiah 43:9." *JBL* 129: 457–61.

Joannès, Francis. 1994. "Amours contrariées." *NABU* 1994/72.

———. 2000a. "Relations entre intérêts privés et biens des sanctuaries à l'époque néo-babylonienne." Pages 25–41 in *Interdependency of Institutions and Private Entrepreneurs*. Edited by A. C. V. M. Bongenaar. MOS Studies 2. Istanbul: Nederlands Historisch-Archaeologisch Instituut te Istanbul.

———. 2000b. *Rendre la justice en Mésopotamie: Archives judiciaires du Proche-Orient ancien (IIIe–Ier millénaires avant J.C.)*. Saint Denis: Presses Universitaires de Vincennes.

———. 2002a. Camb 412. Achemenet. Online: http://www.achemenet.com/pdf/cambyse/cambyse412.pdf.

———. 2002b. Cyr 311. Achemenet. Online: http://www.achemenet.com/pdf/cyrus/cyrus311.pdf.

———. 2002c. Cyr 312. Achemenet. Online: http://www.achemenet.com/pdf/cyrus/cyrus312.pdf.

———. 2002d. Cyr 328. Achemenet. Online: http://www.achemenet.com/pdf/cyrus/cyrus328.pdf.

———. 2002e. Dar 189. Achemenet. Online: http://www.achemenet.com/pdf/darius/darius189.pdf.

———. 2002f. Dar 260. Achemenet. Online: http://www.achemenet.com/pdf/darius/darius260.pdf.

Jursa, Michael. 1999. *Das Archiv des Bēl-Rēmanni*. Uitgaven van het Nederlands Historisch-Archaeologisch Instituut te Istanbul 86. Istanbul: Nederlands Historisch-Archaeologisch Instituut te Istanbul.

———. 2001. "Kollationen." *NABU* 2001/4, 102 (pp. 98–100).

———. 2004a. "Auftragsmord, Veruntreuung und Falschaussagen: Neues von Gimillu." *WZKM* 94: 109–32.

———. 2004b. "Eine Landkaufurkunde mit historisch-juridischem Prolog." *TUAT, NF* 1. 109–10.

———. 2005. *Neo-Babylonian Legal and Administrative Documents: Typology, Contents and Archives*. Guides to the Mesopotamian Textual Record 1. Münster: Ugarit Verlag.

———. 2010. *Aspects of the Economic History of Babylonia in the First Millennium BC:*

Economic Geography, Economic Mentalities, Agriculture, the Use of Money and the Problem of Economic Growth. AOAT 377. Münster: Ugarit Verlag.

Jursa, Michael, Joanna Paszkowiak and Caroline Waerzeggers. 2003–4. "Three Court Records." *AfO* 50: 255–68.

Kleber, Kristin. 2008. *Tempel und Palast: Die Beziehungen zwischen dem König und dem Eanna-Tempel im spätbabylonischen Uruk.* AOAT 358. Münster: Ugarit Verlag.

———. 2012. "Aspekte des spätbabylonischen Gerichtsverfahrens." *BiOr* 69: 182–96.

Kohler, Josef and Felix Ernst Peiser. 1890–98. *Aus dem babylonischen Rechtsleben* 1–4. Leipzig: Pfeiffer.

Koschaker, Paul. 1966. *Babylonisch-assyrisches Bürgschaftsrecht.* Aalen: Scientia.

Kozuh, Michael G. 2006. "The Sacrificial Economy: On the Management of Sacrificial Sheep and Goats at the Neo-Babylonian/Achaemenid Eanna Temple of Uruk (c. 625–520 BC)." Ph.D. Dissertation, University of Chicago.

———. 2008. "Temple, Economy, and Religion in First Millennium Babylonia." *Religion Compass* 2: 929–48.

Krecher, Joachim. 1970. *Das Geschäftshaus Egibi in Babylon in neubabylonischer und achämenidischer Zeit.* Habilitationsschrift, Westfälische Wilhelms-Universität.

Kümmel, Hans Martin. 1979. *Familie, Beruf und Amt im spätbabylonischen Uruk.* ADOG 20. Berlin: Gebr. Mann.

Labat, René. 1999. *Manuel d'épigraphie akkadienne* (6th edition). Paris: Geuthner.

Lambert, W. G. 1965. "Nebuchadnezzar King of Justice." *Iraq* 27: 1–11.

MacGinnis, John. 2008. "A Judgment of Darius the King." *JCS* 60: 87–99.

Magdalene, F. Rachel. 2007. *On the Scales of Righteousness: Neo-Babylonian Trial Law and the Book of Job.* BJS 348. Providence, RI: Brown University.

Magdalene F. Rachel, Bruce Wells and Cornelia Wunsch. 2008. "Pre-Trial Negotiations: The Case of the Runaway Slave in *Dar*. 53." *Iraq* 70: 205–13.

Marx, Victor. 1902. "Die Stellung der Frauen in Babylonien gemäss den Kontrakten aus der Zeit von Nebukadnezzar bis Darius (604–485)." *Beiträge zur Assyriologie und semitischen Sprachwissenschaft* 4: 1–77.

Mendelsohn, Isaac. 1949. *Slavery in the Ancient Near East: A Comparative Study of Slavery in Babylonia, Assyria, Syria, and Palestine from Middle of the Third Millennium to the End of the First Millennium.* New York: Oxford University Press.

Moore, Ellen Whitley. 1935. *Neo-Babylonian Business and Administrative Documents.* Ann Arbor, MI: University of Michigan Press.

Nies, James B. and Clarence E. Keiser. 1920. *Historical, Religious and Economic Texts and Antiquities.* BIN 2. New Haven: Yale University Press.

Oelsner, Joachim, Bruce Wells, and Cornelia Wunsch. 2003. "The Neo-Babylonian Period." Pages 911–74 in *A History of Ancient Near Eastern Law.* Edited by Raymond Westbrook. Handbook of Oriental Studies 72/2. Leiden: Brill.

Oppenheim, A. L. 1940. "Additions au 'Syllabaire Accadien' de F. Thureau-Dangin." *Or* 9:25–28.

———. 1941. "Idiomatic Accadian (Lexicographical Researches)." *JAOS* 61: 251–71.

———. 1944. "Assyriological Gleanings II." *BASOR* 93: 14–17.

Parker, Richard A. and Waldo H. Dubberstein. 1956. *Babylonian Chronology 626 B.C.–*

A.D. 75. Brown University Studies 19. Providence, RI: Brown University Press.

Peiser, Felix Ernst. 1888a. "Studien zum babylonische Rechtswesen." *ZA* 3: 69–92.

———. 1888b. "Eine babylonische Verfügung von Todes wegen." *ZA* 3: 365–71.

———. 1896. *Texte juristischen und geschäftlichen Inhalts*. KB 4. Berlin: Reuther & Reichard.

Petschow, Herbert. 1956. *Neubabylonisches Pfandrecht*. Abhandlungen der Sächsischen Akademie der Wissenschaften zu Leipzig Philologisch-historische Klasse 48, vol. 1. Berlin: Akademie-Verlag.

Pohl, Alfred. 1933. *Neubabylonische Rechtsurkunden aus den Berliner Staatlichen Museen*. AnOr 8. Rome: Pontifical Biblical Institute.

Powell, Marvin A. 1987. "Maße und Gewichte." *RlA* 7:457–517.

Ragen, Asher. 2006. "The Neo-Babylonian *širku*: A Social History." Ph.D. dissertation, Harvard University.

Renger, Johannes. 1971. "Notes on the Goldsmiths, Jewelers and Carpenters of Neo-Bablyonian Eanna." *JAOS* 91: 494–503.

Revillout, Victor and Eugène Revillout. 1886. "Appendice sur le droit de la chaldée au XXIIIe et au VIe siècle avant notre ère." Pages 273–530 in *Les obligations en droit égyptien comparé aux autres droits de l'antiquité*. Eugène Revillout. Paris: Ernest Leroux.

Ries, Gerhard. 1984. "Ein neubabylonischer Mitgiftprozeß (559 v. Chr.)." Pages 345–63 in *Gedächtnisschrift für Wolfgang Kunkel*. Edited by Dieter Nörr and Dieter Simon. Frankfurt: Vittorio Klostermann.

Roth, Martha T. 1988. "'She Will Die by the Iron Dagger': Adultery and Neo-Babylonian Marriage." *JESHO* 31: 186–206.

———. 1989a. *Babylonian Marriage Agreements: 7th–3rd Century B.C.* AOAT 222. Neukirchen: Neukirchener Verlag.

———. 1989b. "A Case of Contested Status." Pages 481–89 in DUMU-E$_2$-DUB-BA-A: *Studies in Honor of Åke W. Sjöberg*. Edited by Hermann Behrens, et. al. Philadelphia: University Museum.

———. 1989c "Marriage and Matrimonial Prestations in First Millennium B. C. Mesopotamia." Pages 245–55 in *Women's Earliest Records from Ancient Egypt and Western Asia*. Edited by Barbara S. Lesko. BJS 166. Atlanta: Scholars Press.

———. 1991–93. "The Neo-Babylonian Widow." *JCS* 43–45: 1–26.

———. 1995. *Law Collections from Mesopotamia and Asia Minor.* WAW 6. Atlanta: Scholars Press.

———. "Tašmētu-Damqat and Daughters." Pages 387–400 in *Assyriologica et Semitica: Festschrift für Joachim Oelsner*. Edited by Joachim Marzahn and Hans Neumann. AOAT 252. Münster: Ugarit Verlag.

———. 2007. "On Amputation, Beating, and Illegal Seizure." Pages 207–18 in *Studies Presented to Robert D. Biggs*. Edited by Martha T. Roth, Walter Farber, Matthew W. Stolper, and Paula von Bechtolsheim. AS 27. Chicago: The Oriental Institute of the University of Chicago.

Rutten, M. 1947. "Contestation au sujet d'une donation d'une mère à ses fils." *RA* 41: 99–103.

Sachs, Abraham J., and Hermann Hunger. 1989. *Astronomical Diaries and Related Texts from Babylonia*, Vol. 2: *Diaries from 261 B.C. to 165 B.C.* Österreichische Akademie der Wissenschaften-Philosphisch-Historische klasse Denkschriften 210. Vienna: Österreichische Akademie der Wissenschaften.

Sack, Ronald H. 1994. *Neriglissar King of Babylon.* AOAT 236. Neukirchen: Neukirchener Verlag.

San Nicolò, Mariano. 1932. "Parerga Babylonica VII: Der §8 des Gesetzbuches Ḫammurapis in den neubabylonischen Urkunden." *ArOr* 4: 327–44.

———. 1933a. "Parerga Babylonica IX: Der Monstreprozeß des Gimillu, eines *širku* von Eanna." *ArOr* 5: 61–77.

———. 1933b. "Parerga Babylonica XI: Die *maš'altu*-Urkunden im neubabylonischen Strafverfahren." *ArOr* 5: 287–302.

———. 1939. "Ein Urteil des Königlichen Gerichtes in Babylon aus der Zeit des Nabonid." Pages 179–88 in *Symbolae ad Iura Orientis Antiqui Pertinentes Paulo Koschaker Dedicatae.* Edited by J. Friedrich, et. al. Studia et Documenta 2. Leiden: Brill.

———. 1945. "Eine kleine Gefängnismeuterei in Eanna zur zeit des Kambyses." Pages 1–17 in *Festschrift für Leopold Wenger.* Edited by Leopold Wenger and Mariano San Nicolò. MBPF 35, Vol. 2. Munich: Beck.

San Nicolò, Mariano and Arthur Ungnad. 1935. *Neubabylonische Rechts- und Verwaltungsurkunden.* Leipzig: Hinrichs.

Sandowicz, Małgorzata. 2009. "Depositaries, Depositors and Courthouse in Sixth-Century B.C. Babylon." *Palamedes* 4: 15–25.

———. 2012. *Oaths and Curses: A Study in Neo- and Late Babylonian Legal Formulary.* AOAT 398. Munster: Ugarit Verlag.

Scheil, V. 1915. "La libération judiciaire d'un fils donné en gage sous Neriglissor en 558 av. J.-C." *RA* 12: 1–13.

Stolper, Matthew. 1976. "The Genealogy of the Murašu Family," *JCS* 28: 189–200.

Strassmaier, Johann Nepomunk. 1889a. *Inschriften von Nabonidus, König von Babylon (555–538 v. Chr.).* Babylonische Texte 1–4. Leipzig: Pfeiffer.

———. 1889b. *Inschriften von Nabuchodonosor, König von Babylon (604–561 v. Chr.).* Babylonische Texte 5–6. Leipzig: Pfeiffer.

———. 1890a. *Inschriften von Cambyses, König von Babylon (529–521 v. Chr.*). Babylonische Texte 9. Leipzig: Pfeiffer.

———. 1890b. *Inschriften von Cyrus, König von Babylon (538–529 v. Chr.*). Babylonische Texte 7. Leipzig: Pfeiffer.

———. 1892. *Inschriften von Darius, König von Babylon (521–485 v. Chr.*). Babylonische Texte 10–12. Leipzig: Pfeiffer.

Tallqvist, Knut L. 1905. *Neubabylonisches Namenbuch zu den Geschäftsurkunden aus der Zeit des Šamaššumukîn bis Xerxes.* Acta Societatis Scientiarum Fennice 32.2. Helsinki: Societatis Litterariae Fennicae.

Tremayne, Arch. 1925. *Records from Erech, Time of Cyrus and Cambyses (538–521 B.C.).* YOS 7. New Haven: Yale University Press.

Waerzeggers, Caroline. 2003–4. "The Babylonian Revolts Against Xerxes and the 'End of Archives.'" *AfO* 50: 150–73.

Wallis, Gerhard. 1964. "Aus dem Leben eines jüdischen Sklaven in Babylon." Pages

14–20 in *... und fragten nach Jesus: Beiträge aus Theologie, Kirche und Geschichte, Festschrift für Enrst Barnikol zum 70. Geburtstag*. Edited by Udo Meckert, Günther Ott and Bernt Satlow. Berlin: Evangelische Verlagsanstalt.

Weidner, Ernst. 1954–56. "Hochverrat gegen Nebukadnezar II." *AfO* 17: 1–9.

Weisberg, David B. 1967. *Guild Structure and Political Allegiance in Early Achaemenid Mesopotamia*. YNER 1. New Haven: Yale University Press.

Wells, Bruce. 2004. *The Law of Testimony in the Pentateuchal Codes*. Beihefte zur Zeitschrift für Altorientalische und Biblische Rechtsgeschichte 4. Wiesbaden: Harrassowitz.

———. 2008. "What Is Biblical Law? A Look at Pentateuchal Rules and Near Eastern Practice." *CBQ* 70: 223–43.

———. 2010. "Competing or Complementary?: Judges and Elders in Biblical and Neo-Babylonian Law." *Zeitschrift für Altorientalische und Biblische Rechtsgeschichte* 16: 77–104.

Wunsch, Cornelia. 1993. *Die Urkunden des babylonischen Geschäftsmannes Iddin-Marduk: Zum Handel mit Naturalien im 6. Jahrhundert v. Chr.* Cuneiform Monographs 3A, 3B. Groningen: Styx.

———. 1997–98. "Und die Richter berieten ...: Streitfälle in Babylon aus der Zeit Neriglissars und Nabonids." *AfO* 44/45: 59–100.

———. 2000a. *Das Egibi-Archiv: I. Die Felder und Gärten*. Cuneiform Monographs 20A, 20B. Groningen: Styx.

———. 2000b. "Die Richter des Nabonid." Pages 557–97 in *Assyriologica et Semitica: Festschrift für Joachim Oelsner anlässlich seines 65. Geburtstages am 18. Februar 1997*. Edited by Joachim Marzahn and Hans Neumann. Münster: Ugarit Verlag.

———. 2002a. "'Du hast meinen Sohn geschlagen!'" Pages 355–64 in *Mining the Archives: Festschrift for Christopher Walker on the Occasion of His 60th Birthday, 4 October, 2002*. Edited by Cornelia Wunsch. Babylonische Archive 1. Dresden: Islet.

———. 2002b. "Debt, Interest, Pledge and Forfeiture in the Neo-Babylonian and Early Achaemenid Period: The Evidence from Private Archives." Pages 221–53 in *Debt and Economic Renewal in the Ancient Near East*. Edited by Michael Hudson and Marc Van De Mieroop. Bethesda, MD: CDL.

———. 2003. *Urkunden zum Ehe-, Vermögens- und Erbrecht aus verschiedenen neubabylonischen Archiven*. Babylonische Archive 2. Dresden: Islet.

———. 2006 . "Metronymika in Babylonien: Frauen als Anherrin der Familie." Pages 459–69 in *Šapal tibnim mû ilakkū: Studies Presented to Joaquín Sanmartín*. Edited by Gregorio del Olmo Lete, et al. Aula Orientalis Supplementa 22. Sabadell: AUSA.

———. 2007. "Marriage Secretly Arranged: Cyr 311 and Cyr 312." ETANA. Online: http://www.etana.org/node/571.

———. 2010. "Neo-Babylonian Entrepreneurs." Pages 40–61 in *The Invention of Enterprise: Entrepreneurship from Ancient Mesopotamia to Modern Times*. Edited by David S. Landes, Joel Mokyr, and William J. Baumol. Princeton: Princeton University Press.

———. 2012. "Legal Narrative in Neo-Babylonian Trial Documents: Text Reconstruction, Interpretation, and Assyriological Method." Pages 3–34 in *Law and Narrative in the Bible and in Neighbouring Ancient Cultures*. Edited by Klaus-Peter Adams, Friedrich Avemarie and Nili Wazana. Tübingen: Mohr Siebeck, 2012.

Wunsch, Cornelia and F. Rachel Magdalene. in press. "Freedom and Dependency: Neo-Babylonian Manumission Documents with Oblation and Service Obligations." In *Extraction and Control: Studies in Honor of Matthew W. Stolper.* Edited by W. Henkelman, et. al. Chicago: The Oriental Institute of the University of Chicago.

Zadok, Ran. 1985. *Répertoire Géographiques des Textes Cunéiformes 8: Geographical Names According to New- and Late-Babylonian Texts.* Wiesbaden: Reichert.

———. 2003. "The Representation of Foreigners in Neo- and Late-Babylonian Legal Documents (Eighth through Second Centuries, B.C.E)." Pages 471–589 in *Judah and the Judeans in the Neo-Babylonian Period.* Edited by Oded Lipschitz and Joseph Blenkinsopp. Winona Lake, IN: Eisenbrauns.

Index of Personal Names

The following symbols are used:

~ the name in the particular entry
/ son or daughter of
// descendant of

Men

Adad-ibni
~/Zariqu-zēra-ibni//Šangû-Zariqu (46:18)
Adad-šarra-uṣur
~/Nabû-ušēzib (4:9, 24)
Adad-ušallim
Bēl-aḫḫē-uṣur/~ (4:13)
Adad-zēra-iddin
Aḫūnu/~ (45:7–8)
Aḫḫêa
Nergal-aḫa-iddin/~ (18:4, 11, 16)
Aḫḫē-iddin
Nabû-nāṣir/~ (6:8–9)
Aḫḫēšu
Bēl-aḫḫē-iddin/~//Gimil-Nanaya (26:20–21)
Ahhūšaya
Nabû-zēra-iddin/~ (11:7'–8')
Aḫimme
Šamaš-šarra-uṣur/~ (16:21)
Aḫišaya
Nergal-šuma-ibni/~ (38:135)
Aḫiya
~/Enlil-aḫa-iddin (15:18)
Aḫiya-alidu
Bēl-šarra-uṣur/~ (42:4, 20–21)
Aḫulap-Ištar
Šamaš-zēra-iddin/~//Ekur-zakir (30:31–32)
Aḫu-nūri
~/Nabû-nādin-aḫi (20:3)
Qudāšu/~ (20:6)
Aḫūnu
~/Adad-zēra-iddin (45:7–8)
Aḫu-ṭāb
Iddinaya/~ (38:56)
Amēl-Nabû
~/Bēl-iddin//Arad-Nergal (34:38)
Ammaya
Amurru-natan/~ (22:5–6)
Amurru-nādin-...
~/Marduka (17:1–2)
Amurru-natan
~/Ammaya (22:5–6, 13, 20, 22, 29, 33)
Amurru-šarra-uṣur
royal official (50:2, 5)

Ana-muḫḫi-Bēl-āmur
slave (44:7)
Anu(m)-aḫa-iddin
~/Mušēzib (6:17)
~/Sîn-ibni//Rēʾi-alpi (7:18–19)
Anu-aḫa-bulliṭ
~/Ištar-nādin-šumi//Kurī (41:8)
Anu/Anim-šuma-ibni
~/Nabû-ušēzib//Nabû-šarḫi-ilī (30:8; 31:24)
Anu(m)-šarra-uṣur
15:21
qīpu-official (31:9, 13;38:7, 32–33)
~/Šarru-kīn (42:2–3, 13, 14, 19; 43:4, 6)
Anu-zēra-šubši
~/Lâbāši (41:15, 20)
Anum-šumu-līšir
~/Nabû-apla-iddin (2:3–4, 10)
Apkallu
~/Nergal-nāṣir//Išparu (5:26)
Aplaya
~/Bēl-lēʾi//Egibi (18:29)
~/Enlil-balāssu-iqbi (28:16, seal)
~/Gula-zēra-ibni//Isinaya (8:3)
~/Libluṭ (49:17)
~/Ninurta-iddin (28:23)
~/Šūzubu (24:seal)
~/Šūzubu//Bābūtu (27:23)
Ardiya/~//Nabû-šarḫi-ilī (3:19)
Nabû-šuma-iddin/~ (37:7–8)
Nādinu/~/Aḫḫûtu (2:19)
[PN]/~ (17:7)
Appussa
Ilī-idriʾ/~ (28:21)
Aqubu
~/Zabdiya (9:1–2, 3, 9, lower edge)
Arad-Egalmaḫ
Ninurta-aḫa-iddin/~ (28:19)
Arad-Bēl
~/Bēl-ušallim//Adad-šammê (4:21–22; 33:5')
~/Ṣillaya//Iddin-Papsukkal (2:17; 38:14)
~/Šarru-kīn (16:2–3)
Lâbāši-Marduk/~//Egibi (3:1–2)
Nabû-ēṭir/~//Arrabtu (49:7)
Nabû-ēṭir-napšāti/~//Egibi (2:18; 14:22)
Nabû-nādin-aḫi/~//Iddin-Papsukkal (42:26–27)
Arad-Gula
24:17, 15'
Nusku-iddin/~ (9:15)
Arad-Innin
~/Bēl-iddin//Kurī (8:4;25:61;38:17)
~/Ibni-Ištar//Gimil-Nanaya (2:22; 38:22)
~/Šākin-šumi (26:1, 13, 23)
Nanaya-iddin/~ (38:44)
Riḫētu/~ (40:1)
Arad-Marduk
scribe (42:30; 43:23)
~/Bēl-apla-uṣur (41:27)
~/Zēriya//Egibi (8:2; 38:12; 43:19)
Arad-Nabû
Mušallim-Marduk/~//Šangû-Nabû (39:14–15)
Arad-Nergal
~/Kīnaya//Egibi (30:8)
~/Mukīn-apli//Egibi (43:14–15)
Ardiya
48:18, 20
~/Aplaya//Nabû-šarḫi-ilī (3:19)
~/Lā-tubāšinni (48:18–19, 20)
~/Nabû-ušabši (49:16)
~/Šākin-šumi//Gimil-Nanaya (31:23)
~/Ubar (28:25)

Ina-tēšê-ēṭir/~ (6:10)
Nidintu/~ (38:112)
Rīmūt-Bēl/~//Itinnu (13:18–19)
Ṭābiya/~//Basiya (18:27–28)
Ašaridu
~/Marduk-nāṣir//Šangû-ili (46:14)
Balāssu
judge//Malāḫu (21:48, seal)
~/Marduk-šuma-ibni//Babūtu (25:62)
Ištar-šuma-ēreš/~//Mukallim (25:65)
Nabû-mušētiq-uddê/~//Dāmiqu (25:1)
Zēriya/~ (14:3–4)
Balāṭu
scribe (38:27)
~/Mušēzib-Bēl (7:8)
~/Nabû-ēṭir//Rē'î-sīsî (24:seal)
~/Nasikātu (27:3, 9)
~/Sîn-ibni//Rē'i-alpi (1:26–27; 21:2–3)
~/Zākir//Kidin-Marduk (8:9–10)
Marduk-šarrani/~//Paḫāru (44:16–17)
Nādinu/~ (8:13; 38:6)
Silim-Bēl/~ (12:13–14)
Balti-ilī
Šulaya/~//Ea-ṣalmu-ilī (24:21')
Balṭiya
~/Innina-zēra-šubši (37:12–13, 17, 22)
Bāniya
~/Aplaya (27:28)
~/Bīt-Ea-kitti (15:16–17)
~/Taribi (3:9–10)
Iddin-Gula/~ (4:19)
Marduk-iqīšanni/~//Ilu-tillatī (46:15)
Šamaš-zēra-šubši/~//Andaḫar (41:9)
Bariki-ili
Bēl-uballiṭ/~ (4:12)
Bariki-ilī
slave (20:1, 9, 15, 16, 26)
Basiya
~/Ibni-Ištar (1:6–7)
Bazuzu
slave (19:3, 8)
Bau-ēreš
judge (43:7)
~/Nabû-aḫa-uṣur (16:1, 13, 16)
~/Nabû-bāni-aḫi (12:4, 7, 9, 12)
~/Šullum-mādu (4:18)
Kutka-ili/~ (4:11)
Nanaya-iddin/~ (4:6)
Bau-iqīšā
~/Usātu (15:1–3, 9)
Bēl-aḫa-iddin
Šamaš-šuma-ukīn/~//Rāb-banê (14:26)
Bēl-aḫa-šubši
~/Etillu//Ekur-zakir (14:23)
~/Nabû-iqīša (6:11)
Bēlšunu/~//Amēl-Ea (30:5)
Bēl-aḫa-uṣur
slave/~Lā-tubāšinni (48:5, 9, 11, 16, 21)
Bēl-aḫḫē-erība
~/Bēl-ušēzib//Dābibī (45:9–10)
~/Nabû-bēlšunu//Kurī (10:12–13)
Bēl-aḫḫē-iddin
judge//Nūr-Sîn (22:39, seal; 29:36)
~/Aḫḫēšu//Gimil-Nanaya (26:2–3, 5, 20–21)
~/(Ina)-Esagil-šuma-ibni//Sîn-damāqu (46:1, 9; 47:1–2, 9; 48:3, 18, 23)
~/Nabû-apla-iddin (24:1)
~/Nabû-bēl-šīmāti//Šangû-Ištar-Bābili (44:15–16)

~/Nanaya-ēreš (5:3, 13)
~/Gudādu//Sîn-lēqi-unninnī (26:6, 21, 36)
Ninurta-nāṣir/~ (28:17, seal)
Bēl-aḫḫē-iqīša
Nādinu/~//Egibi (1:27–28; 7:3; 14:27;25:64)
Bēl-aḫḫē-uṣur
~/Adad-ušallim (4:13)
Bēl-aḫḫē-x
24:18'
Bēl-apla-iddin
"temple enterer of Šamaš"//Šangû-Sippar (33:2')
~/Bēl-rēmanni//Ša-ṭabti-šu (39:17)
~/Nabû-šumu-līsir//Mudammiq-Adad (36:2, 6, 8, 9, 37, 40, 43)
Bēl-apla-uṣur
Arad-Marduk/~ (41:27)
Bēl-ēreš
Nabû-aḫḫē-iddin/~ (38:82)
Bēl-erība
PN/~ (24:7")
Bēl-eṭēri-Nabû
royal official (42:28)
Bēl-ēṭir
judge//Sîn-tabni (22:40, seal)
~/Bēl-iddina//Maštukku (34:38–39)
~/Ile''i-Marduk//Dābibī (13:20)
Bēl-ibni
~/Bulluṭ(u)//Bā'iru (8:8;25:58)
Bēl-iddin(a)
scribe//Atû (21:51)
~/Šāpik-zēri//Mandidi (17:9–10)
~/Bēl-ušebši//Šangû-Zariqu (46:17)
Amēl-Nabû/~//Arad-Nergal (34:38)
Arad-Innin/~//Kurī (8:4;25:61;38:17)
Bēl-ēṭir/~//Maštukku (34:38–39)
Šamaš-iddin/~ (26:2)
Bēl-iqīša
scribe//Sîn-tabni (22:42)
~/Ṣillaya (42:9, 22; 43:5–6, 11, 12–13)
Nabû-ēṭir-napšāti/~//Bēl-apla-uṣur (10:14–15)
PN/~ (24:5")
Bēl-ittannu
~/Zabdiya (28:3)
Bēl-kāṣir
scribe//Atkuppu (21:50)
~/Marduk//Kidin-Marduk (8:7; 38:20)
Bēl-lē'i
Aplaya/~//Egibi (18:29)
Bēl-uballiṭ/~//Sîn-ili (36:53)
Karêa/~//Aḫūtu (18:1, 17, 22)
Bēl-nādin-apli
~/Marduk-šuma-iddin//Bēl-apla-uṣur (31:22; 43:21)
~/Kidin-Marduk//Ēṭeru (41:6)
~/Zēru-bābili//Ile''i-Marduk (14:24)
Bēl-nāṣir
~/Bēl-ušēzib (9:13–14)
Bēl-rēmanni
20:4
governor of Babylon//Mandidi (24:4)
Bēl-apla-iddin/~//Ša-ṭabti-šu (39:17)
DN-aḫa-iddin/~ (18:26)
Bēl-šarra-uṣur
~/Aḫiya-alidu (42:4, 7, 20–21)
Bēl-šarrussu
~/Šamaš-iddin (16:20–21)
Bēl-šuma-iškun
~/Bēl-ušallim//Atû (36:56)

Bēlšunu
~/Bēl-aḫa-šubši//Amēl-Ea (30:5)
~/Ninurta-nāṣir (28:26)
~/Nūrea (30:11–12, 21, 24, 27, 30)
Nabû-zērū-līšir/~//Kurī (8:5;25:69)
Nargiya/~ (37:5)
Bēl-uballiṭ
judge//Rāb-līmi (19:17; 32:35)
šangû of Sippar (4:4–5;33:7, 9, 11)
~/Bariki-ili (4:11)
~/Bēl-lē'i//Sîn-ili (36:53)
~/Līšir//Šangû-Ištar-Bābili (34:43–44)
~/Marduk-šuma-ibni, *qīpu*-official of Aḫulla' (27:21)
~/Šuma-ukīn//Sîn-šadûnu (23:1–2; 29:3–4, 14, 21, 28)
Marduk-ēṭir/~ (39:15–16)
Marduk-šuma-uṣur/~//Pūtu (2:20)
Mušēzib-Marduk/~//Amēl-Ea (10:15)
Rīmūt-Bēl/~//Gimil-Nanaya (3:14–15;38:10)
Bēl-ušallim
Arad-Bēl/~//Adad-šammê (4:21–22;33:5')
Bēl-šuma-iškun/~//Atû (36:56)
Rašil-X/~//Eppeš-ili (11:15'–16')
Šaddinu/~ (34:42)
Bēl-ušebši
Bēl-iddin/~//Šangû-Zariqu (46:17)
Bēl-ušēzib
Bēl-aḫḫē-erība/~//Dābibī (45:9–10)
Bēlilitu/~//Ša-nāšīšu (19:1–2)
Bēl-nāṣir/~ (9:13–14)
Bēl-zēri
judge//Rīmūt-Ea (36:52, seal)
Bibēa
PN/~//Bēl-eṭēru (24:32')
Bīt-Ea-kitti
Bāniya/~ (15:16–17)
Bulluṭ(u)
Bēl-ibni/~//Bā'iru (8:8;25:58)
Bunene-ibni
Ubar/~ (9:11)
Dāgil-ilī
~/Zambubu (44:1, 6, 10, 11)
Damqaya
~/Iddinaya (28:18)
Dannu-aḫḫēšu-ibni
~/Šarru-kīn (38:62, 72)
Eli-ili-rabi-Marduk
Mušēzib-Bēl/~ (36:4)
Enlil-aḫa-iddin
~/Enlil-uballiṭ (28:25)
Aḫiya/~ (15:18)
Enlil-balāssu-iqbi
Aplaya/~ (28:16, seal)
Enlil-bana
Erība-Enlil/~ (28:17, seal)
Enlil-iddin
Enlil-ittannu/~ (28:24)
Enlil-ittannu
~/Enlil-iddin (28:24)
Enlil-mukīn-apli
Ubar/~ (28:19)
Enlil-nāṣir
Šuma-iddin/~ (28:23)
Enlil-šuma-iddin
~/Murašû (9:1, 9; 28:2, 5, 8, 10)
Enlil-šuma-ukīn
Nā–id-Ninurta/~ (28:16)
Enlil-uballiṭ
Enlil-aḫa-iddin/~ (28:25)
Erība
~/Nabû-ušēzib (4:10)
Erībaya
Nabû-nādin/~ (40:14)

Erība-Enlil
~/Enlil-bana (28:17, seal)
Esagil-rēṣua
slave/Lā-tubašinni (48:5, 9)
Esagil-šadûnu
judge//Arad-Ea (19:13; 32:31)
Etillu
~/Bēlilitu (19:9)
Bēl-aḫa-šubši/~//Ekur-zakir (14:23)
Iqīša-Marduk/~//Šangû-Sippar (33:3')
Gabbi-ilī-šarra-uṣur
qīpu-official of the Eanna (1:20; 25:3, 21)
Gadalyama
~/Šabbataya (28:20–21)
Gimil-Gula
~/Itti-Esagil-zēri (35:21'-22')
Gimillu
~/Innin-šuma-ibni (37:6–7, 20, 24; 38:2, 38, 42, 48, 49, 50, 53, 56, 59, 64, 73, 76, 81, 84, 87, 90, 95, 99, 100, 103, 107, 109, 111, 113, 116, 120, 121, 124, 126, 128, 134, 136, 137, 139, 144, 145, 146; 39:5; 40:7, 10, 13, 25; 41:16, 23)
~/Innin-zēra-iddin (3:21;39:18)
~/Nabû-šuma-iddin//Ea-ilūta-bāni (10:11–12)
~/Nabû-šuma-iddin//Gimil-Nanaya (38:25)
~/Nūrea (37:2)
Innin-šuma-uṣur/~//Kurī (30:6; 31:24–25)
Madānu-aḫḫē-iddin/~//Šigûa (1:23–24; 7:2; 14:21;21:1)
Gubaru (Gobryas)
30:19
Gudādu
Bēl-aḫḫē-iddin/~/Sîn-lēqi-unninnī (26:6)
Gudaya
~/Ḫinni-ilī (12:1–2)
Gula-šumu-līšir
governor (15:12–13)
Gula-zēra-ibni
Aplaya/~//Isinaya (8:3)
Ḫabaṣīru
~/Sîn-aḫa-iddin (34:39–40)
Ḫagūru
Katimuʾ/~ (12:5–6)
Ḫananyama
~/Udarnaʾ (28:20)
Ḫanunu
Nargiya/~ (49:10–11)
Ḫašdaya
~/ Lâbāši-Marduk//Egibi (3:10)
Ḫašdiya
~/Ištar-šuma-ēreš//Adad-rabû (38:26)
~/Nabû-mušētiq-uddê (38:61, 62, 63)
Ḫinni-ilī
Gudaya/~ (12:1–2)
Ḫiraḫḫa
Marduk-dīna-īpuš/~ (39:2–3)
Ibnaya
~/Nabû-aḫḫē-šullim (38:45–46, 47)
~/Nādin (34:37)
Nabû-balāssu-iqbi/~//Ekur-zakir (3:17)
Zēriya/~//Egibi (1:21–22)
PN/~//Rāb-banê (11:14'–15')
Ibni-Ištar
~/Nabû-aḫḫē-šullim (7:7)
Arad-Innin/~//Gimil-Nanaya (2:22;38:22)
Basiya/~ (1:6–7)

Iddin-Ištar/~ (6:1)
Innin-aḫḫē-iddin/~ (1:6–7)
Lū-dānu/~[//PN] (1:1)
Nabû-apla-iddin/~//Ekur-zakir (5:26–27)
Šākin-šumi/~//Sîn-tabni (3:15; 14:18–19; 38:18)
Šumaya/~//Ašlaku (5:31;7:4)
Iddin(a)-aḫa
~/Nabû-aḫḫē-šullim (31:1, 2, 4, 5, 6)
Mušēzib-Bēl/~//Bābūtu (27:24–25)
Mušēzib-Marduk/~//Ša-nāšišu (27:26–27)
Rīmūt-Bēl/~//Bēl-pattanni (17:8–9)
Iddinaya
20:14, 21
brother of Gimillu (38:81, 84, 85)
~/Aḫu-ṭāb (38:56)
~/Innin-šuma-uṣur//Sîn-lēqi-unninnī (16:19)
~/ Lâbāši-Marduk//Egibi (3:7–8)
Damqaya/~ (28:18)
Iddin-Enlil
Ninurta-nāṣir/~ (28:22)
Iddin-Gula
~/Bāniya (4:19)
Iddin-Ištar
~/Ibni-Ištar (6:1, 4, 7, 15)
Iddin-Marduk
22:1, 3, 9, 27
35:1', 3', 11', 18', 28', 34', 36'
~/Iqīšaya//Eppeš-ili (36:54)
~/Nabû-ittiya (12:14–15)
Šāpik-zēri/~//Šigûa (47:5–6)
Iddin-Nabû
26:35
slave/Nuptaya (31:7, 16)
Idiḫi-ilī/~ (37:4)
Innin-šuma-uṣur/~//Kidin-Marduk (3:16; 25:66; 38:16)
Nabû-bulliṭsu/~//Dābibī (18:27)
Idiḫi-ilī
~/Iddin-Nabû (37:4)
Ile''i-Marduk
scribe//Eppeš-ili (20:30)
Bēl-ēṭir/~//Dābibī (13:20)
Ilī-idri'
~/Appussa (28:21)
Iltammeš-baraku
/Nabû-zēra-[X] (1:2, 17)
Iltammeš-kīni (7:13)
Imbi-Sîn
šangû of Ur (27:20)
Imbiya
~/Nanaya-ēreš//Kidin-Marduk, governor of Uruk, *qīpu*-official (26:16–17; 41:1–2)
(Ina)-Esagil-šuma-ibni
45:2, 6
Bēl-aḫḫē-iddin/~//Sîn-damāqu (46:1–2, 10; 47:1–2; 48:13);
Nabû-aḫḫē-bulliṭ/~//Sîn-damāqu (46:1–2, 10; 47:1–2)
Ina-Esagil-zēri
~/Ša-pî-Bēl//Amēl-Ea (8:6;25:63)
Nabû-uballiṭ/~//Amēl-Ea (30:7)
Ina-qībit-Nabû
Rīmūt/~ (29:5)
Ina-tēšê-ēṭir
~/Ardiya (6:10)
Innin-aḫḫē-erība
38:99
Innin-aḫḫē-iddin
~/Ibni-Ištar (1:6–7)
Innin-līpī-uṣur
Kīnaya/~ (42:29)
Innin-šarra-uṣur
~/Nergal-ušallim//Sîn-lēqi-unninnī (14:19–20)

Innin-šuma-ibni
Gimillu/~ (37:6–7; 38:2; 39:5; 40:7)
Innin-šuma-uṣur
~/Gimillu//Kurī (30:6;31:24–25)
~/Iddin-Nabû//Kidin-Marduk (3:16;25:66;38:16)
~/Nergal-ušallim//Sîn-lēqi-unninnī (26:34–35, 38)
Iddinaya/~//Sîn-lēqi-unninnī (16:19)
Ištar-aḫa-iddin/~//Nabû-šarḫi-ilī (3:5–6)
Rīmūt/~ (7:9–10)
Šamaš-zēra-iqīša/~ (38:66)
Innin-zēra-ibni
~/Nabû-aḫḫē-šullim//Šangû-Ninurta (38:23)
Innin-zēra-iddin
Gimillu/~ (3:21;39:19)
Innin(a)-zēra-šubši
Balṭiya/~ (37:12–13)
Iqīša(ya)
~/Šamaš-šarra-uṣur (4:14)
Kalbaya/~//Basiya (7:5)
Kinaya/~ (11:1', 9'–11')
Iqīša-Marduk
~/Etillu//Šangû-Sippar (33:3')
~/Nabû-bēlšunu//Nabûnaya (18:23–24)
Ištar-aḫa-iddin
~/Innin-šuma-uṣur//Nabû-šarḫi-ilī (3:5–6, 12)
~/Nabû-šuma-uṣur//Ekur-zakir (41:7)
~/PN (1:6)
Ištar-ālik-pāni
30:9, 26
Ištar-mukīn-apli
~/Nabû-bāni-aḫi//PN (31:25–26)
Ištar-nādin-šumi
Anu-aḫa-bulliṭ/~//Kurī (41:8)
Ištar-šuma-ēreš
~/Balāssu//Mukallim (25:65)
Ḫašdiya/~//Adad-rabû (38:26)
Itti-Anum-balāṭu
~/Šamaš-šuma-iddin (5:22–23)
Itti-Bēl-tabni
Tabnêa/~ (37:1)
Itti-Bēl-ṭābu
Nabû-zēra-iddin/~ (4:20)
Itti-Enlil-balāṭu
~/Usātu (15:2–3, 7, 11)
Itti-Esagil-zēri
Gimil-Gula/~ (35:21'-22')
Itti-Marduk-balāṭu
scribe (42:30)
~/Nabû-aḫḫē-iddin//Egibi (20:23;29:1, 15, 25, 31, 32)
Marduk-nāṣir-apli/~//Egibi (13:3–4; 18:29–30)
Kabti-Marduk
judge (50:31)
Kabtiya
~/Marduk-šuma-ibni//Amēl-Ea (47:16–17)
Marduk-apla-uṣur/~//Šigûa (5:27)
Mušēzib-Marduk/~//Šigûa (3:20)
Nūrea/~ (21:6–7)
Kalbaya
~//Ir'anni (36:49)
~/Iqīša//Basiya (7:5)
~/Silim-Bēl (26:1, 13, 24)
Karêa
~/Bēl-lē'i//Aḫūtu (18:1, 5, 8, 10, 13, 22)
Katimu'
~/Ḫagūru (12:5–6)
Kidin-Marduk
Bēl-nādin-apli/~//Ēṭeru (41:6)
Kīnaya
38:71

scribe (38:27)
~/Innin-līpī-uṣur (42:29)
~/Iqīšaya (11:1', 4', 9'–10', 11')
~/Nergal-ina-tēšê-ēṭir//Dannea (14:2–3, 6, 7, 9)
~/Raḫimmu (16:5, 9–10, 16)
~/Zēriya (1:24–25)
Arad-Nergal/~/Egibi (30:8)
Kiribtu
kizû (20:seal)
~/Nādinu//Babūtu (38:19)
Kiṣir-Nabû
Nabû-ušallim/~ (16:22)
Kudurru
Marduk-šāpik-zēri/~//Nagāru (25:68)
Kurbanni-Marduk
~/Zēriya//Sîn-damāqu, *šatammu* of Eanna (8:14)
Kutka-ili
~/Bau-ēreš (4:11)
Lâbāši
~/Šamaš-aḫa-iddin (37:3)
Anu-zēra-šubši/~ (41:15)
Ṣillaya/~//Šigûa (47:14–15)
PN/~ (24:13")
Lâbāši-Marduk
~/Arad-bēl//Egibi (3:1–2, 13)
~/PN (30:3)
Ḫašdaya/~//Egibi (3:10–11)
Iddinaya/~//Egibi (3:7–8)
Lāqīpi
slave (38:122)
~/Nabû-šuma-ukīn (38:89)
Libluṭ
~/Nabû-mīta-uballiṭ//Mudammiq-Adad (13:1, 10, 16, 18)
Aplaya/~ (49:17)
Līšir
Bēl-uballiṭ/~//Šangû-Ištar-Bābili (34:43–44)
Lū-dānu
~/Ibni-[Ištar//PN] (1:1)
Lūṣi-ana-nūri-Marduk
~/Nabû-aḫḫē-bulliṭ//Dābibī (42:28–29)
Madānu-aḫḫē-iddin
~/Gimillu//Šigûa (1:23–24; 7:2; 14:21; 21:1)
Marduk-nāṣir/~//Šigûa (16:23)
Šamaš-mukīn-apli/~//Šigûa (39:13–14;42:27)
Marduk
~/Nabû-zēra-iddin (5:2, 13)
Bēl-kāṣir/~//Kidin-Marduk (8:7; 38:20)
Marduka
Amurru-nādin-[X]/~ (17:1–2)
Marduk-u
PN/~ (24:14")
Marduk-aḫa-iddin
Šumaya/~ (38:52)
Marduk-apla-uṣur
~/Kabtiya//Šigûa (5:27)
Marduk-dīna-īpuš
~/Ḫiraḫḫa (39:2–3, 6)
Marduk-erība
governor of Uruk (27:19)
~/Nergal-iddin//Ea-ṣalmu-ilāni (25:15, 17)
Nabû-bāni-aḫi/~//Ea-ṣalmu-ilāni (25:15)
Marduk-ēṭir
~/Bēl-uballiṭ//Amēl-Ea (39:15–16)
~/Nergal-iddin//Bābūtu (44:17–18)
Marduk-iqīšanni
~/Bāniya//Ilu-tillatī (46:15)
Marduk-nāṣir
scribe// Bāne-ša-iliya (50:33–34)
~/Madānu-aḫḫē-iddin//Šigûa (16:23)

Ašaridu/~//Šangû-ili (46:14)
Nabû-zēra-ibni/~//PN (25:25)
Marduk-nāṣir-apli
~/Itti-Marduk-balāṭu//Egibi (13:3–4, 13, 16; 18:29–30)
Marduk-šākin-šumi
judge//URU$_3$.DU$_3$–mansum (36:51, seal; 48:25)
Marduk-šāpik-zēri
~/Kudurru//Nagāru (25:68)
~/Mušēzib-Marduk//Šuḫaya (36:58)
Marduk-šarranu(i)
11:4'
~/Balāṭu//Paḫāru (44:16–17)
Marduk-šarra-uṣur
~/Mušēzibbu (15:15–16)
Marduk-šuma-ibni
~/Nabû-apla-iddin (24:1, 6)
~/Šākin-šumi//Šigûa (36:55)
Balāssu/~//Babūtu (25:62)
Bēl-uballiṭ/~ (27:21)
Kabtiya/~//Amēl-Ea (47:16–17)
Nabû-mušētiq-uddê/~ (6:18–19)
Marduk-šuma-iddin
judge//Esagilaya (21:47, seal)
~/Nabû-aḫḫē-bulliṭ//Balāṭu (8:1)
~/PN (30:1)
Bēl-nādin-apli/~//Bēl-apla-uṣur (31:22; 43:21)
Nabû-mukīn-apli/~//Balāṭu (42:26)
Sūqaya/~//Gimil-Nanaya (38:15)
Marduk-šuma-uṣur
governor (35:5')
judge//Adad-šammê (19:14; 32:32)
scribe (35:edge)
~/Bēl-uballiṭ//Pūtu (2:20)
PN/~ (24:10")
Marduk-šumu-līšir
~/Rīmūt//Bēl-usātu (25:56)
Marduk-zākir-šum(i)
governor of Babylon (50:29)
Marduk-zēra-ibni
Nabû-mukīn-zēri/~//Šangû-Ištar-Bābili (44:18–19)
Mār-Esagil-lūmur
21:18
Mina-imbuka
~//Bakiya-rimiya (18:30–31)
Mukīn-apli
Arad-Nergal/~//Egibi (43:14–15)
PN/~//Sagdidi (18:24)
Mukīn-zēri
~/Tabnêa//Egibi (36:57)
Mūrānu
scribe (38:27)
~/Nabû-bāni-aḫi//Ekur-zakir (1:25–26)
Murašû
~/Nādin//Nūr-Sîn (18:28)
~/Zēra-ibni (1:5, 13)
Enlil-šuma-iddin/~ (9:1)
Mušallim-Marduk
~/Arad-Nabû//Šangû-Nabû (39:14–15)
Mušēzib-Bēl/~ (38:91)
Mušallimu
PN/~ (24:6")
Mušebši-Marduk
Šamaš-nāṣir/~//Šangû-Šamaš (34:17)
Mušēzib
Anum-aḫa-iddin/~ (6:17)
Mušēzib-Bēl
governor/Eli-ili-rabi-Marduk (36:3, 47, seal)
judge//Eppeš-ili (21:44, seal; 29:39)
slave (49:1)
~/Iddina-aḫa//Bābūtu (27:24–25)

~/Mušallim-Marduk (38:91)
~/Nādinu//Rāb-banê (32:4–5, 8, 11, 14, 19, 21)
~/Nanaya-ēreš (25:4, 8–9, 11–12, 16, 20, 23, 24, 27, 43)
~/Šamaš-mudammiq//Eppeš-ili (2:15;25:54)
Balaṭu/~ (7:8)
Mūšēzib-Marduk
judge//Bālīḫû (19:15; 32:33)
~/Bēl-uballiṭ//Amēl-Ea (10:15)
~/Iddin-aḫa//Ša-nāšīšu (27:26–27)
~/Kabtiya//Šigûa (3:20)
Marduk-šāpik-zēri/~//Šuḫaya (36:58)
Nabû-aḫḫē-šullim/~//Šangû-Ištar-Bābili (33:4')
Mušēzib-Nabû
chief of the troops (15:14–15)
Nā'id-Ninurta
~/Enlil-šuma-ukīn (28:16)
Nabû-aḫa-ittannu
slave/Nuptaya (31:8, 16)
Nabû-aḫa-iddin
royal official, administrator of the Eanna (3:4; 26:15;31:10–11, 14; 38:9, 34, 36; 39:8; 40:2, 20; 43:18)
~/Nabû-balāssu-iqbi (49:15)
Nabû-aḫa-uṣur
Bau-ēreš/~ (16:1)
Nabû-aḫḫē-bulliṭ
provincial governor (26:3, 12, 18)
~/(Ina)-Esagil-šuma-ibni//Sîn-damāqu (46:1, 10; 47:1–2)
~/Nargiya (49:6; 50:9, 17, 23, 26)
~/P[N], overseer of the city of Šaḫrīnu (4:1–2, 25)
Lūṣi-ana-nūri-Marduk/~//Dābibī (42:28–29)
Marduk-šuma-iddin/~//Balāṭu (8:1)
Nabû-gāmil/~//Miṣiraya (32:1–2, 7–8)
Nabû-aḫḫē-iddin
~/Bēl-ēreš (38:82)
~/Šulaya//Egibi (12:15–16; 19:4–5, 6, 7, 11; 29:24; 46:7–8)
judge (22:37, seal; 23:7')
scribe (32:39)
~/Zākir//Amēl-Isin (47:13–14)
Itti-Marduk-balāṭu/~//Egibi (20:23; 29:1, 15, 25, 31, 32)
Nabû-aḫḫē-šullim
~/Mušēzib-Marduk//Šangû-Ištar-Bābili (33:4')
~/Nabû-šuma-ukīn//[X]-Ninurta (25:59)
Ibnaya/~ (38:45–46)
Ibni-Ištar/~ (7:7)
Iddin-aḫa/~ (31:1)
Innin-zēra-ibni/~//Šangû-Ninurta (38:23)
Nabû-apla-iddin
judge (50:31)
~/Ibni-Ištar//Ekur-zakir (5:26–27)
~/Nabû-šuma-išku//Šangû-Nin-Eanna (18:31–32)
Anum-šumu-līšir/~ (2:3–4)
Marduk-šuma-ibni/~ (24:1, 11, 15, 16', 19'); Nabû-mušētiq-uddê/~ (24:1); Bēl-aḫḫē-iddin/~ (24:1)
Nabû-balāssu-iqbi
24:2, 6, 9', 10', 13', 14', 17', 20', 22', 25', 27', 29', 31'
judge (50:31)
judge//Amēlû (21:43, seal; 23:9';29:37)
~/Ibnaya//Ekur-zakir (3:17; 38:21)
Nabû-aḫa-iddin/~ (49:15)

Nabû-bāni-aḫi/~//Sîn-lēqi-unninnī (5:25;14:25)
Nuptaya/~ (18:2, 12)
Nabû-bāni-aḫi
~/Marduk-erība//Ea-ṣalmu-ilāni (25:15, 27)
Rīmūt-Bēl/~ (25:15);
Šamaš-ēṭir/~ (25:15);
Nanaya-aḫa-iddin/~ (25:15);
Nabû-mušētiq-uddê/~ (25:15)
~/Nabû-balāssu-iqbi//Sîn-lēqi-unninnī (5:25; 14:25)
~/Šūzubu//Šangû-parakki (46:13; 47:12–13)
~/PN//Kurī (38:31–32)
Bau-ēreš/~ (12:4)
Ištar-mukīn-apli/~//PN (31:25–26)
Mūrānu/~//Ekur-zakir (1:25–26)
Nanaya-iddin/~//Ekur-zakir (7:6)
Nūr-Sîn/~//Nūr-Sîn (5:28)
Zēriya/~//Arad-Ea (13:19–20)
Nabû-bēl-šumāti(šīmāti)
Bēl-aḫḫē-iddin/~//Šangû-Ištar-Bābili (44:15–16)
Nabû-ṭāriṣ/~ (10:4–5)
Nabû-bēlšunu
~/Nūrea (37:25)
Bēl-aḫḫē-erība/~//Kurī (10:12–13)
Iqīša-Marduk/~//Nabûnaya (18:23–24)
Nabû-ēṭir-napšāti/~ (18:25–26)
Nabû-bulliṭsu
~/Iddin-Nabû//Dābibī (18:27)
Nabû-ēda-uṣur
slave (45:1; 46:4; 47:4, 8; 48:11)
~/Lā-tubāšinni (48:5, 9)
Nabû-erīb
Nergal-iddin/~ (33:3)
Nabû-etel-ilāni
judge (50:32)
judge//Adad-šammê (21:46, seal; 29:41)
Nabû-ēṭir
~/Arad-Bēl//Arrabtu (49:7)
Rīmūt-Nabû/~ (49:8)
Anum-šuma-ibni/~//Nabû-šarḫi-ilī (30:8)
Balāṭu/~//Rē–î-sīsî (24:seal)
Nabû-ēṭir-napšāti
qīpu-official of the Sealand (27:15)
~/Arad-bēl//Egibi (2:18; 14:22)
~/Bēl-iqīša//Bēl-apla-uṣur (10:14–15)
~/Nabû-bēlšunu (18:25–26)
Nabû-gāmil
~/Nabû-aḫḫē-bulliṭ//Miṣiraya (32:1–2, 7–8, 25, 28)
Nabû-iddin/~//Suḫaya (13:21–22)
Nabû-iddin
judge//Mudammiq-Adad (48:26)
~/Nabû-gāmil//Suḫaya (13:21–22)
Nabû-iqīša
Bēl-aḫa-šubši/~ (6:11)
Nabû-ittannu
Nidintu/~//Šangû-Šamaš (34:39)
Nabû-ittiya
Iddin-Marduk/~ (12:14–15)
Nabû-lū-dāri
slave (3:9)
Nabû-mīta-uballiṭ
Libluṭ/~//Mudammiq-Adad (13:1, 7)
Nabû-mukīn-apli
šatammu/Nādinu//Dābibī (31:9–10, 13–14; 43:16–17)
sukkallu (48:2, 24)
~/Marduk-šuma-iddin//Balāṭu (42:26)
Nabû-mukīn-zēri
goldsmith (6:13)
~/Marduk-zēra-ibni//Šangû-Ištar-

Bābili (44:18–19)
~/Nabû-šuma-ēreš//Ēreb-bīti (49:18–19)
~/Nādinu//Dābibī, *šatammu* of the Eanna (3:3;38:8, 33–34)
Nidintu-Bēl/~//Dābibī (26:14)
Nabû-mušētiq-uddê
~/Balāssu//Dāmiqu (25:1, 23, 37, 45, 50)
~/Marduk-šuma-ibni (6:18–19)
~/Nabû-apla-iddin (24:1)
~/Nabû-bāni-aḫi//Ea-ṣalmu-ilāni (25:15)
~/Nanaya-iddin (38:78, 96)
Ḫašdiya/~ (38:61)
Nabû-mutīr-gimilli
scribe//Gaḫal-Marduk (48:27)
Nabû-nādin
administrator of Kî-Nabû/Erībaya (40:14, 18, 26)
Nabû-nādin-aḫi
38:90
~/Arad-Bēl//Iddin-Papsukkal (42:26–27)
Šamaš-mudammiq/~ (20:5)
Nabû-nādin-šumi
Nādin/~//Rāb-banê (32:3–4)
Ṭābiya/~ //Ḫunzû(25:2, 52)
Nabû-nāṣir
~/Aḫḫē-iddin (6:8–9)
Nabû-rēṣua
slave (3:1)
Nabû-rēšu
~/Šamaš-iddin (25:10, 13, 19, 20, 44, 47)
Nabû-(u)ṣuršu
slave (18:3, 9)
~/Šamaš-kāṣir//Isininnaya (34:18–19, 26)
Nabû-šama'
Nabû-uballiṭ/~ (50:6)
Nabû-šarra-uṣur
royal official, administrator of Eanna (1:19; 5:12, 14, 22; 7:1; 14:12; 25:1, 21, 42, 51)
sukkallu (50:30)
Nabû-šuma-ēreš
Nabû-mukīn-zēri/~//Ēreb-bīti (49:18–19)
Nabû-šuma-iddin
~/Aplaya (37:7–8, 11, 16, 21, 22, 23)
~/Nanaya-ēreš (38:93)
Gimillu/~//Ea-ilūta-bāni (10:11–12)
Gimilllu/~//Gimil-Nanaya (38:25)
Sîn-aḫḫē-bulliṭ/~//Supê-Bēl (41:4)
Nabû-šuma-iškun
35:4', 12'
scribe//Rāb-banê (21:49; 22:41; 23:10'–11'; 29:42)
Nabû-apla-iddin/~//Šangû-Nin-Eanna (18:31–32)
Rīmūt/~//Gaḫul (46:19)
Nabû-šuma-ukīn
judge//Ir'anni (22:38, seal; 23:8')
Lāqīpi/~ (38:89)
Nabû-aḫḫē-šullim/~//[X]-Ninurta (25:59)
Šamaš-aḫa-iddin/~ (38:117)
Nabû-šuma-uṣur
Ištar-aḫa-iddin/~//Ekur-zakir (41:7)
Nabû-šumu-libūr
judge//Gaḫal-Marduk (29:38)
Nabû-šumu-līšir
24:20'
~/Bēlilitu (19:9)
Bēl-apla-iddin/~//Mudammiq-Adad (36:2, 6, 7, 10, 15, 18, 21, 22, 26, 30, 40)

Sîn-ēreš/~//Ibni-ilī (1:22–23;2:16;25:55;38:13; 43:20)

Nabû-šuzzizanni
- *šanû* of the Sealand (27:17)

Nabû-ṭāriṣ
- ~/Nabû-bēl-šumāti (10:4–5)

Nabû-uballiṭ
- ~/Ina-Esagil-zēri//Amēl-Ea (30:7)
- ~/Nabû-šamaʾ (50:6, 8, 15, 22)

Nabû-udammiqanni
- 38:130

Nabû-ušallim
- judge (50:32)
- ~/Kiṣir-Nabû (16:22)

Nabû-ušēzib
- Adad-šarra-uṣur/~ (4:9)
- Anu-šuma-ibni/~//Nabû-šarḫi-ilī (31:23–24)
- Erība/~ (4:10)
- Nargiya/~ (4:10)

Nabû-zabādu
- Sîn-ibni/~ (40:8)

Nabû-zēra-ibni
- 15:13
- 24:26', 28'
- ~/Marduk-nāṣir//PN (25:25)

Nabû-zēra-iddin
- ~/Aḫḫūšaya (11:7'–8', 13')
- ~/Itti-Bēl-ṭābu (4:20)
- Marduk/~ (5:2)

Nabû-zēra-iqīšā
- Nergal-īpuš/~ (5:5)

Nabû-zēra-ukīn
- //Bāʾiru (24:seal)

Nabû-zēra-[X]
- Iltameš-baraku/~ (1:2)

Nabû-zēr-kitti-līšir
- judge//Šulmānu (19:16; 32:34)

Nabû-zēru-līšir
- ~/Bēlšunu//Kurī (8:5; 25:69)
- ~/Nādinu//Išparu (5:28–29)
- Nanaya-[X]/~ (7:11–12)

Nādin(u)
- 35:13', 26'
- governor of Uruk/Balāṭu (8:13; 38:6, 39)
- scribe (38:27; 42:30; 43:22)
- scribe//Paḫāru (23:10')
- scribe/Nergal-ina-tēšê-ēṭir//Sîn-lēqi-unninnī (25:70)
- ~/Aplaya//Aḫḫûtu (2:19)
- ~/Bēl-aḫḫē-iqīša//Egibi (1:27–28; 2:23; 7:3; 14:27; 25:64)
- ~/Nabû-nādin-šumi//Rāb-banê (32:3–4)
  - Mušēzib-Bēl/~//Rāb-banê (32:4–5, 8)
- Ibnaya/~ (34:37)
- Kiribtu/~//Babūtu (38:19)
- Murašû/~//Nūr-Sîn (18:28)
- Nabû-mukīn-apli/~//Dābibī (31:9–10; 43:16–17)
- Nabû-mukīn-zēri/~//Dābibī (3:3; 38:8, 33–34)
- Nabû-zēru-līšir/~//Išparu (5:28–29)
- Nidintu/~//Rēʾi-sīsî (34:37)
- Šamaš-mukīn-apli/~//Egibi (16:18; 31:26; 41:3)
- Šamaš-uballiṭ/~//Amēlû (38:24)

Nādin-apli
- Rīmūt/~//Išparu (30:6)

Nanaya-aḫa-iddin
- ~/Nabû-bāni-aḫi//Ea-ṣalmu-ilāni (25:15)
- ~Nergal-ina-tēšê-ēṭir (38:92)

Nanaya-ēreš
- Bēl-aḫḫē-iddin/~ (5:3)
- Imbiya/~//Kidin-Marduk (41:1–2)
- Mušēzib-Bēl/~ (25:4, 8–9, 11–12, 25, 28)
- Nabû-šuma-iddin/~ (38:93)

Sîn-ibni/~ (38:93, 128)
Zēriya/~//Kidin-Marduk (3:18;41:5)
Zumbu/~ (38:104)
Nanaya-ibni
Nergal-nāṣir/~ (1:3–4)
Nanaya-iddin
~/Arad-Innin (38:44)
~/Attar-ramât (5:7–8, 18, 20)
~/Bau-ēreš (4:6, 24)
~/Nabû-bāni-aḫi//Ekur-zakir (7:6)
Nabû-mušētiq-uddê/~ (38:78, 96)
Šamaš-zēra-ibni/~/Ḫanap (2:21)
Nanaya-[X]
~/Nabû-zēru-līšir (7:11–12)
Napuštu
~/Bel-aḫḫē-iddin//Rēʾi-sīsî (34:40–41)
Nargiya
~/Bēlšunu (37:5)
~/Ḫanunu (49:10–11, 13; 50:1)
Nabû-aḫḫē-bulliṭ/~ (49:6: 50:17, 23–24)
~/Nabû-ušēzib (4:10)
Nergal-aḫa-iddin
~/Aḫḫêa (18:4, 5, 9, 11, 16, 23)
Nergal-aḫa-uṣur
judge (20:29, seal)
Nergal-bānûnu
scribe//Rāb-banê (19:19;32:38)
Nergal-ēṭir
~/Ša-Nabû-šū//Naggāru (33:4)
Šamaš-uballiṭ/~ (33:6)
Nergal-iddin
~/Nabû-erīb (33:3)
Šamaš-iddin/~ (33:5, 10)
Ḫammaya/~//Bābūtu (44:1–2)
Marduk-ēṭir/~//Bābūtu (44:17–18)
Šamaš-erība/~//Sîn-tabni (25:67)
Nergal-ina-tēšê-ēṭir
judge//Rāb-banê (36:50, seal)
Kīnaya/~//Dannea (14:2–3)
Nādin/~//Sîn-lēqi-unninnī (25:70)
Nanaya-aḫa-iddin/~ (38:92)
Nergal-īpuš
~/Nabû-zēra-iqīša (5:5, 10)
Nergal-nāṣir
~/Nanaya-ibni (1:3–4, 8, 16)
Apkallu/~//Išparu (5:26)
Nergal-rēṣū–a
slave (22:1, 28)
Nergal-šuma-ibni
~/Aḫišaya (38:135, 137)
Nergal-ušallim
judge//Šigûa (22:36, seal; 23:7'; 29:35; 32:36)
Innin-šarra-uṣur/~/Sîn-lēqi-unninnī (14:19–20)
Innin-šuma-uṣur/~/Sîn-lēqi-unninnī (26:34–35)
Šāpik-zēri/~//Sîn-karābi-išme (46:16)
Šuma-iddin/~ (38:142)
Nergal-ušēzib
25:28
Nergal-zēra-ibni
~/Šulaya//[Miṣiraya] (5:29–30)
Nidinti-Marduk
~/Šamaš-šumu-līšir//Ileʾʾi-Marduk (34:36)
Nidintu
~/Ardiya (38:112, 115)
~/Nabû-ittannu//Šangû-Šamaš (34:39)
~/Nabû-uṣuršu (34:24)
~/Nādin//Rēʾi-sīsî (34:37)
~/PN (38:67, 69)
Nidintu-Bēl
~/Nabû-mukīn-zēri//Dābibī, *šatammu* of Eanna (26:14–15; 39:7)

Ninurta-aḫa-iddin
~/Arad-Egalmaḫ (28:19)
Ninurta-ēriba
Ninurta-iddin/~ (28:15)
Ninurta-ēṭir
Šamaš-aḫa-iddin/~ (28:15, seal)
Ninurta-iddin
~/Ninurta-ēriba (28:15)
Aplaya/~ (28:23)
Ninurta-nādin-šumi
~/Uballissu-Marduk (9:12)
Ninurta-nāṣir
~/Bēl-aḫḫē-iddin (28:17, seal)
~/Iddin-Enlil (28:22)
Bēlšunu/~ (28:26)
Ninurta-uballiṭ
Šuma-iddin/~ (28:18)
Niqudu
Ribat/~ (9:13)
Nūrea
~/Kabtiya (21:6–7, 10, 17, 27, 41)
Bēlšunu/~ (30:11–12)
Gimillu/~ (37:2)
Nabû-bēlšunu/~ (37:25)
Nūrīšu-Enlil
~/PN (28:24)
Nūr-Sîn
~/Nabû-bāni-aḫi//Nūr-Sîn (5:28)
Nusku-iddin
~/Arad-Gula (9:15)
Parnakku (Pharnaces)
30:20
Pir'u
PN/~ (24:8")
Puṭiya
slave (16:4)
Raḫim'il
Udarna'/~ (28:1)
Raḫimmu
Kīnaya/~ (16:5, 9–10)
Ubar/~ (16:20)
Rašil-X
~/Bēl-ušallim//Eppeš-ili (11:15'–16')
Ribat
~/Niqudu (9:13)
Riḫētu
~/Arad-Innin (40:1, 10, 19, 22)
Rīmūt(u)
10:7
judge (43:7)
~/Ina-qībit-Nabû (29:5, 11, 20, 21, 22, 23, 27)
~/Innin-šuma-uṣur//Ḫunzu (7:9–10)
~/Nabû-šuma-iškun//Gaḫul (46:19)
~/Nādin-apli//Išparu (30:6)
~/Šamaš-lē'i//Arrabtu (35:7', 9', 24')
~/Šullum-mādu (4:18–19)
~/TUK?-*ia*//Rē'î-sīsî (18:25)
Marduk-šumu-līšir/~//Bēl-usātu (25:56)
Zumbu/~ (41:11–12)
Rīmūt-Bēl
judge (50:32)
judge//Miṣiraya (21:45, seal; 29:40)
~/Ardiya//Itinnu (13:18–19)
~/Bēl-uballiṭ//Gimil-Nanaya, *šešgallu* of Eanna (3:14–15; 38:10)
~/Iddina-aḫa//Bēl-pattanni (17:8–9)
~/Nabû-bāni-aḫi//Ea-ṣalmu-ilāni (25:14–15)
Rīmūt-Nabû
~/Nabû-ēṭir//Arrabtu (49:8)
Rīmūt-Nergal
judge//Saggilaya (32:37)

Silim-Bēl
~/Balāṭu (12:13–14)
~/Šuma-ukīn//Ḫanap (25:60)
Kalbaya/~ (26:1)
PN/~ (24:4")
Silim-ili
royal official in charge of the chest (38:11; 42:25)
Sîn-aḫa-iddin
Ḫabaṣīru/~ (34:39–40)
Sîn-aḫḫē-bulliṭ
~/Nabû-šuma-iddin//Supê-Bēl (41:4)
Sîn-ēreš
~/Nabû-šumu-līšir//Ibni-ilī (1:22–23; 2:16; 25:55; 30:2; 38:13; 43:20)
Sîn-erība
sartennu (32:5–6, 30)
Sîn-ibni
~/Nanaya-ēreš (38:93, 128)
~/Nabû-zabādu (40:8, 10, 17, 21, 23)
Anu-aḫa-iddin/~//Rē'i-alpi (7:18–19)
Balāṭu/~//Rē'i-alpi (1:26–27;21:2–3)
Nuptaya/~ (10:2–3)
Sîn-iddin
qīpu-official (26:31)
Sîn-ili
šešgallu//Sîn-ili (36:48)
Sîn-nādin-šumi
Šamaš-mukīn-apli/~ (40:5)
Sîn-šarra-uṣur
royal official (41:17, 23)
Sîn-šēzib
sukkallu (20:28)
Sîn-tabni
25:31
Sūqaya
14:10, 11, 15
slave/Nuptaya (31:7, 15)
~/Marduk-šuma-iddin//Gimil-Nanaya (38:15)
Ṣillaya
~/Lâbāši//Šigûa (47:14–15)
~/Šamaš-aḫa-iddin (38:124, 125, 130)
~/PN//Eppeš-ili (35:7'–8', 11', 19')
Arad-bēl/~/Iddin-Papsukkal (2:17; 38:14)
Bēl-iqīša/~ (42:9; 43:5–6, 12–13)
PN/~ (24:12")
Šabbataya
Gadalyama/~ (28:20–21)
Šaddinu
~/Bēl-ušallim (34:42)
Šākin-šumi
~/Ibni-Ištar//Sîn-tabni (deputy of Uruk) (3:15; 14:18–19; 38:18)
Arad-Innin/~ (26:1)
Ardiya/~//Gimil-Nanaya (31:23)
Bunanītu/~//Eppeš-ili (36:1)
Marduk-šuma-ibni/~//Šigûa (36:55)
Šamaš-aḫa-iddin
~/Nabû-šuma-ukīn (38:117, 120, 121, 122, 124)
~/Ninurta-ēṭir (28:15, seal)
Lâbāši/~ (37:3)
Ṣillaya/~ (38:124)
Šamaš-aḫḫē-lu-irši
~/Šamaš-kāṣir//Isinnaya (34:18–19, 20, 26, 28, 29, 30, 31, 32, 33, 35)
Šamaš-erība
/~Nergal-iddin//Sîn-tabni (25:67)
Šamaš-ēṭir
~/Nabû-bāni-aḫi//Ea-ṣalmu-ilāni

(25:14–15)
Šamaš-ibni
šangû of Amurru (27:30)
Šamaš-iddin
~/Bēl-iddin (26:2, 13, 24, 47, 49)
~/Nergal-iddin (33:5, 10, 12)
Bēl-šarrussu/~ (16:20–21)
Nabû-rēšu/~ (25:10)

Šamaš-kāṣir
Nabû-uṣuršu/~//Isinnaya (34:18–19)
Šamaš-aḫḫē-lu-irši/~//Isinnaya (34:18–19, 24)
Šamaš-lē'i
Rīmūt/~//Arrabtu (35:7')
Šamaš-mudammiq
~/Nabû-nādin-aḫi (20:5, 26)
Mušēzib-Bēl/~//Eppeš-ili (2:15; 25:54)
Šamaš-mukīn-aḫi
15:14
Šamaš-mukīn-apli
~/Madānu-aḫḫē-iddin//Šigûa (39:13–14;42:27)
~/Nādin(u)//Egibi (16:18; 31:26;41:3)
~/Sîn-nādin-šumi (40:5)
Šamaš-nāṣir
~/Mušebši-Marduk//Šangû-Šamaš (34:17, 23, 25, 32, 33, 35)
Šamaš-šarra-uṣur
~/Aḫimme (16:21)
Iqīšaya/~ (4:14)
Šamaš-šuma-iddin
~/Šulaya (5:4)
Itti-Anum-balāṭu/~ (5:22–23)
Šamaš-šuma-ukīn
~/Bēl-aḫa-iddin//Rāb-banê (14:26)
Šamaš-šuma-uṣur
//Šigûa (24:seal)
Šamaš-šumu-līšir
Nidinti-Marduk/~//Ile''i-Marduk (34:36)
Šamaš-uballiṭ
~/Nādinu//Amēlû (38:24)
~/Nergal-ēṭir (33:6, 8)
~/Tirriyama (28:18)
~/PN (34:41)
PN/~ (24:9")
Šamaš-zēra-ibni
~/Nanaya-iddin//Ḫanap (2:21)
[PN]/~ (4:20–21)
Šamaš-zēra-iddin
~/Aḫulap-Ištar//Ekur-zakir (30:31–32)
Šamaš-zēra-iqīša
~/Innin-šuma-uṣur (38:66)
Šamaš-zēra-šubši
brother of Iddin-aḫa (31:4, 8, 17, 19, 20)
~/Bāniya//Andaḫar (41:9)
Ša-Nabû-šū
Nergal-ēṭir/~//Naggāru (33:4)
Ša-Nabû-taqum
slave (16:4, 11)
Ša-pî-Bēl
Ina-Esagil-zēri/~//Amēl-Ea (8:6;25:63)
Šāpik-zēri
~/Iddin-Marduk//Šigûa (47:5–6)
~/Nergal-ušallim//Sîn-karābi-išme (46:16)
~/Šuma-ukīn//Sîn-šadûnu (29:3–4, 12, 13, 21, 26, 28)
~/Zērūtu (27:2, 7, 10, 12, 14)
Bēl-iddin/~//Mandidi (17:9–10)
Šarru-kīn
Anu-šarra-uṣur/~ (42:2–3, 13; 43:4, 6)
Arad-Bēl/~ (16:2–3)
Dannu-aḫḫēšu-ibni/~ (38:62)

Šulaya
~/Balti-ilī//Ea-ṣalmu-ilī (24:21')
Nabû-aḫḫē-iddin/~//Egibi (12:15–16; 19:4–5; 46:7–8)
Nergal-zēra-ibni/~//[Miṣiraya] (5:29–30)
Šamaš-šuma-iddin/~ (5:4)
Šullum-mādu
Bau-ēreš/~ (4:18)
Rīmūt/~ (4:18–19)
Šullumu
24:18'
Šuma-iddin
~/Enlil-nāṣir (28:23)
~/Nergal-ušallim (38:142, 144)
~/Ninurta-uballiṭ (28:18)
~/Tēšê-ēṭir//Sîn-damāqu (44:13–14)
Šuma-ukīn
judge (20:29, seal)
~/PN (30:4)
Bēl-uballiṭ/~//Sîn-šadûnu (23:1–2; 29:3–4)
Silim-Bēl/~//Ḫanap (25:60)
Šāpik-zēri/~//Sîn-šadûnu (29:3–4)
Šumaya
~/Ibni-Ištar//Ašlaku (5:31;7:4)
~/Marduk-aḫa-iddin (38:52, 53)
Šūzubu
Aplaya/~ (24:seal)
Aplaya/~//Bābūtu (27:23)
Nabû-bāni-aḫi/~//Šangû-parakki (46:13; 47:12–13)
Tabnêa
~/Itti-Bēl-tabni (37:1)
~//Šamaš-abāri (24:seal)
Mukīn-zēri/~//Egibi (36:57)
Tattannu
~/Nanaya-ḫussinni (21:5–6, 37, 39)
Taribi
Bāniya/~ (3:9–10)
Tirriyama
Šamaš-uballiṭ/~ (28:18)
Ṭābiya
~/Ardiya//Basiya (18:27–28)
governor of Uruk/Nabû-nādin-šumi//Ḫunzû (25:2, 21, 52)
PN/~//Kidin-Marduk (25:57)
Tēšê-ēṭir
Šuma-iddin/~//Sîn-damāqu (44:13–14)
TUK$^{?}$-*ia*
Rīmut/~//Rē'î-sīsî (18:25)
Uballissu-Marduk
Ninurta-nādin-šumi/~ (9:12)
Ubar
~/Bunene-ibni (9:11)
~/Enlil-mukīn-apli (28:19)
~/Raḫimmu (16:20)
~/Zambubu (45:3)
Ardiya/~ (28:25)
Zēriya/~ (49:17)
Udarna'
~/Raḫim'il (28:1, 7, 8, 10, 12; seal)
Ḫananyama/~ (28:20)
Usātu
Bau-iqīša/~ (15:1–3)
Itti-Enlil-balāṭu/~ (15:2–3)
Zababa-iddin
~/Nuptaya (20:13–14, 21)
Zabdiya
28:3, 6
Aqubu/~ (9:1–2)
Bēl-ittannu/~ (28:3, 6)
Zākir
Balāṭu/~//Kidin-Marduk (8:9–10)
Nabû-aḫḫē-iddin/~//Amēl-Isin (47:13–14)

Zambubu
Dāgil-ilī/~ (44:1)
Ubar/~ (45:3)
Zariqu-zēra-ibni
Adad-ibin/~//Šangû-Zariqu (46:18)
Zēra-ibni
Murašû/~ (1:5, 13)
Zēriya
~/Balāssu (14:3–4)
~/Bēlilitu (19:9)
~/Ibnaya//Egibi, *šatammu* of Eanna (1:21–22; 2:7–8)
~/Nabû-bāni-aḫi//Arad-Ea (13:19–20)
~/Nanaya-ēreš//Kidin-Marduk (3:18;41:5)
~/Ubar (49:17)
Arad-Marduk/~//Egibi (8:2; 38:12; 43:19)
~/Kīnaya (1:24–25)
Kurbanni-Marduk/~//Sîn-damāqu (8:14)
Zēru-bābili
Bēl-nādin-apli/~//Ile''i-Marduk (14:24)
Zērūtu
Šāpik-zēri/~ (27:2, 7)
Zumbu
~/Nanaya-ēreš (38:104, 105)
~/Rīmūtu (41:11–12, 26)

Women

Aḫat-abīšu
17:3
Attar-ramât
Nanaya-iddin/~ (5:7–8, 11)
Banitumma
slave (46:4)
Bēlilitu
~/Bēl-ušēzib//Ša-nāšīšu (19:1–2, 7, 9, 11)
Etillu/~ (19:9); Nabû-šumu-līšir/~ (19:9); Zēriya/~ (19:9)
Bunanītu
~/Šākin-šum//Eppeš-ili (36:1, 5, 10, 13, 17, 19, 21, 25, 26, 33, 35, 41, 45)
Etellitu
36:14, 17, 33, 34, 38, 41, 45
Gagaya
~/Bēl-nāṣir (20:1, 19, 22)
Nuptaya/~ (20:11–12, 20)
Gimillini
slave (46:5; 48:21)
~/Lā-tubāšinni (48:6, 10)

Ḫammaya
~/Nergal-iddin//Bābūtu (44:1–2, 4, 8)
Lā-tubāšinni/~ (44:3, 12)
Iṣṣur-[X]
sister of Nabû-zēra-iddin/Aḫḫūšaya (11:8'–9', 13')
Kišrinni
slave (46:5, 48:16, 21)
~/Lā-tubāšinni (48:5, 10)
Kurunnam-tabni (23:4, 7, 2')
Bēl-uballiṭ/~ (23:1–4)
PN_X/~ (23:1–4)
Kuputtu
49:5
Kuttaya
35:2', 14', 17', 27', 30'
Kuzbaya

slave (18:3, 7)
Lā-tubāšinni
~/Ḫammaya (44:3, 5, 9, 12; 48:1, 4, 8, 17, 19, 20)
Ardiya/~ (48:18–19, 20)
Bēl-aḫa-uṣur/~ (48:5, 9); Esagil-rēṣua/~ (48:5, 9); Gimillinni/~ (48:6, 10); Kišrinni/~ (48:5, 10); Nabû-ēda-uṣur/~ (48:5, 9)
Nanaya-ḫussinni
slave (21:3–4, 11, 16, 21, 37, 39)
Tattannu/~ (21:5–6, 37, 39)
Nasikātu
Balāṭu/~ (27:3)
Nuptaya
female slave (31:1, 15)
Sūqaya/~ (31:16); Iddin-Nabû/~ (31:16); Nabû-aḫa-ittannu/~ (31:16)
~/Gagaya (20:11–12, 20, 22)
Zababa-iddin/~ (20:13–14, 21)
~/Nabû-balāssu-iqbi (18:2, 6, 8, 10, 12, 13, 17)
~/Sîn-ibni (10:2–3, 6)
Qudāšu
~/Aḫu-nūri (20:6, 27)
Rēšat
~/Šūzubu//Šangû-parakki (46:2–3)
Bēl-aḫḫē-iddin/~ (46:1–3, 11; 47:1–3, 9–10); Nabû-aḫḫē-bulliṭ/~ (46:1–3, 11; 47:1–3, 9–10)
Tabluṭu
50:8, 13, 16, 22, 25

Kings

Amēl-Marduk, 3, 74, 76, 78, 118, 193
Artaxerxes, 38–39, 110–12
Cambyses, 57–59, 103, 118–21, 131, 147, 166–68, 171, 173–76, 178–80
Cyrus, 3, 8, 20–22, 24–25, 102–3, 121, 122–24, 129–31, 151–62, 163–64, 166, 171, 198–200, 201–4
Darius, 48–50, 62–65, 121, 132–36, 147, 169–71
Nabonidus, 3, 8, 13–15, 17–19, 27–30, 31–32, 34–35, 36–37, 41–42, 52–54, 55–56, 60–61, 67–69, 70–73, 74–79, 80–83, 84–86, 94–100, 103, 114–17, 125–28, 129–30, 137, 147–50, 151, 155, 157–58, 204
Nabopolassar, 3
Nebuchadnezzar, 3, 7–9, 45–46, 70–71, 87, 92, 94, 96, 97, 102–5, 107–9, 137, 143, 146, 182–85, 186–87
Neriglissar, 3, 67–68, 84–85, 129–30, 141–46, 182, 188–89, 193, 194–96
Xerxes, 3

INDEX OF PLACE NAMES

Babylon, 4–6, 8, 10, 32, 45, 48–50, 55–56, 60–61, 67–69, 73, 74–79, 80–83, 84–86, 88, 90, 107–9, 110, 114–17, 125–28, 141–46, 148, 163, 183–85, 186–87, 188–89, 191–93, 194–96, 198–200, 201–4
Bitqa-ša–Bēl-ēṭir, 169–71
Bīt-Lugalbanda, 28
Bīt Šar Bābili, 70–73
City of Nabû-šuma-iddin, 148–50
Ḫazuzu canal, 114–15
Ḫurri-ša-uṣur-amāssu canal, 95
Kî-Nabû, 167
New canal, 57–59
Nippur, 4–5, 38–39, 55, 110–12
Opis, 45–46
Sippar, 4, 24–25, 129–31, 132–36
Šaḫrīni, 62–65
Takkiru canal, 14
Uruk, 4, 13–15, 17–19, 20–22, 27–30, 31, 34–35, 36–37, 41–42, 52–54, 58, 76, 94–100, 102–6, 108, 118–21, 122–24, 129, 151–62, 163–64, 166, 171, 173–76, 178–80

SUBJECT INDEX

accusation, 23–24, 38, 43, 52, 57, 83, 110, 178
Achaemenid Empire, 3, 5, 8, 121, 204
appeal, 55, 76, 163
apprehension of criminal, 13, 17, 27, 34, 114
Aramaic, Arameans, 4–5, 35, 107
archival text, archives, 1–5, 36, 43, 110, 132
  Eanna, 4, 31, 94, 121, 129, 147–49, 152, 172
  Ebabbar, 4, 129, 136
  Egibi, 8, 50, 60, 67, 80, 84, 110, 114, 125, 137, 183, 191
  Murašû, 5, 38, 110
branding
  livestock, 52, 118, 121, 148–49, 154–58, 161, 163, 173, 178, 180–81
  slaves, 74, 79, 122, 201
conditional verdict, 38, 41
confession, 10, 13–14, 20, 27, 70, 80, 151–52, 201
contract, 1, 67, 80, 89–90, 100, 102, 126, 141, 148, 157, 166, 169, 182–83, 185
counterclaim, 52, 57, 87
courts, 2, 5–8, 102, 199
  royal court of law, 8, 55, 76, 163
debt-note, 5–6, 45–46, 48–50, 102–4, 114–17, 125–26, 129–30, 137–38, 143, 146, 150
documents, 1–7, 13, 17, 24, 36, 40, 45, 57, 60, 62, 79, 84, 94, 100–101, 102, 129, 132, 135, 151, 161, 183, 185–86, 198
  copies, 79, 101, 129, 133, 146, 148, 196
  possession of, 36, 84, 129, 183
  provenance, 4–5, 45, 60, 67–68, 131, 191, 193
dowry, 50, 70–72, 84–85, 141–46, 182–85
Eanna bureaucracy, 9, 52, 75, 94, 102, 118, 129, 147–48, 172, 178
  chief brewer, 52, 74, 76, 165, 172

herd management, 52, 95, 118, 147–48, 150, 163, 171–73
qīpu-official, 94, 103, 123, 152, 154, 156, 160, 169
royal official, 9, 15, 17, 20–21, 27, 34, 53, 94–95, 103–4, 118, 121, 123, 153, 163–64, 166, 169–70, 172–74, 180
šatammu, 9, 15, 18, 21, 31, 37, 94, 102, 104, 123, 129, 153–54, 164, 166–67, 169, 172, 180
evidence, 1, 7, 13–14, 17, 27–28, 36, 38, 41, 45, 67, 94, 102, 166, 172, 186
preservation of, 13–14, 17, 125, 166
false claims, fraud, 68–69, 80–81, 114–17, 132
guarantees, 17, 31, 43, 81, 148–49, 178, 198–99
clear title, 67, 74, 188–90, 191–92
loans, 45–46
inheritance, 48, 74–75, 84, 87–90, 107, 123, 132–34, 137, 141–42
division of, 87–90, 115
interrogation, 13–14, 20–21, 27–30, 31, 77, 82, 110, 116, 120, 148–49, 173–74, 201–2
investigation, 1, 6, 10, 31, 74–75, 172–74, 195
judges/judicial authorities, 7–9, 17, 20, 27, 31, 34, 36, 45, 52, 55, 57–58, 62, 75, 122, 129, 147, 151, 163, 172
assembly, 9, 21, 37, 52–53, 57–58, 94, 97, 110, 118, 120, 129, 155–61, 166, 169–70, 173–75
collegium of Eanna, 120, 129
elders of Sippar, 129130, 132, 135
"Great Ones," 70–72, 201–2
governor of Babylon, 88, 142–46, 203
governor of Uruk, 36–37, 94–100, 102–4, 108, 151–52, 155
kizû, 73
mār banî, 9, 34–37, 43, 57–58, 118–20, 149, 170
qīpu-officials, 9, 15, 55, 61, 94–100, 103–5, 108, 123, 152, 154–61, 169–70
provincial governor, 102–4
royal judges, 7–9, 45, 55, 57–58, 75–76, 85, 115, 172, 178, 181, 204
sartennu, 8, 125–27, 203
sukkallu, 8, 71–73, 194–96, 203
šangû, 24, 70, 108, 129
šatammu, 9, 15, 17–18, 20–21, 31, 36–37, 94, 102–4, 123, 129, 151, 153–54, 163, 166–67, 169, 172, 180
"temple enterers," 129–30
jurisdiction, 9, 58
land, 1, 2, 4, 38, 84, 94, 114–15, 125, 144
sales of, 100, 114–15, 125, 137
law codes, 1, 8, 141
loans, 45, 70, 125
misappropriation, 1, 31, 41, 52, 57, 74, 80, 148, 151–62, 178
names, 2, 4, 51, 60, 73, 102, 113, 120–21, 150, 172, 191, 193, 198–99
family names, 4, 30, 69, 107, 183
oaths, 48–49, 62–64, 137–39, 169, 173, 175, 201–2
parental authority, 84–85, 182–83, 198
penalty, 38–39, 43, 57–58, 60, 65, 67, 151–62, 178, 185, 198
thirtyfold, 39, 52–53, 57–58, 118, 148, 150–62, 178–81
personal status, 60, 64–65, 70–72, 74–75, 147, 182, 186, 189, 194–96

prebends, 129, 132–36
preliminary proceedings, 17, 31, 199
    documentation of, 62
rituals, 17, 20, 132–36
ruling (decision), 1, 5–8, 55, 62, 75–76, 93, 107, 118, 121, 142, 163, 172, 178, 194
scribes, 1, 6, 8, 30, 31, 51–52, 60, 73, 84–85, 94, 114, 117, 128, 154, 160–61, 172, 181, 198–99
    parchment-scribe, 77–79, 168
seals, 7, 17, 40, 70–71, 73, 79, 83–85, 89–90, 92–93, 100–101, 106, 108, 112–13, 127, 131, 140, 145–46, 166, 168, 196, 199, 202–3
slaves, 20, 57–58, 60, 62–65, 67–68, 70, 74–75, 80, 84, 122, 141, 182–83, 186, 188, 191–92, 198, 201
    manumission, 70, 74, 194
    payments to/for, 65, 67, 186, 191–92
summoning/summons, 6–8, 10, 17, 43, 55, 57–58, 60, 62, 76, 118, 163, 169
temples, 1–4, 7–9, 39, 57–58, 74–75, 129, 132
    Eanna, 4, 13–14, 17–18, 20–21, 27–30, 31, 34–35, 36–37, 41, 52–53, 57–58, 74–78, 94–95, 102–6, 118–21, 122–23, 129, 147–71, 172–81
    Ebabbar, 4, 129, 132, 136
    Esagil, 60
testimony, 9, 20, 27, 34–35, 41, 52–53, 57, 67–68, 72, 74, 82, 118–20, 122, 139, 151–62, 166–68, 173–75, 201–2
    guarantee of testimony, 148–49, 199–200
theft, 5, 13–14, 16, 20–22, 24–25, 27–29, 34–35, 38–39, 52–53, 57–58, 110, 118, 151
witnesses, 9, 17, 21, 38–39, 41, 45–46, 52, 60, 67–68, 89, 102, 105, 113, 118, 120, 151–52, 172, 185, 198–99, 201

CPSIA information can be obtained at www.ICGtesting.com
Printed in the USA
BVOW02s0722060314

346845BV00002BA/3/P

9 781589 839434